Aspects of Educational and Training Technology

Volume XXIV

Aspects of Educational and Training Technology
Volume XXIV

Realizing Human Potential

Edited for the Association for Educational and Training Technology by

Roy Winterburn

Kogan Page, London
Nichols Publishing Company, New York

First published in 1991

Kogan Page Limited
120 Pentonville Road
London N1 9JN

British Library Cataloguing in Publication Data

A CIP record for this book is available from the British Library.

ISBN 0-7494-0353-5
ISSN 0141 5956

US Library of Congress Cataloging-in-Publication Data

LC Card 90-662392
ISBN 0-89397-406-4

Printed and bound in Great Britain by
Biddles Ltd, Guildford and King's Lynn

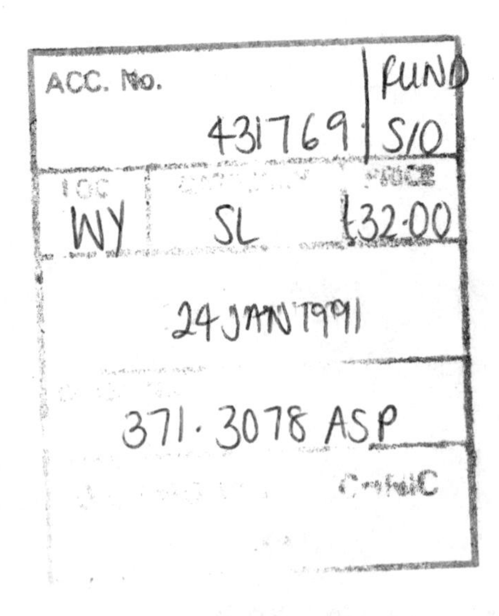

Contents

Contributors 8

Editorial 9

Section 1: Recognizing potential - the meanings, quality and evaluation of competence 11

1. **Opening keynote address: education for capability** 13
   John Stephenson

2. **Competence-based approaches to the realization of human potential - current issues and research** 22
   Paul Ellis

3. **Realizing human competence** 29
   Phil Race

4. **Assessing the performance of crew resource management skills** 37
   J.M.Artiaga and D.J.Sullivan

5. **A quantitative method of measuring performance improvements** 43
   Rosemary A.Greene

6. **Measuring the quality of training** 50
   H.M.Brown

7. **Realizing potential through quality vocational education** 55
   Dave Muller and Peter Funnell

Section 2: The contribution of experiential learning to realizing potential 59

8. **Talking with Christopher Gable** 61
   Christopher Gable and Maureen Pope

9. **Developing human potential experientially** 69
   Jane Henry

10. **The accreditation of prior learning on in-service education courses for teachers** 77
    Michael Bloor and Christine Butterworth

11. **Effective training - some tools for industry** 83
    Karen J.Saunders

12. **The award of academic credit for sandwich placements in Higher Diploma courses by means of learning contracts** 89
    Iain S.Marshall

13. **Travelling to change: an analysis of an international travel/study programme on participants' attitudes** 93
    I.D.Talbott

14. **Introducing simulation/games into the curriculum of a Singapore college** 98
    Henry Ellington, Martin Allinson and Jimmy Chen

15. **A simulation workshop for staff development and vocational guidance** 103
    Danny Saunders

Section 3: The teaching and learning of mathematics 109

16. **Teaching logic: why and how** 111
    Donatella Persico

17. The THE CAI system with learning environment for enhancing problem solving — 117
N.Nakamura, M.Takeya, T.Shakushi and F.Terada

18. Description of problem solving using Petri Nets — 122
Guglielmo Trentin

19. Curriculum supported by computer - mathematics through 'NATTOKU' — 129
T.Matsui, N.Nakamura, M.Takeya and F.Terada

20. The reform of Italian teacher training in computer science — 135
A - Teacher training in computer science: an example of realization — 136
Paola Forcheri, Fulvia Furinghetti and Teresa Molfino
B - A large scale teacher training programme in informatics: chances and limits — 140
Rosa Maria Bottino and Fulvia Furinghetti

21. The 'Basic Maths Project': a CBL approach to basic mathematics and numeracy in further education — 146
Peter J.Clare

Section 4: Computers as aids to realizing potential — 151

22. The role of computers in education and training — 153
Noel Thompson

23. Practical considerations on the introduction of CAL into university teaching — 161
Stephen Fallows, Kathryn Huckbody and Terry King

24. Supporting learner strategies in CBT — 166
Neville Stanton

25. Some difficulties in describing human potential in educational and training technological systems using computers — 173
W.Weston-Bartholomew

26. Computer-mediated seminars: realizing the potential of both students and tutors through interactive distance education — 178
Alexander J.Romiszowski

27. A CAI and CMI system considering student's achievement and consciousness — 185
Yoshikazu Araki

28. Computer based testing and drill and practice at a cross-roads: converging or diverging? — 192
Clement Dassa and Jesus Vasquez-Abad

29. Developmental reading and writing disorders: courseware as a remedial tool — 197
Camillo Gibelli and Michela Ott

30. Developing informational technology skills for nurse teachers — 204
Helen J.Betts

31. Tools for hyper-media authoring — 208
Philip Barker

Section 5: The use of technology — 213

32. Bridging the gap between seeing and doing — 215
Andy Finney

33. **The utilization of media in the lecture from a didactical perspective** 219
C.J.Nel

34. **Students: they also can tell us something about the new technologies** 225
Antonio R.Bartolome

35. **Intellectual enrichmenta and cooperative learning through interactive video in a whole-class situation** 230
Pedro Hernandez Hernandez

36. **Electronic audience response** 236
Stephen C.Day

37. **Using training technology requires more than money!** 238
Ted Hutchin

38. **The hidden technology: societal mechanisms now hampering realizing human potential** 242
E.M.Buter

Section 6: Human aspects of educational technology 249

39. **Keynote - Achieving potential** 251
Tony Buzan

40. **Concept mapping as an adjunct study technique for unlocking human potential** 260
P.David Mitchell and Stephen G.Taylor

41. **A systems approach to the evaluation of a University's teaching, research and community service programme in a post-apartheid society** 265
W.S.H.du Randt

42. **Improving managerial productivity through information technology** 273
Clive Holtham

43. **The new enfranchisement: who types the text?** 278
Roslyn Petelin

44. **Streamlining computer-based training production: improving communication between commissioners and contractors** 283
Elaine England

45. **The human elements of introducing a new computerized system to the workplace** 289
Jacqueline Jeynes

46. **The potential takeup of mass training** 295
Alison Fuller and Murray Saunders

47. **Realizing the potential of disabled people by promoting mainstream educational opportunities: a case study** 301
Peter Funnell

48. **Should the principles of self-management be taught as standard curricula for developmentally delayed children?** 306
Lutfi Elkhatib

49. **Realizing human potential through staff development in an educational context** 311
Dave Muller

50. **Sociometric analysis applying fuzzy theory** 315
Kazuko Nishimura and Hajime Yamashita

Index of contributors

Author	page
Allinson	98
Araki	185
Artiaga	37
Barker	208
Bartolome	225
Betts	204
Bloor	77
Bottino	135,140
Brown	50
Buter	242
Butterworth	77
Buzan	251
Chen	98
Clare	146
Dassa	192
Day	236
Elkhatib	306
Ellington	98
Ellis	22
England	283
Fallows	161
Finney	215
Forcheri	135,136
Fuller	295
Funnell	55,301
Furinghetti	135,136
Gable	61
Gibelli	197
Greene	43
Henry	69
Hernandez	230
Holtham	273
Huckbody	161
Hutchin	238
Jeynes	289
King	161
Marshall	89
Matsui	129
Mitchell	260
Molfino	135,136
Muller	55,311
Nakamura	117,129
Nel	219
Nishimura	315
Ott	197
Persico	111
Petelin	278
Pope	61
Race	29
du Randt	265
Romiszowski	178
Saunders D	103
Saunders K	83
Saunders M	295
Shakushi	117
Stanton	166
Stephenson	13
Sullivan	37
Takeya	117,129
Talbott	93
Taylor	260
Terada	117,129
Thompson	153
Trentin	122
Vasquez-Abad	192
Weston-Bartholomew	173
Yamashita	315

Editorial

This book represents the Proceedings of the Twenty-Fifth Annual Conference of the Association for Educational and Training Technology, held at City University, London, England, on April 9/10/11/12 1990. The fact that this is only the Twenty-Fourth volume in the series Aspects of Educational and Training Technology is an historical accident which stems from the very first Conference.

The major theme of the Conference, that of **Realizing Human Potential**, was in part intended to build on but also to extend that of the 1989 Conference held at Birmingham Polytechnic, which considered some of the human problems associated with non-traditional ways of delivering education and training. The key words in training and education at the beginning of the nineties are those such as capability, competence, enterprise; words which are - perhaps deliberately - vague as to their meaning in the educational and training context. What do they mean, how are they attained, and how are they recognized, both internally and externally?

The contributions to this Conference go some way towards answering parts of these questions, though there are still considerable areas which have been addressed insufficiently, if at all. This is an understandable deficiency in a Conference which invites contributions to a broad theme and then makes a selection from those offered so as to make up an overall programme. Some factors are not addressed at all, while others appear to be being looked at in great depth by considerable numbers of workers in many countries. The teaching and learning of mathematics has been one such topic this year, with international concern about it being shown by the papers included and also by the fact that several other papers, perhaps no less worthy, have had to be left out due to shortage of space.

The Training Agency provided an interesting and useful Conference-within-a-Conference, but the papers which were given in that have not been included in this volume.

The Conference always attracts a considerable international participation, with Italy and Japan being particularly strongly represented this year. Overseas contributions form a particular feature of this volume.

Aspects XXIV is divided into six sub-themes to aid presentation, but as is almost inevitable there is a lot of overlap, with some papers having claims to be included in any of two or three different sections; computers, for instance, are almost ubiquitous.

The book opens with a section reflecting the concerns expressed above - what is competence; how do you measure it or changes in it; how acceptable is it as a concept, and are there quality connotations attached to it?

This is followed by a section on experiential learning methods. Sections Three and Four deal with the teaching and learning of mathematics, and with the uses of computers as aids in education and training; Section Three could quite easily be subsumed within Section Four, though.

Considerations with regard to the use of media other than, or in conjunction with computers form Section Five, while the Sixth takes human aspects as its theme.

The normal papers were supplemented by four very differing keynote speakers dealing with disparate concepts - the achievement of competence (or capability) by encouraging learner responsibility (Stephenson);

capabilities that are shared and those that distinguish one individual from another (Gable); problems and possibilities with computers (Thompson); and using one's brain to the best effect (Buzan). In reporting their contributions, an attempt has been made to reflect - be it ever so palely - their idiosyncratic approaches.

In some cases papers appearing in this volume have been edited, but whether they have or not it has been assumed that readers may well wish to contact contributors, whose addresses have been included after each paper.

The interrelationship between Conferences continues with the Twenty-Sixth International Conference, to be held at the Polytechnic of Wales, when the subject of competence will be investigated further, the Conference theme being **'Developing and Measuring Competence'.**

Roy Winterburn
City University.

Section 1: Recognizing potential - the meanings, quality and evaluation of competence

1. Education for capability

John Stephenson, Director, Education for Capability Project

Abstract: The theme of the Higher Education for Capability project is to encourage the development of qualities of capability through the processes by which students learn. Many forward-looking companies base their in-house education on similar principles. Thus, we ought to be able to promote an alliance between higher education and the outside world which is mutually beneficial, based on the quality of the students' learning experiences. This paper outlines the progress made so far, and the inevitable problems encountered, in this attempt to affect the culture of British higher education.

The Royal Society of Arts, (or RSA), tends to be associated by people with examinations of one kind or another. The full title is the Royal Society for the Encouragement of Arts, Manufactures and Commerce, but the RSA doesn't do anything concerned with the arts, manufactures and commerce - it does the encouraging bit, and this has been the RSA's role for well over 200 years. That is why it has an educational activity, because it sees education in those terms. Its role is to stimulate, to argue and to bring people together, but then to allow them to get on with it while the RSA retreats and does something else.

Because education is not formally the business of the RSA it actually is able to take a fairly neutral stance and to provide a forum for discussion and exchange, and that is proving to be very important.

The RSA is a charity and has to secure funds from a number of sources for its various projects. This particular project is sponsored by a mixture of private individuals, considerable numbers of them contributing small amounts, and by multi-national companies which are active in sponsoring higher education such as BP, IBM, Digital Equipment, Unilever and the Training Agency.

The Education for Capability project is now more than ten years old, though the Higher Education part has been established for less than three years. It started in 1978, and began out of a general feeling of frustration about the artificial split between education and training, which was felt to be a wholly unhelpful distinction to make. Training can be high level or low level, but a level of education is needed to go with the training; similarly, education without the abilities and skills for which training might be useful is less useful than it could otherwise be. The division between education and training has had a kind of apartheid effect, where education was thought to be superior and was associated with the higher level institutions, while training was regarded as being inferior and associated with lower level institutions and lower level activities. As a consequence, some of the difficulties of the British economy and way of life can be traced to the way we have organized our educational system.

It was out of that frustration that the capability movement was established, with the intention of bridging the gap between education and training. That has been done over the period of this project by focusing on the concept of capability as a unifying concept which crosses both education and training. We regard capability as:

CONFIDENCE IN YOUR ABILITY TO	take effective action; explain what you are about; live and work with others; continue to learn from experiences;	IN A DIVERSE AND CHANGING SOCIETY

Confidence in one's ability to take general effective action, to explain what you are about, to live and work with others, to continue to learn from experiences in a diverse and changing society, are genuine human qualities and abilities.

A number of our sponsors, and critics as well, would prefer us to go further and itemize individual competences. In our literature, we do succumb slightly to that and we list consequences of skills and qualities developed through educational experiences which are focused on that kind of capability. Our principle concerns, though, are with the quality of life and the personal qualities which contribute to effective living both at work and in society generally.

One of the reasons why we are so well supported by industry is that it feels misrepresented by Government, as when Government says to higher education, "You shall be relevant to the economy and the economy requires this, this, this and this". But the more thoughtful representatives of industry say, "Well actually, that's not what we want", and they feel somewhat frustrated; what they are concerned about is the quality of the individuals who make up society as a whole, because if one takes the long view, the higher that quality is, the better it is for society (as a whole) and thus better for employers and others working within it. The notion of levels of personal qualities, of taking effective action, of capability, has wide appeal.

Taking that further, Higher Education for Capability

combines excellence: in the traditional areas of knowledge acquisition and skills of analysis

with excellence in doing, organizing, designing, communicating, creativity, imagination, working without supervision, working with others, the use of skills and knowledge

In effect, by focusing on the processes by which students learn we are attempting to combine the traditional areas of excellence of higher education - excellence in knowledge acquisition and skills of analysis, on which universities and polytechnics pride themselves as being their proper function - with other activities which we argue are of equal importance (doing, organizing, etc).

The process that we are promoting through the capability project can be summarized in the two words 'responsible' and 'accountable', i.e. giving students the opportunity to be responsible and accountable for their own learning, both as individuals and in collaboration with others. We are concerned to improve and change the nature of the relationship between the teacher and the taught, such that the students can actually claim major responsibility for most of their learning, at the expense of being accountable for it.

A lot of the current activities, of course, 'bolt on'. Learning leadership on Friday afternoon, learning how to listen on Tuesday morning, or as weekend activities - these are well done in many institutions and quite effectively, but what we want to do is to overcome the problem that the bolt-on classes in those skills tend to be regarded as less important than learning about Jacobean tragedy (or whatever the subject matter of the course happens to be) and therefore tend always to be squeezed and under-resourced. That then creates problems over the allocation of priorities by students and staff. These problems are not always as extreme as I have indicated, but by and large if these activities are part of the main stream then we can be more successful in ensuring that they happen. Put bluntly, an old slogan, 'The medium is the message' is perhaps the best way of summarizing what this project is about - that if you get the experience of having to be capable through the management of and responsibility for your course, then you are more likely to develop the qualities of capability mentioned above.

An issue that frequently arises in the context of higher education is to identify a notion of level when talking about capability. How can one talk about honours degree level for listening skills, or for collaboration, or for any of the other component skills that one might care to identify? This is a problem which exercises people's minds and time considerably.

If one considers the nature of capability, and the different kinds of capabilities that might be identified, there is a continuum of situations in which capability needs to be exercised. At the extremes there is a dependent capability (position Y), and an independent capability (position Z). Position Y, for example, is a situation of familiar problems and a familiar context for which people can be prepared quite adequately. This may be the training end, but it is also where quite a lot of higher education takes place. Many higher education courses which have a capability (or practical) besides an intellectual

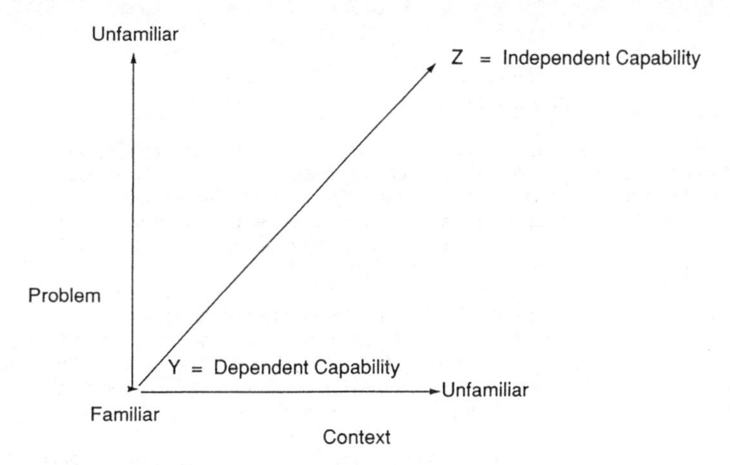

Figure 1: Dependent and independent capabilities

base, prepare people by exposing them to familiar problems in a defined context, and the students learn through exercises and similar activities. These can be quite high level - in some senses some of the most sophisticated skills can still be at position Y.

Position Z is at the other extreme, where neither the context nor the problem is wholly familiar. The student is to some extent alone, either because it is the self that is being changed, or (s)he is moving from one context to another, or the context in which the student works is constantly being changed. In higher education we may be talking about levels of capability, or kinds of capability that are appropriate to the Z end of that continuum rather than the Y end. There is no reason, of course, why they both cannot be done; where there can be preparation for

Y when there is an immediate job in mind, but to prepare in such a way as to be capable and at ease in position Z when it (inevitably) arises.

For people to survive under conditions of uncertainty, unfamiliarity and pressure (position Z), the kinds of personal qualities needed go beyond the familiar lists of areas of knowledge and skills. There are major debates about filling in the top circle in Figure 2 with what skills are useful and important in modern life: personal skills, transferable skills and the rest are all very important, but they can be lumped together, to make the point that there are other qualities that people need.

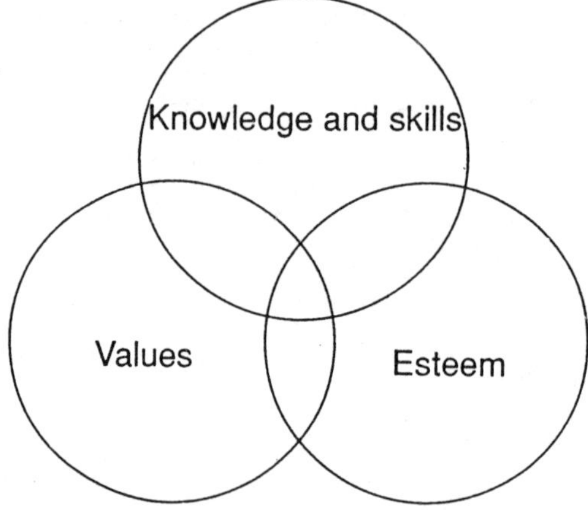

Figure 2: Components of capability

Not enough emphasis, in my view and in the view of the sponsors of our project, is given to the two other aspects - the esteem of the individuals concerned and their capacity to address issues of value or to be clear about their own values. To be able to survive and to flourish in conditions of uncertainty (towards position Z) needs a high level of personal esteem, because a major factor in position Z is the prospect of failure. This contrasts with position Y, which involves training for predictable contexts and predictable problems, with tried solutions and skill in their implementation. High personal self-esteem is therefore an important aspect of capability at the Z end, together with the ability to make decisions using conflicting information. For these, a well developed value system and a capacity to deal with issues of values are needed.

If one looks at the differences between people who have a dependent capability and those who have an independent capability, the former are likely to have received knowledge and skills rather than taken initiative in learning them, and they will have been tested by others externally - by course tutors, by external examiners, by examining boards, by a whole range of external validators and testers. The greater the level of independence in the process the more self-monitoring becomes important, for testing competence and capability and self-mastery of the knowledge and skills that are being acquired.

A similar situation holds with regard to the relevance of what is learned. In a dependent course, this is determined by others - by those who control the curriculum, those who set examinations, by professional associations, and so on. Students can get by quite happily without ever questioning the relevance of items one with another in a programme of study. At the other extreme, the relevance has to be negotiated by the students themselves and therefore understanding is much greater. As a consequence the former type of course might turn out in terms of the students' total experience as being rather fragmented, but where there is a high degree of independence it is more likely to be integrated and coherent as a result of the arguments, discussions and negotiations of the students themselves.

There is an esteem which comes from achievement in higher education. On dependent courses the esteem can come from getting A++ or B++-+ when everybody else in the class had C-s; or from gaining a degree and the status which comes with that. If work is done independently, though, with responsibility for completing work for which the student is accountable then it is self-work that has been proved and the student gains confidence in that as a consequence. There is confidence in one's own ability rather than relying on qualifications given by others.

In position Z, decisions depend as much on intuition as on precise knowledge and skills, and to have confidence in your own intuition in uncertainty requires a high level of internal confidence, in self-esteem and in self-work to be able to back that intuition. The same happens with values - on a dependent programme, priorities are set by others and as a consequence students are encouraged to avoid judgements. Indeed, there are undergraduate courses where students have been forbidden by their staff to make judgements: "Rely on the things that we tell you". The opposite is the case for the independently capable, where the students are developing their own programmes.

Now those are two extremes juxtaposed, and no doubt most experience fits in neither context but somewhere in the middle. My caricature of the dependent course in higher education I'm sure doesn't exist in any institution, but by posing it in that way it indicates the importance of trying to look for opportunities to give students as much responsibility for what they do as is possible within the constraints that we all have to accept, such as external validation.

At the many universities and polytechnics we have visited, there has been a generally warm reception to the kinds of things that I have been talking about - in particular, to the suggestion that higher education ought to be about the quality and capability of the students going through it. That is one of the reasons why many institutions resist enterprise: it disagrees with their understanding of the independence and the mission of higher education. The notion of capability for the quality of life, of which work is a part, has more attraction than preparation for the economy.

Another reason why it is proving successful is that the one thing that higher education will readily agree as being part of its mission is to promote excellence: academic, educational and intellectual excellence. We are not challenging that interest in excellence; we want to help achieve that, preferably at an even higher level. The self-monitoring element of being responsible and accountable clearly promotes excellence in traditional activities of higher education. To self-monitor, the student has to have greater understanding of what is being done, and what has been achieved. The student inevitably begins to think in terms of self-set goals and how well they are being met; that self-monitoring, in turn, leads to an examination of the relevance of what is currently being done in other study areas.

Testing, though, becomes rather more difficult. If all are doing the same thing then it is possible to say, "Well, I'm 7th out of 25 in my group, therefore I'm above average, therefore I'm doing all right" - in other words a purely arbitrary judgement which has no substance to it other than as a simple comparison.

I was talking to a polytechnic student who claimed that he really began to understand or realize he was making progress when he started writing obscenities in the margins of some of the learned journals that he read (he rubbed them out afterwards, they were in pencil), because when he had the confidence to argue with acknowledged experts then he really knew that he understood it and was making progress. So one tests against specialists rather than makes arbitrary comparisons, and in order to monitor progress the outcomes of what has been learnt have to be communicated, which again promotes understanding.

Our concentration on the hard mainstream process of higher education protects everybody's interests. It protects the academics because they say, "Yes, well we would like our students to have all those qualities and be able to develop these capacities", but it also protects the external interests. One of the things industrialists have said to me is, "What really annoys us about higher education is that they keep coming up to us and saying 'Tell us what you want and we'll do it'. We don't want you to do that," they say, "We want you to be good at your job, because if you are good at your job in the way that we are describing here, in other words if you are producing capable people who know what they're about, can take effective action and so on, they'll be good as people for themselves, but they will also be good employees if we take them on".

One of the biggest multi-national companies, noted for its business activities, refuses to take business studies graduates because they are the opposite of capable. They have stuff poured into them, being taught very intensively. The company would much rather have people with other qualities, so that those qualities can then be developed by the company.

The question therefore arises, "How do you do it?" which is a very important part of the work of our project and one of the reasons why we are anxious to visit as many institutions as possible. From my own teaching experience I have the confidence to encourage people (and there are many who have got comparable experience to my own) to work or to move in the direction of student responsibility for their own learning. It is possible to look at the range of possibilities, or rather actualities, on a continuum from whole schemes through to components:

WHOLE SCHEMES	**PARTIAL SCHEMES**	**SPECIFIC COMPONENTS**
Independent study programmes	Medicine in NSW	Integrated placements
Associate students	Final year contracts	Student-negotiated projects
	Progressive responsibility	Collaborative learning
	Blank modules	Self/peer assessment

Table 1: Learner responsibility and accountability

An interesting development is the use of associate students; students who come into a polytechnic off the street and register, the polytechnic charging them a little for registration. They use the library and sit around, then come along after 12 months and say, "Well I've done this and I've done that, can I have a certificate?" Sure you can have a certificate, fine. Twelve months later, "I've done this and I've done that and I've done this writing, can I have a diploma?" Well, that's a bit more difficult, because a certificate anyone can get, a certificate is not threatening us, but a diploma, we'll have to think about that seriously. But what happens two years later, when those same students come along and say, "I've done the assignments the other students have done, and I've handed them in and I know they are at least as good as those others , but I haven't attended any classes. Can I have a degree? Not for participating in any of the courses but for demonstrating that I am as good as the others"?

Now this is an interesting development, and it is happening in a number of institutions. And how threatening is that? Where somebody doesn't attend any of the things which highly paid academic staff have carefully planned and delivered, but still does well or better than well at the end simply by moving around, by absorbing, by being responsible and accountable and asking that that accountability be assessed by the same criteria as are applied to the 'normal' students.

There are quite a lot of partial schemes. Of the medical scheme in New South Wales, many might say that it is important that a doctor knows the difference between an arm and a heart, which is probably true but the experience in New South Wales is that anybody who is aspiring to be a doctor doesn't need to be told that. And it demeans students, I feel, when people say, "You can't have student responsibility in medicine because we need doctors who know the difference between... " In fact, students who go through that programme are much better than conventional GPs at diagnosis and patient relationships.

There are a number of institutions in this country where contracts are introduced into the final year. The education is traditional for foundation studies in Years 1 and 2, but much more responsibility is given to them in Year 3. Or, as a variant of that, there are schemes where students start on their projects in Year 1, and the project gradually takes up more time in Years 2 and 3, so that it dominates Year 3. An interesting development in the modular schemes, of which there are many, is the use of blank modules where students can say, "I want 60 credits for doing this as part of my Year 2 programme". There are many, many more specific components and I have mentioned only a few, and there are encouragingly large numbers of such innovations going on over a very wide continuum.

Our project's current activities include talking to groups in institutions; running major enquiries into capability in the professions; capability and links with industry; capability and validation of higher education, and capability and strategies for institutional change. We are establishing networks where subject specialists - engineers, scientists, psychologists or whatever - can make contact with others in the same field who are grappling with similar problems, some of the many problems which I have glossed over in this paper.

After three years our sponsors will expect us to have changed the culture of British education. We are carefully preparing them for a great disappointment, in that we will _not_ have changed that culture in such a short period. What we hope to have done is to have started something going, through the groups and through the enquiries and support networks, which will have the effect of gradually changing the culture beyond that three year period.

AUDIENCE: This may sound like a cynical question, but having worked in a lot of institutions now for two years, do you still remain optimistic that change is possible?

STEPHENSON: Yes, and let me give you an instance of how things happen and why they make me optimistic. I went to an institution in Northern Ireland, and was shown the usual 'prestigious bits' by the chief executive, but we came across two people in a very unfashionable department who were wrestling with the notion of self and peer assessment, and that turned out to be the most interesting thing I saw. I encouraged them to talk about their work, to persons both inside and outside their institution including the RSA. It has enormously raised the profile and the status of that sort of activity in their institution; I don't know whether that will be a lasting effect, but I can only work on the basis of a confidence that that sort of thing will continue and progress.

AUDIENCE: How do you see the relationship between your concerns and those of the National Council and others with regard to course skills?

STEPHENSON: Discussion of course skills is entirely healthy and useful, and it gives a useful starting place for those who are bound by traditional practices of content delivery, because it opens up discussion as to what is important and what is possible. The difficulty arises over the issue of what you do about it and how you make a good response. We're clear that we very much favour the essential process approach, where people acquire these qualities and skills willy nilly, by virtue of the mainstream activities in which they are involved. Now I agree that this is a departure from the norm for some groups, so I suppose the direct answer to your question about how we relate is that we have some interesting debates, not about the merits of course skills but about the different ways in which they can be achieved.

AUDIENCE: When you start to provide an ideological basis for what you propose, will there not be questions as to whether it will undermine the existing order?

STEPHENSON: I would hesitate to say that I hope it does undermine the existing order, but I think the opening up of existing systems is to be encouraged, as is clearly implied by what I have been saying. The idea that we are actually radical is I think eccentric. We're talking about institutions of higher education being communities of learners, where people have different roles but they relate to each other as learners. You can't get a more traditional view of education than that, but the structures that surround us are aberrations of what might be called good education.
Where tutors have the confidence and the support to move in the directions we favour, they feel as much liberation as the students. There is for most of us nothing worse than delivering the same old turgid material on the same old curriculum, which you have had no hand in developing: but some people get conditioned into that and feel threatened if they move out of it. Perhaps idealistically, all we want is a move towards quality in learning, where everybody celebrates everyone else's learning.

AUDIENCE: What is the cost of bringing your team to a college?

STEPHENSON: I've never been asked that before. Our sponsors underwrite us to visit every institution, so if we haven't been to your institution before and we come as part of giving our message or stimulating debate, it will cost you nothing. For that to happen though, we do insist that we have a letter of invitation from your chief executive, because we do want to maintain the leverage of getting your chief executive to understand our mission, to participate in the visit and to hear about what is going on. If we have been before, and you invite us back to help with a particular problem you may have, we undercut all other consultants by only charging you expenses.

AUDIENCE: Could I ask if the age of the learner is significant? From experience in my own institution, it seems that lecturers are far more interested in and conditioned to teaching a 20 year old than a 40 year old, and one way of changing lecturers' attitudes is to get mature students to attack this kind of attitude. Have you any evidence that this is a factor which needs changing?

STEPHENSON: Certainly it is an important factor, but let us look at some of the trends. The nature of the 18 year old intake is going to change: in schools particularly, the changes stemming from TVEI and some of the GCSE activities, and the likely changes in A level, are going to result in youngsters coming to higher education with different experiences and changed expectations. Secondly, and this is more a personal response, I've always opposed the notion that what we propose is all right for mature students but not for 18 year olds. It's all right for young children; its all right for older people; its all right for the less able because it is an opportunity for them to catch up; its all right for the most able because they have the ability to go on, and I'm left with the only group for whom it is not possible - the people between 18 and 21 who are on formal mainstream courses. Now there must be something odd that happens to human beings at the age of 18 which denies them their capacity to live, learn and grow in the same way that they did from the age of zero on, and are expected to do from 21 onwards.

I used to receive all the first year students in the School of Independent Study on their very first day and say, "Well, you're in higher education now, here is a lecture". I gave them a lecture, on nothing in particular, because they were expecting higher education to have lectures, at the end of which I asked, "Do you want any more because if so you can have them?" Once they realized this was a real choice, I'm glad to say they didn't. You have to start where people are, but the opportunities for giving them freedom in learning are there.

Professor John Stephenson has been for many years Head of the School for Independent Study at the Polytechnic of East London, and is currently seconded to the Directorship of the project, Higher Education for Capability.

Address for correspondence: **Prof.J.Stephenson,**
Director, Higher Education for Capability Project,
R.S.A., 8, John Adam Street, London WC2N 6EZ

2. Competence-based approaches to the realization of human potential - current issues and research

Paul Ellis, National Council for Vocational Qualifications

Abstract: An overview is provided of the many issues which arise in designing and implementing competence based education and training founded on defining standards of performance. The basic concept is not new, but in contrast to previous limited applications it is now being developed in the UK into a comprehensive national system. The result will be National Vocational Qualifications which promote flexible learning in its widest sense. Progressing an initiative on this scale has required a thoroughgoing exploration of all aspects of the underlying concept and the implications for implementing it coherently. The issues which have emerged as a result are identified and discussed. Particular emphasis is given to identifying the further research which needs to be done.

BACKGROUND

In Britain fundamental changes are being implemented in Vocational Qualifications. Qualifications are being reformed to base them on competence defined in terms of standards of performance. The basic concept is not new. However in contrast to previous limited applications it is being developed into a comprehensive national system. The result will be National Vocational Qualifications which promote flexible learning in its widest sense. Before exploring some of the issues that this has thrown up, it would be helpful to recap briefly on why this initiative was set in motion and the terminology used.

The Government created a National Council for Vocational Qualifications (NCVQ) in 1986. NCVQ's remit is to bring about strategic change in vocational qualifications. Needless to say this is not welcomed by all; change never is. There is the instance of the fabled letter, attributed to the Wigan Observer, in which the correspondent complained, "I'm sure that this change to decimal currency is a good thing and in the long run will benefit the country. But couldn't the Government at least have waited until all the old people had died off to avoid confusion." But the change which NCVQ is bringing about is not change for change's sake.

The 1986 Review of Vocational Qualifications pinpointed the impetus for changes as weaknesses in existing arrangements which were producing a qualifications system (or non-system) which was:

* not closely related to the needs of employment;
* over complex;
* resulting in too few of the working population having relevant qualifications.

The aims of NCVQ are therefore:

* to improve vocational qualifications by basing them on the standards of competence required in employment;
* to establish a National Vocational Qualifications framework which is comprehensible and comprehensive and which facilitates access, progression and continued learning.

The basic idea is quite simple. Start off by defining the standards of performance required in employment - standards developed by representatives of the employment sector to ensure relevance and accuracy. A qualification is then created which incorporates these standards. The standards lead the creation of the qualification, they do not follow it.

A standard is made up of an element of competence, e.g.

'receive and assist visitors'

and of performance criteria which detail proficient performance, e.g.

'visitors greeted promptly and courteously'
'visitors' needs identified'
'reasons for any delay or non-availability explained politely'.

The standard is not unique to a particular company or location. It is nationally applicable throughout an employment sector. It can therefore form the basis for national recognition in a unified system of vocational qualifications.

Elements and their performance criteria are grouped into units which can be separately credited to an individual and which have a value in employment. Because units can be separately credited they can be built up into a full award.

The competence which is required in order to gain the award is fully specified in the standards; no requirement is made on the individual other than to provide suitable evidence of that competence. In particular, the award is independent of the route followed to acquire the competence. This creates inherent **FLEXIBILITY** in devising education and training opportunities.

Ready **ACCESS** is built into the assumptions of the system. The intention is to encourage participation in the Vocational Education Training and Qualifications system; the principle is one of including rather than of excluding people.

In the light of this it is interesting to reflect for a moment on the nature of the criterion referenced standards which are at the heart of the system and are written in go/no-go terms. They indicate clearly what is expected for **PROFICIENT** performance to meet employment requirements. They are not graded, nor do they describe features of exceptional performance, rarely attained by most individuals. The system is thus one which is accessible to those of us of ordinary ability.

The implementation of these apparently simple ideas raises complex issues. These are briefly reviewed under three headings:

* describing competence;
* assessing competence;
* delivering competence.

The review is selective, which is inevitable, and to an extent personal and idiosyncratic, for which I accept full responsibilty.

DESCRIBING COMPETENCE

It seems only sensible to start with the intellectual puzzle of how to analyse occupations into competences.

We have already seen that competence is described in terms of standards to be achieved; standards take the form of elements of competence each of which has associated performance criteria. This deceptively simple formulation does, however, hide much of the complexity involved in deriving standards which will assist rather than hinder our purposes.

In pursuit of a skilled and flexible workforce we need standards which take a broad view of competence. Qualifications and the standards on which they are based should reflect **OCCUPATIONAL** competence rather than just the ability to carry out a particular job in a particular organization, which means that all aspects of performance relating to a whole work role must be included. The ability to apply competence in different contexts and environments will also be important.

The breadth which is seen to characterize occupational competence must be considered alongside the very practical nature of competence. Competence within the NVQ framework is the ability to perform the activities within an occupation or function to the standards expected within employment, and a competence is a full and complete description of something which a person who works in a given occupational area should be able to do and achieve.

Some early attempts to produce statements in this form were naive and lacking in precision. Experience, reflection and the development of more systematic analytical processes has brought about substantial improvements. One particular approach which has become known as **FUNCTIONAL ANALYSIS** (unfortunately a term used in other circles to describe an unrelated methodology) has contributed much to this field.

The strategy utilized in functional analysis involves starting analysis by identifying the key purpose of an occupational area. The question is then asked, 'What needs to happen for this to be achieved?', thereby identifying functions. The analysis is then repeated at subsequent levels. The effect, through a systematic top down approach, is to retain throughout the analysis the relationships to the objectives of the activity being considered, thereby emphasizing the broader aspects of competence. We are seeking to see the trees as part of the wood.

The effect is reinforced by continually checking to see if four interrelated components of competence are reflected in the standards:

* **TASK SKILLS** - for the performance of relevant tasks;
* **TASK MANAGEMENT SKILLS** - for planning and organizing the application of task skills;
* **CONTINGENCY MANAGEMENT SKILLS** - the management of breakdowns in routines, procedures and sequences;
* **JOB/ROLE** environment skills - for dealing with the constraints and relationships of the situation.

The explicit identification of these facets of competence assists in making the full nature of competence clear, and the drafting of units, elements and performance criteria can then incorporate these more demanding specifications. For instance, in commercial horticulture, consideration of task management aspects might lead to the drafting of an element of competence:

'Contribute to the overall cultivation plan by maintaining seasonal records of propagation and planting'.

Meanwhile contingency management might dictate that one of the performance criteria associated with another element should be:

'Adverse soil conditions likely to have a detrimental effect on cultivation are recognized and reported to an appropriate authority'

Functional analysis can help ensure that the full role requirements are adequately represented in the elements and performance of a statement of competence. Even so it has become apparent that in the form outlined the statement of competence cannot adequately convey all the necessary information with respect to breadth.

Someone who is occupationally competent should be able to produce the required outcomes in a variety of situations and contexts. Their competence is transferrable, not bound to a single set of circumstances. But suppose that we have an element of competence:

'Maintain soil conditions and physical appearance of bed'.

What then do we know about the different situations in which we would expect this competence to be able to be applied? The answer is, of course, that we cannot be sure. Based on the concepts of occupational competence outlined earlier, it is fairly certain that it is not intended that the competence be limited to one plot on a particular site at one time of year. But if more than this is intended, how much more?

The totality of different circumstances is virtually infinite; further statements are needed which set some boundaries on these circumstances in the interests of common interpretation. Acid and alkaline soils; fast draining and waterlogged sites; chemical and biological treatments, might, for instance, be specified as lying within the realm of required competence. Because of the importance of including this information the use of **RANGE STATEMENTS** is being explored as a medium for conveying the necessary context information in a standard form.

Range statements have a key role to play in the way competence is specified. They extend and broaden the statement of competence by making it clear that full competence requires the ability to master a range of circumstances, putting bounds or limits on the specification so that a consistent and **REALISTIC** interpretation of its extent is encouraged.

Combined with the improvements in the quality of elements and performance criteria which can be achieved by use of functional analysis, range statements ensure that the statement of competence specifies breadth with great clarity.

So what are the further research and development needs in relation to describing competence? I would suggest they are:

* to develop the idea of range statements and develop guidance on good practice;
* to establish the degree to which statements in the form described are, in practice, interpreted consistently;
* to develop techniques which will readily allow the 'quality' of a statement of competence to be evaluated;
* to investigate the applicability of this approach to descriptions of professional competence.

ASSESSING COMPETENCE

The assessment process for NVQs is driven by the statement of competence, or standards, which are at the heart of an NVQ. Assessment is seen as a process of **COLLECTING EVIDENCE** that these standards have been met. The evidence may be derived from any of a number of different sources; the key consideration is the validity and efficiency of these sources in providing evidence that the required standards have been met.

The model allows for evidence to be derived both from prior achievements and current assessments. What is not supported by this model is commitment to any particular method of assessment prior to a consideration of the nature of the competence as specified in the elements and performance criteria. Essentially, assessment involves balancing the weight of evidence that an individual is competent, derived from a number of different sources, against the laid down standards.

Given the practical nature of the requirements described in a statement of competence there is of necessity going to be considerable emphasis on assessment of performance. Certainly this will have a much higher profile than has commonly been the case in the past.

As we are interested in occupational competence the workplace is an obvious place to look for evidence, but there is only limited experience of using assessments in the workplace as a basis for national certification. One piece of research carried out by Psychometric Research and Development therefore set out to evaluate assessments carried out by supervisors or trainers in the workplace. The researchers concluded that:

'workplace assessment is viable and should become credible in time provided it receives care and support in delivery, and continuing attention and support once in place.'

Key points identified as maintaining the validity of assessment were:

* assessments should be made of real work performance as far as possible;
* there should be a point to point correspondence, as far as possible, between the assessment instrument and the critical elements derived from job analysis;
* the more work put into getting the performance criteria right the less problematic assessment becomes;
* more than one method of assessment or source of evidence (for instance observation, products, customers) should be used to enrich validity.

For consistency of assessment decisions the researchers recommended:

* assessment on multiple occasions;
* assessment by multiple assessors;
* measures to harmonize assessors' judgements.

COMPETENCY TESTS are probably the most commonly used approach to gaining evidence about the performance of individuals. They tend to be held in relatively high regard because they standardize and control assessment conditions and mimic the characteristics of high status examination based systems.

The researchers suggest that competency tests are methods of particular use for those who are unable to access other forms of assessment through training and work. They note with concern, however, that many systems appear to have sacrificed validity, in terms of the replication work reality, in favour of standardization, and conclude that the central concern surrounding competency tests must be the reliance placed on them as the sole means of gaining performance evidence of an individual's competence, as they are likely to give **INSUFFICIENT EVIDENCE.**

The indications seem to be for:

* more use of combinations of assessment methods;
* more use of performance evidence;
* more use of assessment in the workplace.

A number of research or development priorities arise out of this, e.g.

* an exploration of decision theory and professional judgement modelling in order to clarify the issues of combining evidence and sufficiency of evidence;
* an investigation of the principles which underlie the identification of the key features to be replicated in maintaining realism in simulations;
* the specification of the competences required by assessors and establishment of procedures to ensure harmonization of standards;
* the development of rigorous approaches to identifying the skills and knowledge which underpin competent performance so that they can be incorporated within the mix of evidence.

DELIVERING COMPETENCE

How will individuals attain the competences they are eventually to be credited with? The question is important, for although NCVQ's remit does not extend directly to the vocational education and training system, the ultimate reason for being concerned with qualifications is because of the power that they have to shape education and training provision.

In one way the question is difficult to answer because, to introduce flexibility, NVQs specifically preclude prescription of a particular course or mode of study to be followed. There will be more people participating in education and training activities; more individuals and organizations, with different contexts of operation, offering them help.

It is, however, possible to anticipate trends and patterns. Most conspicuous amongst these is a move from the full-time course as the only, or primary, way of gaining access to learning and accreditation, to the use of a variety of modes of learning. The college, workplace practice, open learning, full-time study, part-time study, experiential learning... all have a role. Colleges will frequently but not of necessity be involved: the workplace will increasingly be recognized as a valid location for learning. In place of the course is emerging a client-led model of provision incorporating guidance; assessment; the preparation of individual action plans; access to a broad spectrum of learning opportunities; credit accumulation and continuing learning.

Partnerships between industry and education in delivering these opportunities are likely to become common, as is access on demand. Managing learning will increasingly describe the role of the lecturer or trainer rather than 'teaching' - a switch by colleges away from being teaching institutions to becoming centres of learning.

One Local Education Authority has sought to implement these ideas in a number of colleges. The leaders of the initiative concluded that colleges need to shift their overriding purpose to one of facilitating the personal, academic and vocational achievement of the individual rather than one of providing courses.

A group of university researchers, drawing on information arising from a number of different interventions, suggested that:

* college wide preparation for the implementation of competence-based qualifications should address both what and how changes are to be introduced;
* college-industry partnerships need to be nurtured prior to the implementation of competence-based programmes;
* competence-led changes require the identification of learning opportunities across a range of learning environments;
* work-related learning offered through colleges needs to be designed, modified and coordinated jointly with industry.

There is a key issue which mediates progression down the path which is emerging. All systems have performance indicators and criteria by which they are judged, but it is not always the case that these measures have been devised to encourage the next step down the path, yet this is essential. Developments in performance indicators and criteria need in turn to be supported by developments in management information systems, if these ideas are to be operationalized.

There are difficulties to be overcome. It is worth overcoming them. A progress report from within one London borough noted the demands which change was making on staff. It then says:

> Students feel motivated. They can choose areas of interest to them and study at the time and pace they prefer. The atmosphere is relaxed and they like to have responsibility for their own learning..... Both groups, staff and students, are working together to make their course a success. The end results are perceived to be greater satisfaction for staff and better qualified students, able to take responsibility for their development and able to integrate their vocational skills in the workplace .

The possibilities are becoming increasingly evident, but much of the detail still remains to be worked through. Priority needs to be given to:

* developing appropriate systems performance indicators and criteria and devising management information systems in support of these;
* giving guidance on operating open access, client led provision;
* establishing approaches to cementing college/employer partnerships;
* exploring the contribution which mastery of underpinning knowledge and skills makes to the acquisition of competence.

CONCLUSION

I am frankly encouraged; the groundwork is being laid to enable truly flexible learning in the widest possible sense. Too much of what has passed for flexible learning in the past has been limited in its horizon and limiting to the individual. I have two thoughts to conclude on.

Firstly, the infrastructure within which we work must be supportive of our objectives. If this is not the case then our initiatives and interventions will be short-lived because they will not establish mutually supportive external links. As educational technologists we must therefore concern ourselves with the system macrotechnology as well as the method's microtechnology.

Secondly, the measures which a system applies, its performance indicators or criteria are profoundly important - it is essential that they support the aims which any system purports to have.

BIBLIOGRAPHY

Ellis, P.(1986): The macro-technology of training. In, Rushby, N. and Howe, A.(eds), Aspects of Educational Technology XIX. Kogan Page, London.
Fennel, E.(1989): The analysis of competence - an overview. Competence and Assessment, Special Issue 1, pp.5-10.
Haffenden, I.G. et al.(1990): Preparing for competence-led curricula in further education. Competence and Assessment, 10, pp.3-5.
HCTB (1989): The Caterbase Project: Workplace Assessment and Accreditation for the Hotel and Catering Industry. MSC Research and Development Technical Series Report. Sheffield.
Jessup, G.(1989a): Building a Framework for Progression - Qualifications and Standards. Paper for IPM/BACIE Conference, April.
Jessup, G.(1989b): The Emerging Model of Vocational Education and Training. Paper to AETT International Conference, April.
London Borough of Enfield (1990): Second Report of Cross-Colleges Project for the Implementation of Competence Based Qualifications (NVQs). Steering Group Progress Report.
Mansfield, B.(1989): Functional analysis - a personal approach. Competence and Assessment, Special Issue 1, pp.5-10.
Mitchell, L. and Cuthbert, T(1989): Insufficient Evidence? The Final Report of the Competency Testing Project. SCOTVEC, Edinburgh.
MSC/DES(1986): Review of Vocational Qualifications, England and Wales. HMSO London
NCVQ (1988): NCVQ Information Note 4. Assessment in National Vocational Qualifications. National Council for Vocational Qualifications, London.
NCVQ (1989a): Criteria and Procedures. National Council for Vocational Qualifications, London.
NCVQ (1989b): Information Note 5. Assessment in NVQs: Use of Evidence from Prior Achievement. National Council for Vocational Qualifications, London.
Stanton, G.(1989): The contribution of Further Education colleges to delivering NVQs. Competence and Assessment, 9, pp.11-13.
Training Agency(-): Development of Assessable Standards for National Certification, Guidance Notes 1-6. Training Agency, Sheffield.
Wood, R. et al.(1989): Boning, Blanching and Backtacking: Assessing Performance in the Workplace, Research and Development, No.46. Training Agency, Sheffield.

Address for correspondence: **Paul Ellis**,
National Council for Vocational Qualifications,
222, Euston Road, London NW1 2BZ, UK

3. Realizing human competence

Phil Race, The Polytechnic of Wales

Abstract: At a time when education and training are becoming increasingly preoccupied with 'competence' this paper is an attempt to bring the discussion back to **people.** After proposing suitable definitions for competence (and its reverse) the paper explores how learners may be helped to acquire a positive feeling of **ownership** of the competences they develop.

COMPETENCE

'Competence' seems set to be the buzz-word of the 90s in training and education. What does 'competence' mean? Attempts to define competence abound - but in general seem to cause confusion by their diversity. Perhaps sometimes it means something similar to 'capability', perhaps something more specific - ability to do, ability to perform, ability to make judgements, ability to decide, ability to take responsibility, and on and on! Or maybe competence means a whole range of such abilities?

There is a simple solution: **Competence = can do**

This allows **any** kind of competence - from the simplest to the most complex - to be expressed in suitable terms. A competence statement becomes a 'can do' statement. This is better than a 'will do' statement in that it retains the choice of the individual. It is important that people feel **ownership** of the competences they develop - describing competence in terms of 'can do' statements adds to such a feeling.

When competence is inadequately described (for example by vagueness in the wording of competence statements) it becomes in danger of being one of those things where "you know it if you see it". If competence statements are vague, it becomes hard to see how we may measure competence. There is then a tendency to think, "If we can't measure it, it doesn't exist". But at the same time, if competence is not properly described, when trying to measure it the wrong things may be measured - leading to the feeling, "If you **can** measure it, it isn't **IT**".

How can competence be measured? it needs to be measured in some way if credit is to be awarded for having it. It may be difficult to measure particular competences directly - we can measure what people **do**, we can measure what people **have done** - but that does not necessarily mean we've measured what they **can do.** However, the **result** of competence being exercised is often measurable. Such results can take many forms - actions, products, judgements, ideas, decisions and so on. Since **results** are needed to measure competence, let's call them **evidence.** One piece of evidence may reflect several competences, or it may take several pieces of evidence to reflect a single competence.

THE REVERSE OF COMPETENCE?

The word **incompetence** comes to mind. Unfortunately, this word carries overtones - it is usually taken to mean something more sinister than 'can't yet do'. Perhaps we can use:

Incompetence = can't EVER do?

UNCOMPETENCE!

Let's adopt this word to get over the problems with the word 'incompetence'. **Uncompetence** can have a number of meanings without the degrading overtones of incompetence. Uncompetence can incorporate choices, making it easier to feel ownership. (No-one would want to own incompetence!).

uncompetence = can't YET do
uncompetence = don't NEED to do
uncompetence = don't WANT to do
uncompetence = WON'T do

LEVELS OF COMPETENCE

It's easy enough to express competences in terms of **'can do'** statements. It is more difficult to describe **how competent**. The level of competence may depend on several things, for example:

* the requirements of the job;
* other people's assessments of competence;
* the particular dimensions chosen for its measurement.

It would be useful if we could define some sort of **'absolute'** competence which was completely independent of assessment - formative or summative. After all, people can often be highly competent at something - but not prove so in assessment. This is the fault of the process of assessment or of the content being assessed. If someone were to have 'absolute' competence, this should be reflected by any valid kind of assessment.

However, we can think of some sort of scale of competence, spanning several levels.

Highly competent (e.g. can do very well);
quite competent (e.g. can do quite well);
neither competent nor uncompetent (e.g. can just about do);
rather uncompetent (e.g. can't really yet do - but nearly);
highly uncompetent (e.g. can't yet do at all).

For the purposes of argument, we could imagine an arbitrary borderline between states of competence and uncompetence. The borderline has to be an arbitrary one - if the requirement is to be **highly** competent at some thing, the borderline would sensibly lie between 'quite' and 'highly'.

CONSCIOUS OR UNCONSCIOUS?

Let's think of any manifestation of competence - from a simple specific one (for example solving a mathematical equation) to a broad complex one (for example delivering a training programme). Does the owner of the competence **know about it?** Or is it unconscious?

By 'conscious' I mean 'knowing', and by 'unconscious' I mean 'unknowing' or 'subconscious' or 'unrealized'. I chose to use a scale of unconscious/conscious in the discussion which follows (rather than a knowing/unknowing scale) as I wanted to avoid the danger of getting into cognitive-psychomotor-affective discussions! Competences can be conscious or unconscious in any such domain - and (as in real life!) in complex overlaps of all three.

I was careful to choose the word **'realizing'** for the title of this paper, rather than 'developing'. Realizing can indeed be interpreted as 'developing', but it can **also** be interpreted as 'becoming aware of'. The range from unconscious to conscious can be regarded as another scale, perhaps extending as follows:

deeply unconscious	quite unconscious	on the brink of being conscious	quite conscious	acutely conscious

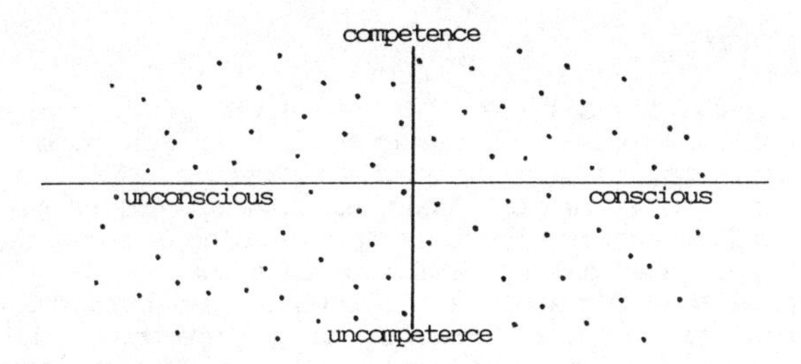

Figure 1: Conscious and unconscious competence and uncompetence.

As before any borderline should be regarded as arbitrary - depending on e.g. * personal perceptions, self awareness;
* help from other people;
* evidence - for example assessment data.

This gives us a way of mapping competence - conscious or unconscious. I should emphasize that I don't see people 'inhabiting' particular boxes, rather owning an array of different competences which at any moment are scattered through ALL the boxes. Most points on the diagram are perfectly all right wherever they are - no need or reason to move them. **Purposeful learning** may be regarded as moving and developing particular competences in a planned way - or acquiring such competences as may be needed for particular purposes.

CONSCIOUS COMPETENCE

This is the box in which we may want to have particular competences - those to do with our jobs, our interests - and our lives in general. All good teachers wish their learners to develop particular competences in this box. Whatever the description of the competence - whatever the form of the evidence - we want it to be 'good' and we want it to be **known** that it is good.

In the context of learning or self-development, conscious competence is the **target** box (see Figure 2a). I hesitate to call it the 'objective' box or the 'aim' box - aims and objectives may only describe **part** of the competence being sought.

Owners of competences already in the **target** box can say or feel:
* I can do it and I **know** I can do it;
* this is one of my strengths.

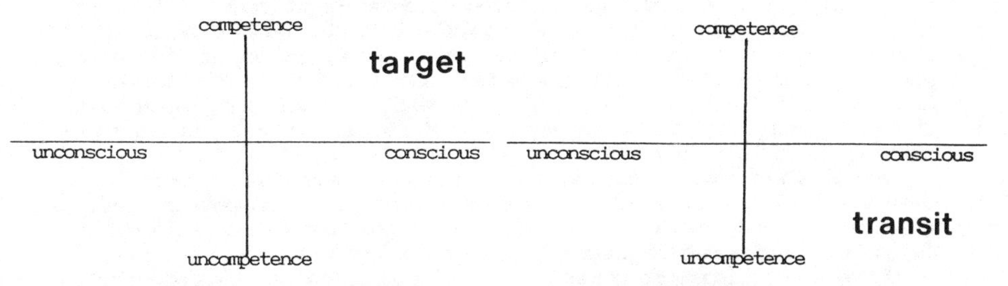

Figure 2a: The **target** box **Figure 2b:** The **transit** box

People who have developed an array of conscious competences are likely to be in a position where it should not be hard to put together a collection of **evidence** on the basis of which credit may be awarded.

CONSCIOUS UNCOMPETENCE

Let's call this the **transit** box. This is because if we have things in this box we're normally either on our way to getting them to the **target** box or we're quite happy to leave them where they are - for example competences we don't want, or don't need, to develop. Only those uncompetences which are to be the basis for learning are the ones 'in transit'. All the rest may safely remain in this box.

Having explained that "It's O.K. to be consciously uncompetent" ask a group of learners (for example), "How many of you are consciously uncompetent at preparing a report?" - many will identify themselves. As far as learning is concerned, conscious uncompetence is a healthy position to be in. People who know exactly what they can't yet do are usually well on the way to becoming able to do it - or at least are receptive to help in learning about it.

It's often a sensible learning ploy deliberately to address conscious uncompetence areas - that's what goes under the name of **revision** before exams, in that there's little point learning what's already mastered!

UNCONSCIOUS UNCOMPETENCE

On the whole, people with things in the **transit** position can move them towards the **target** state - with or without a little help. It's worth planning the journey with some care, so that suitable **evidence** may be accumulated on the way, and in due course the competences can be accredited. But **unconscious** uncompetence is not so simple!

"Hands up those of you who are unconsciously uncompetent?" is a question which should get no replies! "How many of you **know someone** who is unconsciously uncompetent?" gets a vigorous response and some mirth usually. Unconscious uncompetence is the **Danger** box (See Figure 3a).

But this is the **danger** box only if **relevant** and **necessary** competences lie there. It then represents the problem of 'not knowing what you don't know'. If this is not sorted out, the unconscious uncompetence may go on until it is **found out** one way or another - in an exam, job, etc.

We need to do everything we can to help people move important unconscious uncompetences from the **danger** box to the **transit** box. On entry to a programme of study, a friendly 'assessment' can help to do this - if it is ensured that this is not seen as a 'punitive' or 'threatening' exercise. 'Assessment', 'diagnostic test', 'pretest' are not the friendliest of words. The benefits to learners of identifying their elements of unconscious uncompetence need to be spelled out very convincingly to get their wholehearted cooperation in seeking them out.

Self-assessment is particularly good at allowing people the comfort of privacy while they seek out their unconscious uncompetences. Thereafter, **peer assessment** used regularly can feel less threatening than formal assessment. In both, learners usually benefit if given a suitable level of ongoing support - for example help in defining the criteria **they** can then apply to their own work.

Learners who have benefitted from self-assessment and/or peer assessment will be able to see how **past** unconscious uncompetence was discovered - and when relevant, rectified. They then become more willing to use such processes to identify **present** dangers.

There is nothing more powerful than allowing learners the opportunity of **learning by assessing** their own and each other's work. A major criticism of formal assessment devices such as exams is that they are often **lost learning opportunities.** Learners rarely get detailed feedback about exams - other than their final results - despite the skill and care which may have gone into the assessment of their scripts. Poor exam performance is only of limited help (and often too late) in helping learners identify unconscious uncompetences.

Figure 3a: The **danger** box. **Figure** 3b: The **magic** box.

UNCONSCIOUS COMPETENCE

This is the **magic** box. Mature learners in particular have an array of competences they don't know about. Their life experience can often be very valuable for their task of future learning. The more we can help learners **find out** about the competences they have already accrued, the more confident they feel about their ability to succeed.

It has been said that the single most important factor which predetermines success is **confidence**. A quick way to develop confidence is to identify some of the relevant unconscious competences that learners have, and place them firmly in the **target** box.

Evidence for unconscious competences may already exist - for example a learner who has already produced excellent reports may not have realized how many competences were involved in the process. Even in the absence of ready evidence, it may be quite straightforward to collect some, allowing what were unconscious competences to be accredited.

LOSING COMPETENCE

We've been thinking about routes leading to **gain** in competence, but it can be lost too (see Figure 4a). Take for example the ability to drive.

* After passing the driving test - and after a bit more practice - the skills involved are probably well into the **target** box.
* After a few years perhaps, the competence may still be there - at maybe an even higher level - but less conscious (the **Magic** box).
* Or perhaps the skills deteriorate, albeit subconsciously, and fall into the **danger** box (I see a lot of evidence of this!).

Perhaps with driving, and many other skills and competences, **regular testing** is needed to restore (or maintain) not just competence, but awareness.

TIME - A THIRD DIMENSION?

So far, we've been looking at our model without considering the dimension of time. A map of competences and uncompetences is in a way only a snapshot - the picture is always changing. Some points will stay fixed (the 'don't need to do' and 'don't want to do' uncompetences for example). Learning, however, will involve planned **trajectories** on a three-dimensional model. Naturally, there will be many possible trajectories between a starting position (for example at a point in the **transit** box - or even more remote: the **danger** box) and a desired end-

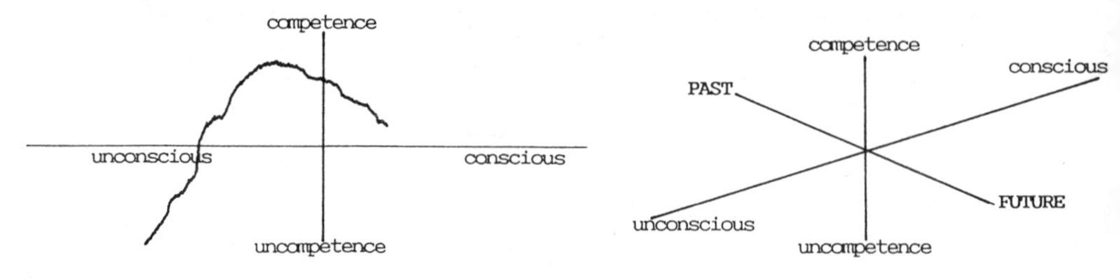

Possible changes of competence with time.
Figure 4a: Unplanned. **Figure 4b:** Planned.

position in the **target** box. Developing effective **learning skills** will be an important aid to being able to choose and use direct trajectories.

This leads us to think about the **processes.** Processes for **developing competence.** Processes for **measuring competence.**

PROCESSES LEADING TOWARDS COMPETENCE

* **What exactly am I expected to become able to do?**
* **How best can I get to a suitable 'can do' state?**
  These are the key questions that learners need to address. They need all the help we can make available to them with these issues.
* Syllabus objectives often give an idea of the sort of standards to be aimed towards - but often in language that is more appropriate to teachers than learners - and sometimes in language which would frighten off all but the most confident of learners.
* Past exam papers can provide an example of some of the things learners should become able to do. However, these too can be frightening if seen too early.
* Competence statements are in similar danger at times. It's all very well to describe successful performance in terms of the competence that it demonstrates, but it is the **PERFORMANCE** that is easier for the learner to anticipate, not necessarily the competence.
* Another alternative is exposure to learners who have already gained competence. 'Proctoring' is a term used to describe (for example) final-year learners working with first-year learners on particular parts of a learning programme. The 'proctors' probably gain a lot of competence by helping their less-competent colleagues! The proctors provide evidence of how it is to have gained competence.

As far as printed words are concerned, I suggest that the best way of alerting learners to what is expected of them is to accompany each competence statement by one or more examples of **EVIDENCE.** These examples need to avoid prescribing too much the way in which the competence can be demonstrated. Learners need freedom so that the ways in which they develop and demonstrate each competence can be as relevant as possible to their job, profession or career.

Both **EVIDENCE** and **COMPETENCE STATEMENTS** may need extra detail - description and specification.

DESCRIPTION - especially of the sort of evidence which may be gathered - should be understandable to learners who have not yet gained a given competence. Though **SPECIFICATION** may not be understandable to learners at this stage, it should be available to them as a means in due course of seeing exactly what sort of criteria may be applied to the evidence they produce. Both DESCRIPTIONS and SPECIFICATIONS can therefore be regarded as bridges between competence and evidence.

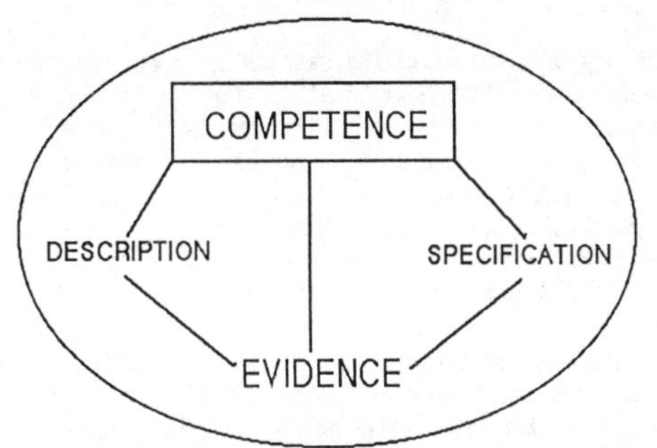

If competence statements are to be successful as a way of describing standards, learners need these extra degrees of information - examples of the **PROCESSES** by which the standards may be recognized and measured once they have been achieved. This points to increased dialogue between learners (individually and in groups) and their teachers or trainers - which can profitably replace some (perhaps all?) of the time normally used in trainers 'transmitting' and learners 'receiving'.

To reach a stable 'can do' position, it is usual to have gone through 'have done often' states. Learning is mainly 'by doing'. The 'doing' needs to fit as closely as possible with the sort of criteria which will be used to measure competence. The 'doing' needs also to be closely related to the sort of evidence which will be judged by such criteria.

Competence and strengths, weaknesses, opportunities, threats

Another set of variables - or a means of assisting the PROCESSES of competence development? 'SWOT' analysis has long been used as an aid to helping people find out where they are, and how best to go on from there. Having addressed the question, **"WHAT EXACTLY AM I EXPECTED TO BECOME ABLE TO DO?"** by identifying the sort of **EVIDENCE** which may be brought for assessment, it can be productive to lead learners (particularly in groups) through SWOT analysis.

strengths	weaknesses
threats	opportunities

One way of applying SWOT analysis is to use sheets with four boxes into which learners write their own feelings about each of the aspects involved in the context (e.g.) of their planned learning programmes.

STRENGTHS -"things you know you're good at already" - are a start for things belonging to the **target** box - they are conscious competences.

EVIDENCE may already be available, or may be collected fairly easily.

WEAKNESSES - "things you know you're not yet good at" - can be regarded as conscious uncompetences - things presently in the **transit** box. Some will matter - and need to move towards the **target** box. Others won't matter at all and can remain where they are. The kinds of **EVIDENCE** that will demonstrate that chosen weaknesses have been overcome can be planned, so that (where needed or wanted) progression to demonstrable competence can be achieved as efficiently as possible.

OPPORTUNITIES - (for example) "Your answers to the question 'what's in it for me?'" - are far more complex. They could be the chance to move things into the **target** box - both from the unconscious competences **(magic)** and from the unconscious uncompetence **(danger)** box (i.e. to overcome the danger by first finding out about it, then rectifying it).

THREATS - (for example) "things that could stop you getting there" - also are more complex. One of the threats could be the shock of discovering things in the **danger** box. Another threat could be not knowing things in the **magic** box - things which could be employed to lead to successful learning. Perhaps the most significant threat could be 'lost competence' - far better to anticipate such a threat and plan accordingly, than to find out too late that a particular previous competence was now absent.

There are many ways of helping learners use SWOT analysis. It can take the form of private self-evaluation. It can be done by learners in groups. It can be done with the help of a facilitator. SWOT analysis can be a productive way of clarifying problems that learners may be facing - and establishing ownership of the problems. The ensuing ownership of the SOLUTIONS which may arise from discussion of the analysis is a vital contribution to success.

CONCLUSIONS

Most of this paper has been about helping people find out where they are at, as a basis for moving on to developing those competences that **THEY** need, and producing the evidence WE need to accredit their performance. It has been also about giving learners a feeling of ownership for the competences they develop and the processes they employ to do so. My suggestion is that we help our learners to gain a day-to-day perspective of the development of their competences, rather than waiting for some day of judgement on which they will find out - maybe too late.

Dr.Phil Race started his career in science, doing his Ph.D in electrochemistry. After appointment as a physical chemist to the Polytechnic of Wales, he became more and more interested in the methodology of teaching and learning. This resulted in him being appointed a Principal Lecturer in Educational Development, and last year being promoted to Reader in the same subject.

Address for correspondence: **Dr.P.Race**, Reader, Educational Development,
The Polytechnic of Wales, Pontypridd,
Mid Glamorgan, CF 37 1DL, UK

4. Assessing the performance of crew resource management skills

J.M.Artiaga and D.J.Sullivan, Hernandez Engineering, Inc.

Abstract Assessing the technical skills of air crews in the military and the airlines has become a routine procedure within all flight training systems. The evaluation of crew resource management (CRM) skills, that contribute to the safe and efficient flying of an aircraft, has proven more difficult. Despite the proliferation of CRM and crew coordination training programs in recent years, little has been done to evaluate objectively the impact of the training on air crew performance during scheduled flights or military missions. This lack of assessment techniques for CRM is directly attributable to the lack of objective, observable performance criteria for evaluating CRM skills, such as interpersonal communications, situation awareness, stress management and decision making. This paper presents the approach used in developing objective performance criteria and evaluation techniques to assess CRM skill acquisition in a large-scale training program for the U.S.Air Force.

INTRODUCTION

Statistics gathered over the last ten years, indicating that a significant number of aircraft accidents and incidents are directly attributable to a lack of crew resource management(CRM), have led to the development of CRM programmes in both civilian and military aviation. Despite this proliferation of such programmes, little has been done to evaluate objectively the impact of the training on crew performance during scheduled flights or military missions. According to Cannon-Bowers (1989), even in programmes in which some evaluation data have been collected, the findings have been incomplete in providing full assessment of programme effectiveness in teaching CRM skills to crewmembers. As a result, there are no conclusive evaluation studies that indicate that CRM training changes crewmembers' behaviours related to mission effectiveness or safety.

The best indicator of the success of CRM training would be a significant, documented decrease in the number of accidents and incidents directly attributable to human error. However, the low incidence of accidents renders these data useless in determining the effectiveness of CRM training. Other measures that have been applied to CRM training have also proven inadequate in providing objective assessment of CRM skill acquisition.

Unlike objectives for technical skills such as flipping the correct switch at the right time, performance-based CRM training objectives, and the criteria to determine successful performance of those objectives are not easily identified or developed. While acquisition of technical skills can be assessed by observing whether the required performance occurs or does not occur, CRM skills must be assessed according to the degree or level of successful performance. Also, according to Helmreich (1986), many of the anticipated changes in behaviour and performance are related to changes in attitudes and commitment, which are the most difficult types of behaviours to evaluate. To compound the problem, acquisition of the desired behaviours may be adversely impacted by specific personality characteristics of some crewmembers.

It is clear that a comprehensive approach to evaluation is needed to determine the effectiveness of CRM programmes in teaching skills that will impact mission effectiveness and safety. Such an approach must begin with a well planned and conducted training requirements analysis that allows for clear and concise programme definition. This definition should include training objectives that are clearly stated in terms of specific measurable skills and abilities; programme content and methodologies based on those performance objectives; and student assessment based on the criteria outlined in the objectives. It is also clear that an innovative evaluation approach is needed in defining the criteria and the techniques that will be used to assess CRM skill acquisition.

APPROACH

Background

The concept of Crew Resource Management emerged from a study conducted by the National Aeronautics and Space Administration (NASA) to investigate the relationship between pilot workload and pilot error (see Ruffel-Smith, 1979). The study found that improper use of available resources often resulted in less effective handling of normal flight operations, as well as the unexpected events that can deteriorate into life-threatening situations; and also large variations in cockpit management and communication behaviours among airline crews, particularly in the areas of leadership, resource management and decision-making. This led NASA researchers to suggest that classical business management concepts might be applied to aircrew operations. In addition to the workload factors identified in the NASA study, Orlady and Foushee (1986) targeted the management areas of communication, situation awareness, problem-solving, decision-making, judgement, leadership/followership, stress management, critique and interpersonal skills as concepts that could be applied to the development of effective CRM.

Most of the existing CRM programmes utilize the traditional concepts of business management and have adapted them to the aircraft environment. Most programmes have also adopted experiential management training techniques in carrying out the training. However, none of the practitioners in the field of CRM have applied the concepts and techniques used by corporations to evaluate employees' business management skills to the evaluation of aircrews' performance of CRM skills.

Assessment Centre Techniques

Assessment Centres have been used by corporations to evaluate the leadership potential of management trainees for the last fifteen years. This technique involves the design of a simulation of a management job in which candidates assume the role of the manager for a two or three day period. Candidates' performance in various activities that make up the simulation is observed by a team of assessors. Candidates are evaluated on a variety of dimensions, such as leadership, analytical skills, oral and written communication skills, decisiveness and other managerial requirements.

During the simulation, a candidate participates in a series of exercises that are samples of specific managerial jobs and responsibilities. The exercises might require candidates to respond in writing to a series of letters and memos, counsel a poorly performing subordinate, meet with an irate customer, analyse the organization's

DIMENSION \ EXERCISE	GROUP DISCUSSION 1	ANALYSIS PROBLEM	GROUP DISCUSSION 2	IN-BASKET
ORAL COMMUNICATION	✓		✓	✓
ORAL PRESENTATION	✓			
STRESS TOLERANCE	✓		✓	✓
LEADERSHIP	✓		✓	
SENSITIVITY	✓	✓	✓	✓
TENACITY	✓		✓	✓
RISK TAKING	✓	✓	✓	✓
INITIATIVE	✓	✓	✓	✓
PLANNING & ORGANIZATION	✓	✓	✓	✓
PROBLEM ANALYSIS	✓	✓	✓	✓
DECISION MAKING	✓	✓	✓	✓
DECISIVENESS	✓	✓	✓	✓
RESPONSIVENESS	✓	✓	✓	✓
WRITTEN COMMUNICATION		✓		✓
MANAGEMENT CONTROL		✓		✓
DELEGATION				✓

Figure 1: Assessment Centre Dimensions and Simulation Activities

financial situation and compete for resources in a budget meeting. Dimension ratings for each exercise are integrated by the assessors to obtain an overall evaluation of each candidate's performance on each dimension. Finally, an overall assessment of managerial potential is made based on these dimension ratings. Sackett (1988) outlined the leadership dimensions that were assessed in a sample assessment centre simulation. Figure 1 contains these dimensions and the types of activities used to assess them.

According to Klimoski and Brickner (1987), assessment centres have been used for a variety of purposes, including training and development, career planning, improving managerial skills and promotion and selection. The centres have been used in diverse situations to include manufacturing companies, government agencies, the military and utility companies, and have proved successful with a majority of the participants regardless of educational level, race, gender or other personal characteristics.

The design of most assessment centres is based on the results of job analyses, which provide the basis for the identification of managerial job requirements, or the traits to be assessed. This in fact serves to produce the construct validity for assessment centres (Sackett and Harris, 1988). Job analysis can also be used to create the actual simulations and thus provide the content validity for the centre as well. Dulewicz (1989) contends that accurate samplings of relevant work situations are critical in establishing the job relatedness of the assessment activities. Accurate job sampling and translation of those job activities into the simulations is necessary to ensure that good performance on the exercises relates directly to good performance on the job.

Mission Oriented Simulator Training Sessions (MOST)

In many of the existing CRM programmes, the final phase is a MOST session. This session provides the equivalent of a job sample based simulation of the resource management performance requirements of an aircrew. The MOST session is normally a three to six hour simulator session consisting of a CRM pre-brief and a videotaped MOST session, and is followed by a CRM performance critique. The objectives of these sessions are:

* to present crews with realistic operational scenarios designed to represent their actual job requirements;
* to elicit CRM behaviour in individuals and the entire crew;

* to provide practice and reinforcement of concepts and skills presented in earlier phases of training; and
* to provide the basis for a critique by the crew and a facilitator of the crew's performance during the videotaped simulation.

Although the simulator sessions have served as the basis for self-criticism by crews, this critique is conducted in an informal, non-threatening environment. No formal checklists are used to evaluate performance, no data are kept on crew performance, and the videotapes are erased after the critique. As a result, no forms of objective evaluation data are collected to determine the crews' CRM skills levels following training, or the effectiveness of the training in changing crew behaviour and performance. In the CRM programme being developed by the International Training Division of Hernandez Engineering, Inc., selected MOST sessions will be used as the basis for a crew resource management assessment simulation to provide the first objective evaluation of the acquisition of CRM skills using job-analysis based performance criteria.

CRM ASSESSMENT SIMULATIONS

In the initial stages of designing the present CRM programme, a comprehensive training requirements analysis was conducted to identify job specific CRM performance requirements to be used in developing performance objectives and evaluation criteria and to provide detailed CRM related job analyses for the design and development of real-world mission scenarios.

1: Crew Communications
- Responsibility
- Assertiveness
- Timeliness
- Listening
- Barriers
- Feedback

2: Situation Awareness
- Perception of Reality vs. Reality
- Role Fixation
- Monitoring
- Total Awareness
- Incapacitation

3: Behavioural Styles and Response Strategies
- Common Styles
- Personal Style
- Interpersonal Skills

4: Stress Management
- Perception and Accommodation in Others
- Anticipation and Recognition in Self
- Stress Management Techniques

5: Mission Management
- Conflict Management
- Decision Making
- Situational Leadership
- Team Building
- Critique

Figure 2: CRM performance dimensions

The job analyses data were obtained from interviews with crewmembers, evaluators, instructors and staff personnel; from CRM-related incident information provided by crewmembers and evaluation personnel; from Air Force accident and incident data; from existing simulator mission scenarios and from subject matter experts on the International Training

Division staff. The information gathered from these sources provided the background and expertise to build realistic mission scenarios for the simulations. These scenarios were designed to include the routine operations of each phase of flight, as well as problem situations that might lead to disaster if not handled appropriately. The scenarios were also designed to focus on activities requiring effective crew resource management and the involvement of all crewmembers.

The job-based performance requirements, generated from the training requirements analysis data sources given above, were used to develop detailed performance objectives which were categorized into the five major CRM dimensions contained in Figure 2.

The performance objectives provided the framework for development of the content, media, and methods of the prework and workshops, and the criteria established in the performance objectives provided a basis for identification of the CRM performance criteria to be used in the MOST sessions and in the operational environment. These criteria were designed to be specific to job-related CRM activities and to be readily observable by the evaluator/assessor.

CREW COMMUNICATION				
Preflight:				
1. Took responsibility for communicating critical information	NO	NE	E	VE
2. Open communication among crewmembers	NO	NE	E	VE
3. Tone set by group leader	NO	NE	E	VE
4. Barriers to communication dealt with	NO	NE	E	VE
5. Addressed coordination, planning and anticipated problems	NO	NE	E	VE
FLIGHT:				
1. Took responsibility for communicating critical information	NO	NE	E	VE
2. Open communication among crewmembers	NO	NE	E	VE
3. Tone set by group leader	NO	NE	E	VE
4. Barriers to communication dealt with	NO	NE	E	VE
5. Critical information communicated in a timely manner	NO	NE	E	VE
6. Feedback provided to confirm communication	NO	NE	E	VE
NO=Not Observed, NE=Not Effective, E=Effective, VE=Very Effective				

Figure 3: CRM Simulation Checklist for Crew Communication

In order to provide precise and objective evaluation of the CRM skills as they occur during a simulator session, a checklist was developed which contains a list of the criteria and the degree or level of successful performance of the specific CRM skills. This checklist would be used by an evaluator/assessor during the simulator session and/or during the replay of the videotape of the session. The checklist could also be used by crewmembers to evaluate their own performance during the replay of the videotape in the critique session. Figure 3 provides an example of the CRM checklist.

CONCLUSIONS

At this time (April 1990), neither the evaluation criteria, nor the assessment centre technique proposed for the evaluation of CRM skill acquisition, has been field tested. This will be accomplished in July 1990, when the first complete CRM course will be validated. During validation of the courseware, the evaluation approach will also be validated and then revised based on the results. The validation will provide information on the content validity, the construct validity, and the face validity of the criteria and the assessment technique.

If the approach and the criteria prove effective in providing objective evaluation of actual, job-requirements-based CRM skills, it may be possible to establish a CRM assessment centre that would not only evaluate a crewmember's CRM skills, but also predict the actual CRM performance during a mission.

REFERENCES

Cannon-Bowers, J., Prince, C., Salas,.(1989): Determining aircrew coordination training effectiveness. Proceedings of the Interservice/Industry Training Systems Conference.

Dulewicz, V.(1989): Assessment centres as the route to competence. Personnel Management, 21, 11, pp.320-325.

Helmreich, R.(1986). Theory underlying CRM training: psychological issues in flight crew performance and crew coordination. Proceedings of the NASA/MAC-Workshop (NASA CP 2455), pp.15-22.

Klimoski, R., and Brickner, M.(1987): Why do assessment centres work? The puzzle of assessment centre validity.Personal Psychology, 40, pp.243-248.

Orlady, H., and Foushee, H.(Eds),(1986): Cockpit resource management training. Proceedings of NASA/MAC Workshop (NASA CP 2455).

Ruffell-Smith, H.(1979): A simulator study of the interaction of pilot work-load with errors, vigilance and decisions. NASA Technical Manual 78482.

Sackett, P., and Harris, M.(1988): A further examination of the constructs underlying assessment centre ratings. Journal of Business and Psychology, 3, 2, pp.214-225.

Dr.Jeanne M. (Hebein) Artiaga is Technical Project Manager for Hernandez Engineering Inc.'s (HEI) International Training Division. Her SAC CRM program responsibility includes management of the technical aspects of design, development and production of the CRM training curriculum. Dr. Artiaga has had over 20 years experience in instructional systems design, front-end analysis, program evaluation and computer-based and interactive video training since obtaining her Ph.D. in Instructional Technology, and has authored over 30 publications in the fields of instructional technology and training systems design.

Dennis J.Sullivan is the Deputy Division Manager for HEI's International Training Division, and served as Manager for the development of the SAC CRM program that is the subject of this paper. While with HEI, he has been responsible for the definition of European Space Agency astronaut training requirements and the design of the training system for the COLUMBUS Attached Pressurized Laboratory module of Space Station Freedom. Mr. Sullivan has a Master's degree in Instructional Technology and has authored more than 40 papers in that field, while gaining over 20 years' experience in the design, development and evaluation of operational and training systems.

Address for correspondence: **Dr.J.M.Artiaga and D.J.Sullivan**
Hernandez Engineering, Inc., International Training Division,
650 S. Cherry, Suite 102, Denver, CO 80222, U.S.A.

5. A quantitative method of measuring performance improvements

Rosemary A. Greene, Greene R and D International, Inc.

Abstract: This paper summarizes the results of a project in which a quantitative method for measuring the effects on student performance of a change to a technical course was developed and validated. Changes were made to a well-established technical course for adult industrial technicians, and the effect on the technician's post-course knowledge on exiting the course was measured. The measurement approach was validated using data from over 20 courses, each with 15-20 students. The measurement method gives management a tool for evaluating the effectiveness of changes made in instructional design or presentation, and offers the potential to reduce significantly training time and costs.

DEFINITION OF THE PROBLEM

Managers of adult technical training are under continual pressure to prevent technical obsolescence, and at the same time remain within the tight schedule and costs indigenous to 'hi-tech' industries. Courses must be constantly reviewed for technical content and cost effectiveness, and in a rapidly changing technical field, courses must be provided on a continuing basis to ensure the technicians performing installation and service functions have expertise in the latest products, operation and procedures. This type of training can be a drain on company profits, or a source of income depending on the effectiveness of management control over course efficiency. The purpose of this project was to provide a management tool for quantitative measurement of course efficiency, especially the impact of changes implemented to reduce course costs. For this project, course efficiency was defined as a reduction in learning time over other instructional methods without a reduction in learning gained (see Henderson & Nathenson,1976).

REVIEW OF POTENTIAL SOLUTIONS

Approaches favoured for reducing costs include course presentation advances such as computer-assisted instruction (CAI), or computer-based training (CBT). The first has potential for reducing course time, the second for allowing technicians to take courses at home sites, reducing travel and subsistence costs, but takes longer to implement. A measurement technique was needed to show that these changes were effective, and ensure that knowledge and skills remained at acceptable levels.

Any measurement technique requires a method of defining an upper and lower limit to the range of the measurement, and a scale that allows interpolation between these limits (as defined by Horvath, 1985). The biggest problem in 'soft sciences' such as education and management is defining the limits of measurement. The basic tenet of the measurement technique used in this project is comparison of final examination results from two groups. If a significant increase (or decrease) is found between the 'control' and the 'modified' group's examination results, it can be claimed it is due to the change made to the course. However, only that a change has occurred is known, not its quality.

The approach taken to develop the measurement scale was to use the final exam results from a group of technicians that had been previously classified as having superior ability as an upper limit of required expertise or knowledge. The lower limit could be defined in a similar manner, choosing a group having the minimum ability or performance characteristics, but in this instance an open-ended lower limit to the range was allowed. This is not unusual in the hard sciences, for example the Richter Scale used to classify the intensity of earthquakes is an open-ended measurement approach. The trick is to provide an interpolation scale that measures the required property below (or above) the chosen datum level.

This was achieved by assuming technicians taking a modified course belong to a new population, that this population has performance characteristics significantly different from the performance characteristics of the national pool of technicians, and that the difference between the populations can be described using standard statistical techniques. In statistical terms, any random sample of technicians drawn from a national pool of technicians will have examination results that have only one chance in twenty groups (0.05) of lying outside predefined limits. The chance factor and limits are those recommended by statisticians (per Horvath, 1985). Thus if the examination results for the technicians taking the modified course fall outside these limits it is unlikely to be from chance, and probably due to the modification made to the course.

This is where the datum measurement technique using a special group of technicians becomes of value; their deviation from the national population scores allows a quantitative indication of the improvement achieved with the course change. If average technicians taking a modified course match the achievement of the special advanced group it can be implied that the course has improved their performance to the advanced level. This may be a case of over-training, (relative to the course objectives), thus training time could be reduced with attendant reduction in cost. Similarly, if the 'modification' was a change in presentation techniques from a lecture/laboratory course to a computer-based course, it would indicate such a presentation approach has improved technician training.

The first objective of the project was to confirm the basic hypothesis that any reasonably sized group of technicians drawn from the nationwide pool of technicians performed in a predictable manner, and did in fact belong to a single 'average' population. The next objective was to confirm that a quantitative measurement of the change could be developed based on the performance of the 'advanced' technician population. The final objective was to examine the impact of course modifications on the performance of 'average' technicians, and confirm the modifications resulted in a different technician population whose performance could be quantified relative to the standard achieved by the 'advanced' group.

The timescale and financial resources available for the project were limited, but great care was taken within these limitations to minimize any impact of extraneous variables. Therefore this study should be considered to be a feasibility assessment of a management tool and care should be taken in extrapolation beyond the structure considered. However, it is the author's belief it will be shown that the techniques tested have wide applicability, and deserve further investigation to confirm their generality.

IMPLEMENTING THE MEASUREMENT AND EVALUATION TECHNIQUE

The course chosen for the project was given at regular intervals by a major manufacturer of telecommunications equipment to groups of technicians to upgrade their knowledge of a specialized type of telephone equipment. The project was conducted in two phases; in Phase 1 a measurement scale was developed, in Phase II a change was made to the course delivery strategy, and the impact of this change evaluated against the measurement scale. Care was taken during Phase 1 and Phase II to minimize the effect of extraneous variables by retaining the same course instructor, course content and classroom environment. This provided a stable database of post-course test performance against which the post-course test performance of the experimental groups could be measured. A student's 't' statistical test was used for comparing the final examination results (Used when a decision is to be made as to whether a small sample is part of a larger population. The decision is formulated in the form of a 'null hypothesis', such as 'no difference exists between the sample and the specified population').

It was postulated that three distinct populations existed, differentiated by the following characteristics:

1. technicians drawn from a nationwide pool who attended a lecture based training course. This will be called the 'average' technician population. Groups selected from this population will be referred to as 'control'groups;
2. a pre-identified subset of this population who were known to be of superior ability. They will be considered to belong to a population of 'advanced' technicians, and the groups drawn from this population will be referred to as 'advanced' groups;
3. a randomly selected subset of the first population who will attend a modified course and as a result belong to a new population called the 'experimental population'. Groups drawn from this population will be referred to as 'experimental' groups.

The technicians from these populations were unaware that they were participating in the project until the course had been completed and the final examinations taken. Course participants were mainly male, and had extensive training and field experience with various aspects of PBX telecommunication equipment. In general, sequential courses were chosen in the project to aid the random selection of technicians, and to allow a check on courses before and after the modified course to identify any 'carry over' of the change by the instructor to subsequent courses.

Every technician completed a 29 question criterion referenced final examination (pass mark 80%). The mean and variance of the final examination results was calculated for each individual group, and for the integrated results from those groups belonging to defined populations.

ANALYSIS OF PERFORMANCE RESULTS

In Phase 1, five control groups were selected, three prior to modifying the course and two following the experimental courses. The data from each course was analysed to obtain the mean and variance (standard deviation) in final examination results. The initial three courses were compared with each other, and the final two courses. Each course was then compared with the integrated results from all five courses. The results are summarized in Table 1.

Several conclusions were drawn from this analysis:

1. all the technicians belong to the same population;
2. each course has the same characteristic as the population from which it was drawn, suggesting that the sample size represented by a single course is sufficiently large to make predictions about the population;
3. there was no 'carry over' of the modification to courses following the experimental courses.

	GROUP 1		GROUP 2		GROUP 3	
	Means and standard deviations of each class					
	Mean	StdDev	Mean	StdDev	Mean	StdDev
CONTROL	89.1	4.6	89.4	7.0	90.8	6.3

	(Student's 't' test)		
	1 to 2	2 to 3	1 to 3
CONTROL	.3019	.302	.224

(Note: a value of greater than 0.05 is indicative that the groups are from the same population)

Table 1: Comparison of Control Groups

Since the p values for the Control group (0.224 to 0.302) are all much greater than .05, it is very probable that these samples are from the same population. Also,they are very similar values, indicating the stability between classes. This implies that the course was very stable, with no major increases or decreases in test performance over time.

Having confirmed a stable population of average technicians exists, the next step was to develop a measurement datum by analysing the performance characteristics of the advanced technicians. The data were analysed in a similar fashion, and are summarized in Table 2.

	GROUP 1		GROUP 2	
	Mean and standard deviations of each class			
	Mean	StdDev	Mean	StdDev
ADVANCED	94.8	4.0	94.2	4.9

	T-Test within populations	
	1 to 2	2 to 3
ADVANCED	.338	-

(Note: a value of greater than 0.05 is indicative that the groups are from the same population)

Table 2: Comparison of Advanced Groups

The advanced group contained field technicians, a specially selected group of technicians trained for the most demanding servicing tasks. These technicians are expected to have a greater knowledge of the technology, and so would be expected to assimilate the course material more easily and to perform at a higher level in the final examination. This is confirmed when the two populations are compared using the student's 't' test: the results are shown in Table 3.

	Advanced vs Control Groups
LEVEL OF SIGNIFICANCE (p):	0.0008
CHANCE FACTOR :	1 in 1250

Table 3: Comparison of Control and Advanced Populations

The comparison indicates there was a significant increase in the performance of the advanced groups (compared to the average technician). The population of advanced technicians was then defined as a datum; any group/population having the same characteristics will be considered to have achieved a superior performance.

After a change is made to the course the results obtained by the experimental groups will be considered to come from a new population, the experimental population. The effectiveness of change will be measured by how close the experimental population approaches the characteristics of the advanced population measured with the 't' test.

EFFECT OF CHANGE IN PRESENTATION TECHNIQUE (COMPUTER-AIDED INSTRUCTION)

The control groups attended classes taught by lecture only, and the experimental groups attended classes taught with lecture and CAI. The CAI system consisted of both hardware and software, including the computer, student terminals, and electronics to control the interface between the computer and terminals. The instructor controlled the presentation from a master computer, and students viewed the information on their terminals. Each terminal was used by two technicians.

A commercially available computer software program was used to enable the instructor to present course materials using a CAI approach. The software was selected for its ability to structure and present complex information sequentially and in logically meaningful chunks. The design of the CAI software used a hierarchical format that makes the relationship between the items visually apparent. The chunks (of information) per screen were deliberately kept to seven items, plus or minus two. The information in a 'chunk' presented a single concept or fact (as described by Slak, 1985) and these facts, taken as a chunk, formed a more complex concept, relationship or procedure.

Course information was displayed on students' terminals, but required no student response. No technical changes were made to course content or teaching strategy during the project, other than using the CAI.

The data obtained from the control, advanced and experimental (or CAI) groups is presented in Table 4. A student's 't' test was also run on this data. A value of $p>0.05$ (a chance factor of 1 in 20) indicates that the samples are from the same population. Any value less than 0.05 indicates that samples are most probably drawn from two different populations. The greater the magnitude is above 0.05, the more probable that the samples are from the same population. The 'p' values within the groups classified as Control, Advanced and CAI populations are all much greater than 0.05. (Table 4). This indicates the groups were drawn from a stable population and the students accurately represent the population.

DISTRIBUTION STATISTICS

	GROUP 1		GROUP 2		GROUP 3	
	Mean	StdDev	Mean	StdDev	Mean	StdDev
CONTROL	89.1	4.6	89.4	7.0	90.8	6.3
ADVANCED	94.8	4.0	94.2	4.9	-	-
CAI	92.6	5.8	92.5	6.1	-	-

Means and standard deviations of groups

COMPARISON OF GROUPS

	No. of Groups	Groups 1 and 2	Groups 2 and 3	Groups 1 and 3
CONTROL	3	.3019	.302	.224
ADVANCED	2	.338	-	-
CAI	2	.339	-	-

't' test within populations

Table 4: Each Population's Statistics.

The means and standard deviation were calculated for each of the three populations, average, advanced and experimental, using all of the data from each population (Table 4). The use of the total number of students in each population increased the sample sizes, and therefore the accuracy of the statistical 't' test. The results when comparing the populations using the Student`s 't' test on the total populations are shown in Table 5.

	LEVEL OF SIGNIFICANCE (p)	HYPOTHESIS
Advanced vs.control	0.0008	False
CAI vs control	0.0164	False
Advanced vs CAI	0.1736	True

(Null hypothesis tested was "Exam results between groups with CAI and those without CAI will not be significantly different")

Table 5: Student's 't' test on Population Means

The difference of means between the CAI and control groups in a p value of 0.0164, which indicates these groups are not from the same population. Alternatively, one can say that there is only a 1 in 61 chance that these sample groups, the CAI and control groups, would have the same exam results by chance. The CAI group consisted of average technicians trained in a special way; CAI with lecture. If CAI made no significant difference in post-course test performance, the results from the 't' test could have shown that the groups were from the control population. Since the 't' test results showed a significant difference in means, the two groups of students can be assumed to be from different populations. Since all other variables in this project were held constant, it can be concluded that the use of CAI was the cause of the increase in technicians' post-course test performance.

The positive increase in the performance of the CAI group is confirmed by comparing the examination results of the advanced group and the CAI group. The p value of 0.1736 indicates that these two groups are from the same population (Table 5). In other words, the scores of the experimental group trained with CAI match those of the advanced group. It is concluded the measurement technique shows the average technician's knowledge, when instructed by CAI, was increased to approach the level of the advanced technician's performance.

EFFECT OF DIFFERENT COURSE INSTRUCTOR ON PERFORMANCE

The same instructor was used for both phases of this project to reduce the impact of uncontrolled variables. As an adjunct to the project, data was also collected for the same course given by a second instructor and analysed using the same techniques. Results of this analysis show potential for the measurement technique developed in this project to provide a quantitative measure of the effectiveness and consistency of instructors teaching the same course. However it would require a more comprehensive, controlled study to confirm this potential.

EFFECT OF USING CAI ON COURSE EFFICIENCY

All the statistical tests show that CAI increased student performance in this course with this Instructor. Additionally, student comments on a post-course evaluation form indicated that they liked the use of CAI and found it easier when trying to understand complex information. They particularly liked the manner in which the information was presented in a very organized and logical way. During the CAI course, students were observed to be more attentive to the information displayed on the screen and to take more notes than during lecture only courses.

Interviews with the instructors before, during and after the project indicated that CAI was useful in several ways. The instructor reported that using CAI software to develop the course materials had helped him organize the information in his own mind in more meaningful ways, and the result was a set of course materials that he felt was better organized technically. In fact, originally, only one module within the course was to have been converted to CAI for the project. When the instructor began to use the program, he liked it so much that he converted and presented the entire course with CAI. It is interesting to note that student performance levels in the same course following the CAI course (delivered by the same instructor but using lecture/lab method method) reverted to performance levels of the average population. This indicates that the instructor's comments on organizing material better (with CAI) did not carry over to subsequent courses using other presentation techniques.

The instructor reported that students were impressed by the use of CAI because they considered it to be the most current technology. The instructor further observed that the students also appeared to have a high regard for his knowledge and skill as a result of using a CAI system. The instructor felt that the use of CAI had provided a more professional-looking course which reflected well on his reputation as a technically competent instructor, and on the company's reputation for offering high quality courses.

CONCLUSIONS

The benefits to industry of increasing the performance of technicians can be translated into large cost savings. Minimizing training time while maintaining acceptable performance levels translates into significant cost savings in terms of less travel and living expenses when bringing technicians to courses only offered in one corporate location. More importantly, technicians with more advanced knowledge and skill could be expected to be more effective and efficient, with attendant cost savings that result from increased job productivity.

REFERENCES

Borg, W.R. and Gall, M.D.(1983): Educational Research, An Introduction (4th edition). Longman, New York.

Henderson, E.S. and Nathenson, M.B.(1976): Developmental testing: an empirical approach to course improvement. Programmed Learning and Educational Technology, 13, 4, pp.31-42.

Horvath, T.(1985): Basic Statistics for Behavioural Sciences. Little, Brown and Co., Boston, Mass.

Slak, S.(1985): Short-term memory for figural items as a function of the number of variable dimensions. Bulletin of the Psychonomic Society, 4, pp.381-383.

Rosemary A. Greene is the Director of Education for Greene R&D International, Inc.

Address for correspondence: **Rosemary A.Greene**,
16, Boydell Close, Liverpool L28 6YA, UK

6. Measuring the quality of training

H.M.Brown, Royal Air Force

Abstract The Royal Air Force uses a Systems Approach to Training which includes several validation processes; however, as part of the introduction of the New Management Strategy, we have been investigating additional, and more quantitative, methods of measuring the quality of training. This paper gives an overview of Performance Indicators and stresses the need to include performance on quality as a focus for the attention of training management. The paper describes a trial which has been initiated using questionnaires to assess numerically 'consumer' valuation of training quality. An insight is given into the difficulties faced in the early stages of the trial and how the results are expected to be used.

INTRODUCTION

The Royal Air Force uses a Systems Approach to Training which involves a high level of control, especially in the area of flying training. The system relies on the clear specification of objectives - knowledge, skills and to a lesser extent attitudes - both at the Training Performance Standard and the Operational Performance Standard, to be achieved later in the work environment. We have a well-proven system of both internal and external validation, backed by a range of other mechanisms including the Central Flying School (which both trains and examines our instructors), the movement of staff between training and operations, and the Training Standards Committees for different aircraft roles.

However, as part of the New Management Strategy (NMS) we are also developing Performance Indicators (PIs) for functional areas such as training. The basis for this development lies in a perceived need for monitoring which is faster and more quantitative than that now used.

THE FOCUS OF THE NEW MANAGEMENT STRATEGY

The development of managerial approaches is common to all in the public sector, indeed not just to those in this country. Some might see this development in terms of a growth of management at the expense of professional independence and react accordingly, e.g. resistance to Local Management Initiatives (LMI). One guiding principle of managerial approaches is that of comparing performance either cross-sectionally or by year-on-year. The Treasury guidelines for management focus on three PIs as follows:

$$\text{Economy} = \frac{\text{Input}}{\text{Cost}} = \frac{\text{Training Days}}{\text{Training Budget}}$$

$$\text{Efficiency} = \frac{\text{Output}}{\text{Input}} = \frac{\text{Qualified Students}}{\text{Training Days}}$$

$$\text{Effectiveness} = \frac{\text{Output Value}}{\text{Physical Output}} = \frac{\text{Operators}}{\text{Qualified Students}}$$

Hence, deriving

$$\text{Value for Money} = \frac{\text{Output Value}}{\text{Input Cost}} = \frac{\text{Operators}}{\text{Training Budget}}$$

One approach is to see PIs as either 'dials or can-openers' (see Cave et al, 1988) and the answer to the question - Why are we measuring performance? - should then determine which type of use will be required of the PI.

The use of output-defined objectives in training makes it marginally easier to apply PIs than in education, particularly if one tends to see training as a production process. The danger is that, as the associated budget system develops, identifying actual rather than allocated cost, the first two PIs, being primarily financial and more easily gathered, could become the over-riding focus of managerial attention.

The assumption of both MNS and LMI is that managers are going to change things: hence, if we do not have some performance measure of quality it may be perceived as being of less importance than budget out-turns within management's overall strategy. Thus, there is a need to have some measure of quality which is linked to the effectiveness of operators and not just to the number of trainees graduating. The difficulty lies in trying to produce numerical measures of subjective quality judgements which can then be compared with the financial measures.

DEFINING QUALITY

Relying solely on the traditional questions of external validation e.g. difficulty, importance and frequency of tasks, could lead to an acceptance of minimum standards, particularly when there are several stages in the training process. Although the output and input standards of two serial stages of training should be the same we also need to be aware of intangible factors such as 'airmanship and captaincy' which may be longer-term products of the total package. A focus on minimum, and often mechanical, standards of trainee performance may be inadequate for getting a true perspective of effectiveness.

Hence, the nature of quality may be longer term and part of what is sometimes called the hidden curriculum. The question one might ask of course graduates is, perhaps, 'What do you remember as the highlight of your education?'. The answer may reveal much about longer-term influences, particularly the nature of staff/trainee relations.

Setting a PI for quality may be more to do with maintaining a culture of success than trying to measure it objectively to an exact degree. Nevertheless, there is a link to investment appraisal methods e.g. Cost Benefit or Cost-Effectiveness Analysis, aided by the development of actual/real cost data. This methodology can be compared with that of the Department of Education and Science which seems to rely primarily on input-orientated statistics (see overview in Education, 8th Dec 1989) and assumes, since investment appraisal is limited, that education (and training) is a 'good thing'.

So, we are attempting to develop measures which are simple and easy to collect, with the aim of using quarterly returns to build a quality index. The methodology is based on our experience with external validation and, in particular, our recent use of the Army's computerized system Exval.

EXVAL

Exval is a well-proven, computer software package which uses an Optical Mark Reader to input quickly the data from questionnaires. We have recently confirmed its value by comparing Exval results with those gained from interview-based validation and were impressed with the overall similarity of outcomes.

The questionnaire requires recipients to give a numerical score (1-4) for each of the training objectives for the course. The questionnaires are completed by both course graduates and their supervisors/trainers at the next stage. The nature of the questions requires that, on completion, the forms are handled with due confidentiality.

We have spent 3-4 months developing the questionnaires with the specialist staff at our training headquarters. It was at this stage that we identified the need for templates to achieve some standardization of the numerical scores. Four levels were produced ranging from unsatisfactory through to excellent, with appropriate word-pictures describing each one. Figure 1 shows the template to be used by the course graduate.

Level 1: Unsatisfactory

I have had to be retaught many of the basics of this item and feel that, at my previous stage of training, this item suffered because of the following reasons (delete as necessary):

It required excessive private study.
Instructional time was not well used.
It was rushed.
Adversely affected by weather.
Poor assessment.

Level 2: Satisfactory

Confident of a sound basis having been given. Happy that previous training provided sufficient chance to practise and understand. Occasional slight revision needed in the early stages of current training.

Level 3: Good

Smooth transition to current work. Previous training developed both skills and an awareness of the fundamentals.

Level 4: Excellent

Very confident of progress. Previous training fully developed my ability and gave a thorough understanding of nature and importance of the fundamentals.

Figure 1: Student Template

We anticipate that since students will have successfully completed the final test of their previous course it is unlikely that Level 1 would occur very often. This does raise the problem of whether the trial should be extended to include inputs from those who have failed. Further questions focus on which part of the course provided the best preparation, which the worst, and what factor might have caused this difference e.g. workload spread. From this we will derive an index based on arithmetic means, with frequency monitoring for sub-groups e.g. helicopter pilots.

In February and March 1990 we discussed the first questionnaires with staff at our Advanced Flying Training School and carried out initial trials with students. The trial year commenced in April and will see approximately 200+ questionnaires being completed in Flying Training and several thousand in a related trial in Ground Training. The sample size of the latter has advantages for developing our statistical analysis.

DIFFICULTIES

As we move into the trial year, we have become increasingly aware of some of the difficulties involved with assessing quality. Since the approach is consumer and not producer orientated there has been some staff resistance to student comment, although this is not uncommon in more traditional validations (see Education, 1st Dec 1989 for similar use in Maryland). It may be that managerial strategies, which seem to emphasize quality control rather than the perhaps greater focus on quality assurance of professional strategies, are seen as implying distrust of the trainer. Hence, as part of our change strategy we have taken great care to involve all interested parties during the implementation phase. The strategy has included 'marketing' which stressed the potential benefits to the trainers themselves.

Despite some acceptance of the production process metaphor, a further difficulty is raised when we try to go on to associate outputs directly with inputs. The problem in systems terminology is that of **emergent properties,** in which we cannot clearly specify in advance exactly what will arise from a given soft system e.g. intangibles such as airmanship. Even when we can use training objectives for outcomes it still remains very difficult to pin down exactly what is happening within the 'black box'. These problems of relating inputs and outputs are quite common within non-market provision, particularly of services; indeed this is usually why they are non-market (for similar problems elsewhere in the public sector see Jowett and Rothwell, 1988). Related to this are difficulties of comparability associated with the absence of control groups in a changing environment.

Perhaps the most difficult problem of all relates back to defining quality i.e. asking the right questions. If we cannot agree on what we are describing how can we hope to agree on numerical measures of it! Of critical importance is our concern with the 'quality of the training not the trainee', hence our focus on developing appropriate templates. Without this emphasis, and some knowledge of input standards, it becomes impossible to account for the 'value added' by the training process and consequently investment appraisal becomes somewhat meaningless. Unfortunately, these fairly common problems of public sector economics are sometimes ignored in the desire to create a market for all services as well as commodities.

USING THE RESULTS

At the start, it was suggested that our trial may be of importance solely in keeping managerial focus on quality; nevertheless, we do anticipate that numerical measures will be of value either as simple dials to let senior management know that all is still well or, occasionally, to delve more deeply under the surface (hopefully not into the proverbial can of worms). The aim is that the quality index will be updated quarterly and included in reports to our senior management. The information will be included with the other PIs and budget data and should moderate management strategy accordingly. We also believe that, if used correctly, quality PIs can act as both a motivator for training schools and as evidence for supporting budgets in times of constraint.

The NMS includes a Performance Review and Objective Setting Exercise (**PROSE**) which involves a need for comparison and investigation of how we best use our resources e.g. planned versus actual wastage on courses. However, we need to be aware of the context, e.g. changes in the selection of recruits for input to the system and/or indeed even the weather, within which changes in performance are taking place. This is where information from other sources such as the Central Flying School (akin to a combination of Local Education Authority and Her Majesty's Inspectors) remains paramount. The DES approach to quality in schools may be more limited than that of PROSE, in that many of the statistics recommended tend to be Yes/No, which gives limited indication of performance change (see Education, 8th Dec 1989).

In terms of investment appraisal one might consider such questions as "How would further investment in our instructional techniques appraisal and categorization system compare with more investment in recruiting?". Similarly, one might monitor for links between improved instructor categories and assessment of student quality. However, we anticipate that it will take three to five years to develop any meaningful analysis of trends even using complex packages such as SPSS.

Taking a wider view we hope that our work may be of value to those training organizations which wish to measure their output (see OECD 1989). Perhaps when some of our training journals begin to run Which-style reports on courses, we might see some improvement in the quality of training which many civilian organizations are currently delivering. Within a European market of increased competition in training services we ought to remember the plight of those UK manufacturing industries which in the past did not devote sufficient attention to their quality.

REFERENCES

Cave, M., Hanney, S., Kogan, M. and Trevett, G.(1989). The Use of PIs in HE: A Critical Analysis of Developing Practice. Jessica Kingsley, London.

Jowett, P. and Rothwell, M.(1988): PIs in the Public Sector. Macmillan, London.

OECD (1989): Schools and Quality: An International Report. HMSO, London.

Performance Indicators DES Aide-Memoir. Education 174, 23 (8th December 1989) pp.514-515.

Week by Week. Education 174, 22 (1st December 1989) p.471.

Squadron Leader H.M.Brown, MA MSc MITD RAF is a member of the Flying Training Support Cell at Headquarters Royal Air Force Support Command. The Cell's work includes the external validation, provision of equipment for, and design of flying training courses.

Address for correspondence: **Sqn Ldr H.M.Brown,**
Room F90, HQ RAF Support Command,
RAF Brampton, Cambridgeshire PE18 8QL, UK.

7. Realizing potential through quality vocational education

Dave Muller and Peter Funnell, Suffolk College

Abstract: Much current debate in vocational education and training focuses on the provision of quality services and products as a means of realizing the potential of learners. However, despite the attractiveness of the concept of quality, its application in the educational arena remains problematic. A workshop was run to provide an opportunity for senior practitioners to explore the concept of quality and to provide illustrative case studies of quality provision. The workshop illustrated the difficulty in defining the concept of quality whilst enabling individuals to provide examples from their own experience of high quality provision. Participants recognized that by working through their own experience as deliverers of education and training they were able to develop performance indicators relating to quality.

INTRODUCTION

The term 'quality' was used extensively in both an educational and a business context towards the end of the last decade and is prominent in the early 1990s. It is noticeable that many job advertisements in the educational press focus on the provision of quality services. However, it is only recently that there have been serious attempts to relate the concept of 'quality' to the educational system, both in terms of delivering quality in vocational education (FEU, 1987) and in recognizing it once it has been achieved (McVicar, 1989). More recently Muller and Funnell (1991) have examined the concept from a variety of different perspectives and have provided a range of case studies illustrating quality provision in vocational education.

The use of the concept 'quality' has been derived primarily from the private sector and relates specifically to a managerial approach which aims to understand and to deliver precisely what the customer wants.The emphasis is on the producer developing a 'zero defect' approach such that the final product is exactly in line with that demanded by the market. Quality is not seen as something which can be reviewed after the event has taken place or the product produced, but as part of the process of delivery or production. Hence, quality is built into the process rather than inspected out of the product. It can therefore be seen as customer-driven in terms of clearly defined outputs.

From an educational perspective this raises a wide range of fascinating issues. What, for example, constitutes quality? Who evaluates it? How can this process be undertaken? What is the product of vocational education? Who is the customer? These questions and a wide range of related issues need exploring within an educational context if vocational education is to benefit from the model developed in industry.

A workshop was run by the authors focusing on two specific questions which were addressed sequentially as separate activities:

1. What criteria define quality in a vocational educational context?
2. How can quality vocational educational provision be facilitated?

DEFINING QUALITY

In the workshop, two groups set about producing a list of criteria with which to evaluate quality vocational education in training. Each group brainstormed and then produced a selective list of main criteria which were then shared at a plenary session.

Group 1 produced four main criteria:

* linking theory to practice;
* developing a social learning climate to foster learning;
* developing reflective behaviour and individual ownership of learning;
* creating individual learner 'stress' as a stimulus to effective learning.

Group 2 produced a list of five main criteria:

* standards;
* quality of output of both tutors and students;
* developing learner-centred approaches;
* meeting needs or providing benefits;
* 'you know it when you see it'.

A wide range of other issues was discussed including the development of performance indicators and the difficulties in defining learning objectives. There was also considerable discussion concerning whether or not there was a difference from a vocational perspective between education and training.

The plenary session indicated clearly the difficulties the two groups faced in defining quality in a vocational context. The criteria provided ranged from the creation of stress in individuals through to the quality of the learning environment and the externally defined standard of the product. Neither group was convinced that it had produced a list which fully defined quality. However it was possible to conclude that quality related in some way to:

* outputs;
* the quality of the learning process (production);
* individual development and ownership (commitment).

Thus although the concept of quality would appear difficult to define it does seem possible to derive a broad framework within which to explore its relationship to vocational education and training.

DELIVERING QUALITY

Both groups were then invited to provide examples of good practice of the ways in which quality vocational education and training can be promoted. Without focusing on the nature of quality or on defining specific performance indicators, both groups readily produced examples of what were generally agreed to be good practice in vocational education. Four of these case studies are noted below and the criteria by which they were defined indicated.

Case Study 1: Learning to Ski

This case study focused on what can be seen as the development of sophisticated perceptuo-motor skills. Nevertheless, from this example the following criteria were noted:

* the standards were defined externally by a National Body;
* individualized learning programmes were designed;
* emphasis was given to helping the learner co-ordinate skills through cognitive reflection and motivation.

This case study illustrated clearly the complexity of developing skills-based learning and the need to motivate the individual.

Case Study II: Learning to Fly (Royal Air Force)

This case study illustrated the need to focus on externally defined criteria where high level cognitive skills were being developed which could be defined in terms of 'high risk'. The main criteria to control quality were:

* clear and explicit statements of learning outcomes;
* carefully built-in review procedures;
* the involvement of experienced colleagues.

Given the nature of this case study greater emphasis was quite properly placed on the product.

Case Study III: Teaching about teaching

Two groups used teaching of teachers as examples of delivering quality vocational education and training. Four main criteria to facilitate quality were defined:

* the use of quality circles;
* the learner ownership of knowledge;
* the use of peer-and self-assessment;
* a problem-solving approach.

The focus from both groups was on the role of the learner and the process of education rather than the product. Again, this reflects the nature of learning how to teach which itself depends upon the development of reflective critical practitioners.

Case Study IV: British Rail Consultancy

A consultancy project with British Rail was described which illustrated the importance of learner participation. The consultancy undertaken showed clearly that those individuals being made responsible for implementing the products of training need themselves to 'own' the solution (product). Ownership facilitated commitment to the proposed course of action.

CONCLUSIONS

Following the first activity it was recognized that quality is difficult to define but the second activity led to a wide range of examples of good practice and the development of appropriate performance indicators. The breakdown of quality into outputs, the quality of the learning process and individual development and ownership was confirmed through the criteria derived to illustrate good practice. Of particular interest was that vocational education and training is in itself extremely broad as was illustrated by the case studies. This does mean that it is likely that the definition of quality in relation to vocational education and training must be in itself broad and cover a wide range of criteria. For example, teaching teachers to teach would seem to focus very much on the quality of the learning process whereas teaching pilots to fly focuses much more on the product. In both cases it is possible to define quality in such a way that it can be evaluated externally.

The final plenary session of the workshop went some way towards defining both the 'customer' and the 'product' of vocational education and training. In the first case the 'customer' was felt to be the individual learner or the student, and the 'product' a set of skills and more advanced knowledge. It was also felt that being able to motivate the learner is in itself an important product. The reciprocal nature of teaching people to teach, where the product is itself harder to define was commented on. Finally, a potential tension between the development of a person-centred individual approach to vocational education and training and the pre-determination of externally set goals was recognized.

This distinction might in itself be a means of exploring possible differences between vocational education and vocational training.

ACKNOWLEDGEMENTS

The authors would like to acknowledge the contribution made by the following participants in the workshop:
Helen Betts; H.Brown; Dr. Rien Buter; Beth Campbell; Bob Farmer; Jack Oakley; Karen Saunders; Brian Stanford.

REFERENCES

Further Education Unit (1987): Quality in NAFE. FEU, London.
McVicar, M.(1989): Performance Indicators and Quality Control in Higher Education. Portsmouth Polytechnic, Portsmouth.
Muller, D.J. and Funnell, P.(1991): Delivering Quality in Vocational Education. Kogan Page, London.

Dave Muller is Vice Principal of Suffolk College of Higher and Further Education, with responsibility for staffing and course development. He was previously Dean of the Faculty of Science at Lancashire Polytechnic. He has published a number of papers applying psychology to a wide range of topics, including education, medicine and nursing. More recently he has been exploring the links between the development of policy statements, their implementation and the role of individuals in this process.

Peter Funnell is currently Head of the Research and Development Unit at the Suffolk College with responsibility for cross-College curriculum initiatives, staff development and training, and the generation of research and consultancy activity. Previously senior lecturer in Social Policy and Organizational Theory he has been a researcher and operational manager in local government and a service planner in the NHS. His current research interests include the interface between humanistic educational practice and the developing entrepreneurial culture within the UK educational system.

Address for correspondence: **Prof.D.Muller** and **P.Funnell**,
Suffolk College, Rope Walk,
Ipswich, Suffolk IP4 1LT, UK

Section 2: The contribution of experiential learning to realizing potential

8. Talking with Christopher Gable

Christopher Gable, Northern Ballet Theatre, with
Maureen Pope, University of Surrey

Abstract: The beliefs and vision for a ballet company and a ballet school, which are to compensate for the increasing emphasis on physical skills by stressing also the interpretive aspects of the profession are outlined. The comparative problems of instilling both capabilities into sixteen-year-old and ten-year old pupils are considered, and contrasts made with the Russian system. Finally, the recognition of quality in the context of dance is considered, and Mr.Gable's thoughts on and approaches to teaching summarized.

POPE: Recently I came back from Berlin Chris, and there is a film that is causing quite a lot of interest that has just come out, called "Dancing for Mr B"; Mr B is or was the director of the New York City Ballet, and in fact if we hadn't been given a title, I was going to call this "Conversations with Mr G"! So that is quite useful, but in fact there is perhaps another title which is on a video which we want to show you which is called "Talent Is Work", which is perhaps a somewhat more serious title, but it would be useful, I think, if we showed a little bit of the video, don't you?

GABLE: Well, yes if you'd like to folks. It is always nice to see a picture show before you have the words isn't it, and this is a video that we made which was fundamentally a promotional video and it took material for a film that was made for Granada, I think, on me and what I was doing. But the first part of this film is just seven minutes and it gives you a little bit of a flavour of what the school is about and what dancers are about, and it might give what we say afterwards more context for you. So do you want to see a movie? Yes?

(Video shown)

Well there doesn't seem to be a lot left to say really, we've said it all haven't we?

POPE: I think we've ended it at the point where you should begin, which is what are your beliefs and what's your vision for the company? Lets carry on from there .

GABLE: The thing that I felt was important for the company - if we are going to talk about a vision first and I guess one does have to have a vision first - the vision that I had for the company was really a reaction to what I saw happening in the theatre. You will agree, I think, that in any physical skill, the physical ability seems to get better and better and better. You are probably, most of you, much too young to remember something that happened when I was quite young in that somebody ran a mile in four minutes and everybody said "Woho, it's impossible, how have they done it?" Roger Bannister did it in four minutes; now, as you are very aware plenty of people can run as fast as that, and faster.

When I first watched television as a youngster I watched gymnasts and skaters doing single turns and double turns in the air, and then some very clever man learnt to do three turns in the air, and then some strong girl managed to do three turns in the air, and now a fellow is doing four turns. In other words, what I am saying is technical ability does seem to keep on going up and up and up (there must be a cut-off point) and the demands of higher spins, higher legs, stronger muscles and a greater physical potential keeps growing all the time. I thought the danger is that the theatre is a communicating art form, it is a place of communication, it is a place where you share things with people, like I'm hopefully going to try and share anything that I might know that is interesting with you now; one is sharing. And I thought that if all you're thinking about is how many spins and how high you go then the central essence of what you do in a theatre, which is share, is being neglected, seriously neglected: so the idea was to produce, to help to develop dancers who were like two sides of an apple if you like - the green side is the nuts and bolts of being a physically expert dancer who can do physically anything that a choreographer requires, and then the rosy side of the apple is the part of the dancer that has a creative imagination and perception that will pick out what the human quality of the situation is on the stage, and be able to share it with the public so that will give them another colour; so the idea of the company was to make a dancer who is both sides of an apple. Was that an answer?

POPE: That's a good answer, but maybe we could move from the company, although I think we'll come back to that. Really perhaps apple for the teacher: what's the teacher bit in you in the school trying to achieve there?

GABLE: Well, obviously dance is something which has to begin very young and that is something that I was saying on the video, you have got to start very early with them and all that happens is as the years go by you find out how you don't know anything about it really. I just keep on coming up with lots of different questions. I think what one has to impress on the young dancers that are coming to us at sixteen is this balance between the creative imagination and the sheer technical nuts and bolts of what dance is. By definition, they are attracted and motivated by the virtuosos. All the young dancers that come to us basically only want to spin and jump like maniacs and be Baryshnikov and Makarova; that's their focal point, they don't perceive the theatre as being a place of communication at all. So that's the first thing that one has to try to persuade them of, that the interpretive part of their work is in effect their only unique thing. That seems to me to be very important in dance, because there is a set of rules in dance that aren't arguable, the rules of being a classical dancer or indeed any other kind of dancer are laid down very, very firmly and you spend your life in a room with mirrors trying to conform to those rules. Classical ballet most particularly is hard because it is all sort of renaissance circles, everything has got to fit into a circle, it's all got to balance, there's got to be a harmony. To do the steps at all you have to have a fair degree of physical facility; you've got to have long achilles tendons, you have to have long hamstrings, you have to have a lot of mobility in your hip sockets because the whole thing is built on turnout, so you've got a lot of physical criteria governing it before you start.

So there you are in those great rooms with these great big mirrors, and you look in that mirror every day and you've got your series of physical tasks to perform and you can't evade the fact that you're not doing them properly; that the muscles do give up, and the feet aren't fully stretched, and the elbow has dropped, and you aren't supporting - you can see all of that, and you can also see not only the muscular shortcomings that are to do with strength, but also the fact that God in his infinite wisdom didn't give you a long enough achilles tendon, and you're stretching the damn thing as hard as you can but it's only going to go to a certain point before it'll snap. So you're faced with your physical limitations all the time. Now what I`ve discovered is that the hook through to people who are faced with that every day, is to remind them that their creative imagination is the only thing that is utterly unique to them. You can look at a dancer and say that the legs are low, he's too fat, she's too thin, but you can't really say anything about the creative imagination because that is totally individual, nobody else has got anything quite like it, and what I find is that the students that are coming into the school won't trade development of their creative imaginative self for hundreds of pirouettes . But if you talk about the totally individual, unique aspect of the student which nobody else can reproduce, that has got a hook because they are much more into what is more unique about me - who isn't, we're all looking to find if we've got anything unique about us.

POPE: There is a dilemma in what you are saying though, because in the video we saw an emphasis on discipline, a word which could be interpreted in a range of ways. In terms of the attitude, if you like, of the sixteen year old to the kind of discipline you are talking about, does the teacher have to impose a particular discipline because of the rule system, or is it some other form of self-discipline, or is it both together on occasions in dance.

GABLE: Well it starts off as both. There are two ways that you can do it, and obviously, educationally, you want to persuade the student of a mode of working and an approach to work which is highly disciplined and which will protect them long-term, and you want them to do it for themselves. Our sixteen year olds don't like doing that. I've now got a twenty-one year old and a twenty year old who when you try to impose certain types of discipline on them say "I have to be me, I have to develop, I have to have a year out to find myself". That's what I mean about being so young in the video I showed; dancers haven't really got time to go and find themselves because by the time you've found yourself, it's all too late because your career is all pressed into the first bit of your life. What I would say is that, strictly speaking, the kind of discipline that is needed to support a career as a dancer doesn't come very comfortably or naturally to a sixteen year old because a sixteen year old is already formed and all the rules of discipline - their background, the kind of home they come from - make such a huge impact on them that ideally for a dancer you get them at ten. This is going to sound appalling, but it does seem to me that at ten years old what you can do is build up a kind of discipline that is largely mindless. Isn`t that awful? I can remember going along at ten years old to the Royal Ballet School, and they said, "This is the bar and you hold it like that and you relax your elbow and that's what you do, and you always turn towards it and you stand in the position until I say go, and you don't get out of the position until I say stop". And at ten, maybe I was a retarded ten year old, you say all right and you stand there, and then they say, "That's no good, get your elbow up" and they whack it and it hurts and you think, Huh. I know you're not allowed to smack anybody anymore, but then you could get smacked so it was all right: they'd smacked up your elbow and then they'd smack this and smack that and they shouted at you and they abused you and they said "It's rubbish".

Whatever you came up with, "It's rubbish, it's rubbish", but there's something about you, you're terribly resistant at ten, I assume, and eleven and twelve, and you do it.

Then what happens is, when you get to those terrible adolescent years of thirteen and fourteen and you start saying, "I won't" and, "I don't want to" and, "Why should I" and, "I hate you", and all of that, by that time your elbow is up because it's been up seven days a week for three years, so it's all been built. In other words, you've built a physical scaffolding which your physical technique can stand on and you've built it up in those unquestioning years which will accept it. Well, I suppose I accepted it all because I went to a school, the Royal Ballet School which was going to teach me to be a dancer. I wanted to be a dancer, I wanted to be successful, I wanted to be a star. They said this is how you do it; I said you must know best (if I thought about it logically at all) so if it means being smacked and shouted at and abused all day long, then that is obviously how you do it, and so I accepted it.

Now what we have at the school at sixteen is something quite different, and that is why we have discovered there is in effect no point, I don't think, in trying to train a dancer if you start at sixteen unless they are pretty bright. That's not to say intellectually bright; they've got to be intelligent, but you've got to be able to replace those years when the muscular memory has been trained in the same way as a pianist trains - you go up and down there for four or five hours a day so that in the end your fingers will move and have a life of their own, I think it's to do with synaptic bypasses or something - anyway, they operate on their own, they'll do all that stuff, and so you don't have to think about them any more. So you are then free, your creative energy is free because the machinery will operate, to a large extent, without you.

If you start a dancer at ten you can also get a muscular memory built, which operates largely without conscious thought; it does on me. I can get up here and I can do this now, and that too, and I can do it without thinking about it because all the muscles know about how to do it: even though I'm semi-geriatric, I can still do that because all those muscles know it. Now those starting at sixteen can't do that, so what I have to do is to explain to the dancer how their spine has to be balanced over their feet, how their feet have to be put onto the floor, to explain all the rules, and they have to understand those rules. I also have to say "It will hurt". I have to explain to them what the prices they are going to have to pay will be, and they have to accept those prices, so it's a much more rational process. Curiously enough though, what I have discovered in the school is that the sixteen year olds are very highly motivated. I'll talk about boys, simply because I have been most responsible for the boys in the school. The boys have come through that terrible background of "You must be gay if you want to be a dancer at all", so they've had merciless ragging, even these days, for being in dance at all. They've also had Mum and Dad saying "But you've got seven, eight O levels at A grades and B grades, why don't you do a proper job - go to university and do a real job", and all of that, and so these lads arrive - this is something else I should tell you, slight digression, but what we discover when we interview at the school is that there is in the education system a sort of set-up (my son went through it), that if you're clever you go for the sciences, you do maths and all the other scientific bits; then there's this other range of stuff you do if you're a half wit, which is music, religious instruction, cookery, and a whole range of those. At my son's school they were quite definitely set aside as what you did if you were a bit thick; you did sort of creative things!

So they've had parental opposition, these lads, they've had merciless ribbing from their peer group, and when they arrive at a vocational school such as ours, they've already overcome a tremendous amount of opposition, so they want it very badly. And in the end, I would say my experience is that that hunger, that motivation is at the root of all success. If somebody wants something badly, they will pay virtually any price for it. What has been very dispiriting, the most dispiriting thing for me in the training of youngsters is how much one meets a lack of want, that "It doesn't matter much anyway" and the whole ethos of trying to succeed without trying. We all want to succeed without trying; I've spent my life trying to find a way of succeeding without trying, and what I've discovered is that you don't actually achieve anything without trying. You can try very, very hard indeed and still not succeed, but I've never yet met anybody who has succeeded without trying. And yet there seems to be this idea, I think the Beatles and the rock scene had a lot to do with that, in that lots of people saw a mate who had been sitting in the changing room at school going "la la la" and suddenly they've made a thousand million pounds with a pop record and they've rocketed, so it looked like success was easy. But that kind of fluke success is another thing altogether: that's not success, you can't build a life on a fluke. Well, you could try I suppose.

POPE: Can I ask you perhaps a final question because I know at the school a lot of your training is based on the Vaganova method which originates in a cultural context quite different from this society. Have you got any observations about this?

GABLE: Yes, I think it is without question the most complete training - physical training - system in the world. The lady was very much a scientist. She broke down all the movements of dance/classical ballet into their component parts, looked at the best order to teach them and then did assessments. She had experimental groups so she could check whether you approached it that way, did A first and then B, or whether you did B then A; what order you did it in to get the best results. That's the reason why the Russians are producing by far the best and most complete dancers, because they were the first to take a really scientific interest in how the muscles were formed, how much pressure you can put on them before it starts to become counter productive. They took it seriously in the same way as they took their gymnastics and all such. The difficulty is that the whole social framework in Russia is so different. You see, in the way that in this country everybody pushes their kids to be doctors and surgeons and those jobs that are perceived as good jobs with good money and good rewards. There are those jobs, and there are dance and theatre and the arts generally that are so far down that they're under the carpet somewhere, whereas in Russia to be a dancer is practically the best job you can get. You get better food, you get better living conditions, you get a better pension, you might even get somewhere to live in the country, so it's right up at the top with the brain surgeons, being a dancer. Consequently every parent is pushing their child to the ballet. You know 85,000 people apply each year to the Kirov Choreographic Institute to be dancers? They see 3,000 of which they take 85 and they reckon that half of those will have dropped out before the end of their training, either broken somewhere along the way or dropped out for other reasons. The 40 that they get left with are guaranteed jobs because there's eleven ballet companies in Leningrad alone, I think, and every theatre is packed to see those dancers because that's the national pastime, to go and see the ballet. I think that is terribly wasteful and I hate the idea of that waste. I hate the idea that anybody is expendable in that way, that if it doesn't work out, throw them away; "If they split, fine, we'll get another one." I think that's a horrid idea.

What we've been forced to do in the school is at completely the other end of the scale. The people who've survived the system and the parents and the bantering and have got themselves into a vocational school, are relatively few. If you then look at the ones who have got a long achilles tendon, and a long hamstring, and an ability to turn out in a natural spring, and natural co-ordination - and that's not the end of it because once you've got the right physical specimen, you're also trying to find somebody who's got the emotional availability and creative imagination of an actor, but who is also sensitive to and responsive to music, who has an idea for line and colour - you're looking for a very complex package of natural skills that you are then trying to develop. They are so thin on the ground that you've got to use every resource: you've got to try and encourage, develop, stroke, otherwise we'd end up with nobody.

POPE: Fine, thank you because I think perhaps we should give the audience some possibility to ask questions. If I could just make a quick comment from my own experience working occasionally at the school, and that is that Chris has emphasized the complexity of what it means to be a dancer, but one of the things that I admire in Christopher is his capacity to try and communicate to people outside of the world of dance quite what that's about. Dance can often be seen as a mystique, a rarefied atmosphere, and in fact I think in this country it's been somewhat promoted like that. So my comment in terms of thanks for the conversation is that as an educationalist, I have learnt a lot about education by going in to a school of dance, but perhaps others might like to ask Chris some questions.

AUDIENCE: What is quality and how do you assess it?

GABLE: Well, maybe the best way I could answer that would be to describe one of the greatest performances I have ever seen. I was very lucky, when I was sixteen years old and I was at the Royal Ballet School. It was 1956 and the Bolshoi came for the first time after all the horrors, and they came with a lady called Galina Ulanova, and one of the ballets they danced was 'Romeo and Juliet'. She was playing Juliet and it was impossible to get in, except that they needed 10 boys to carry food on their head to the Capulet Ball, and they came to the Royal Ballet School to choose them. So I got smoked salmon, I think, papier-mache smoked salmon, and all we had to do was just march across the front cloth with this stuff on our heads, but what it gave you was this magic little thing with your photograph on it which got you through the stage door, because the security was terrifying. I very quickly realized that if you put on a dressing-gown and make-up, and stood in the wings, 'cos we were told very firmly that we'd to stay down - there's a cellar they keep the extras in at Covent Garden, and they said very firmly stay down in the cellar - but I realized that if you put on make-up and a dressing-gown and said something Russian-sounding occasionally, nobody really knew, so it meant that I was in the wings to watch every one of those performances by Ulanova. And I thought it, and subsequently I defined it as a great performance. There was a large part of the audience that went there, as always at Covent Garden, covered in their jewellery and diamonds and to be seen and say, "My darling I was at the Bolshoi last night", and they really just wanted an evening out at the theatre, and they got that. There was the Ben Hur syndrome, the people who actually love to go and see massive sets and costumes and the whole thing come to life on the stage and a great spectacle; that was provided for them. Then there are always people in a ballet audience who go to see the athleticism. To go to see how many spins, how high the jumps are, what the technical expertise is: the company provided that for them, to the limit - wonderful! There are the people who go, which is called the Anna Neagle syndrome, to see a lady of 45 pretending to be 16. "My dear you wouldn't believe it would you?" And she provided that because a more effervescent expression of being 16 I've never yet seen. Isn't it curious that only old people know about being young - have you ever noticed that? And young people don't know anything about it. So she was the essence of youngness and there was that. But for the people who went to see an in-depth psychological study of a young girl in torment - you know in Shakespeare's text, she's not even 14, and there's the whole family pressing towards a marriage when she's already married and nobody is telling and she doesn't know what to do. Now I was perhaps 10 yards away from that performance night after night, and that was the most staggering, in-depth study of a girl in torment. So I subsequently defined it in my mind as a great performance - a performance which is accessible and communicates on whatever level the audience is able to reach it.

AUDIENCE: Could you teach someone to dance who didn't want to dance or didn't know that they wanted to dance?

GABLE: I think yes, for sure, and I think that's to do with the imagination. It's to do with the teacher's ability to create that hunger and enthusiasm. We ran at the school sessions where we were looking at the next generation, the little ones, and the thing about dance is you have to start so little. What we didn't want was the 'Good toes, naughty toes' syndrome, we wanted to get real proper kids coming in. So we sent round to all the schools that were within striking distance of our base, which is up the road here, and we said, "Can we come and have a look at your kids that are, in your school, good at sport, good at games, athletic, basically athletic rather than artistic", because artistic can be terribly dangerous. Athletic, and so we went and we got in a whole lot of kids and they were every colour and every kind of kid from every kind of background. It was really a very interesting bunch, and it was all free, and it was an experience of dance - you come in and you just do it. The example I am thinking of is, we have a lady who graduated from the Kirov and we were fascinated to see what she would do with these athletic little ten/eleven year olds. So she gathered her group together and she took them into the studio and she said "This is a very special place because this is the place where you will become a dancer". And they looked, and then she said "And the first thing you will do to become a dancer is...", and she showed them, "and then you'll stand like this, and this is..." and the eyes got bigger and bigger and bigger. Now the traditional approach to the teaching of dance in this country, which I think is so insulting to children, is that they can't handle that; what you've got to say is "When the music goes high be on your tipitoes, and when the music goes low be a big giant". That's insulting to children. If you say to a child "You have to do this and this and this, let's try," and you give the child time to think about it, what was magical for me watching those classes was seeing the concentration and realizing that they want to know how to do it properly; they don't want to be fobbed off with feathers, they want the real thing. Inevitably, as it went through, some of them found it too difficult and fell away: some of it was to do with parents in fact, who didn't like them getting so obsessive about this training that they were doing, "It's not healthy for a youngster is it? She should be watching television", there was a lot of that. But some of those, we still have one boy particularly who's actually gone from step to step to step. He had an additional skill of course, which was that he was able to keep that whole life private and completely secret. His training gear had to be kept at the bottom of the bag; there had to be no chance that anybody would ever see that he was actually doing it because that could damage it all, and he had to keep it very precious and to himself. But to answer your question properly and quickly, the bottom line was the encouraging thing that youngsters do want to do things properly, but it's crucial that you feed it to them in the right way. And that's the teacher's skill in the end isn't it; that's why I say I don't know anything about it. I'll tell you why I think I'm a reasonably good teacher - I hate saying that because maybe I'm not, I don't know - but the reason I think I'm reasonably good at it is because I'm an actor and have been for over 30 years, and all of you must be actors because that's what you are, and it means that if all your working life is spent trying to hear the feeling of the place you're in, the people you are with, the people you're talking to, trying to sense when they start to get bored, when they start resisting - and that's why phones are so frightening aren't they, because you don't know what's happening at the other end - but when I can see you I can see when you're bored, when you think that's a load of old rubbish, but then that gives me the opportunity to think, "Well wait a minute, do they think what I'm saying is rubbish or have I said it wrong?" So I can say it in another way, and then if you still think it's rubbish then you think it's rubbish. But we're all doing that all of the time, all of us, and so I now begin to feel that the most skilled teachers in the school and in the company have been successful performers. There are some performers who are obviously no use at it at all, like Harold Turner. You probably won't remember Harold Turner, but he taught me a lot. He was an absolutely natural intuitive dancer, and you'd say, "Mr Turner, how do you do this double turn in the air?" and he'd say, "Well you jump up in the air and you go round twice. Look, like this," and there are lots and lots of boys who kind of went whoops splat, and you'd be saying "No it doesn't work for me". " Yes it does, you just jump up and go ..." So there are some performers who can't do it at all, but I think the part of the performer that is crucial is you play the class. Every day when I go into the company and when I go into my class at the school, I feel where they are. There is a kind of sixth sense which you all must have experienced a hundred times; you've got to decide whether to kill, whether to go in and go "Pow pow pow and I'm sick to death of this lazy sloppy class, I can't stand another minute of it", or "You must be tired my darlings, let's go easy" and you just know which line you're going to take to get the best results: if it starts to go wrong you shift, and I think that's crucial.

Christopher Gable Trained at the Sadler's Wells Ballet School and then worked successively with Sadler's Wells Opera Ballet, their Theatre Ballet and then the Royal Ballet, where he danced the entire range of classical roles. He retired from the Royal Ballet in 1966 to pursue an acting career in theatre, television and film. Christopher became Artistic Director of Northern Ballet Theatre in 1987, and is also Artistic Director of The Central School of Ballet in London. He divides his time between the Company and the School, which work in close association, especially on educational developments.

Dr.Maureen Pope lectures at the University of Surrey, and is a Governor of The Central School of Ballet.

9. Developing human potential experientially

Jane Henry, The Open University

Abstract: This paper examines approaches to experiential learning and their place in realizing human potential. It attempts to clarify what experiential learning and realizing human potential mean in practice. Experiential learning methods are grouped into schools with different orientations and routes to realizing human potential. The schools are personal development, prior learning, placement and project work. The paper discusses similarities and differences in the goals, processes, assessment procedures and outcomes claimed by practitioners.
The study draws on an international survey of experiential learning practitioners which included contributions from the fields of nursing, management, education, agriculture, language learning, outward bound etc., in Europe, Australasia, North America and elsewhere.

INTRODUCTION

Experiential learning (EL) means different things to different people: to a mathematician it may imply the use of activities like building blocks to convey mathematical principles; to those in the human potential movement it may imply learning about the self through experience; to experiential educators it may imply the provision of structured learning experiences that aim to bring a flavour of the outside world into the classroom. These learning experiences have different goals, processes and outcomes and yet my analysis of a survey on experiential learning suggests practitioners share a common philosophy that is very much concerned with developing human potential. (See Appendix A for questions used.)

Most of the experiential learning advocates in my study were happy to cite Kolb's (1975) description of the experiential learning cycle by way of theoretical justification. Kolb's cycle outlines four stages; concrete experience, observation and reflection, abstract conceptualization and generalization, and active experimentation in which new behaviours and approaches are tested out (1). Many people opt for more user friendly definitions of these stages and adapt Kolb's original - Figure 1 offers my version.

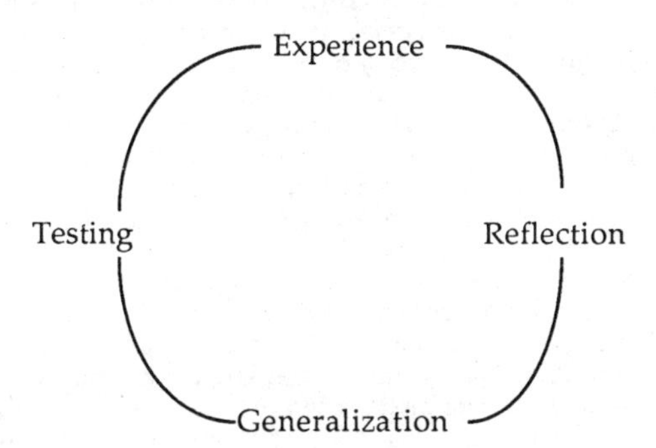

Figure 1: The Kolb learning cycle.

HUMAN POTENTIAL AND EXPERIENTIAL LEARNING

Both members of the human potential movement and those in experiential education use the term experiential learning to describe their kind of 'teaching'. My study suggested a tendency for theorists practising personal development and involved in the human potential movement to interpret the Kolb EL cycle somewhat differently than experiential educators involved in independent learning and problem-based learning. Those interested in human potential and personal development tend to interpret the third stage (abstract conceptualization and generalization) as coming to a personal sense of meaning; for instance James Kilty, (from the Human Potential Programme at Surrey), used puzzling out and making sense of experience (Kilty, 1982). Educators tended to refer to a more abstract kind of thinking, for instance Gibbs (1987) retains conceptualization.

Stages

The survey (Henry, 1989a) highlighted other differences between the human potential and experiential learning camps; most of the personal development/human potential advocates perceived EL as a two stage process - an experience followed by reflection, normally mediated by sharing. Here the participant is expected to articulate an experience or express feelings about it in some other way and then discuss and reflect on the meaning of that personal experience with others.

Human potential: Experience → Reflection

Experiential learning advocates in the field of education usually cited a three stage model of EL, in essence: experience, reflection and action. This was particularly true of those practising project work, problem-based or independent learning.

Experiential learning: Experience → Reflection → Action

The actual naming of the stages varied, and some used four stages, e.g. reflect, conceptualize, decide and act or expanded substages, e.g. synthesize, generalize. (See Henry, 1989a for more examples).

Goal

In either case the goal was to involve the student personally and offer a practically useful outcome. Though the various experiential methods take different routes to get there, all are distinguished from more conventional approaches by their disdain for mere knowledge and determination to treat the student as a person rather than a knowledge machine; and to meet student determined needs. The desire for **personal involvement** requires that the learning experience is meaningful for the student. This may be personally meaningful in terms of their own development and/or practically useful.

Realizing human potential is generally taken to refer to the process which requires students to become conscious of their own feelings and desires and ultimately gain more autonomy through the capacity to exercise choice effectively. Personal development and human potential focus on affective goals like understanding oneself, along with the idea of a personal empowerment that allows the student to be assertive enough to ask questions and challenge received knowledge.

EL stresses the **practical** side of learning as much as its scope for personal development, and normally leads to some new understanding, skill or practical application relating theory to practice. It generally gives the learner more control of the learning process, assuming that this will produce a more autonomous human being.

EL claims to develop higher order skills that are generalizable and transferable. It is commonly believed to be more motivating for the students, because the choice and responsibility placed on the student is more involving. Finally because the learning is often based on real needs it is perceived to be more directly useful, (Henry, 1989a).

EXPERIENTIAL LEARNING METHODS

Experiential learning encompasses many teaching traditions covering a wide range of learning methods. These include:

* personal development;
* activity based learning;
* action learning;
* project work;
* prior learning;
* placement;
* problem solving;
* independent learning.

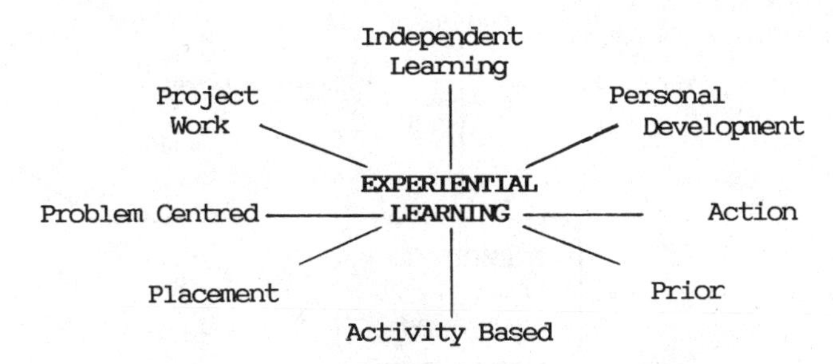

Figure 2: Experiential learning approaches.

Personal development work focuses on affective learning. The usual method employed centres round sharing feelings, e.g. co-counselling, but may employ other methods from the human potential armoury such as drama, guided imaging, meditation, narrative exercises based round autobiography, bodywork or creative expression, e.g. drawing.

Action learning is a means of learning from doing, where a group meet to discuss their progress and decide on future action at intervals. Action learning can also imply participation in actions that are new to the learner, for example through accessing resources not normally available to the learner (2).

Prior learning involves the assessment of previously completed work for accreditation towards an educational qualification. Typically students submit a portfolio demonstrating competences arising from their past work and life experience; this may include essays, an autobiography, testimonials and references. Sometimes performance measures such as competency check-lists, tests, discussion and extended papers are used.

Activity based learning includes practicals, simulations, games, role plays or expressive approaches like drama, art and imaginative activities (e.g. visualization).

Placements take various forms. The classic apprenticeship with an individual master who has the skills to be acquired; attachment to a mentor; or shadowing one or more individuals. Students may be assigned to a particular role, for instance as a trainee teacher; they may undertake a project, e.g. as part of a sandwich course; take part in day-to-day activities on a work attachment; or familiarize themselves with the work environment on an internship.

Project work refers to an extended piece of work in which the student (or group of students) selects a topic, collects relevant information and organizes this material into a presentation. Research projects may involve surveys, interviews or experiments. Information projects include literature reviews, and work with primary documents and secondary sources. Design projects may involve building something tangible or just producing plans to do so (Henry, 1977).

Problem-based learning follows a similar sequence of stages to

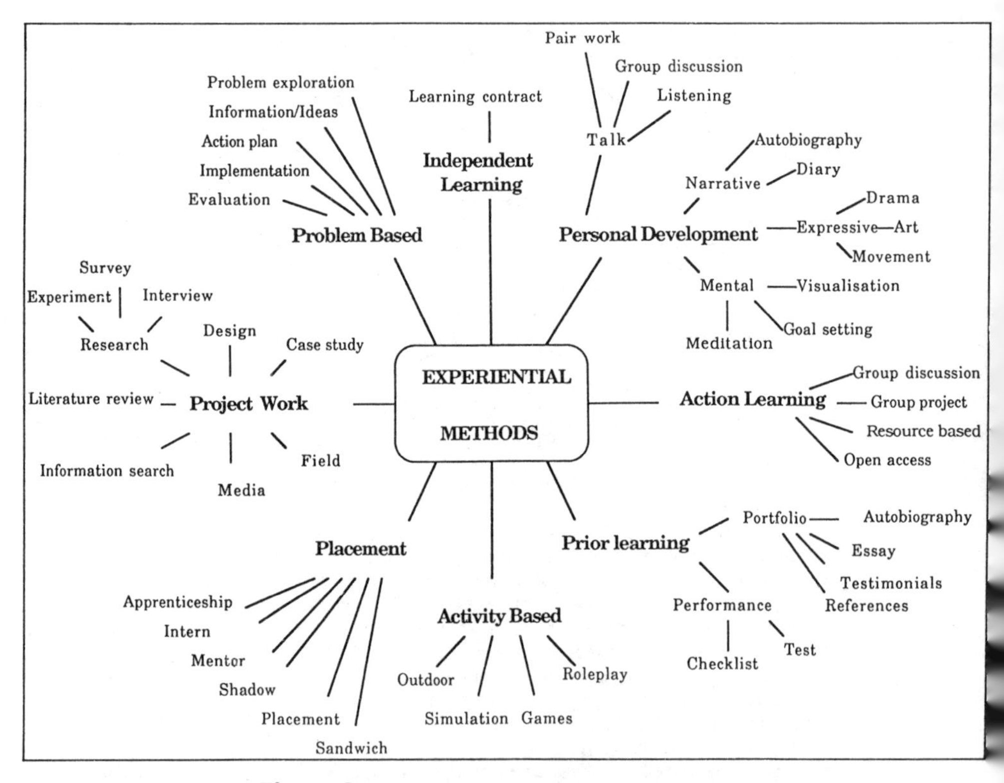

Figure 3: Experiential learning methods.

project work. The student starts with a problem, explores it, collects information, generates ideas, selects a way forward, implements it and revises as necessary, so gaining experience of design, evaluation and feedback procedures through extensive involvement in a problem central to the field of study.

Independent learning gives students control of the learning process, typically by a learning contract which offers the participants the chance to study situations of interest to them. It often uses problem solving and project based approaches.

SCHOOLS OF EXPERIENTIAL LEARNING

The various forms of experiential learning offer a variety of educational experiences and develop human potential in different ways. I will summarize some differences in concern or focus, process, assessment and outcome with illustrations from four main schools of experiential learning:

* project work;
* personal development;
* prior learning;
* placement.

It comes as no surprise that certain of these activities are more common in some disciplines than others. Work placements, activity-based learning and problem-solving approaches are found especially in the teaching of applied subjects, for instance agriculture, nurse training, engineering and business. Prior learning is usually available to mature students and though theoretically of use to all, personal development features especially in training for the human service professions, for instance teachers, the police, and psychologists.

1. Concern

Each of these orientations to experiential learning has a different focus. The **project** school (in which I am including independent learning and problem-centred learning) focuses on developing student autonomy. In contrast the school of **personal** development focuses on affective learning. **Prior** learning is ostensibly concerned with granting the student acceptence for skills and knowledge he or she already possesses. (In practice many prior learning programmes will include a development programme which seeks to add skills and knowledge in areas where the student is lacking). **Placements** by their very nature are focused on showing the student the practical application of the profession or activity concerned.

2. Process

But what of the processes in each of these different schools? A distinctive feature of the project method is that it places responsibility on the student for both choosing the topic and carrying out the study. Much personal development work is centred round a process of reflection. In non-educational settings this may be linked to other processes such as catharsis. Prior learning ostensibly asks the student to document his existing life and work skills in a reasoned manner, but of course the process of working out what these are involves considerable reflection. Placement involves a respect for the professionals and environment into which the student enters, and a faith in the possibility of conveying some of this understanding and skill to the novice student.

Approach	PROJECT	PERSONAL	PRIOR	PLACEMENT
Concern	Autonomy	Affective	Acceptance	Application
Process	Responsibility	Reflection	Reason	Respect
Assessment	Presentation	Peers	Portfolio	Practical
Outcome	Capable	Confident	Credible	Competent

Table 1: Features associated with **Experiential Learning Schools**

The amount of time allowed for these activities varies. Project-based learning is often allocated relatively large chunks of time ranging from a few weeks in schools to months in higher education. This allows the student considerable flexibility as to how to order and when to do the work. Personal development activities can be brief, lasting anything from half a day to two weeks, or a series of on-going sessions lasting several hours each. Work placements tended to be shorter for school age students (perhaps a few days to a week), and often much longer for undergraduates (e.g. four months to a year). Work placement and project based learning are more common late on in a course.

3. Assessment

Projects are usually assessed by some form of presentation: normally this comprises a written report. Assessment in independent learning can be student initiated, and take the form of the students presenting an oral case for their graduation backed up by a presentation of their written work and staff and supervisors' written comments on performance. Personal development often uses informal self-assessment and peer feedback. Where formal assessment is required, academics sometimes resort to setting conventional assignments (such as a literature review), which are unrelated to the affective learning that forms the major part of the course.

Prior learning is often assessed via a portfolio documenting outcomes of past experience and in some cases by dissertations and written papers.

Work placements are often assessed by an analysis of the student's performance in practice, often jointly by the academic facilitator and the work supervisor; sometimes the student is required to complete a project as well. School children are not always assessed on their placements.

4. Outcome

All these approaches aim to empower the individual.

Projects prove to students that they are capable, granting the kind of self-respect that comes from the satisfaction of completing a difficult task, and partly the knowledge that they could do it again. On large projects and in independent learning students can develop a belief in themselves which allows them access to their personal power. They sometimes report improved communication and decision-making skills (Henry, 1977).

Personal development seems to remove emotional blocks and give students confidence in themselves. The outcome of personal development is often an increase in self-awareness, plus improved interpersonal skills.

In addition to the credibility offered by a qualification, the process of assessment in prior learning can enhance self-awareness and offer new skills as well as saving time and money.

Placements foster an appreciation of the realities of the work environment and the part the student could play. Ideally the students emerge competent in the role they have been trained to practice or at least appreciative of what is involved.

CONCLUSION

This paper has given a brief resume of some experiential ways of developing human potential. All experiential learning approaches aim to offer something more human and relevant to student life than the traditional cognitive emphasis. Experiential approaches recognize educationally neglected sides of humanity like affective, conative, integrative and practical skills alongside cognitive abilities, and encourage people to take responsibility for their actions. Such methods aim to develop confidence, competence and capability. The educational shift from a focus on retaining knowledge to developing the knower should favour EL processes, and their goal of training capable individuals with sufficient initiative, awareness, confidence and skill to think and act flexibly and effectively in a changing world.

This is not to say that such approaches are suited to all types of learner or every kind of knowledge, skill, behaviour or attitude that can be learned. Determining whether certain experiential methods are better matched to certain learning styles than others and more appropriate for studying some kinds of knowledge, skills, behaviours and attitudes than others are important questions beyond the scope of this paper.

REFERENCES

Boydell, T.(1976): Experiential Learning, Monograph 5, Manchester.
Carkhuff, R.R.(1960): Helping and Human Relations. Holt, Rhinehart and Wilson
Dewey, (1916): Democracy and Education.
Gibbs, G.(1987): Learning by Doing. Further Education Unit, London.
Henry, J.(1977): The course tutor and project work. Teaching at a Distance, 9.
Henry, J.(1987): Variety in Experiential Learning. Project Memo 15, IET, Open University, Milton Keynes.
Henry, J.(1989a): Meaning and practice in experiential learning. In Warner Weil, S. and McGill, I.(eds), Making Sense of Experiential Learning. SHRE/OU Press,
Henry, J.(1989b): The human side of project work. In Farmer, B., Eastcott, D. and Lanz, B.(eds), Aspects of Educational and Training Technology, XXIII, Making Learning Systems Work. Kogan Page, London.
Kilty, J.(1982): Experiential Learning. Human Potential Research Unit, Surrey University, Guildford.
Kolb. D. and Fry, R.(1975): Towards an applied theory of experiential learning. In Cooper, C.L.(ed), Theories of Group Process. John Wiley, Chichester.

NOTES

1 - The idea of learning as a cycle is not new and one is reminded of other attempts to define the learning process, e.g. Dewey's process of observation, design, development and testing (1916) or Carkhuff's (1969) model of understanding, exploration and action. (See Boydell 1976 for a review of experiential learning theories).

2 - A previous attempt at categorizing experiential learning methods (Henry, (1989a) did not itemize action learning as a separate category. I have included it here in response to suggestions by participants at my AETT and Learner Managed Learning workshops.

APPENDIX A

If you complete the following questions and return them to the address below, I will forward an analysis of the survey.

Experiential Learning Questionnaire

Please describe briefly:

1 i What the term experiential learning means to you.
 ii What you see as its purpose.

2 Describe one example of experiential learning in practice, preferably one that you are associated with. If possible please note the following:
 i Why this learning experience is offered; what is its purpose?
 ii What the process is; what the student does.
 iii Who the students/participants are, e.g. age, numbers.
 iv When this takes place: time allowed, how often, optional, compulsory.
 v Where this takes place: e.g. school, university.
 vi How it is assessed.
 vii What the outcome is; what the students get out of it.

Jane Henry is a lecturer at the Open University. Currently she is developing and chairing their MBA course on Creative Management. She is a director of a management consultancy, and her research interests include experiential learning, project-based learning, intuition and imaging.

Address for correspondence: **Jane Henry**,
86, Mount Pleasant, Aspley Guise,
Buckinghamshire MK17 8JU, UK.
Tel:0908 582941; Fax 0908 653744

10. The accreditation of prior learning on in-service education courses for teachers

Michael Bloor and Christine Butterworth, Thames Polytechnic, London

Abstract This paper provides an account of an approach used at Thames Polytechnic to facilitate the accreditation of prior learning (APL) on an in-service education (INSET) programme for teachers. It begins by reviewing the range of INSET courses provided and then considers some general theoretical issues involved in the accreditation of prior learning. An account of the counselling procedures used to develop the portfolios, which provide evidence of professional development, is then given. Finally, the paper briefly considers some implications of these procedures - in particular issues of staff development.

INSET COURSES AND ACCREDITATION OF PRIOR LEARNING

The range of in-service education and training (INSET) courses at Thames Polytechnic in which the accreditation of prior learning (APL) is currently being used includes:

BEd in Further Education;

A range of Diplomas in Professional Studies in Education (DPSE) including an Open DPSE;

MA in Post-Compulsory Education and an Open MA.

('Open' means that the student chooses her/his own combination of units to make up the course or pathway).

All of these courses are modular, with a large 'menu' of units to choose from at Levels 3 and M of the Council for National Academic Awards Credit Accumulation and Transfer Scheme (CNAA CATS). This gives students maximum flexibility in the pattern of units they take, and in how long they take to accumulate the credits needed to gain the award. It also gives them the freedom to fit the study programme in with the demands of their job, and to buy the award in stages if they are self-financing.

These study routes are called pathways rather than courses, to reflect the amount of individual choice that is possible. To ensure that the chosen study route has coherence, and to maintain progression, each student has a counsellor who advises on the choice and sequence of units to meet the personal, professional and institutional needs appropriate to each student.

Our work on APL has been done to give students advanced standing on the route to their award, rather than access to the pathway. APL can also be used to get exemption from a core unit on a particular pathway, if it can be shown that their previous learning has met all of the aims of the core unit. Advanced standing can be gained either by certification from relevant previously-taken courses of an appropriate level (normally done within the last 5 years, to ensure that the learning is current), or by documenting previous experience in a portfolio to show how that experience has contributed to the student's professional development. This APL portfolio work is the focus of this paper.

THEORIES OF EXPERIENTIAL LEARNING UNDERPINNING APL

In order to claim for accreditation of prior learning, students must develop a portfolio which consists of:

1 a description of relevant experiences they have had;
2 identification of the learning resulting from those experiences;
3 some indication of how these (1 and 2) meet the criteria for either Professional Development (Level 3) courses or Advanced Professional Development (Masters' Level) courses (see note at end of this article).
4 some supporting evidence that verifies the learning claims, e.g. testimonials, curriculum development documentation, etc.

The underlying theoretical rationale for this approach to APL draws upon several models of experiential learning. One excellent review of these models is provided by Boud et al (1985). The simplest model is that initially proposed by Kolb (1975), and further considered by Gibbs (1988), where learning is regarded as a four-stage cycle,

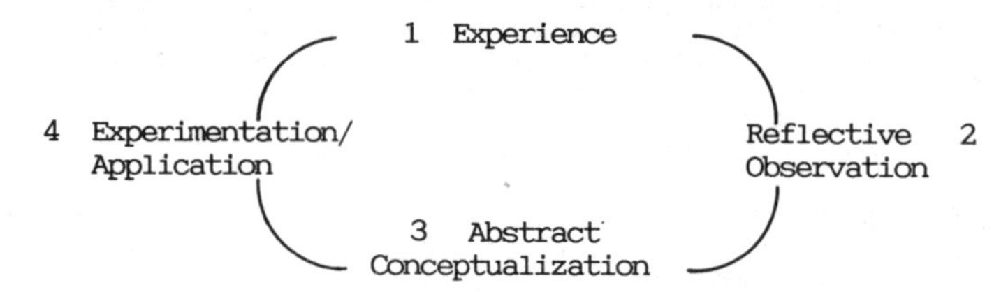

Figure 1: Kolb's description of the experiential learning cycle (Gibbs, 1988)

Concrete experience is the basis for reflection and observation; these observations are assimilated into a conceptual framework which serves to illuminate further experience. The student's portfolio is intended to provide documentation and evidence of all four stages of this cycle.

A second model is proposed by the Further Education Unit (FEU, 1981) which clarifies the need for organized reflection and the crucial role the tutor plays in helping the student to consolidate, interpret and develop pertinent concepts and theories. The counselling procedure used in the portfolio development therefore uses a 'learning conversation' approach (Candy et al, 1985) to explore pertinent theory which will help illuminate these experiences.

THE STRUCTURE OF THE APL PORTFOLIO

We are working in a specific context, seeking to establish relevant prior learning according to preset criteria for particular courses of professional development. Our working methods derive from this particular situation, and will not suit all possible instances of portfolio development. However, our experience so far leads us to offer the following as a model of a 'typical' portfolio for our purposes:

Section 1: Abstract, summarizing the learning claim.
Section 2: List of learning outcomes.
Section 3: Extended reflective writing describing the experience(s) and analysing how this produced the learning claimed, and meets the criteria for professional development.
Section 4: Evidence to support and prove the claim (working papers, testimonials, etc.).

THE PROCESS OF WRITING FOR APL

The writing process is a complex one which presents the student with different problems from those encountered in other parts of the course. Recording learning in a portfolio is by now an accepted method, the psychological value of which has been accepted by teacher educators. Walker (1985), in reviewing his work on using portfolios as a means of achieving reflection in learning, provides a useful guide for facilitating reflective writing. This kind of writing is essentially a solitary and deliberate process, during which the writer analyses her/his experience from a new perspective, and brings the past into present consciousness in a new way.

Though the purpose of the portfolio is partly to provide student credits, it helps develop the 'reflective teacher' (Ashcroft and Griffiths, 1989). The writing up and documenting process is hard work, as the writers realize that what is needed is not free writing but a new kind of written product, one that is both highly personal and intellectually rigorous, because of the need to meet the criteria for professional development. If successful, the process is genuinely developmental because it has made the writers conscious of what their professional development has been. This changes their perception of their own competence and initiates a continuing process of development. The conflict, though, between allowing the students the freedom to produce an original document and yet one which has to meet the same academic criteria as the products of traditional study routes, is a dilemma which we have not yet resolved.

THE COUNSELLOR'S ROLE

It has been documented elsewhere (Evans, 1987) that it is important to keep the counsellor's supporting role separate from the role of assessor, and our experience bears this out. Our role as APL counsellors in supporting the documentation process is complex, in that four distinct roles can be distinguished:

The Counsellor: Especially important in the early stages, to build up the students' confidence that their experience is adequate/relevant. Later they need support and encouragement when they find the thinking or writing difficult, while in the final stages the writers may use reflective discussion with the counsellor to clarify ways in which they feel they have developed, to look at the process objectively and to recognize their enhanced professional competence.

The Supervisor: At certain times the writers need academic advice on how to add theoretical depth and coherence to their accounts of how learning happened. This deepens their analysis and ensures the portfolios are equivalent to products of more traditional academic study.

The Editor: The organization and structuring of what is often a substantial amount of written work so as to present it well can be a considerable task, especially if the student has little recent experience of writing.

The Audience: As someone familiar with academic standards, the tutor can represent the academic audience to the writers as the work progresses, while still seeking to ensure that they feel free to write it up in their own way. This is discussed in more detail below.

SOME DIFFICULTIES IN THE COUNSELLING PROCESS

Grundy (1982) highlights the nature of the relationship which must be established between teacher and student to facilitate critical reflection. She stresses the importance of the ability to make a genuine free choice as being a pre-requisite for some self-reflection. This is the first of our difficulties: having evolved a format for presenting and framing claims for learning which seemed to work well, we found that some students resisted our efforts to 'impose' this structure on them.

Another conflict we experienced was that some students felt that our insistence on the conceptualization part of the cycle, making them relate their experiences to a wider theoretical framework, was unnecessary and indeed devalued and negated their experiences rather than enriched them. In view of research on deep and surface approaches to learning (e.g. Säljö 1980, Gibbs et al 1982), and that Entwistle and Ramsden (1983) describe the deep approach as integrating personal experience and formal learning - the sort of learning we are encouraging our students to demonstrate in their portfolios - we are exploring using the Kolb model in the introductory portfolio workshops to justify and explain the procedures we adopt.

SOME IMPLICATIONS OF THE PROCEDURES

1 Staff Development

We have found an increasing demand for APL on our courses, though more by college lecturers than by school teachers (the latter need to be encouraged to apply for APL), which has necessitated a programme of staff development to provide a pool of expertise in APL counselling procedures. We are not sure whether the lecturer/teacher difference is a real one arising from variations in professional development, or results from differences in perceptions of self and their relative professional developments.

We have used two models for staff development in APL expertise:

* staff development workshops, in which the staff identify their own significant experiences and document the resulting learning. They then begin to work with students of their own, while we act as 'consultants';
* staff simply sit in on APL sessions.

Our initial impression is that the former is more satisfactory, as staff take over responsibility sooner and tend to be more actively involved throughout.

The Professional Development Portfolio

INSET staff at Thames Polytechnic are currently involved in developing a portfolio that can be used for professional development on a wider scale, along the lines suggested by Graham (1989). The format allows the individual teacher to record details of courses attended, work tasks undertaken and areas of private study or research, as briefly or in as much detail as they choose. It is intended to have several purposes:

* to record personal and professional development, for instrumental purposes (job applications, APL) or to use for systematic reflection;
* to give to student teachers on completion of initial training. This 'keys them in' to Thames' INSET provision as a recruitment strategy, and introduces them early in their careers to the idea of continuing professional support and development.

professional support and development.

Negotiations are currently going on between Thames Polytechnic and local education authorities (LEAs) to tie in distribution of the Professional Development Portfolio (PDP) with the LEAs' own polytechnic-accredited INSET provision. The PDP can be used in staff appraisal schemes; provides evidence of achievements; and can be used to identify future lines of professional development.

In this paper we have given an account of the procedures we are developing to support the accreditation of prior learning on INSET courses. Although we are concerned with the professional development of in-service teachers, it does indeed seem that emphasis in the field of education is currently being placed on this model of the 'reflective practitioner': see, for example, Ashcroft and Griffiths (1989) who describe the course rationale of a BEd degree course as being based on Zeichner's (1987) concept of the 'reflective teacher' - the idea that student teachers, in initial training, need to be able to reflect on their practice and personal ideologies in order to evolve effective theories of practice. We would be interested in others' experiences.

REFERENCES

Ashcroft, K. and Griffiths, M.(1989): Journal of Education for Teaching 15, 1, pp.35-52.

Boud, D. et al.(1985): Reflection: Turning Experience into Learning. Kogan Page, London.

Candy, P. et al.(1985): Reflection and the self-organized learner: a model of learning conversations. In Boud, D. et al (eds):Reflection: Turning Experience into Learning. Kogan Page, London.

Entwistle, N. and Ramsden, P.(1983): Understanding Student Learning. Croom Helm,

Evans, N.(1987): Assessing Experiential Learning: A Review of Progress and Practice. Longman for FEU, London.

Further Education Unit (1981): Experience, Reflection, Learning. FEU, London.

Gibbs, G.(1982): Better teaching or better learning. In Habeshaw, T. (ed): SCEDSIP Occasional Paper 12, Three Ways to Learn. Bristol Polytechnic, Bristol.

Gibbs, G.(1988): Learning By Doing. FEU, London.

Graham, J.(1989): Professional development portfolios and their implications for portability in modular schemes. British Journal of In-Service Education, 15, 1 (Spring).

Grundy, S.(1982): Three modes of action research. Curriculum Perspectives, 2, 3, pp.23-44.

Kolb, D. and Fry, R.(1975): Towards an applied theory of experiential learning. In, Cooper,C.L. (Ed):Theories of Group Processes. J.Wiley, Chichester.

Säljö, R.(1980): Learning approach and outcome. Instructional Science, 10, pp.47-64

Walker, D.(1985): Writing and reflection. In, Boud, D. et al (eds): Reflection: Turning Experience into Learning. Kogan Page, London.

Zeichner, K.M. and Liston, D.P.(1987): Teaching student teachers to reflect. Harvard Educational Review, 57, pp.23-48.

Address for correspondence: M.Bloor and C.Butterworth,
Thames Polytechnic, Roehampton Campus,
Downshire House, Roehampton Lane,
London SW15 4HR, UK

NOTE

Professional development at Level 3 (BEd or DPSE level) is defined as an activity which leads to one or more of the following:

1 development of the person's specialist skills, knowledge and understanding in support of her/his professional role;
2 advanced educational or professional enrichment. This is to do with students, the classroom, the curriculum or the processes and understanding integral to a person's professional practice;
3 re-orientation of the individual as her/his roles change or to prepare her/him to undertake new roles.

Advanced professional development (Masters' level) is defined as an activity which shows all of the following:

1 the ability to reflect on the significance and inter-relationships of knowledge derived from the experience of the knower (on the basis of experience and institutionally focused and similar investigation) and knowledge derived through scholarship;
2 the formulation, on the basis of such reflection, of original ideas and/or innovative proposals;
3 the ability to initiate change on the basis of such informed ideas/proposals. Such action could relate to personal professional practice or a wider context;
4 the ability to do the above with a reasonable level of autonomy. This need not imply lack of tutorial support but does relate to the individual's ability to initiate, plan and organize her/his own development.

11. Effective training - some tools for industry

Karen J.Saunders, Taytec FTS Ltd

Abstract: There are many training methods used at present in industry. This paper looks at a series of methods and techniques (tools) which can be used to make training more effective by developing a total quality attitude through all levels of the workforce. It has been found from experience that the perceived quality of the training offered, by whichever method, and the effect this has on learning, are directly related. This can generally be measured by an increase in the quality of the output, whether this be widgets or decisions.
The practical application of educational theory in the development and design of systems, which can make this come about, are discussed. It will be seen that some time spent thinking carefully in planning may have more effect than spending thousands of pounds in the heat of the moment.

INTRODUCTION

Training is a buzz word in industry today. There are many initiatives funded by the Government, which is keen to enhance the profile of training, particularly vocational training. With 1992 approaching, and with the emergence of National Vocational Qualifications (NVQ), many organizations are now prepared to invest a significant amount of money to take part in the training game.

This has not always been the case. In the past training was often seen as a perk and was always the first budget to be cut when money was short. Open learning was given Government support through the MSC Open Tech Project to provide reduced cost training to meet the prevailing needs of industry. This method received a bad press; it was seen as being cheap and nasty. On the whole, the materials were considered shallow, almost remedial in their content and were often irrelevant to training needs. Open learning was seen as being aimed at individuals such as the unemployed or those unable to attend college on a regular basis. It was perceived as being of poor quality not suited to industry's needs.

Taytec Ltd. was set up under the Open Tech Project in 1984. The training content of the programmes produced was of varying quality. Programmes were written by individuals who did not necessarily have a background in open learning and were seconded to the company from other organizations. The workbooks and packaging were professionally designed, however, and from this point of view were thought of highly when compared to other Open Tech produced materials.

In order to succeed commercially and prove that open learning was a viable form of training, we had to be seen to be producing for the corporate market quality training materials that would fit the purpose for which they were intended - to train people so that there would be a measurable benefit such as increased productivity with improved quality output which would arise from a decrease in waste or rejects. It was this requirement which led us to review our programme development systems to produce programmes with two major objectives in mind:

* benefit to the individual (by development);
* increase the profitability of the client organization.

In this paper I will discuss how a simple set of tools was developed to enable the company to progress to meet the needs of clients through the provision of quality training materials. These tools were built up from the application of educational theory related to the concept of experiential learning (Kolb's theory). Over about three years, the tools have been expanded, using a total quality attitude developed throughout all tiers of the organization, increasing the overall efficiency of training programmes and therefore the efficiency of the organization as a whole.

THE THEORY

Over a period of about three years now, we have been producing training programmes based on a model of experiential learning developed by Kolb (1984). Kolb described a four-step learning cycle (Figure 1) which involved four adaptive learning modes:

* concrete experience;
* reflective observation;
* abstract conceptualization
* active experimentation.

Kolb relates these learning modes to experiences which the trainee has had and to which new learning can be related. He also defines learning as a 'process where knowledge is created through the transformation of experience'. We thought that if we could develop training programmes which would take trainees through each of the four modes as Kolb prescribed, the training would be more effective. There would be more chance of the training programme meeting its objectives - developing the individual and increasing the profitability of the organization. We set about designing a model which would allow us to apply this theory.

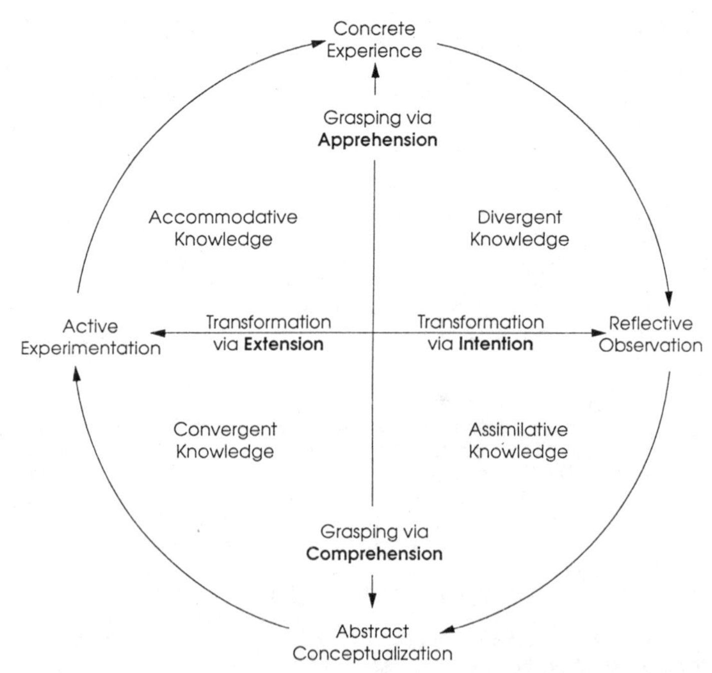

Figure 1: Kolb's learning cycle

APPLYING THE THEORY

We first tackled the immediate issue which was to improve the quality of the training materials to ensure that they would meet the needs of our potential clients, i.e. that the trainees (the client's employees) would learn from them and that the company as a whole would benefit.

We studied the four learning modes described by Kolb and developed a range of systems which would take the trainee round each of them while working through the training materials. The systems were designed to **actively involve** the trainee in the learning process. This was done by taking the trainee through a series of activities which encouraged:

* relating new information to previous experiences; (Concrete Experience)
* thinking skills to be developed; (Reflective Observation)
* discussing new concepts with colleagues/line managers; (Abstract Conceptualization)
* experimenting/using other resources - learning from doing. (Active Experimentation)

These systems improved the quality of the learning materials and encouraged self-development in the individual. This in turn would fulfil the objective for the organization.

PROGRAMME DESIGN

The next stage was to ensure that the quality in design and presentation was maintained. We found that we already followed the quality procedures specified by the MSC (MSC, 1988). This reinforced our case for adopting a total quality attitude. We were now in a position to fit the new learning systems to our established house style.

The workbooks were designed giving plenty of space to note observations, write down checklist procedures, make notes and fill in answers. Case studies were included, to help put new ideas into context. Question and answer systems were designed to test knowledge and understanding.

The questions themselves were designed so that the trainee had to inter-act with the information given and build on this rather than merely copy what was printed in the previous paragraph. A range of different styles of question was developed, which would test the trainee's understanding and grasp of the material to assess if the training objectives had been met.

Illustrations played an important part in the learning material. A good many of our programmes are very technical and the diagrams give vital information and help put the text into context. Sometimes cartoons were used to make points, break up the text and give some visual impact.

In the past, audio was an integral part of all Taytec programmes. In discussions with users it was found that in most cases, trainees did not bother with it. Of those that did, few saw any benefit.

Although most of our material is text based, additional media is used to fit the required need. Video has also been used but only where seen as necessary to enhance the learning and give information which could not suitably be handled by text. CBT is a medium which we have not used much as the programmes which have been produced to date would not have benefited from it. CBT is being considered for a current project where it would be most suited to managing and mapping the learning. We also intend to use it as an interactive assessment and record system.

PILOT STUDY

In order to test our new ideas, the first programme to be produced was piloted with a sample from an identified target audience. It was also sent to a group of 'experts in the field' to comment on the technical accuracy of the content. We did unfortunately, mainly due to pressure of time, make an error at this stage. The materials were not piloted in their published landscape format, with boxes to write in, visual cues to identify activities, questions, etc. Instead, although produced by word processor through a laser printer, they were in portrait format with only changes in point size to differentiate text from activity. Space was allowed to write in but not all of the illustrations were included.

The feedback from the pilot was disappointing, but to be expected. All those involved met to put their comments to the project team. The major point to come out of the meeting was that the presentation was unacceptable: the participants had been so distracted and misled by the presentation that they could not give us the information we required relating to the content and effectiveness of the training materials.

This raised an important point and confirmed our previous thought - the quality of the materials **is** noticed and does have an effect on the perceived value of the training and how much is taken from it. This point would be taken on board in the development of our next project.

Subsequent programmes were piloted with the two groups of people, as before, but in as near published form as possible. Participants were informed of any illustrations, etc., which were missing (so they did not spend time considering this) and to explain what type of feedback we required. Questionnaires were sent out covering all aspects of the package. These questionnaires are refined with every new programme to be piloted in order to maximize the quality of the feedback and allow us to make accurate changes to the content, where called for.

WINNING THE TRAINEE

We thought we had developed our first new package, in theory, to work. Would it work in practice? To achieve this we had to win the confidence and commitment of the trainees which needed the support of the company. We knew from experience the trainees were apprehensive about participating in training programmes. It had often been several years, perhaps since school, since a trainee had been involved in any formal learning. Many did not want others to see their mistakes. We developed a set of tools to help make the learning experience easier and more fun, i.e. to motivate the trainer to **want to learn**, to develop knowledge and skills already possessed and take responsibility for their own learning. The first of these tools was designed to 'put the trainee in the picture'.

Learner Guide

This is a short booklet which is intended to:

* provide an outline of the training programme;
* explain the expected outcomes;
* discuss the benefits to the individual and the organization;
* explain how the package works;
* help the trainee devise a plan of study;
* offer tips to maximize learning.

At this stage the trainee is more or less alone and needs the contact and support of others. Someone within the organization had to be responsible for ensuring that the learning was taking place within a reasonable timescale, if it was to benefit the organization. The training also had to be organized to ensure that people and other resources such as television, video, computer and a place to work in were all available when required. It was agreed with client organizations that the best person to take this responsibility was the trainee's line manager or supervisor. Even if some of the duties were delegated to a more suitable/knowledgeable person, the line manager was the person who knew the trainee best and the job to be done, so we designed a set of guidelines to help the manager help the trainee obtain the most from the package.

Manager's Guide

This is a brief set of notes which is intended to:

* outline the content of the programme;
* explain the benefits to the organization of proper implementation and successful completion of the training programme;
* give model answers/checklist notes for activities;
* give tips for supporting the training;
* provide a checklist to ensure that any resources will be available when required.

Progress Chart

It was recognized by us and confirmed by the pilot feedback that with 'off-the-shelf'training programmes,some trainees may be more experienced than others in certain areas and may not need to complete the entire package in depth. This led us to produce the progress chart (based on Training Targets) as a multi-functional tool. Its suggested uses are:

* to help trainee and manager agree which areas should be studied in depth and which can be skimmed over or used for reference;
* to allow the trainee to check progress;
* to allow deadlines and goals for completion to be set.

The chart was designed as a poster to be a visible record of achievement and has had very favourable reactions. We found people actually like having something to put up in their work area which encourages colleagues to ask how they are getting on with their training.

Training Contract

As new programmes were being developed, it was emerging from post-pilot feedback that trainees were still lacking support from their line managers and were becoming demotivated. It was this factor which led us to develop the training contract.

This is a set of guidelines which form the basis of a commitment between the trainee and the organization, where the line manager would normally represent the organization. The concept was that before training began, the trainee and manager would agree a training plan, using the progress chart as a base. The trainee would then agree what had to be achieved within the timescale, and the manager would agree on behalf of the organization that everything necessary would be done to facilitate and support this learning. This formalized the situation, making commitment between both parties. From the information which we have received to date, this system seems to be having some success. Studies are continuing in this area with programmes which are being developed at present.

WINNING THE ORGANIZATION

Until this point we had really only dealt with the issue of individual trainees, or small groups with the same particular training need within an organization. Situations were arising where we had to consider the organization as a whole. This is our current area of development and we are in the process of applying what we have learned by developing the tool set to meet the whole needs of organizations. We have found that it is critical to the success of the project to gain commitment from the most senior levels.

In 1989 we produced an induction programme for a manufacturing company dedicated to total quality. They had previously been successful in implementing open learning training programmes and the resultant benefit was managing to reduce machine downtime by 20%.

The organization now wished to pass the quality message through all the workforce. The project was initiated by the personnel manager who won the support of the factory manager. On the basis of previous success, company HQ agreed it. The enthusiasm was quite overwhelming. Managers and supervisory staff completed the package themselves before acting as tutors for the rest of the workforce. The attitude to quality seems to have passed through the shop floor to the product with its improved standards and production rates. Studies are, however, continuing.

Our present project is with a small bakery firm and we are in the process of applying all we have learnt over the past three years. There is total commitment from the management who see the need to improve all standards within their production by improving the skills of their workforce. Their aim is to save money through efficiency which can ultimately be passed to the employees via enhanced conditions.

IN CONCLUSION

Through the application of Kolb's Theory of Experiential Learning a framework has been developed to allow the creation of a basic tool set, which coupled with a quality design process and training support system produces a quality training programme. **Only** the application of an effective learning system and a quality design process will meet the real identified needs of **both** the individual and the organization.

REFERENCES

Kolb, D.A.(1984): Experiential Learning. Prentice-Hall, New Jersey
Rowntree, D. et al(1988): Ensuring Quality in Open Learning - A Handbook for Action. Manpower Services Commission, Sheffield.

Karen Saunders is Programme Development Coordinator with Taytec. The company specializes in producing all types of training materials for the corporate market. She is involved in the research and development of open learning programmes and manages the entire production process.

Address for correspondence: Karen J.Saunders, Taytec FTS Ltd.,
6, North Isla St, Dundee DD£ 7JO, Scotland

12. The award of academic credit for sandwich placements in Higher Diploma courses by means of learning contracts

Iain S. Marshall, Napier Polytechnic of Edinburgh

Abstract: When people undertake responsibility to learn something on their own authority, what they learn may be learned more deeply and retained for longer than what they learn by being taught (Knowles, 1980). In part, this philosophy underpins the placement element of sandwich courses. Difficulties arise from the fact that in field-based learning there is a strong possibility that what is to be learned from the experience will be less clear to both the learner and the supervisor that what work is to be done. One way to make the learning objectives of the placement experience clear and explicit to both is by means of a negotiated agreement, referred to here as a learning contract. For the student, the process of identifying and agreeing goals for learning, appropriate in the workplace setting, is a significant responsibility and can engender powerful ownership of the proposal and strong commitment to achievement of the goals agreed. The experience of using initiative, taking responsibility and assuming one's own authority, can contribute to developing enterprise as a value system for the individuals involved.

THE PROCESS

When people undertake responsibility to learn something on their own authority, what they learn may be learned more deeply and retained for longer than what they learned by being taught (Knowles, 1980). In part, this philosophy underpins the placement element of sandwich courses. However, the weakness in planning for existing sandwich placements provision can result in inadequate learning by the students, particularly when they fail to recognize valuable learning opportunities.

One way to make the learning objectives of the placement experience clear and explicit, for learners and teachers, is by means of a student-driven, three-way negotiated agreement which is referred to here as a Learning Contract (see Figure 1).

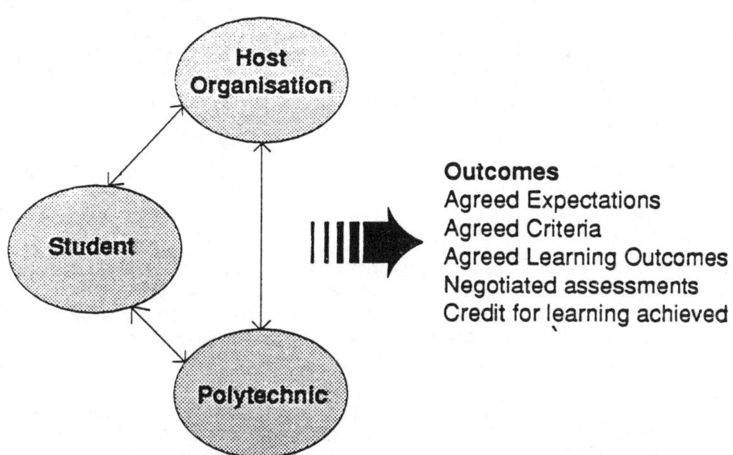

Figure 1: Model of student-driven three-way Learning Contract.

For the students, the process of identifying and agreeing suitable goals for learning, that are appropriate in a workplace setting, is a significant responsibility that can engender powerful ownership of the proposal and strong commitment to the achievement of the goals agreed. The experience of using initiative, taking responsibility and assuming ones' own authority, can contribute to developing enterprise as a value system for the individuals involved.

For the host employer, the negotiation of agreed learning outcomes may encourage an active role in helping students learn, and an increasing awareness of new possibilities in the students' potential contribution.

For academic staff, engaging in the process of negotiating appropriate learning goals with students can result in a clearer recognition of the significance of work-based learning as an effective activity, and may lead to its wider application.

The entire process of developing a Learning Contract and assessing it is shown in diagram form in Figure 2.

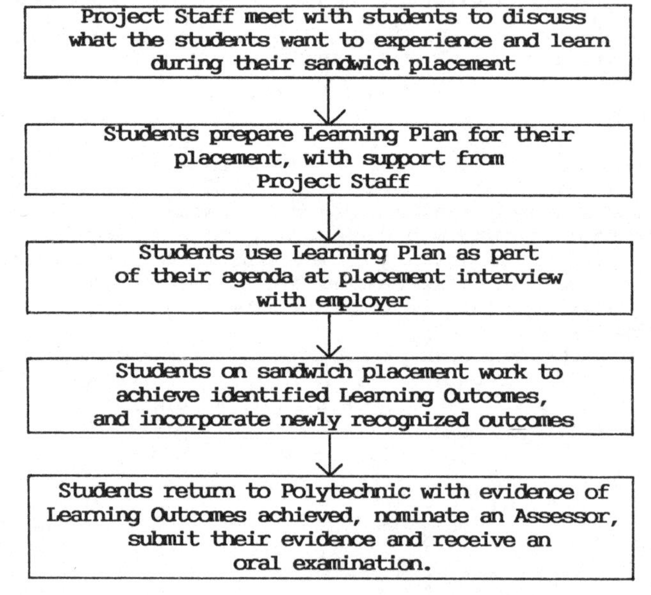

Figure 2: Model of the Work-Based Learning Process for Students

DISCUSSION

From the very first learning plan preparation workshops there was a focus on encouraging the student to reflect upon how they learn, and to share that information with one another and with the staff involved.

Points which consistently emerge from students include:

* the importance they place on being actively involved in learning;
* the need to see the relevance of material which is to be learned;
* the low value they place on the lecture as an aid to learning;
* their wish to have some say in what is to be learned, and in how they might learn it.

One consequence of repeated exposure to these staff/student workshops is that staff reflect upon their own learning methods and experiences, and begin to re-examine the teaching methods currently adopted by them in teaching those same students on other parts of the course.

"Learning is necessarily a phenomenon of both teachers and learners. Teachers should not expect to remain unaffected by what they do." (Carr and Kemmis, 1983). However, not all staff are ready or able to work in this way, which raises the question of appropriate staff development. Where possible staff should-self select into this system, and be encouraged to identify appropriate staff development opportunities. Many staff accustomed to the 'teaching' role will experience difficulty in adapting to a 'facilitating' role. It may be useful to pair an experienced facilitator with an inexperienced one, as a form of staff development.

Staff should be encouraged to develop closer contact with industry and commerce. As the model suggested here involves the student's placement host employer, this ought to be a natural development which emerges from negotiating the three-way agreement.

Experience from the project suggests that:

* **employers are likely to be attracted by students they perceive to be enterprising;**
* **employers are likely to be pleasantly surprised to discover that educational institutions are prepared to involve them in three-way negotiated contracts.**

Workplace supervisors and managers should be involved as much as possible in the assessment of the student's work-based learning. It may be that existing employee appraisal systems can be easily adapted to encompass the learning outcomes/competences which the student is achieving.

Many qualities associated with Enterprise such as: taking responsibility, using initiative, coping with uncertainty, tolerance of risk, and negotiating skills are fostered by learner-centred methods such as contract learning. It should be borne in mind that in the future, employers will be competing for quality employees, and colleges giving effect to models such as the one described here will be recognized as sources of competent and able people.

One of the aims of this project was to use the contract learning model to reduce the length of the courses. In a credit-based system, the opportunity to obtain credit from sandwich placement allows the number of credits required for the award of a qualification to be achieved during a period which previously did not give academic credit, and can shorten the overall length of the course. Already, Higher Diploma courses have been reduced from three to two years, and models such as the one presented by this report provide a means of awarding credit for relevant learning outcomes achieved.

In degree programmes the same opportunity exists to shorten courses which have a sandwich placement. However, in the case of degree courses the task will become easier if and when they are expressed in learning outcome terms. Students will then have scope for achieving these learning outcomes in a variety of ways, including work-based learning.

Malcolm Knowles, in 'Using Learning Contracts' (1986), makes the point that in America, "Institutions of higher education are without doubt currently the most prolific users of contract learning". On a recent visit to North America, I found evidence of the widespread use of learning contracts in a range of educational institutions. At Empire State College, which is part of the State University of New York, most academic work is organized through learning contracts.

So, the question being addressed is not of the student's ability to learn by using a learning contract, but of the ability of staff to devise systems and procedures which can support and assess learning which is relevant to the course of study being pursued.

The lessons learned from this pilot study are contributing to the learning contract model currently evolving through a Training Agency funded project, and, as other courses and institutions express an interest, the expertise being developed at Napier will be available to them.

REFERENCES

Carr and Kemmis (1983): Becoming Critical - Knowing Through Action Research. Deakin University Press, Geelong.

Knowles, M.S.(1980): The Modern Practice of Adult Education. Cambridge Book Co.

Knowles, M.S.(1986): Using Learning Contracts. Jossey-Bass.

State University of New York(1988/89): Empire State College Bulletin. p.15.

Address for correspondence: **Iain S. Marshall,**
Educational Development Unit,
Napier Polytechnic of Edinburgh,
10, Colinton Road, Edinburgh EH10 5DT, Scotland

13. Travelling to change: an analysis of an international travel/study programme on participants' attitudes

I.Duke Talbott, Glenville State College

Abstract: Based on surveys of participants in four different programmes, this paper examines the impact of a number of variables on the effectiveness of an international travel/study activity in expanding individual horizons relating to perceived understanding of other cultures and the ability of the individual to function in them for pleasure or business purposes. The study indicates that participants see their experiences as very beneficial in a number of ways.

INTRODUCTION

Since 1986 Glenville State College has developed and implemented international travel/study programmes in western Europe. The programmes have been designed to provide an experiential education in a European cultural environment for traditional students, continuing education students, and alumni. It is the aim of this study to measure the degree of success that the programmes have had on participants' attitudes regarding confidence in themselves for functioning in an international context and for expanding their international consciousness for social, cultural and professional purposes. (For a bibliographic essay on previous related research see Welds, 1986).

SCOPE AND OBJECTIVES

Glenville State College is a comprehensive baccalaureate institution having evolved from a publicly-supported teacher training 'normal school' of the nineteenth century to its twentieth century mission of offering bachelors degrees in education, business, and the liberal arts. The college is unique in the particular geographic area it serves. Located in West Virginia in the heart of the Appalachian Mountain region of eastern North America it provides educational opportunities to a preponderantly rural population with a majority of less than national median income families (overwhelmingly descendents of immigrants from the British Isles and Germany). The general educational level of the service area and the university attendance rate are among the lowest in the United States. The economy, however, is highly internationally orientated with much of its product tied to commodity and manufacturing export markets and with significant external ownership of resources.

The international travel/study programmes were developed to remedy the limited availability of activities for expanding international understanding. In identifying the objectives and scope of the programmes the background of potential participants based on the socioeconomic characteristics of the service area were taken into account. Two objectives for the travel/study programmes were thus defined:

* to develop confidence in the individual in operating independently in an international environment; and
* to provide an opportunity for expanded understanding of other cultures resulting in a greater international consciousness and awareness.

The programmes tried to meet the objectives by providing participants with two sets of activities:

* coordinated group functions (seminars, discussions, visits, to business establishments, cultural sites and activities);
* planned opportunities for operating independently (given time, instruction, recommendations, encouragement and guidance);

intended to extend horizons, to enhance self-reliance, and to gain an understanding and appreciation of the historical, social and cultural attributes of nations in western Europe.

TRAVEL/STUDY PROGRAMME DESIGN

Beginning in 1986 four annual programmes were developed. The 1986 and 1987 programmes emphasized international business while the 1988 and 1989 programmes stressed history and culture.

The 1986 programme was centred in Britain, France and the Netherlands. In London specific activities included a seminar with a representative of Lloyd's of London on its history and operation; a seminar with an economist from a major clearing house bank followed by lunch in a traditional 'City' pub; a discussion visit to the London Stock Exchange; a visit to St. Katherine's Docks; and a Red Bus tour. In the southeast of England there was a coach trip with commentary through export-orientated horticultural areas and an escorted visit to and discussion of the workings of the Dover Docks. The time in Paris was devoted to a discussion visit to the Centre Commerciale de la Defense and a seminar on retail marketing with its director; a discussion visit to the Paris Stock Exchange; a visit to a hypermarket; a river excursion on the Seine by 'Bateau Mouche'; and dinner in a typical regional restaurant. In Amsterdam there was a seminar on the operations of the European Options Exchange; a discussion visit to the van Moppes Diamond Company; and a boat excursion through the city's canals and harbour. Rail, ferry, tram, and passenger trip travel were included in the schedule of activities.

The 1987 programme was similar in scope and itinerary to the 1986 programme, but a guided tour and seminar on the operations of the port of Antwerp; a seminar on trade policy with the American consul in Belgium; a video presentation and seminar by company officials on comparative advertising techniques of Heineken Brewery; and a discussion visit to a Dutch cheese processing and exporting facility replaced the Paris Centre Commerciale and the Amsterdam European Options Exchange.

The 1988 programme emphasized history and culture of England and was characterized by visits to the British Museum, Tower of London and Tower Bridge, Windsor Castle, Stratford upon Avon, National Gallery, Tate Gallery, Victoria and Albert Museum, Shakespeare Memorial Theatre and Hampton Court. Participants also had a boat trip down the Thames, a discussion visit and lunch at the Guinness Brewery, and a guided tour of Oxford University. They took the opportunity for an optional day trip to Calais in France. Participants lived in a London School of Economics hall of residence and gained an idea of the British student experience.

The 1989 programme included visits to Iceland, Luxembourg, Germany, Switzerland and Italy. The stay in Iceland included a guided tour of the city of Rekjavik with optional visits to points of interest including an opportunity to swim in the thermally heated outdoor swimming pool surrounded by several inches of snow. The Swiss itinerary included a walking tour of Basel; an optional day trip to Lucerne for independent visits; a seminar with representatives of the Cantonal Tourist Office; a day trip to Milan with escorted visits to il Duomo and da Vinci's Last Supper; tours of the castle, cathedral and university in Heidelberg; and an individual day in Karlsruhe with a visit to its palace. They also planned an optional day trip to a location of their choice (the Black Forest and Strasbourg being the two principal selections).

In all programmes participants were exposed to cultural and social activities unique to the host countries, and especially to practices that might be expected to differ from those they could meet at home. For example, the varieties of transportations used could not be found in their particular area of primary experience. In land-locked and rural central West Virginia, expressways, or more commonly John Denver's country roads, are the primary modes of travel: virtually every family has a car. Intercity passenger trains, underground railroads, passenger ships and trams cannot be found, so travel on these systems was made a part of the programme. In addition, dining at a variety of restaurants which included both host country national and other ethnic cuisines, was developed as a regular scheduled aspect of the programme. These ranged from a Soho pub supper in London to an Indonesian 'rijstafel' in Amsterdam and an Indian banquet in Dover.

In meeting the objective of making participants feel comfortable while operating independently in an international environment participants were provided with maps and encouraged to move about on their own. They were given an opportunity to identify particular individual or small group activities, and plan, in consultation with an instructor or with each other, which to carry out. After a few days of group experience all were encouraged and expected to operate independently.

EFFECTIVENESS OF THE TRAVEL/STUDY PROGRAMMES

To evaluate the success of the programmes as an educational experiential approach for developing human potential within the context of the stated objectives a survey of participants was initiated in the summer of 1989. The survey was mailed to 76 former participants. (The duplicated count of participants, some having been part of two programmes was 111). A total of 55 responses was returned.

When asked "Do you feel that your travel/study expanded your intellectual horizons?" 80% answered in the highest category, while another 16.4% answered in the next highest category. (All questions had four levels of answer). Similarly, in response to the question "Do you feel more confident about international travel as a result of your travel/study tour?" 74.1% replied in the top category and 20.4% replied in the next to highest category. To the question "Overall did your travel/study have a positive impact on your ability to function independently in an international environment?" 56.4% responded with "Yes - A lot" while another 32.7% answered "Yes - Some" the third highest category.

Carrying the line of questioning a step further with the query, "Would you travel alone for pleasure in a European country of your choice?" the responses dropped dramatically with only 41.8% replying, "Definitely - Yes" and 25.5%, "Probably". A relatively large 18.2% answered, "Definitely Not", the lowest ranked response. It appears that many respondents still needed some reassurance or companionship in utilizing international travel for pleasure. On the other hand, in response to the question,"Would you travel for pleasure with just one friend in a European country of your choice?" the answers jumped to 74.1% with, "Definitely -Yes", and another 20.4%, "Probably". The ,"Definitely - Not" lowest ranked response dropped to 1.9%. The more positive responses were slightly higher to the question, "Would you feel comfortable travelling alone in a European country if required for a business or job assignment?", which elicited a response of 50% for "Definitely - Yes", and 29.6% for, "Probably".

Those who felt they had attained a greater positive impact on their ability to function independently in an international environment were also those who were the most willing to travel independently for business or pleasure. A linear regression analysis (Student's t) indicated a beneficial association between degree of positive impact of international travel/study on ability to function independently and willingness to do so for either business or pleasure.

Security with having an acquaintance nearby was expressed in response to the question, "Did you feel comfortable making group visits to various sites and facilities" with 74.5% replying, "always", the highest category, but when the question was changed to individual visits, only 51.9% said, "Always" and 33.3% replied, "Usually".

As a method of personal development participants overwhelmingly endorsed international travel/study. When asked, "Would you recommend travel/study to a fellow student, friend or colleague as a means of expanding one's horizons?" 89.1% replied "Definitely yes", the highest ranked response, with 9.1% "Probably" (the next highest) and none responding to the answer "Definitely not".

In identifying the degree to which their international travel/study experiences had been incorporated into their societal and professional activities upon their return home a majority indicated a positive response but not as strongly as their endorsement of international travel/study as a means of expanding one's horizons.

In regularly-scheduled class sessions prior to departure students were instructed in various aspects of the cultures they would be visiting, including a discussion of the concept of 'culture shock' as a possible psychological phenomenon (utilizing the definition developed by Copeland and Griggs, 1985) which they might experience. When subsequently asked whether they felt they experienced 'culture shock' at any time during their travel/study programme, 56.6% replied "Sometimes" and 32.1% "Not at all", the two lowest categories. To "Were you able to purchase personal items you needed in the countries visited?" 53.7% replied "Always" and 37% "Usually", the two highest categories. 83.6% classed themselves in the "Always/Usually" categories with regard to feeling comfortable with the different eating and drinking habits in the countries visited.

There was little relationship between age or prior educational achievement as factors in participants' responses. A linear regression analysis (Student's t) was computed to compare the effects of age and education on responses. Educational level could be significantly correlated (95% confidence level) with culture shock in that those having a higher educational level experienced less culture shock. However, with an r^2 of .11 this explains little. No other dependent variables in the study could be significantly correlated with educational level.

Only three of the dependent variables correlated significantly with age as the independent factor (95% confidence level). These, however, all had extremely low r^2 coefficients and consequently little explanation of variability. There was a negative correlation between age and willingness to travel alone for pleasure (r^2 = .11) and willingness to travel alone for a business or job assignment (r^2 = .08). When age was the independent variable correlated with degree of comfort with eating and drinking habits a positive correlation was indicated but also with a low correlation coefficient (r^2 = .096).

SUMMARY AND CONCLUSIONS

Based on participants' responses the international travel/study programmes achieved their stated objectives of:

* developing confidence in the individual in operating in an international environment, and
* providing an understanding of other cultures for greater international consciousness and awareness.

In meeting the first objective of developing confidence in oneself the willingness to travel independently is less pronounced than is the willingness to travel with others, although in this connection it is the whole venture that is more intimidating rather than its integral parts. Individual activity within a country, provided there is access to an associate, is more readily accomplished. In addition, participants generally felt comfortable with personal activities such as dining and shopping.

For the second objective participants had an overwhelming feeling that international travel/study contributed to one's intellectual horizons, and that it was something that could be recommended to others. However, specific utility of international travel/study upon return was less positively pronounced in expanding participants' horizons and providing them with greater international understanding and awareness which could be incorporated into actual societal and professional functions.

The study indicates that participants saw their experiences as beneficial in expanding their thought processes, broadening their understanding of other cultures, and building confidence in themselves in operating independently in an international context. The extent to which this took place varied from individual to individual, although there was little or no significant correlation between age and prior educational level and extent.

REFERENCES

Copeland, L. and Griggs, L.(1985): Going International: How to Make Friends and Deal Effectively in the Global Marketplace. pp.195-197.

Welds, K.(1986): Psychosocial impact of international education: what dimensions of attitude change and personal growth are associated with cross-cultural experiences? International Education, 16, 1, pp.36-50.

I.D.Talbott is currently Director of Community Services and Continuing Education and Research Associate Professor of History and Economics at Glenville State College in West Virginia. He has conducted a number of collegiate international travel/study programmes in western Europe and Canada.

The full analysis of this investigation can be obtained from
Dr.I.D.Talbott, Glenville State College, Glenville, WV 26351, USA

14. Introducing simulation/games into the curriculum of a Singapore college

Henry Ellington, Martin Allinson* and Jimmy Chen*
Robert Gordon's Institute, Aberdeen: *Ngee Ann Polytechnic, Singapore

Abstract: This paper describes a highly ambitious attempt to introduce simulation/games into the curriculum of the Electrical Engineering Department of a Singapore polytechnic in 1989. Teaching in Singapore is in the main highly traditional, with both staff and students being accustomed to their respective roles. In this project electrical engineering staff at Ngee Ann Polytechnic were trained to take on a radically different role - that of facilitators - and all 500 students in the second year of the Department's Diploma course were introduced to student-centred experiential learning by taking part in a two-day simulation/game. The paper describes how the project was conceived and planned, how the simulation/game on which the project was based was developed, how staff at Ngee Ann were trained to supervise the exercise, and how the exercise was organized and run. It concludes by looking at what was learned from the project and showing how it may well lead to more widespread use of experiential learning methods in Singapore - both within Ngee Ann and in other schools and colleges.

INTRODUCTION

Teaching in Singapore tends to be highly traditional, with both staff and students being well accustomed to - and apparently quite happy with - their respective conventional roles of **presenters** and **passive receivers** of information. This paper describes an attempt by the three authors to introduce interactive simulation/games into the curriculum of the Electrical Engineering Department of one of Singapore's two polytechnics - Ngee Ann Polytechnic. This involved training 25 members of staff to take on a radically different role - that of **facilitators** - and then introducing all 500 second-year Diploma students in the Department to the type of **student-centred experiential learning** that such exercises make possible. As we will see, the experiment was a great success, and could well lead to widespread use of such instructional methods in Singapore - both within Ngee Ann and in other schools and colleges.

HOW THE PROJECT WAS CONCEIVED AND PLANNED

In March, 1989, one of the authors (Dr.Ellington) visited Ngee Ann Polytechnic as a consultant to their Educational Technology Centre, carrying out staff development work in the areas of individualized and group-based student-centred learning. In the course of a seminar held in the Electrical Engineering Department, Dr. Ellington introduced the staff to some of the educational games and simulations that he and his colleagues have developed for the Institution of Electrical Engineers - games (such as 'The Power Station Game' and 'Power for Elaskay') that have played a key role in the IEE's Schools Liaison programme in Britain during the last 15 years, and have also been used in schools and colleges throughout the world.

As a result of this seminar, the Head of Ngee Ann's Electrical Engineering Department (Dr. Chen) decided that his own students would benefit greatly from the type of student-centred experiential learning that exercises such as 'The Power Station Game' make possible. He therefore asked one of his senior members of staff (Mr. Allinson) to discuss with Dr. Ellington how this might best be done. It was eventually decided that Dr. Ellington would develop a 'custom-designed' version of one of the existing IEE games, ('Power for Elaskay') specially for use with Ngee Ann students and would return to Ngee Ann at the end of July in order to help run the exercise with all 500 students in the second year of the Department's Diploma Course in Electrical Engineering.

HOW THE EXERCISE TO BE USED IN THE PROJECT WAS DEVELOPED

'Power for Elaskay' was originally developed as part of a 'structured lesson' on alternative energy for use in British schools (Ellington and Addinall, 1979). It involves the class first being given an introductory lesson on the different methods that can be used to generate electricity from 'alternative' energy sources. The class then divides into five working groups in order to investigate the technical and economic feasibility of exploiting the five such sources of energy that are available on the (imaginary) Scottish island of Elaskay (peat, solar energy, wind energy, tidal energy and hydroelectric power) and report on their findings. Finally, the class is asked to take on the role of Elaskay's Island Council, and has to develop a 50-year rolling programme for meeting the island's future electricity needs by making optimum use of these various energy sources.

In the course of the discussions that took place between Dr. Ellington and Mr. Allinson in March, 1989, it was decided that 'Power for Elaskay' was not ideally suited for use with Singapore students in its existing form. Firstly, it was based on a Scottish scenario, and it was felt that student motivation and interest would be greatly increased if this could be changed to a more local scenario to which Singaporeans could more easily relate. Also, the original scenario had been written in 1978, and was somewhat dated. It was therefore decided to re-design the exercise round a contemporary scenario in which the students would take on the role of teams of Singaporean 'consultants' who had been asked to produce a plan for meeting the future electricity needs of the (imaginary) SE Asian island of 'Pemang'.

Secondly, it was felt that the timescale for the original exercise (roughly 3 hours) was far too short for Singapore students, who would probably require much more time than British students to become familiar with the exercise and carry out the various tasks that it involved. A longer timescale would also enable a much greater 'communication skills' element to be built into the exercise, thus providing the students with an ideal vehicle for developing such skills and practising the use of English (which is not the native language for the majority of Singaporeans). It was therefore decided to re-design the exercise so that it could be run over a two-day period, and to place a much greater emphasis on formal group presentations than in the original version.

Thirdly, it was felt that the type of student resource materials that had been produced for use in the original exercise would probably not be suitable for use with Singapore students. These, it was agreed, would almost certainly require much more guidance than British students, and might well have difficulties with some of the language used in the original documents. It was therefore decided to produce a completely new set of resource materials, designed so as to make it as easy as possible for such students to master the contents and follow the instructions. The new resource materials would also be extremely 'user-friendly' from the point of view of the teaching staff who would have to run the exercise - another very important consideration. As in the case of the original resource materials, they would all be produced as photocopy masters in order to facilitate reproduction.

Work on the development of the new exercise, which was given the name 'Power for Pemang', was carried out by Dr. Ellington once he returned to Aberdeen. A detailed description of how this was done is given elsewhere (Ellington, 1990). Master copies of all the resource materials were then sent to Ngee Ann so that the multiple copies that would be needed to run the exercise - a total of over 6,500 sheets in all - could be produced.

HOW NGEE ANN STAFF WERE TRAINED TO RUN THE EXERCISE

One of the major problems faced by the authors in planning the 'Power for Pemang' project was that none of the 25 members of the Electrical Engineering staff who would actually have to run the exercise had any previous experience of this type of teaching. Because of this, several had considerable misgivings about the project, wondering (a) whether they would be able to run the exercise and (b) whether their students would be able to cope with the work involved. It was therefore decided to mount a series of staff development workshops during the week prior to that in which the exercise was to be run so that all the staff who would be involved could be given the necessary training.

These workshops, each of which involved roughly 6 staff, were run by Dr. Ellington and Mr. Allinson, and had the following objectives:

1. To convince the staff that 'Power for Pemang' would be a valuable learning experience for their students, and that their students would be perfectly capable of carrying out the work of the exercise (the latter took some doing!).
2. To introduce the staff to the 'Power for Pemang' scenario, make them familiar with the resource materials that they would be using, and provide them with detailed instructions on how to run the exercise with a class so that they would be able to do this with confidence.

The success of the staff development programme can be judged from the fact that on no occasion did any member of staff have to come to the authors for help during the subsequent running of the exercise.

HOW THE EXERCISE WAS ORGANIZED AND RUN

As can be imagined, running a highly complicated two-day simulation exercise with 500 students was no mean logistical feat, and required considerable planning and preparation on the part of the authors - particularly on the part of Mr. Allinson, who was given overall responsibility for the organization of the project. He and Dr. Ellington finalized the arrangements and prepared the individual 'teachers' packs' of resource materials during the staff development week that preceded the week in which the exercise was run, much midnight oil being burned in the process!

For the purpose of the exercise, the 500 second-year students were divided into 25 classes of 20 students, with a member of the Electrical Engineering staff being assigned to each class for the entire two days (all normal classes were cancelled for the week of the exercise). For logistical reasons, the exercise was run on a 'staggered' basis, with the first group of classes starting on the Monday and finishing on the Tuesday, a second group starting on the Tuesday, a third on the Wednesday and a fourth on the Thursday. Each group of classes was given an introductory talk by Dr. Ellington at the beginning of the first day, after which the individual classes were taken to their designated work rooms by the members of staff responsible for looking after them.

On reaching their work rooms, each class was given a further briefing by their supervising lecturer, who then divided the students into five working groups each containing four people. Each group then had to carry out a detailed technical and economic feasibility study on the possibility of exploiting each of the five natural sources of energy available on Pemang - wood from the island's one remaining tropical rain forest (this replaced peat as the source of fossil fuel), solar energy, wind energy, tidal energy and hydroelectric power. Each group had then to prepare an oral presentation on its findings, the day ending with the five groups presenting their reports and the students entering the technical and economic data relating to the various possible schemes on a specially-prepared worksheet.

On the second day of the exercise, each class was divided into two competing teams of 10 people, each team containing two of the members from each of the five specialized working groups from day 1. Using the information that had been presented at the end of Day 1 as a starting point, each team then had to draw up a 50-year rolling programme for meeting Pemang's future electricity needs and prepare a detailed group presentation on their proposed scheme. They then took turns to present their proposals, after which the supervising lecturer brought the exercise to a close by announcing which scheme was to be adopted and debriefing the students.

WHAT WAS LEARNED FROM THE PROJECT

The most important thing that was learned from the 'Power for Pemang' project was that participative simulation exercises of this type can be just as effective with Far Eastern students as they are with western students. When the project was being planned, many of the staff who were to be involved maintained that such exercises could not possibly work with Singapore students, since these had no experience of enactive, student-centred learning; would not be able to work effectively in groups; would be too inhibited to take part in the various presentations; and would find the content too difficult from both a technical and a linguistic point of view. As it turned out, all these worries proved to be completely groundless, and everyone who was involved was pleasantly surprised at just how easily the students coped with the various demands that the exercise made. Some of the specific comments that were made by the supervising staff in the questionnaire that they were asked to fill in after the completion of the project are given below.

* "The simulation game is a useful tool to stimulate students' thinking power and get them to learn to work as a team."
* "It is a joy to see students thinking aloud, debating among themselves before coming to a collective decision. The students are keen, and they enjoyed the whole exercise."
* "In this game, the students were gaining knowledge without knowing that they were learning".
* "The exercise was very beneficial to me personally because I was able to develop an even closer rapport with the students, to stimulate their minds on problem-solving techniques, on negotiation skill, to hold and chair meetings, and to present facts in a proper manner."

The responses to a student questionnaire were equally encouraging, 93% of the students who took part maintaining that they found the exercise 'interesting' and fewer than 30% indicating that they had any difficulties in understanding the technical content or performing the calculations. The only disappointing result was that only 40% of the students said that they would like to take part in similar activities again - probably because 'Power for Pemang' was not officially part of the examination curriculum (Singapore students like to see a definite return from everything they do!). This point has been well taken, and, when 'Power for Pemang' is run again, the students will almost certainly have their performance assessed in some way.

One of the most encouraging outcomes of the project has been the stimulus that it has given to further developments of this type in Singapore. The staff of Ngee Ann's Electrical Engineering Department are certainly convinced of the value of exercises such as 'Power for Pemang', and plan to make regular use of them in future. Indeed, several of the staff intend to design their own exercises.

Other departments in Ngee Ann seem likely to follow suit - especially when they see the splendid video that their Educational Technology Centre has made of the project. A preliminary version of this video was shown at a public lecture that was given by Dr. Ellington after the completion of the project - a lecture that was attended by representatives of practically every secondary and tertiary educational establishment in Singapore - and aroused considerable interest. Thus, it is hoped that many other schools and colleges will follow Ngee Ann's pioneering example and start to make use of simulation/games with their students. They would certainly find the result well worth the effort.

REFERENCES

Ellington, H.I. and Addinall, E.(1979): Building case study simulations into the curriculum as part of structured lessons. Simulations/Games For Learning, 9, 1, pp.13-19.

Ellington, H.I.(1990): Two case studies in game adaptation. 1: Converting 'Power for Elaskay' into 'Power for Pemang'. Simulation/Games For Learning, 20 (in press).

'Power for Pemang', is being published by the Institution of Electrical Engineers. Further information obtainable from the IEE's Schools Liaison Service, Michael Faraday House, Six Hills Way, Stevenage, Herts SG1 2AY.

Dr.Henry Ellington is Head of the Educational Development Unit at Robert Gordon's Institute of Technology, Aberdeen, Scotland.
Mr.Martin Allinson is a Senior Lecturer in the Electrical Engineering Department at Ngee Ann Polytechnic, Singapore.
Dr.Jimmy Chen is Head of the Electrical Engineering Department at Ngee Ann.

Address for correspondence: **Dr.H.I.Ellington,**
Educational Development Unit, RGIT,
St. Andrew Street, Aberdeen AB1 1HG, Scotland.

15. A simulation workshop for staff development and vocational guidance

Danny Saunders, The Polytechnic of Wales

Abstract: A workshop for staff development is discussed, where a competitive simulation asks participants to play the roles of either a Promotions Panel or employees hoping to be promoted within an organization. A series of dilemmas is devised by participants, based on their own work experiences, and solutions as offered by players are then judged by the Promotions Panel. The workshop is discussed in terms of its original relevance to police organizations, and a case study is presented for the area of Polytechnic lecturing. The workshop has additional applications within the general area of careers guidance, where school leavers may be informed about organizational features associated with their vocational choices.

INTRODUCTION

A **simulation** is a partially accurate representation of reality, and one that exaggerates certain features whilst playing down others (see Crookall and Saunders, 1989). Provided that the participants accept this serious limitation, and become involved in the activity through using their imaginations to make the artificial situation real, the simulation becomes a useful method in training and learning. As emphasized by Miller (1988), the value of such a technique is not so much in the simulation activity itself, but instead it is in the **debriefing** of that activity later on. The present article discusses a workshop involving the application of a simulation to a crucial issue which concerns many personnel within organizations: promotion. Because the simulation contains elements of competition, and is usually associated with enjoyable activity, it also constitutes a **game** (see Jones 1990 for a further discussion of terminology).

INITIAL OBSERVATIONS: POLICE WORK

Three years ago the author became involved with the planning and teaching of a part-time B.A. (Honours) degree in Police Studies for in-service police officers. One of the major observations and insights of working with the police as college students, and in visiting their places of work on several occasions, was the amount of importance attached to promotion and rank within career hierarchies. Especially relevant was the reaction of experienced and long-serving officers who witnessed the rapid promotion of other (often younger) staff to higher status - and salaried - positions for reasons that were not immediately apparent as regards the business of 'being a good officer'. To give one quote: "If I'd known then what I know now, I wouldn't have gone into the force".

This kind of observation prompted further enquiries and research by the author, not least because so many parallels can be seen with other organizations and career structures - including higher education! Of especial importance is the concept of the **the ceiling effect**, where personnel reach a certain level within a career hierarchy and want to go higher but cannot. Another essential consideration is **burn out**, where personnel become exhausted and even 'incompetent' as a consequence of much hard work and effort which proves to be too demanding and that is not sufficiently rewarded. Ceiling effects and burn out refer to the gloomier areas of organizational behaviour and personnel management where employees are frustrated, bitter, demoralized and depressed.

There is much relevance here for staff development programmes which allow people to air their grievances and possibly find some solutions. Furthermore, welltimed training workshops may pre-empt the emergence of such frustrations in the first place - especially when much later difficulty is caused by earlier job expectations that are naive or unrealistic as regards the ambitions, desires and needs of a changing individual as she or he moves through life within an employment sector. This can even include staying with the same organization and the same colleagues for their entire working lifetimes.

To illustrate with a deliberately pessimistic and exaggerated scenario: a twenty year old police officer may look forward to a varied job which involves some excitement, is seen as important, and as reasonably secure. At the age of thirty there may be some financial pressures (such as mortgage and dependents), a weariness or fear of certain kinds of police work, a fuller awareness of how police organizations operate, and ambitions of climbing the career ladder a little further. At the age of thirty eight the work pressures may have increased but the hope of gaining further promotion is gone - and the person is now fed up with the job which they have been doing for years for relatively little further reward. The officer may now be **surviving** until early retirement.

Much depends on the initial reasons for selecting a particular kind of employment. Again, with reference to police work, it is worth referring to some research conducted by Russo et al (1983). They identified three types of officer, based on their interests and their reasons for getting involved with policing as a career: people orientated officers (who prefer to work with others and enjoy talking and listening to people), personal reward orientated officers (who are attracted by conditions of service and financial rewards), and professionally orientated officers (who are attracted by status, authority and prestige). Whilst this study was simplistic in its inability to recognize that people can be some or all of these types at different times in their careers, it was very useful in pinpointing different kinds of reaction to stressful situations and crises. It would seem that the people orientated officers appear to be more capable of coping with stress, especially when compared to the professionally orientated officers.

From a training viewpoint, it is useful to design a workshop that gauges perceptions and expectations about a given employment, and that prepares new applicants who want to enter a particular employment sector for possible frustrations or otherwise unforeseen obstacles. In other words, to warn newcomers about later problems as reported by more experienced personnel. Another focus for training involves a workshop which allows experienced personnel and employees to discuss openly their feelings and perceptions of success and failure within a particular organization.

As a result of these two objectives, the Promotions Workshops has two areas of application:

1. as a staff development activity for experienced personnel;
2. as an aid for vocational guidance.

THE PROMOTIONS WORKSHOP

The workshop involves the use of the PROMOTIONS GAME (Saunders and

Coote and Crookall, 1988; Saunders and Crookall 1989) and deliberately establishes a competitive situation where teams represent individual employee roles within a workforce. In this article it is presented as a **frame** for a workshop, so that interested readers can simply supply their own organization as a context for play. The following section is based on Saunders and Crookall (1989).

THE GAME FRAME

There are few materials involved - coloured cards, dilemma sheets, dice and a stack of curriculum vitae forms. The game begins with a degree of control from the facilitator(s), but quickly hands over power to participants who are selected for a Promotions Panel. There is the added facility of including an expert on personnel management within this 'elite' (in which case the session becomes more of a simulation than a game because the degree of realism is increased).

Reference to Figure 1 suggests that the Promotions Game thus divides participants into two groups: one being the Promotions Panel and the other being the 'new employee'. The Panel draws up a series of dilemmas and a diagram depicting a career hierarchy; this information is based on their own experiences of early employment. The rest of the workshop involves players who draw up curriculum vitaes for fictitious personnel: a throw of the dice can, if the facilitator so wishes, determine outcomes for each area of the curriculum vitae.

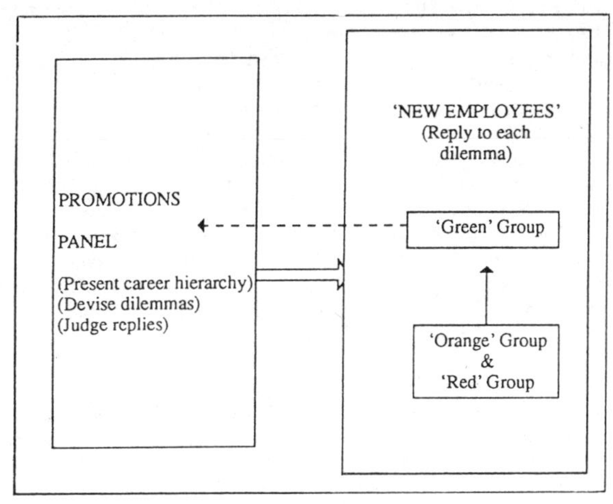

Figure 1: Workshop divisions for The Promotions Game.

Participants have to provide solutions to each dilemma which is presented by the Panel, who in turn judge each reply. The best answers receive a green card, leading to promotion. Average answers receive an orange card, corresponding to a salary increment but no promotion through a 'bar' within the Panel's career hierarchy. Poor answers result in the awarding of a red card - demotion.

The activity is at its most powerful with a homogeneous group of participants who use their own curriculum vitae, and where the Panel involves relatively senior personnel. In this instance, the employment hierarchy and organization is based on fact: a 'lived' career hierarchy is perceived and very real dilemmas have to be solved. If a heterogeneous group of employees is involved then the employment context and career structures may be more distanced and fictitious for some or all participants. It is emphasized that this may be **more** advantageous for 'defensive' groups which have low morale and are associated with job dissatisfaction rather than success and rapid promotion. It is also more effective for workshops consisting of personnel who are relatively inexperienced in business affairs.

Eventually the workshop will probably consist of three separate groups:

* the Promotions Panel itself;
* a green card group which is enjoying itself and doing well;
* orange and red groups, which have teamed together but feel alienated from the greens and the Panel (see Figure 1).

This division can be further emphasized by the award of a gold card to the green table; this allows nominated individuals to join the Panel and have the luxury of presenting dilemmas to their former colleagues.

In most cases the game is played in good spirit and with a certain flair by participants. Debriefing, however, tends to be a serious affair. The organizational pyramid and career ladder as presented by Panel members is applied critically to participants' own employment context, and the dilemmas are expanded and appraised by those people who played the part of 'new employees'. A frequent issue concerns the **lack** of clarity for an organization's promotion criteria. In some cases there is either a bewilderment or suspicion about why some people succeed and others fail. In others there is the fatalistic belief about being in the right place at the right time. And yet at other times the somewhat satirical Peter Principle (Peter and Hull, 1969: wherein people rise to the level of their incompetence) becomes the most popular interpretation of the consequences of advancement within the promotion pyramid. Only rarely does there appear to be a confidence in management's promotion decisions when it comes to recognizing the positive and negative qualities of a workforce.

Of course there are many problems associated with the above observations such as 'sour grapes' from many employees who may be jealous or threatened by other people's success. Another concerns a generally critical appraisal of middle and upper management by employees within many workforces - so that no matter what decisions are made, management simply cannot win. But no matter how 'false' such perceptions may be, they are real in their consequences for areas of an organization which may be affected by job frustrations and poor working relationships.

It is therefore hoped that this single example of a business game offers a valuable insight into the attitudes, opinions and beliefs of its participants. In so doing it acquires a **diagnostic** function, provided the workshop members are protected from prosecution as regards any publicizing of grievances or concerns! This is a strong argument for bringing in outside facilitators to run the game, should serious and irreconcilable management-employee relations be suspected. The presence of a senior member of management, who may well be actively involved in real life promotion decisions, can clearly inhibit open discussion on certain occasions.

A CASE STUDY INVOLVING THE TEACHING PROFESSION

Lecturing in a Polytechnic

At the AETT 1990 Conference, a workshop addressed the career of lecturing within higher education. One person who had a background in the polytechnic sector volunteered to play the role of the Promotions Panel, whilst the rest of the participants formed pairs and drew up their curriculum vitaes for new lecturers who were just starting out in higher education. The Promotion Panel's career sequence is:

Lecturer I → Lecturer II → Course leader →
Head of Department → Assistant Director → Director

Some examples of the dilemmas proposed by the 'Promotions Panel' were:

LEVELS ONE AND TWO

* You are experiencing a lot of anxiety, stage fright and nervousness about teaching your first group of students. What do you do about this?
* Because of your heavy teaching load you are finding it hard to keep up to date and on top of the subject matter. What can you do about this?
* You have just received a complaint from a student who feels that you have marked an assignment unfairly. How do you deal with this situation?

LEVEL THREE

* You have received yet more bad feedback regarding a member of staff about whom the students constantly complain. How do you handle this?
* You have to make some cutbacks in your department and there are some staff who have seriously overspent their budgets. What do you do?

CONCLUSIONS

It is emphasized that there are no right or wrong answers to the above dilemmas, and that in the workshop participants did not progress to the top of the hierarchy. Instead, solutions to the dilemmas were mostly rapid and light-hearted, with a 'green group' breaking away from the rest as they achieved higher positions on the career ladder because of the favourable treatment afforded by the Promotions Panel. The physical distance that appeared between the successful and unsuccessful roles was viewed as an important symbolic feature of the Promotions Game, where people either communicate differently or else stop communicating altogether once higher status is gained. By contrast, the green group communicates more with the Promotions Panel once success is evident.

The actual duration of the game is short - no more than thirty minutes. It is emphasized that it is highly simplistic, and that the dilemmas are very crude and lacking in sufficient detail. Instead it is the debriefing that is essential for staff development and training purposes. To begin with, the Promotions Panel states what their 'real' criteria were for the awarding of red, orange or green cards (in some cases this can be totally arbitrary, such as preferring an answer because the CV states that the person is local and knows the area). This is then followed by a discussion of the dilemmas, and drawing on the experiences of participants as regards whether these dilemmas were realistic enough. In many cases other real dilemmas will be suggested, based on the past experiences of participants. The career pyramid as presented at the beginning of the briefing period is then critically appraised and modified. The final stage involves open and frank discussion about possible paths and obstacles within that pyramid.

Overall, a game of dilemmas is not a new idea (indeed the popular game of SCRUPLES takes the theme of deciding about what to do in crisis situations a lot further), and it is only intended as a catalyst or even an icebreaker for discussion about issues and frustrations which may be very serious and personal for some members of a workforce. The exercise is at its most powerful when representatives are present from management groups who are responsible for deciding the promotion of the personnel present. There are also applications to careers guidance, where school leavers can be warned about the unforseen aspects of their chosen careers. It is feasible, for example, for somebody from that particular employment sector to visit a school or college in order to play the part of the Promotions Panel.

At the AETT '90 Conference a number of modifications were suggested, including the computerizing of the entire operation. One of the disadvantages of the current workshop is that it becomes slow and unwieldy when there are large numbers present: it takes time to listen to all of the proposed solutions to dilemmas, and people may become bored after they have had their turn. It is certainly the case that computer networking allows for faster feedback from the Promotions Panel, who can then also immediately present the next dilemma. As a final ironical comment, we also point out that the workshop has not yet been tried out with police officers - the people who first inspired its design.

REFERENCES

Crookall, D. and Saunders, D.(eds)(1988): Communication and Simulation: from two fields to one theme. MultiLingual Matters, Clevedon.

Jones, K.(1990): On terminology. Simulation/Games for Learning. 20,4.

Miller, A.(1988): Who would like to share their experiences? Debriefing and experiential learning. In, Saunders, D., Coote, A. and Crookall, D. (eds), Learning from Experience Through Games and Simulation. SAGSET, Loughborough.

Peter, L. and Hull, R.(1969): The Peter Principle. Morrow, New York.

Russo, P., Engal, A. and Hatting, S.(1983): Police and occupational stress. In, Bennett, R.(ed), Police at Work. SAGE, London.

Saunders, D.(1988): The Promotions Game. Business Education Today, 14, 4, pp.12-14.

Saunders, D. Coote, A. and Crookall, D.(1988): Learning from Experience. SAGSET, Loughborough.

Saunders, D. and Crookall, D.(1989): Exploring career hierarchies: the Promotions Game. In, Miller, A. and Crookall, D.(eds), Simulation and Gaming: Pathways to Progress. SAGSET, Loughborough.

Address for correspondence: **Danny Saunders,**
Department of Behavioural and Communication Studies,
The Polytechnic of Wales, Pontypridd,
Mid-Glamorgan CF37 1DL, UK.

Section 3: The teaching and learning of mathematics

16. Teaching logic: why and how

Donatella Persico, Institute of Educational Technology, CNR Italy

Abstract: Learning logic can enhance formalization and deduction skills, therefore contributing to the development of cognitive and communication skills. Furthermore, the teaching of logic may be built around a multidisciplinary educational path, by taking advantage of the natural links and analogies between logic and other disciplines. To realize this potential Logiclandia, a courseware for high schools aiming at facilitating and supporting the problem-based learning of logic, has been designed. While Logiclandia's printed material guides students to solve simple problems by using the language and methods of predicate logic, its software environment provides a motivating framework to try out their solutions.

INTRODUCTION

It is widely recognized today that some features relating to the learning of mathematical logic, such as the development of formalization and deduction skills, have a high educational value. It is thus not surprising that logic has been introduced in the experimental curricula of years 1 and 2 of Italian higher secondary schools (14-16 age group) and that several experiments in teaching logic have been carried out both in Italy and abroad. For similar reasons, the teaching of logic programming and declarative languages in the field of computer science education is meeting with increasing interest and approval.

Despite this academic interest, school practice is very different, at least in Italy: logic is generally neglected by teachers and often hated by students, because school books on it are very theoretical and abstract, it imposes the use of a language which is totally unnatural, apparently an end in itself, and is often dealt with as a preliminary theoretical basis to - but detached from - other scientific disciplines.

It was in this context that the Logiclandia project, which aims to develop a different approach to the teaching and learning of logic in higher secondary schools, was started in 1987. To start with, it was essential to investigate whether logic could really contribute to basic education (i.e., identify both the content and methods of logic that could make a contribution, as well as the aspects of basic education that could be contributed to), and if so, how. In the following sections the educational potential of formalization and, to a lesser extent, deduction is shown, and then Logiclandia's approach is discussed.

Learning to communicate clearly in relation to a problem as the first step towards its solution.

How many teachers complain about the inability of their students to express themselves? No matter what the subject is, the improper use of language can reach the point of compromising mutual understanding, if not rendering futile the efforts made to analyse a problem or situation. The importance of the capacity to express oneself clearly, precisely and, when necessary concisely, is often underestimated by students. The fact that "The teacher knows what I mean anyway" demotivates the search for more accurate expressions and terms, and often an assessment which takes account of the proper use of language is even considered 'unfair'.

Logiclandia's approach is based on the hypothesis that the capacity to formalize a problem, or rather to translate its content into a formal language of any kind - graphic, linguistic or any other - is crucial to the activity of solving the problem itself. In other words, understanding the text of a problem also means being able to re-organize the information it contains in an autonomous and appropriate way. Although the ability to formalize is not a necessary condition, even less a sufficient one, for the solution of the problem, one can definitely say that it plays an essential role when one wishes to organize, manipulate and communicate knowledge.

Within this framework, the introduction of an interlocutor capable only of understanding a formal language (e.g. a software environment) provides at a practical level the need to use a formal language.

Logic as the backbone of interdisciplinary reflections

Highlighting connections and analogies within and between school subjects is generally considered appropriate and even desirable. It can foster learning by making links and analogies with already known concepts and theories; it helps broaden horizons by getting students used to considering a problem from various angles; and it enriches and strengthens students' capacity to understand and analyse knowledge autonomously. Encouraging this type of 'transfer', however, is not easy, and it often requires the collaboration of more than one teacher, as well as the presence of a series of conceptual links (i.e. relations of interdependence like analogies) between the various disciplines. Logic offers numerous opportunities of this type, provided that an educational path is designed, highlighting its links with other disciplines. The logical connectives and quantifiers, for example, may be introduced by analysing the student's natural language. This fosters reflections about, on the one hand, the ambiguity and imprecision of this language when expressing a problem, and on the other hand, the inadequacies of artificial languages when compared with the richness and expressive powers of natural languages.

Other 'natural' links between logic and other disciplines are provided by the analogies between logical connectives and the set operators, the logical operators of programming languages, and the logic gates of electronic circuits. Finally, as is shown below, the link between logic and computer science (and in particular data bases) is cemented by Logiclandia's software environment.

LOGICLANDIA'S EDUCATIONAL APPROACH

The Logiclandia project is based on two hypotheses:

* that an operative approach suits the age range we are dealing with (14-18) better than a more abstract and theoretical one;
* that the availability of a software environment in which the language of logic may be used and its concepts and methods put into practice, can motivate and reinforce its acquisition.

Confirmation of this may be found in several experiments (for example Ennals, 1986) which showed that some logic programming languages can be used to teach propositional logic. The major drawbacks of this approach, when trying to adapt it to the teaching of predicate logic are the implicit quantifications of variables (this may be misleading when trying to learn how the logical quantifiers work) and its strong dependence on the deduction mechanism adopted by the interpreter of the

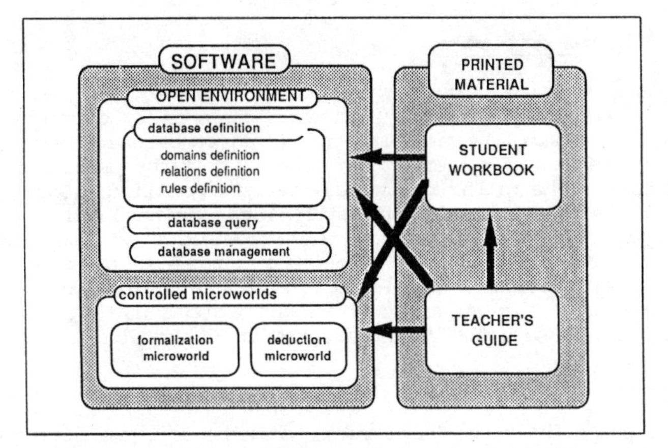

Figure 1: Logiclandia's structure and functions.

chosen language (Persico, 1990). On the other hand, the great strength of this approach is the availability of a software environment (i.e. the interpreter of the chosen language) which allows active learning, motivates the need for formalization and provides feedback on both a syntactic and semantic level.

On the bases of these hypotheses and experience, Logiclandia proposes a 'problem-orientated' approach, where "problems are the starting point of the learning process and organized forms of knowledge are only introduced when needed to solve them" (Ellington, 1989), and provides a software environment in which the problems may be formalized, solved and their solutions automatically checked. This environment is inspired by a class of applications whose theoretical foundations are closely linked to the world of logic - data bases.

The courseware, consisting of the software environment, a student workbook and a teacher's guide (Figure 1), has been designed for use in class or in a computer laboratory, under the supervision of at least one teacher.

The printed material suggests a path for the gradual learning of the fundamentals of predicate logic and familiarization with the software environment. In particular, the material dealt with includes logical connectives (conjunctions, disjunctions, negations, implications); existential and universal quantifiers, the concept of deduction, the modus ponens, the modus tollens, proof ab absurdo.

SOLVING PROBLEMS WITH LOGICLANDIA

Logiclandia's software environment allows the student to create, modify and query small data bases, in order to find a solution to a problem. Part of the data base definition and the query phase require the use of **logichese**, a language based on predicate logic. In particular, logichese uses the logical connectives, **and**($\wedge$), **or**($\vee$), **not**($\neg$) and **implies**($\rightarrow$), the existential($\exists$ and $\exists!$) and universal($\forall$) quantifiers and an operator, **what**, to query Logiclandia about all the values of one or more variables satisfying a given logical condition.

Since there is more than one correct solution to each problem, the student workbook only provides methodological suggestions rather than guiding the student towards a particular solution. Below are described the phases which make up Logiclandia's problem-solving approach.

Understanding the problem

On the basis of the text of the problem, expressed in their own language, students identify the classes of objects (or domains) relevant to the aim of solving the problem, the relations between them, and the query or queries to be answered. From the text of the problem in Figure 2a, for example, the following domains can be identified: **people, places** and **drinks.** The relations might be **sell(places,drinks)** and **drink(people,drinks).** In addition, the 'rules' which will make deduction possible are identified at this stage. One example is the binary rule compatible(people,places), which specifies how a person and a place are compatible when a drink that person drinks is sold in that place. The result of this phase could be the diagram in Figure 2b.

Problem formalization

In this phase the student interacts with the software environment to create a data base whose structure derives from the problem's semantics previously identified. For each domain a table is created and filled out with its elements. The relations can be expressed in two ways. The first consists of specifying its name, the domains it connects and finally filling in a table such as that in Figure 2c, indicating which objects are in relation to each other (the so-called **extensional** definition of a relation). The second way consists of defining 'rules' establishing logical conditions which have to be satisfied for a certain number of objects to be in relation to each other. The rules, i.e. the so-called **intensional** component of the data base, are expressed in **logichese** (Figure 2c) and communicated to Logiclandia by means of a simple text editor. At the end of the input of each rule a syntactic analyser produces possible error messages. Automatic controls to check the coherence of the data bases created by the students are also provided.

Lastly, the queries are formalized (also in **logichese**) and submitted to the software. Figure 2c shows, for example, the solution to the problem of Logiclandia's drinkers. While syntax errors are diagnosed by a syntactic analyser, the questions which are syntactically correct but semantically wrong generally elicit unexpected replies which force the student to check the correctness of the data base and the query to identify possible mistakes. In particular, complex rules and queries are generally defined via a process of trial and error; for example, once the **compatible** rule is defined, the workbook suggests that the students check its formalization, for at least one pair (places,people).

Deduction

Students may solve the problem independently, by making a deduction based on the known data and rules, and then check their solutions against Logiclandia's. If the two results are different, a software option may be used, called 'why' to go back step-by-step through the sequence of deductions deployed by Logiclandia. Alternatively, students may retrace their own deductive steps and query the software about partial solutions reached until the discrepancy is revealed. In the same way as within each phase, the process of solving a problem proceeds in an iterative rather than a sequential way. At any level the need to revise what has been done before can arise.

Formalization and deduction, the two skills that Logiclandia aims to develop, are also the focus of two so-called 'controlled microworlds', which are complementary software components characterized, contrary to

In Logiclandia there live two people, whose names are Kurt and Thoralf. Both of them like drinking in company but of course each has his own preferences: Kurt only drinks beer or wine, while Thoralf doesn't like Coca-cola. In Logiclandia there are three places to go for a drink: the Cocco, which only sells Coca-cola and lemonade; the Mocambo, which only sells beer; and the Britannia, which sells Coca-cola, lemonade, beer and wine.

Kurt and Thoralf meet and Kurt decides to buy his friend a drink. So he asks him where he wants to go. Thoralf thinks about it for a moment and chooses somewhere where they sell at least one drink that he likes and one that Kurt likes, and which isn't the Britannia because he owes the landlord some money. Which place do they go to? What does Kurt drink?

Figure 2a: Text of the problem

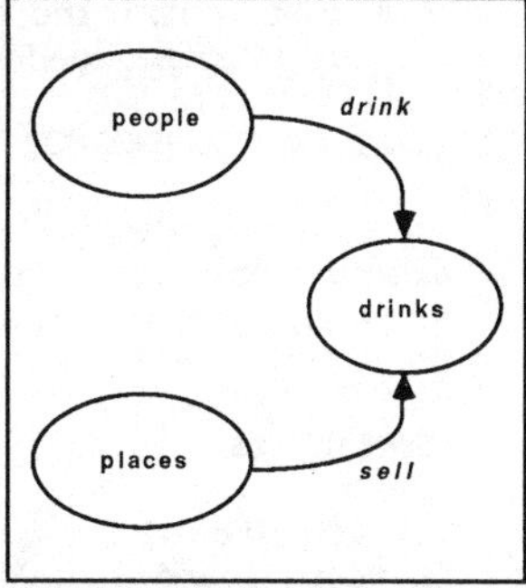

Figure 2b: Output of problem analysis

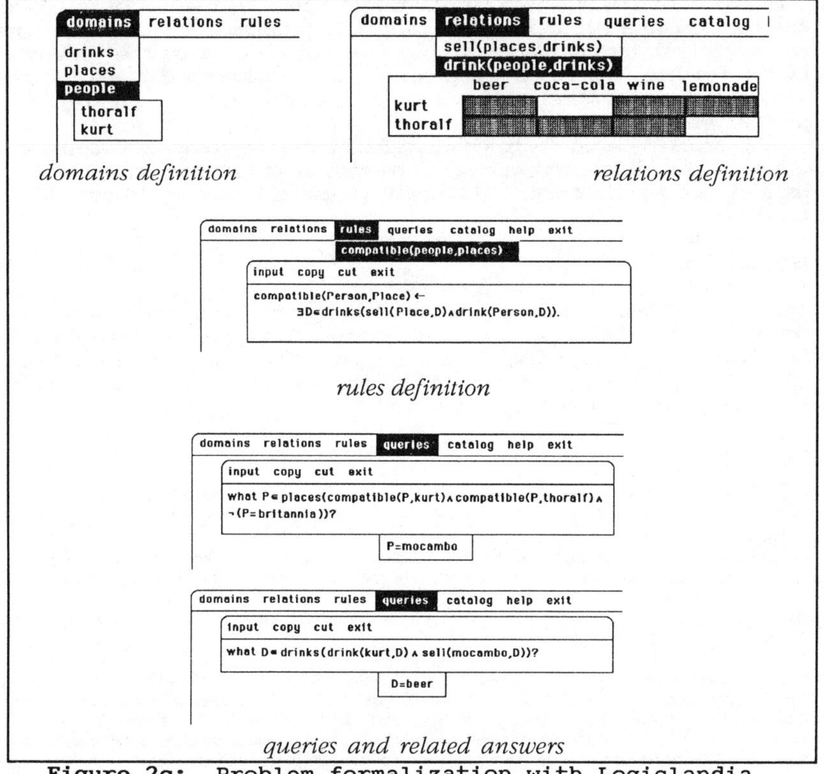

Figure 2c: Problem formalization with Logiclandia

Logiclandia, by a more directive strategy. This directivity is dictated by a more restricted and well-defined objective and by the need to provide precise feedback on students' work.

STATE OF THE PROJECT

A first prototype of the software and a draft of the printed material are now available. Field testing is planned to get a formative evaluation of this material. The final version of the software should operate on IBM/MS-DOS with at least 640K, a hard disc and possibly a mouse.

CONCLUSIONS

Even with the recent introduction of logic in experimental curricula in years 1 and 2 of higher secondary schools, teachers and textbook writers tend to pay little attention to this discipline or to ignore it altogether. Apart from a natural inertia, this can also be attributed to the absence in Italy of a well-established tradition of teaching logic at this level. Possibly even more negative factors are the justified reservations about the educational value of certain exercises in propositional calculus and of the abstract and theoretical treatment of predicate logic, more suited to university than to secondary students.

The alternative approach proposed in this article is based on a teaching environment which guides the students in the use of the language and the concepts of logic to solve simple problems. It should be noted, however, that the 'guidance' is provided not so much by the software as by the teacher, who poses the problems to be solved and plans the educational path, more or less according to the suggestions in the printed material.

The problem-based approach therefore sets the tasks of leading a class to the 'discovery' of logic, by trying to achieve an optimal balance between autonomy and creativity and stimulus, guidance and control.

ACKNOWLEDGEMENTS

The author thanks all those who have co-operated and continue to co-operate in the development of Logiclandia: in particular, teachers Licia Marcegalia and Sandro Rivella and computer programmers Stefano Jesi, Carlo Innocenti and Claudio Massucco for the experience and creativity they have contributed to the project.

REFERENCES

Ellington, H.I.(1989): Problem-based learning in education and training. In Bell, C. and Winders, R.(eds): Aspects of Educational and Training Technology, XXII, pp.177-184. Kogan Page, London.

Ennals, R.(1986): Teaching logic as a computer language in schools. In Van Canegham, M. and Warren, D.H.D.(eds): Logic Programming and its Applications, pp.129-144. Ablex Publishing Corp., Norwood, N.J.

Persico, D.(1990): Imparare la logica con i database. Informatica e Scuola, to be published.

Dr. Donatella Persico is a researcher at the Institute for Educational Technology of the Italian National Research Council, and has been active in the field of Educational Technology - theory and applications - since 1981. At present she is involved in the project 'Educational systems based on multimedia databases' within the EC DELTA programme, and is in charge of the Logiclandia project.

Address for correspondence: **Dr.Donatella Persico,**
CNR, Instituto Tecnologie Didattiche,
via Opera Pia 11, 16145 Genova, Italy.

17. The THE CAI system with learning environment for enhancing problem solving

Naoto Nakamura, Makoto Takeya, Takahiro Shakushi* and Fumiyuki Terada**
Takushoku University; *Bunkyo University; **Waseda University, Japan

Abstract: The THE system (Terada and Hirose Education system) is a multimedia CAI system with a videodisc player controlled by a personal computer. This system was first presented in 1981, and has been improved several times. In this paper we propose various practical uses of mathematical materials through the THE system. After a brief introduction to the development of the THE system, a configuration of the system hardware is shown. Then, a set of strategies -TESSOKU strategy - to find deterministic solutions is introduced, which are particularly applicable to problem solving. Basic tutorial and practice courseware is discussed from the viwpoint of categorization by TESSOKU; two new modes proposed for the implementation of this are included in a data structure of the THE system.

DEVELOPMENT OF THE SYSTEM

The THE system (Terada and Hirose Education system) is a multimedia computer assisted instruction (CAI) system with an optical laser video disc player controlled by a personal computer. The prototype THE system was demonstrated in 1981 (see Terada et al, 1981). The configuration of the hardware, the software and the courseware for high school mathematical education was completed in 1982 (see Terada et al, 1982). That system, though, had the problem that if the entire presentation was longer than two hours the system needed more than one videodisc player. This has been solved by the SWSD (Still with Sound and Data) method which was developed by the Pioneer Electronic Corporation. The second version of the THE system, using SWSD, was introduced in 1985, and it was reported that students who studied using this system performed better than they did before using it (Terada et al, 1985).

The next phase of development, in 1987, allowed the THE system to be applied to various types of learning domains, e.g. English language teaching (see Terada et al 1987). Furthermore, we have been researching how to use the THE system for various types of learning, such as tutorial, practice, reference, guidance and so on. We term these various learning types 'multiple learning environments'. In particular, we are developing multiple learning environments based on the mathematical education needed for problem solving.

THE HARDWARE OF THE THE SYSTEM

The hardware configuration of the THE system is a personal computer (PC)(UC-V102 of the MSX-2 type by Pioneer Electronic Corporation) connected to a videodisc player as shown in Figure 1. The UC-V102 includes an interface for superimposed images. Audio and visual information are recorded on the videodisc and played through the SWSD unit, which is controlled by the RS232C interface of the PC.

The latest THE system has three playing methods - still play, dynamic play and SWSD play. The previous version had only the still and dynamic play methods. The SWSD play system is a voice synthesized method which was not available for the previous system, and which allows more voice information to be obtainable. Thus more versatility is achieved for the

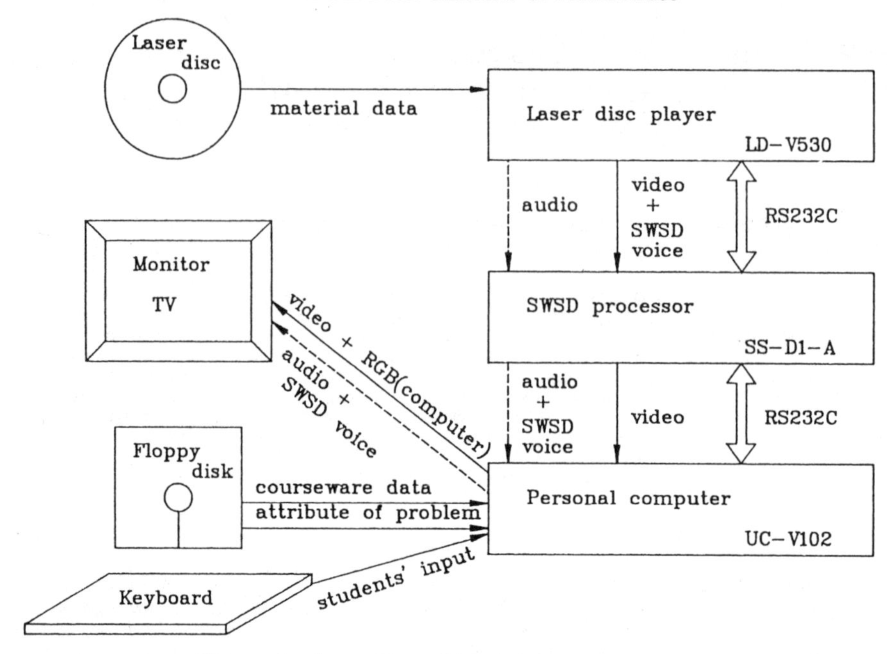

Figure 1: A configuration of the THE system.

courseware. The previous system allowed 30 minutes of voice information each side, but the SWSD method increases this to a maximum of 5,400 events per side, where one event is one still image plus 28 seconds of voice.

MULTIPLE LEARNING ENVIRONMENTS

To develop new learning environments, we analysed students' opinions about the basic courseware and the materials of the THE system (see Takeya et al, 1989b). During this analysis, attention was drawn to the effectiveness of the guidance which TESSOKU gave. TESSOKU is a set of strategies to find a deterministic solution, and comes from a Japanese word meaning 'ironbound rule'. The new learning environment which has replaced the existing basic courseware is thus designed to allow the students to learn TESSOKU efficiently.

Problem solving and TESSOKU strategy

In problem solving, a student uses two kinds of knowledge - mathematical knowledge (MK) and TESSOKU. The MK is a set of mathematical truths, such as definitions, formulae, theorems and so on, which are classified into particular mathematical categories like quadratic functions, trigonometric ratios, finite mathematics, etc. In the traditional THE system, each mathematical category corresponds to one chapter. On the other hand, TESSOKU is a set of strategies for applying MK efficiently to solve problems. Each TESSOKU strategy is generally related to the various mathematical categories, and the various strategies are necessary to solve difficult or complicated mathematical problems.

In considering the students' problem-solving procedures, we classified more than 200 TESSOKU strategies into the following eight categories by analysing about 2000 mathematical problems included in the THE system:

* put given condition into mathematical graph/expression;
* put given/unknown target into mathematical graph/expression;
* decrease unknown elements for simplification;
* transform for simplification;
* use particularity for simplification;
* replace target graph with expression;
* replace target expression with graph;
* trial and error using actual values/graphs.

To clarify TESSOKU categories, some examples are:

* in the mathematical category 'trigonometric ratio' there are the TESSOKU strategies, 'unify the given angles' and 'unify trigonometric ratio'.
  More specifically, the latter strategy means that when sin, cos and tan appear in the same equation, trying to apply MK by means of a formula such as 'tan x = sin x / cos x' is effective in solving the problem;
* in the mathematical category 'vectors' there is a TESSOKU strategy to 'replace all of the given vectors into the linear combination of the basis.'

These examples belong to different mathematical categorizations, but they are contained within the common category 'Decreasing unknown elements for simplification' within the TESSOKU system. We think that learning TESSOKU is very important in increasing students' creativity and to improve their ability to think logically.

Basic courseware

The basic courseware which was implemented on the traditional THE system was termed Tutorial and Practice style (T & P style), and has branches which have been developed as a result of students' practice. This courseware has various phases - lecture phase, training phase, judgement phase, etc. - in each chapter, which are aimed at supplementing incomplete parts of MK through problem solving. An individual TESSOKU strategy is applicable to the given problem without relating it to others, and students are able to learn the various TESSOKU strategies through T & P. However, because the course sequence is based on the mathematical categorizations, it was not sufficient just to teach a student the method of choosing the most suitable TESSOKU strategy for the given problem from the variety of TESSOKU strategies available.

New learning environment

In the new environment, traversing mathematical categories plays an important role. Figure 2 shows the relationships between the problems.

The T & P style courseware has the course sequenced according to the mathematical categorization (shown in Figure 2 by the arrows with continuous lines). Each of the problems has some applicable TESSOKU strategies; for example, TESSOKU strategy TC1 can be applied to problems 1, 5 and 7, and the arrows with dashed lines reconnect the problems according to the applicability of this strategy. Problems 1, 5 and 7 are similar and so related to one another in the TESSOKU strategy but located separately in the sequence in mathematical order.

Students must find any similarities between problems by themselves, and learn the applicability of TESSOKU strategies through practice in

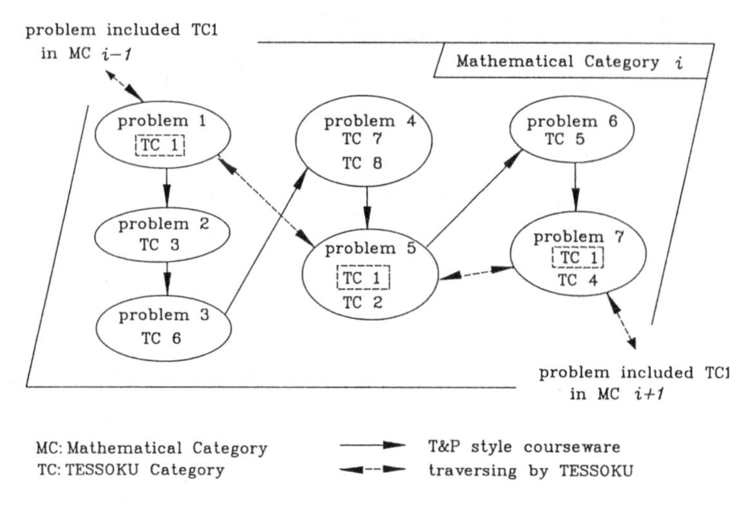

Figure 2: An example of traversing.

problem solving. When they succeed in allocating the right TESSOKU categories to problems, this is regarded as successfully learning general problem-solving strategies, which are embedded into the students' mathematical intelligences.

Why is it easier to learn MK rather than the problem-solving strategies? Probably because MK is taught in an order which is organized specifically for it. In order to encourage a more total mathematical intelligence, we produced a new learning environment which included two traversing modes:

* Strategic Learning mode; and
* Similar Problem Searching mode.

In the Strategic Learning mode, problems are linked into a sequence according to the applicability of TESSOKU strategies. In the Similar Problem Searching mode, problems which are alike in the applicability of a particular TESSOKU strategy to their solution are selected by students from the 2000 problems recorded on the video disc which was prepared for the T & P style courseware. In these ways, students can acquire both problem-solving strategies and also total mathematical intelligence.

Data structure

The data structure needed to implement the new environment is shown in Figure 3. The substructures 'Mathematical Category' and 'Video Disc Address' were prepared for the previous T & P style courseware, and they are re-used under the new environment to access the information on the video disc. The substructures named 'TESSOKU Category' are added to the previous data structures, and each TESSUKO category has two fields - "'Category Number' and 'TESSUKO Number'. The Category Number field has values of 1 to 8 corresponding to the category number of TESSOKU strategies, while the TESSOKO Number field has a value corresponding to each TESSOKU strategy.

CONCLUSION

This paper has described the multimedia CAI system called the THE

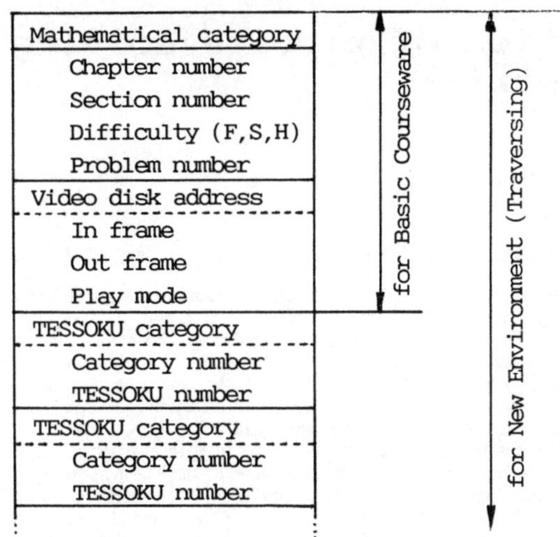

Figure 3: Data structure of a problem.

system, which has been steadily improved as electronic media, computer technology and teaching technology have developed. A basic courseware called T & P style has been created for mathematical education. In this paper, to research the capabilities of the THE system we have proposed a new learning environment which focuses on the problem-solving strategies known as TESSOKU. Two modes are introduced, the Strategic Learning mode and the Similar Problem Solving mode. These two modes appear to be effective in helping students to learn problem-solving strategies, but we need still to analyse the relationship between the learning effect and what appears in the students' logs.

REFERENCES

Takeya, M., Nakamura, N. and Matsui, T.(1989b): An evaluation of the THE CAI system based on students' opinion. Journal of Japanese Science Education, 13, 2, pp.102-108.

Terada, F., Hirose, K. and Ono, T.(1981): Instruction techniques on using video disc system. IFIP Proc. of 3rd World Conference on Computers in Education. pp.343-349.

Terada, F. et al(1982): THE system: instruction using videodisc and a micro-computer. Educational Technology Research, 6, pp.29-36.

Terada, F., Hirose, K. and Handa, T.(1985):Towards a self-paced learning support system. IFIP Proc. of 4th World Conference on Computers in Education. pp.39-44.

Terada, F., Matsuyama, M. and Shakushi, T.(1987): English education using multi-media CAI system: use of the THE system in meeting the needs of English language education. Proc. of the IFIP TC3 Regional Conference on MCSE. pp.319-324.

Addresses for correspondence: **Naoto Nakamura** and **Makoto Takeya**,
Faculty of Engineering, Takushoku University,
815-1, Tatemachi, Hachioji, Tokyo 193, Japan.

Takahiro Shakushi,
Bunkyo University, 1100 Namegaya,
Chigasaki, Kangawa 253, Japan.

Fumiyuki Terada,
School of Science and Engineering, Waseda U.,
3-4-1 Okubo, Shinjuku, Tokyo 169, Japan.

18. Description of problem solving using Petri Nets

Guglielmo Trentin, Institute of Educational Technology, CNR Italy

Abstract This paper explores the possibility of using Petri nets as a formal language for pupils to represent their own personal knowledge. The underlying hypothesis is that the process of identifying and defining the knowledge structure of a given content area, makes it easier for the pupils to use the knowledge itself (solving a problem, expounding an argument, etc....).
The remarks refer to experiments carried out with pupils in the first years of higher secondary school (14-15 years old) and deal with the graphical representation of problem-solving procedures for some simple mathematical problems, with the aim of establishing the most suitable problem-solving procedure. In describing the experiments it will be shown how this type of activity can on the one hand foster self-checking and the consolidation of learning, and on the other hand accustom the pupil to a hierarchical view of a particular knowledge domain, that is, to a distinction between 'preordinate' and 'subordinate' knowledge.

STRUCTURING KNOWLEDGE

An important objective of education is to foster in pupils the activity of structuring their personal knowledge, that is, the creation of a network of permanent connections between information elements (notions) which they gradually receive through educational processes. The basic idea is that being able to represent knowledge is one of the keys to being able to use it (Donald, 1987).

If we start from the observation that learning is generated not only by the activity of the teacher but also by the activity of every single pupil, we can conclude that the main role of the teacher is to create learning situations in which the pupils are stimulated to explore knowledge. In realizing this aim teachers must not limit themselves to providing information but must, first of all, induce and stimulate internalization (Larsen, 1986). With reference to the experiments described in this paper an attempt was made to create a situation which could facilitate both the knowledge representation to be activated during the solving of a particular problem, and communication between the components of the various work groups.

Now, if by representation we mean an 'external' organization of the knowledge in structures, whether the act of representation consists in drawing a diagram which illustrates known facts and their relations, or tables or diagrams are created in order to clarify the formulation of a problem, the effect is to place cognitive elements in structures or schemes which can be put to rapid use.

In our case we chose Petri Nets to schematize problem-solving abilities. There were two specific reasons: firstly, because they represent a graphical formal language, and secondly because they are easy to learn and to use.

Below, it will be shown how Petri Nets have been used to formalize cognitive structures, with the aim of proposing schemes for solving simple mathematical problems.

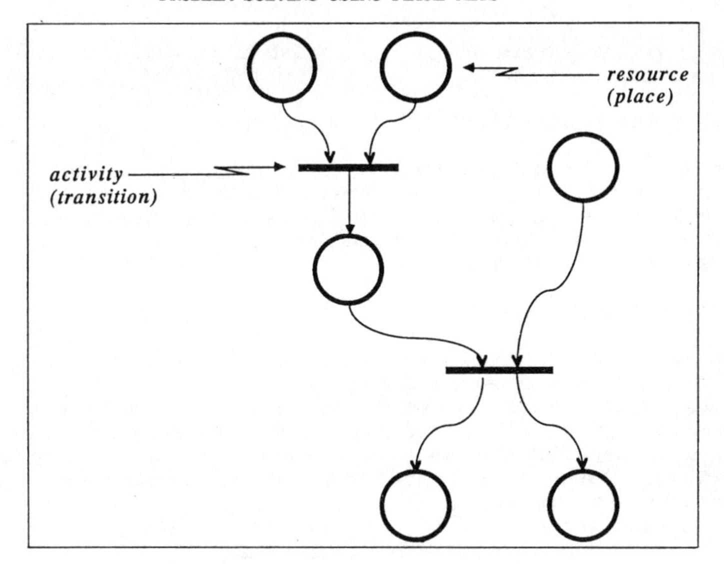

Figure 1: A Petri Net graph.

PETRI NETS AS A FORMAL LANGUAGE

A Petri Net (Peterson, 1981) can be defined as a bipartite directed multigraph in which two types of nodes are represented: a circle represents a 'place'; a bar represents a 'transition' (Figure 1). Directed arcs (arrows) connect places and transitions, with some arcs directed from a place to a transition and other arcs directed from a transition to a place. In the following we will use the term 'resource' instead of place and the term 'activity' instead of transition.

An arc directed from a resource to an activity defines the resource as an input of activity; in other words this means that the resource is necessary for carrying out that activity. On the other hand, an output resource is indicated by an arc from the activity to the resource; it means that the resource is a product of the activity.

In the content representation, the activity corresponds to the ability which must be applied. From another point of view, the activity can be considered the task (or the class of tasks) one must be capable of carrying out: this means that a specific topic has been acquired. In this context the resources identify what is necessary in order to carry out a certain activity or what is produced by it.

Generally, the formalization of a model in terms of Petri Nets occurs in various stages: the first concerns the generalized representation of the model in which it is necessary to analyse the content domain, identify the main activities, represent such activities in terms of Petri Nets and check the syntactic correctness of the net obtained.

In the subsequent stages a so-called refinement of the activities, described in the generalized representation, is carried out. The procedure for each stage is: analyse the corresponding content domain, identify the activities on a subordinate level (which represents the prerequisites for being able to carry out the activity in question), represent such subordinate activities in terms of Petri Nets and verify the syntactic correctness of the refinement.

At each stage of the refinement it is advisable to give a linguistic description of the activities and resources involved. Obviously the levels of refinement are closely correlated to the degree of detail one wishes to give to the model.

DESCRIPTION OF PROBLEM SOLVING

The pupils' work was based on the use of Petri Nets to describe the procedure for solving a simple mathematical problem. On the basis of these descriptions and what arose during their production, some comments are made on the most interesting aspects and on the results produced by the experiments.

The pupils' activities

The pupils were asked to produce a Petri Net associated with a particular knowledge domain, and more precisely, associated with the knowledge to be applied in order to reach the solution of a given problem. In this way it was intended to give the students exercise in:

* **analysing** the information received and the data of the problem;
* **identifying** the portions of their own knowledge which could be used in connection with the subject of study;
* **structuring** (formalizing) the elements of the knowledge domain and establishing logical connections between them;
* **checking** the correctness of the structure which has been produced.

In each of these activities the students have to identify clearly the elements, their graphic and logical connections, and check the linkages according to precise rules.

The proposed experiment

In successive lessons two experimental classes in the second year of secondary school were given exercises which involved the use of algebra notions in the solution of geometrical problems. By way of example, reference will be made below to one of these problems, to the description of the procedure worked out by the pupils and to the comments which this type of work has given rise to. Here is the text of the problem:

> In a right-angled triangle the sum of the sides measures 24cm. and the sum of the squares of the three sides measures 200sq.cm. Determine the area of the triangle. (After solving the problem, construct the related Petri Net, stopping at the second level of refinement.)

Here we show the system as it could be formulated by a pupil:

$$x + y + z = 24$$
$$x^2 + y^2 + z^2 = 200$$
$$x^2 + y^2 = z^2$$

After a few simplifications the system may be written as

$$x + y = 14 \qquad x.y = 48$$

so that the area of the triangle measures 24sq.cm.

In the subsequent phase of drawing up the Petri Nets the pupils are asked to pay particular attention to the linguistic description associated with each stage of refinement, where they are asked to clarify all the conceptual prerequisites needed in order to 'activate the solution of the problem'.

In the same way the pupils were asked to describe the activity in relation to the mathematical abilities involved and to discuss the resources, establishing both their compatibility with the terms of the problem and their geometrical significance.

The following diagrams show one of the formalizations of the problem-solving procedures worked out by the pupils and the related linguistic descriptions.

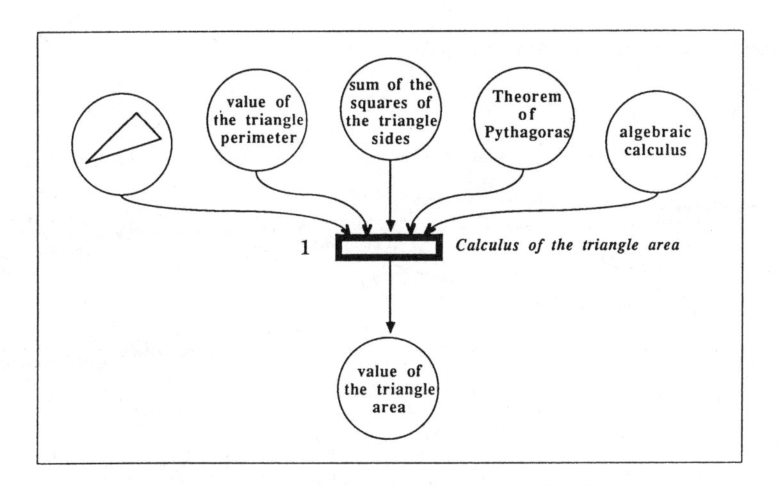

Figure 2: Generalized representation of the model.

Generalized representation of the model (Figure 2)

Activity: given the perimeter and the sum of the sides of a right-angled triangle, determine the area of the triangle.

Input resources: the right-angled triangle and the properties associated with it, the value of the perimeter, the sum of the squares of the sides, the theorem of Pythagoras, notions of algebraic calculus (calculus of radicals, second degree equations, systems of equations, etc...).

Output resources: the value of the area of the right-angled triangle.

First Level of refinement (Figure 3):

View of all activities connected to the achievement of the problem solution.

Activity: formulate the system and reduce it to a symmetrical system; interpret the symmetric system obtained; calculate the area of the right-angled triangle.

Input resources: the right-angled triangle (etc., as for the generalized representation).

Intermediary resources: the symmetric system obtained from the starting system, the sum and the product of the catheti.

Output resources: the value of the area of the right-angled triangle.

Second level of refinement (Figure 4):

From the starting system to the symmetrical system.

Activity: formulate a system starting from the data of the problem (assigning the unknown quantities) and lead it back to the symmetrical system.
Input resources: the right-angled triangle (etc., as before)
Intermediary resources: starting system

$$x + y + z = 24$$
$$x^2 + y^2 + z^2 = 200$$
$$x^2 + y^2 = z^2$$

Output resources: symmetric system

$$x + y = 14 \qquad x.y = 48$$

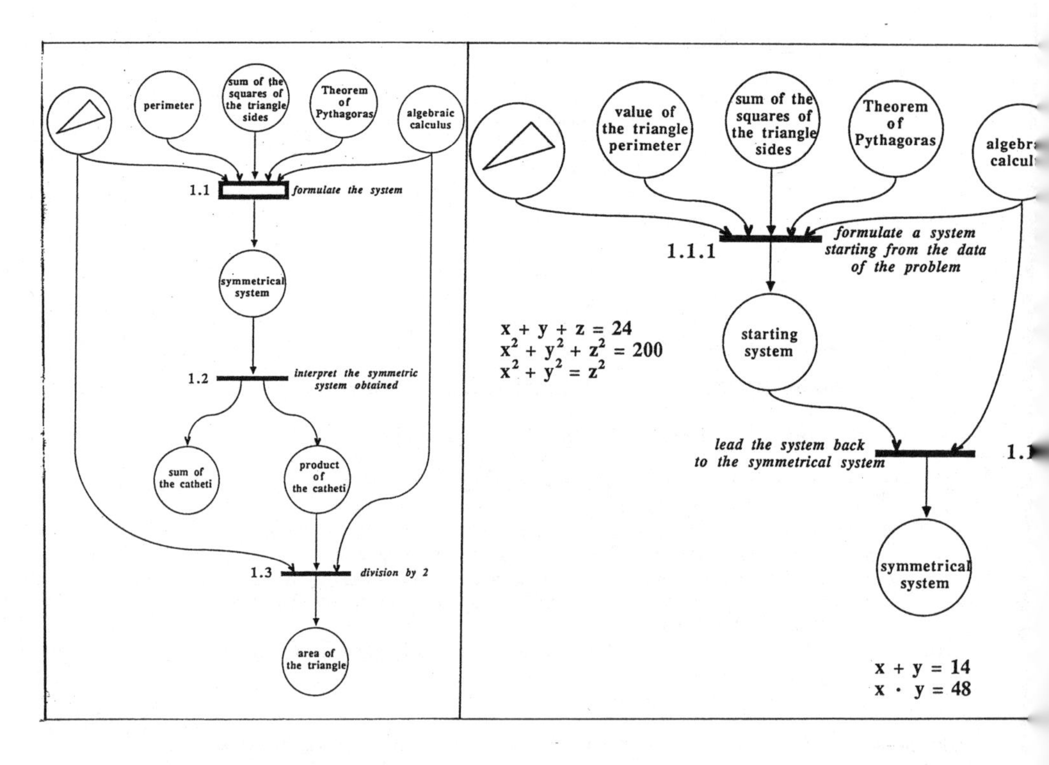

Figure 3: First level of refinement **Figure 4**: Second level of refinement

SOME OBSERVATIONS

The pupils proceeded by alternating individual work (done at home) with group work. The collective activity, based on analysing and comparing the descriptions of the problem-solving procedures, produced individually, led the pupils to examine carefully their own mathematical knowledge and their own mode of operating and to use the skills they had acquired.

From this experiment, we believe that the discussion of individual representation in terms of Petri Nets allows the students to analyse their conceptual convergences and divergences concerning the description of the problem-solving procedure and consequently the related knowledge domain necessary to reach the solution. In fact, the use of Petri Nets to describe how the problem had been solved, led the individuals to re-examine the procedure they had followed, taking care at each stage:

a. to identify the resources;
b. to define each resource in conjunction with the use that was made of it (assign the unknown quantities, establish the type of system obtained, etc...);
c. for each topic to identify and make explicit the prerequisites;
d. to point out possible alternative schemes.

A FORMATIVE ASSESSMENT

The observation of the pupils' schemes and their behaviour when faced with the particular task, has underlined an interesting aspect of the experimentation. This concerns the process of self-assessment that is activated when pupils are called upon to organize their own knowledge (Di Carlo and Trentin, 1990).

In fact during the experimentation pupils were stimulated to take an active and critical role in the creation and assessment of their own knowledge. To create a Petri Net it is necessary to analyse all the elements used, checking whether they are interconnected and identifying possible superfluous or missing resources (is resource x really necessary for the activity in question? is resource x available? is resource x sufficient or must it be used in conjunction with other resources?); this allows the individual pupils to model, improve and if necessary correct a conceptual scheme related to a specific content.

In this way, proposing that pupils create a Petri Net on basic topics in the school curriculum, induces them to use self-assessment in specific subjects. In fact, the difficulties which arise during the creation of a Petri Net lead the pupil to:

* identify the unknown topics, necessary for the complete and correct description of the field in question;
* choose the most appropriate 'learning material' for their remedial activity (the book chapter, the clarifying questions to ask the teacher, etc...).

There is another aspect which should not be underestimated. Sometimes, despite the persistence of cognitive deficiencies, the pupils still manage to solve certain types of problems; in this case it is very difficult to point out the deficiencies as far as prerequisites are concerned. However, the fact of having to 'put down on paper' one's own knowledge, organizing it and justifying it, makes it easier to notice the level of knowledge acquired.

Similarly, the linguistic description, associated with each phase of refinement, is an opportunity for self-assessment. In fact the task of illustrating the individual activities implies the knowledge of that which has to be described and the acquisition of a proper language pertinent to that particular subject.

CONCLUSIONS

Organizing one`s own knowledge often proves to be a difficult task. Generally these problems derive from a poor ability to think abstractly, an ability which if rarely exercised cannot be accessed easily.

The experiments conducted were thus based on stimulating pupils' ability to think abstractly through the use of a specific tool, Petri nets. The task of describing the problem-solving procedure for a given problem induced individuals to become aware of their own level of learning. Moreover it permitted them to operate actively in the recovery of subjects where cognitive deficiencies emerged most clearly.

In fact, the development and refinement of a Petri Net can be compared to observing an object which is increasingly magnified. This should also prevent the possibility of confusion between subjects which appear to be similar. In any case, one is obliged to establish and make explicit the boundaries within which one operates and to focus on the activity to be exercised with the available resources.

It would be interesting if the formalization in terms of Petri Nets of particularly significant subjects became part of educational practice. In this way the pupil would come into possession not only of a series of schemes which represent the knowledge acquired, structured according to explicit, clear and correct connections, but also of an analytical tool which can be used in various fields. In fact these skills, that is, the ability to:

* break up an activity into smaller activities;
* identify the resources relevant to each 'subactivity' and to connect them for the purposes of further refinement;
* distinguish, based on the product of the activity, the assignment of the various resources;

do not seem to be connected exclusively to scientific or mathematical subjects but can also be applied in other sectors too, such as historical analysis or linguistics. The habit of formalizing in different school subjects (and not necessarily just scientific subjects) would probably result in improving student problem-solving skills by means of a structured approach.

REFERENCES

Di Carlo, A. and Trentin, G.(1990): Diagnostic testing in formative evaluation: the students as test developers. In Bell, C.(Ed), World Yearbook of Education 1990 - Evaluation and Assessment. Kogan Page, London (in press).

Donald, J.G.(1987): Learning schemata: methods of representing cognitive, content and curriculum structures in higher education. Instructional Science, 16, pp.187-211.

Larsen, S.(1986): Information can be transmitted but knowledge must be induced. Programmed Learning and Educational Technology, 23, 4, pp.331-336.

Peterson, J.L.(1981): Petri Net Theory and the Modelling of Systems. Prentice-Hall, Inc., Englewood Cliffs, N.J.

Guglielmo Trentin is a researcher at the Institute of Educational Technology at CNR (the Italian National Research Council), working in the field of Educational Technology. In particular he has been involved in the area of learning evaluation through computer. At present he is working on the project 'Educational Systems Based on Multimedia Databases' within the CEC DELTA programme.

Address for correspondence: **Dr.G.Trentin,**
Institute of Educational Technology, C.N.R.,
Via all'Opera Pia, 11,
16145 Genoa, Italy.

19. Curriculum supported by computer - mathematics through 'NATTOKU'

Tatsunori Matsui, Naoto Nakamura, Makoto Takeya* and Fumiyuki Terada*
Waseda University: *Takushoku University, Japan

Abstract: Progress in our highly information-orientated society is accelerating every day as we approach the new century. Socially, great importance is attached to education, particularly mathematical education, to meet future needs. Various uncoordinated attempts have been made to incorporate computers, but we need to consider the entire curriculum from the basis of having computers in both the classroom and in a self-learning environment. The new Japanese mathematical curriculum, already announced and due to take effect in 1994, makes a start on this. To go one step further, the idea of Curriculum Supported by Computer (CSC) is presented in this paper. The design, experimental use and evaluation of the system is described.

INTRODUCTION

In Japanese education, particularly mathematical education, there are two important themes:

1. the need for widespread mathematical literacy in all students so as to improve our highly technological society as the twentyfirst century approaches. The future leaders of this advance need to have by upper secondary school a more demanding mathematical curriculum than normal;
2. in this increasingly information-based society, as many people as possible should have a thorough grounding in computer literacy.

Coordinating mathematical education and information education in upper secondary schools has many problems, and we have been trying to solve these by making effective use of computer capabilities. It is considered that mathematical education should go further than teaching just knowledge, and achieve the following objectives:

* the cultivation of creativity, so that knowledge can be constructed systematically from specific facts;
* the ability to express oneself logically, and give logical descriptions;
* the ability to use an analytical approach to problems;
* always to look for reasons.

The first two, particularly, should be taught to all students.

The Curriculum Supported by Computer (CSC) is an approach to achieving these objectives by using the capabilities of computers. CSC differs from the simple use of a computer for training or simulation, in that it attempts to restructure the existing mathematics curriculum (Terada et al, 1988).

In this paper we outline:

1. the detailed design of the CSC;
2. the results of the experimental lessons designed using the CSC concept;
3. the evaluation of the curriculum using semantic structure (SS) analysis (Takeya, 1987) and factor analysis on the results from the experimental lessons.

THE CURRICULUM SUPPORTED BY COMPUTER

Why was the CSC introduced?

The purpose of our mathematical education is not only to cram a lot of mathematical knowledge into the students' heads, but also to encourage their creativity, and/or to improve their mathematical literacy. It is thought that the effective use of computer capabilities can help to achieve this. In the following sections our approach is described, and compared with conventional teaching.

* At the start of the lesson, definitions and/or theorems are normally taught directly. To encourage creativity, it is important to get students to see the need for the definitions and the theorems.
* Later on, instead of mathematical theorems being taught by describing their complete proofs (the normal way), we prefer to improve students' mathematical literacy by them observing numerical value experiments, and producing graphs and figures from their own calculations.

An idealized mathematical education is difficult to achieve by conventional methods using notebooks, blackboards, etc: the CSC is a method of trying to achieve it by making use of computers' capabilities.

What is the CSC?

CSC aims at improving students' creativity. It also aims at the same time to get the vast majority of students to understand the concept of mathematics. To clarify the creative and mathematical understanding processes, it might help to consider the thought processes of a mathematician, who

* discovers something by trial and error on paper;
* then proposes a theorem;
* constructs the proof;
* establishes the theorem.

The process described is both creative and also very general, and can thus serve as a useful prototype for our method.

The trial and error process on paper is called Trial and Approach in the CSC. At the theorem stage, many students find difficulty in understanding the complete proof, whereas they find the concept easier if the proof is replaced by numerical value experiments which they can observe, and then create graphs and figures which give a more understandable view of the concept. When used in CSC, this latter method is termed NATTOKU (from a Japanese word meaning understanding or actual feeling).

The CSC is built up from six basic elements, as shown in Figure 1 - Trial, Approach, NATTOKU, and the additional elements described below.

Trial leads the students smoothly to a new mathematical world, while giving them the opportunity to overcome any sense of incompatibility they may have with this world.

Approach leads the students on to find something interesting in the mathematical world, while the teacher encourages the students to develop and maintain through experiments a creative attitude along with that interest. The experimental activity should promote more positive participation by the students in the lesson. Approach also aims to show the need for the theorems that appear in the mathematical world.

Teaching is a normal lesson by the teacher. Students are allowed to use computers, to help check their existing knowledge and/or to clarify difficult parts in proofs.

NATTOKU. Many students find great difficulty in understanding fully the definitions and in doing the proofs of theorems. It is considered enough

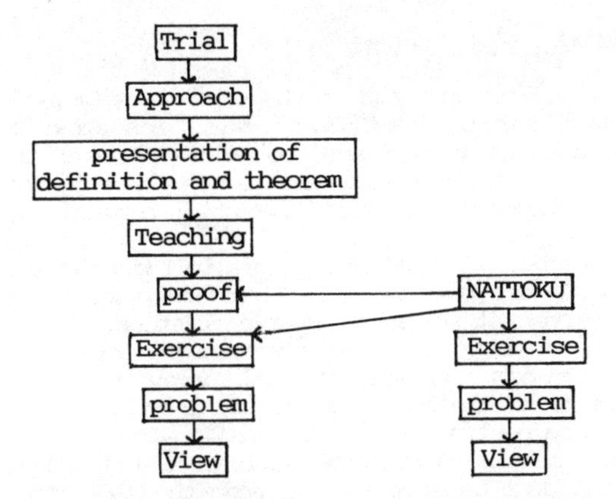

Figure 1: The flow of CSC

if these students have a general understanding, and can use computers to get a rough grasp of the definitions and the theorems, through manipulation and experiment, but without ever reaching or needing to reach full logical understanding. This activity and learning process is NATTOKU. **Exercise** makes the students confirm the material in different ways. The computer is used for drill and practice, based on the NATTOKU activity. **View** shows all students more detail of the mathematical world and how useful its contents are, while the more capable students can get more information about the contents.

AN EXPERIMENTAL LESSON

Basic plan

A number of experimental lessons were presented using the concept of the CSC, emphasizing particularly the Approach and the NATTOKU parts of the six elements in it. The subject matter, taken from the mathematics curriculum at upper secondary school level, was quadratic functions.

Contents of the course

We gave the following four items as learning objectives for quadratic functions:

* direction of translation of a graph;
* maxima and minima;
* descriptive solutions of quadratic equality;
* how to solve second degree inequalities.

AN EVALUATION OF THE EXPERIMENTAL LESSONS

These, using the CSC concept, were given to fortyseven upper secondary school students. Two questionnaires were prepared; one for investigating the students' attitude towards mathematics, and given before the lessons, the other for studying the level of NATTOKU and given after the experimental lessons. Comparing the pre-lesson results with those from the post-lesson questionnaires gave the following information about the effectiveness of the CSC.

Investigation of students' attitudes

The results of students' opinions on the experimental lessons were analysed using semantic structure (SS) analysis. This shows the relationship among questionnaire items, based on the results from them. The analysis gives us a lot of information for evaluating the students' attitudes towards mathematics by the CSC. Partial results are summarized :

* from the high number of affirmative answers to the relevant questions, it would seem that the visualized image was successful in giving students a concept of the quadratic function.
* The general questions about computers showed more informed answers in the post-survey when compared with the pre-survey, which indicates that the students found the experimental CSC lessons very useful.
* Though students were neutral about the benefits for subsequent examinations, they became positive on motivation and on computers, which was regarded as a benefit arising from the CSC lessons.

Study of the level of NATTOKU

In the (post-lesson) questionnaire on NATTOKU, the students chose one of the five levels given below:

5 - I can develop an image of its graph at once and solve it.
4 - I can develop an image of its graph after a while and solve it.
3 - I can develop an image of its graph at once, but cannot solve it.
2 - I can develop an image of its graph after a while, but cannot solve it.
1 - I can not develop an image of its graph and cannot solve it.

The comparison of pre-survey and post-survey results of the level of NATTOKU are shown in Figure 2, which gives the average rating scores of questionnaire items before and after the experimental lessons.

Factor analysis results

Using SS analysis with factor analysis, the SS graph can be grouped into three clusters which correspond to individual factors obtained by the factor analysis as shown in Figure 2. Thus, almost all of the factors are grouped into one of these three aspects:

first aspect - items that are related to knowledge of functions that had already been studied in junior high school. (Item numbers 1,2,3 and 4).
second aspect- items that are related to knowledge of quadratic functions obtained through this experimental lesson. (Item numbers 9,10,11,12 and 13).
third aspect - items that are related to knowledge of the intersection points of some graphs which had already been studied in junior high school. (Item numbers 5,6 and 7).

SS analysis results

The results of students' level of NATTOKU, based on SS graphs, are shown in Figure 2. Partial results are as follows:

* items that are related to the quadratic function are all equivalent items, and average rating scores of these items are four or over. Thus it is considered that students can understand it visually, and apply that understanding to problems of maxima, minima, and of an inequality of second degree.

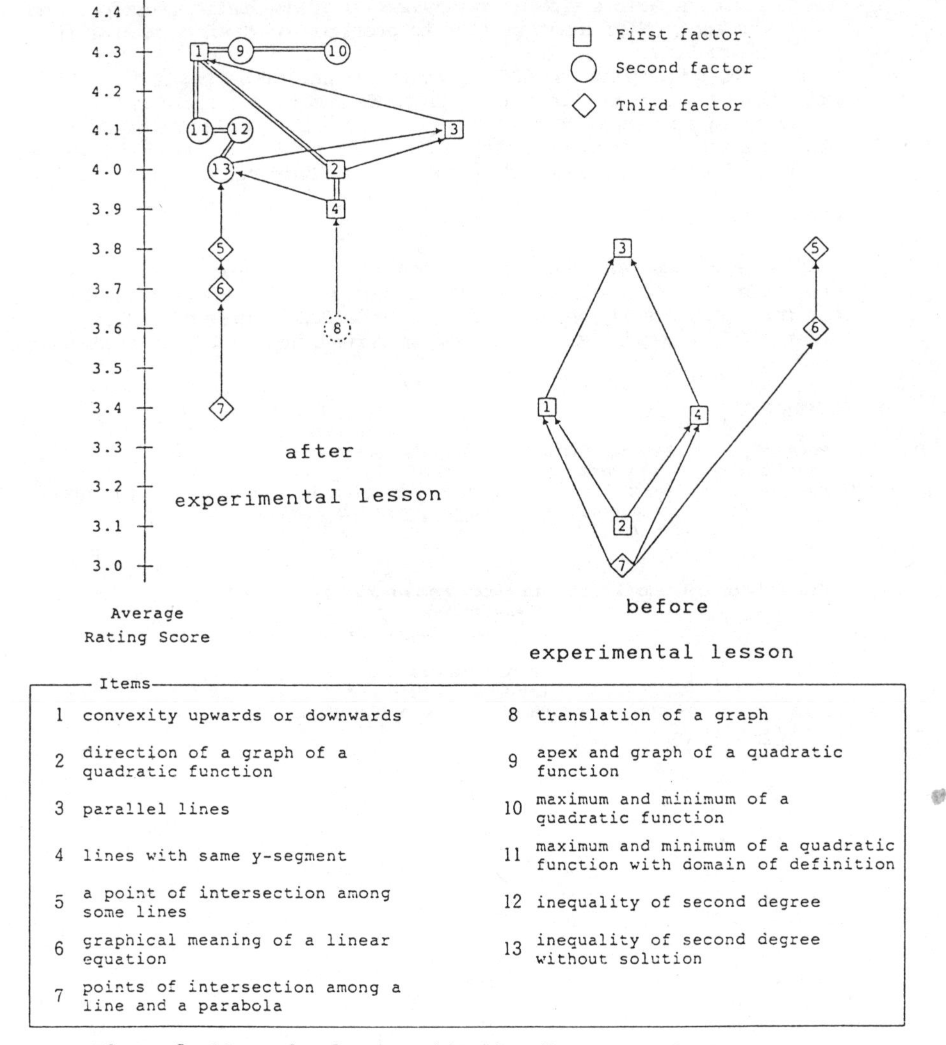

Figure 2: SS graphs for investigating the level of NATTOKU

* comparing the SS pre- and post-survey graphs, the latter is moved up, and four items (1,2,3 and 4) are changed to equivalent items instead of ordered items. From this, it is considered that the students have achieved a deeper understanding.

An evaluation of the CSC

The results of the evaluation are summarized below:

* students who are not good at mathematics learn enough for their needs and capabilities;
* students who are good at mathematics can study the subject in greater depth;

* students have a visual understanding of quadratic function, and can apply that understanding to problems of maxima, minima and inequality.

Thus, we found that the CSC is effective for students, and particularly those weak in mathematics. We are of the opinion that mathematical education through manipulation and experiments rather than full theoretical proofs is suitable for most students, while for gifted students, the CSC motivates them to further learning.

CONCLUSION

This paper has described the concept of the CSC, experimental lessons done under that concept, and an evaluation of it based on students' opinions. As a result, we maintain that the CSC is effective for students of differing abilities, and we hope that it will be implemented shortly.

REFERENCES

Takeya, M.(1987): Semantic structure analysis among questionnaire items using scale method. Behaviometrika, 14, 2, pp.10-17.

Terada, F. et al(1988): Computer assisted curriculum in mathematics. Proceedings of the 14th International Conference on Improving University Teaching. University of Maryland, U.S.A.

Addresses for correspondence: **Tatsunori Matsui** and **Makoto Takeya**,
Waseda University, 3-4-1, Okuba,
Shinjyuku, Tokyo 169, Japan.

Naoto Nakamura and **Fumiyuki Terada**,
Takushoku University, 815-1, Tatemachi,
Hachioji, Tokyo 193, Japan.

20. The reform of Italian teacher training in computer science

Paper 20A
Paola Forcheri, Fulvia Furinghetti* and Maria Teresa Molfino
Paper 20B
Rosa Maria Bottino and Fulvia Furinghetti*
Institute of Applied Mathematics, CNR Italy; *University of Genoa

Abstract: At present, in Italy, a national programme is being carried out aimed at introducing computer science and its technologies in the mathematics course of the first two years of upper secondary school (ages 14-16 years). This initiative contemplates a large-scale programme of in-service mathematics teacher training in computer science and its technologies involving the schools of the entire country. This programme is operated through trainers who are in-service teachers specifically trained for this purpose. Paper A discusses some features of teacher training, the analysis of a course we organized and realized for mathematics teachers of secondary schools, with the intention that this paper gives an operative contribution to the discussion on the organization of teacher training courses in computer science.
Paper B refers to the training of the trainers, and discusses the way in which this training programme is realized and its drawbacks. In particular the approach is analysed to see if it is effective in meeting both the teachers' expectations and the needs for developing correct directions in teaching.

INTRODUCTION

The rapid evolution of new cultural, technological and social aspects of life raises the need for a reorganization of teacher education, with a consequent re-training of in-service teachers. In particular, in the last decade, new technologies (computers above all) have had an impact on education and call for widespread teacher training initiatives.

The status and role of teachers have been changing in recent years: on one hand, teachers have to continue their work in classroom practice; on the other hand, they have to learn new topics and review their teaching methodology in the light of new technologies. The new teachers' status is well synthesized in the title of an interesting paper, 'Teachers as workers and teachers as learners' (see Brown, 1988). This status, while exacting and stressing, may offer teachers the significant advantage of a new role, that of designers of their own didactical itineraries in the classroom, by starting from a body of 'expert knowledge'.

This last point, namely, which body of 'expert knowledge' has to be passed on to the teachers, is the crucial problem of the various attempts at developing teachers' competence. It is the task of researchers in education to design strategies for guiding teachers to face changes in school practice.

These two papers refer to a recent proposal of reform of the mathematics programme in the 14-16 years age range. This reform contemplates, among other innovations, the introduction of computers and of computer science in the mathematics course. Since the majority of in-service mathematics teachers are not trained in computer science, the Italian Ministry of Education (M.P.I.) has launched a large-scale programme of teacher training in computer science and its technologies. It consists of a three-weeks residential course, which should provide teachers with basic elements of programming, with some general pedagogical features and with the first elements in the use of the computer.

20A. Teacher training in computer science: an example of realization

Paolo Forcheri, Fulvia Furinghetti and Maria Teresa Molfino
National Research Council/University of Genoa/National Research Council

In spite of the efforts of the lecturers involved in the national training programme and the considerable resources supplied by the government, the results of the programme rouse some perplexities (see Bottino and Furinghetti, 1990). The most relevant is linked with the shortage of time (three weeks) scheduled for the exacting task of providing teachers with a background suitable for giving an autonomy in the activity of constructing new didactical itineraries, combining two different contents - of mathematics and of computer science - and two different educational paths (we analysed the difficulties of this activity in Forcheri et al., 1990). Thus, when I.R.R.S.A.E. Liguria (Regional Research Institute for Educational Experimentation and Training) asked us to organize a mathematics teachers training course in computer science, we considered this request a good opporunity for rethinking teacher education in computer science and its technologies, and we tried to design a course aimed at giving an adequate background for mathematics teachers wishing to experiment with the introduction of computer science in the classroom.

TRAINING MATHEMATICS TEACHERS IN COMPUTER SCIENCE

Computer science teaching is still under discussion, as this discipline is still evolving and is characterized by the coexistence of theoretical and technological aspects (see the recent debate reported

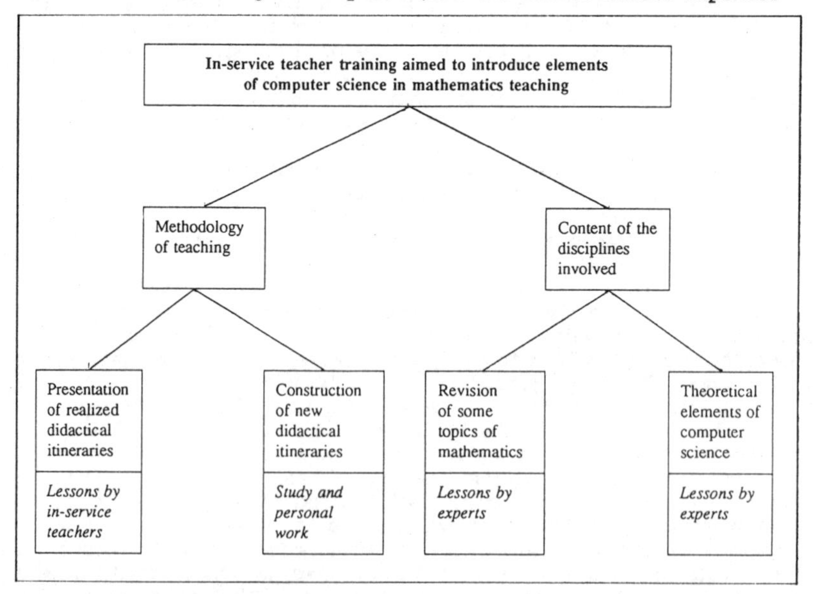

Figure 1: Schematic diagram of the course, 'Integration of computer science and mathematics'.

in Denning, 1989). In our case, these difficulties are increased by the context we work in.

Firstly, the training in question should be aimed at giving general ideas of computer science rather than a specialized education, as the teachers we train will teach only selected elements of computer science within mathematics courses. Secondly, as the teachers to be trained are in-service, there is not much time available for their training: thus drastic choices must be made with regard to the content and teaching strategies, to exploit that time as much as possible. Finally we think that content should be chosen to emphasize aspects of computer science strictly linked to mathematics. This last point concerns our wish to make the training effective for mathematics teaching in school practice.

In fact, it is possible to give students the right ideas on computer science but, at the same time, mathematics teaching can take advantage of computer science only if teachers understand its conceptual crux and if they are aware of the cognitive difficulties which are involved.

Reflections on the previous points are the basis of our proposed training course for in-service mathematics teachers. Figure 1 illustrates its structure. The course title, 'Integration of mathematics and computer science' indicates our intention to introduce the elements of computer science by exploiting the common features of the two disciplines.

The diagram of the proposed course relates to the particular case of introducing computer science as a part of the mathematics programme in the age range 14-16, though it is easily adaptable to more general situations with regard to both the subjects in question and the age. Figure 1 shows the philosophy underlying our work. This is made more explicit in the following Figure 2, in which we stress the crucial

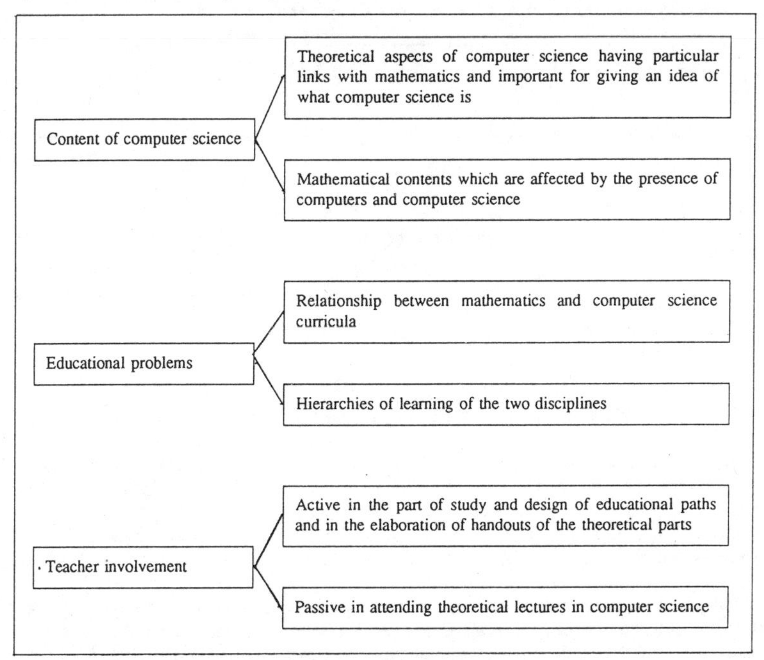

Figure 2: Crucial points of the design of the course and the choices we made for facing them.

points of the design of courses such as those in question and the choices made for facing them.

REALIZATION OF THE COURSE

A significant application of the ideas described above was a course carried out in the school year 1988-1989. Figure 3 shows the overall organization of the course, which was aimed at teachers of mathematics in the first two years of upper secondary school, since as previously stated, these have a realistic possibility of experimenting in the classroom with the introduction of computer science within mathematics

Argument	Integration of computer science and mathematics
Aims	To deepen the computer science basic elements already known by the teachers To introduce new computer science fundamental concepts To address problems of integrating mathematics and computer science from the pedagogical point of view
Requirements	Operative knowledge of microcomputer Capacity to use an operating system Ability to write a simple Pascal program and run it
Participants	Mathematics teachers of upper secondary school
Lecturers	University professors and researchers of C.N.R. with previous experiences of teacher training in computer science
Material	Copy of the transparencies Supporting papers on mathematics and computer science education Booklets (for teachers and for students) Bibliographical references Handouts of the lessons
Number of hours	42 (distributed throughout the entire year)

Figure 3: Overall organization of the course.

courses. The number of participants was limited to 100 in order to facilitate and control the active involvement of the teachers. The training course has not been concentrated in a short period but has been developed throughout the entire year in order to foster the assimilation of the topics, which are objectively difficult to learn, and to give convenient intervals to study.

The course was subdivided in four parts: the first three parts covered the theoretical aspects and the fourth was devoted to educational problems, as is shown in the scheme illustrated in Figure 4.

Part I	**Revising mathematics through the computer** Presentation of two softwares developing mathematical topics. Positional number systems. Error theory; error propagation. Floating point arithmetic (real numbers representation, single precision calculations, accuracy of floating point arithmetic, distribution of floating point numbers).
Part II	**Hints on design and analysis of numerical algorithms** Solvable and unsolvable problems. Problem solving in practice: computational cost. Iterative and recursive algorithms (iterative algorithms, recursive algorithms, from recursion to iteration). Algorithm stability and problem conditioning.
Part III	**Programming languages** The inductive nature of programming languages. The language of integer expressions. A subset of the Pascal language: Syntax (expressions, statements, declarations); Semantics (value, state transformation, environment). More about Pascal: structured data types (record, array, file, pointer); recursion.
Part IV	**Educational aspects of the introduction of computer science and its technologies in mathematics** Illustration and discussion of Italian experiences in the introduction of computer science in the teaching of mathematics.

Figure 4: Programme of the course.

With regard to the computer science content, which was the core of the course, we stress that we tried to choose the most significant from the various streams of this discipline in order to give learners with little or no previous knowledge of it, an idea of what computer science is.

After the theoretical stage, a stage explicitly devoted to the development of the topics in the classroom was scheduled: the study and discussion of the construction of didactical paths by those contemplating the introduction of computer science. A convenient interval of time has been given to teachers in order to give the possibility for self-reflection and self-organization of the topics learned in the theoretical stage. Moreover, to offer the teachers a common starting point for the discussion, we gave them two booklets in which we illustrated the main lines of the project 'Integration of computer science and mathematics', which had already been tried out in several upper secondary school classes (see Forcheri et al., 1990). As a further idea of what can be achieved in the classroom, the last part of the course was dedicated to the presentation of experiences about computer science and its technologies when inserted in mathematics teaching. The presentations were given by the teachers who had carried out the experiments. Different kinds of didactical itineraries were analysed.

REMARKS ON THE COURSE

We would like to come back to the problem of the attitude of teachers with regard to changes in school practice. We consider the course in question a good place for studying this attitude. The feeling we derived may be synthesized in the following observations:

* teachers were interested in what concerns the translation of the introduced topics into school practice;
* teachers were interested in what their colleagues do;
* teachers showed a great interest in the part dedicated to the revision of mathematics;
* teachers showed less interest in theoretical computer science, as they judged that immediate use in the classroom was impossible, i.e. they did not immediately see the usefulness of training that seems to them only aimed at enriching their personal cultures.

In their attitudes the teachers showed a certain passivity in their professionalism, in that they tended to demand decisions on their work from other persons, such as school authorities and/or publishers of text books and didactic software. This lack of criticism is dangerous at the moment with innovations being proposed in school, as teachers tend to accept these depending on the external pressures they have, and do not make decisions on the basis of considerations from their own experience and culture.

ACKNOWLEDGEMENTS

The authors are grateful to Paolo Boieri, Milvio Capovani and Bruno Codenotti for their help in the realization of the theoretical part of the course. They are also grateful to Franca Balbis, Antonella Bontae, Rosangela Cacciabue, Giuseppe Garibaldi, Carlo Ghione and Luisa Pedemonte for presentation of their classroom experiences with students. Authors thank Antonella Bontae who collected handouts of the lessons.

REFERENCES

Brown, M.(1988): Teachers as workers and teachers as learners. ICME 6, Budapest, T1 (Survey lecture).

Bottino, R.M. and Furinghetti, F.(1990): A large-scale teachers training programme in informatics: chances and limits (to appear).

Denning, J.P.(Ed)(1989): A debate on teaching computer science. ACM Communications, 32, 12, pp.1397-1414.

Forcheri, P., Furinghetti, F. and Molfino, M.T.(1990): Integration of computer science and mathematics in upper secondary school: reflections and realizations. Computer and Education (to appear).

20B. A large-scale teacher training programme in informatics: chances and limits

Rosa Maria Bottino, Institute of Applied Mathematics, CNR Italy, and **Fulvia Furinghetti**, University of Genoa, Italy

FROM CURRICULA DESIGN TO CLASSROOM IMPLEMENTATION

It is our opinion that the classroom implementation of new curricula often does not reflect the intentions of the curricula designers with sufficient accuracy. This problem is particularly felt in centralized systems of education (such as the Italian system) in which the detailed control of the development of a reform project is more difficult to monitor (for further considerations see Wojciechowska, 1989).

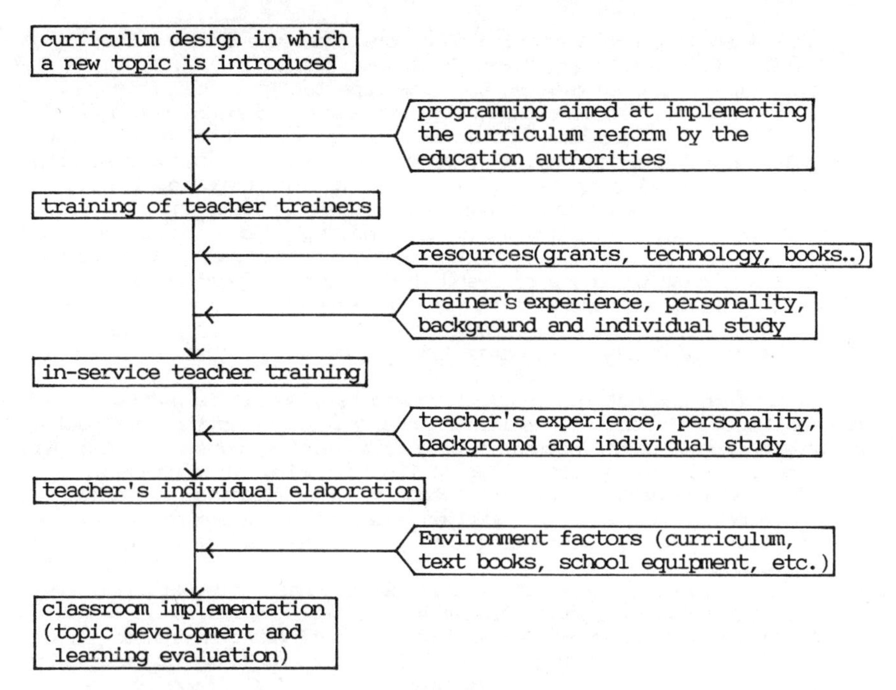

Figure 1: Schematic diagram of an educational path aimed at introducing informatics in schools. The left hand boxes show the different stages of the path; the right hand boxes show the types of factors affecting passage from one stage to another.

This is not surprising if one takes into account the complexity of the global process leading to the introduction of a new topic in a classroom. In Figure 1 we illustrate a schematic diagram of this process, in which teacher training is carried out by teacher trainers who have to be previously trained to perform this task, which is the case we discuss in this paper.

The intermediate stages that are shown in Figure 1 are crucial to the development of any curriculum reform, since it is at these stages that the conditions suitable to realize the teacher's potential are provided and managed (for further considerations see House, 1988).

In this paper we concentrate on these intermediate stages in order to highlight some causes of the inconsistency stressed above between curriculum design and curriculum implementation. Our study considers as an example the introduction of informatics in mathematics courses for students between 14 and 16 years old.

The crucial point in this curriculum reform, which is still under discussion, is the problem of in-service teacher training. In order to evaluate the extent of this problem, consider the informatics contents proposed in the new mathematics programmes (taken from Il menabo, 1987), bearing in mind the lack of familiarity many mathematics teachers have with these topics:

> [...] Abstract developments of algorithms. Graphical and textual representation of algorithms. First introduction to formal languages: automata, alphabet, words and generative grammars [...] Using a computer: command languages and programming languages. Use of a

programming language. Reflexion on errors: syntax and semantics elements. Practical experience in various contexts [...].

It is not our aim to discuss here the opportunity this initiative gives, and the revised curriculum content (see Bottino and Furinghetti, 1990b for this). We are here concerned with the fact that teaching the indicated topics implies having an adequate background in the discipline together with an adequate capability in the use of computing tools. 'Adequate' does not mean that teachers have only to know what they are going to teach; our interpretation of 'realizing teacher potential' is to provide them with a background knowledge (content and methodology) which allows them to have a real and active role in constructing didactic itineraries (see Bottino and Furinghetti, 1990a).

A large scale programme of teachers' training

Taking into account the previous considerations, it is not surprising that an important part of the Italian national plan for the introduction of informatics in school consists of a large-scale programme of teacher training in this field, consisting of the following three phases:

* selection, from in-service teachers, of a number of potential teachers' trainers, who will do this for a limited number of years, usually two (during this period they do not teach in school);
* training of the previously selected teachers' trainers;
* training of in-service teachers.

The first two phases are managed by four national centres for educational computing technologies, while the third phase is managed by teacher trainers in a number of centres throughout the country. The training courses (for both teachers and for trainers) are residential and last three full, non-consecutive weeks. From published data (NUMI, 1989), it is possible to deduce that this programme has involved about 40% of all existing Italian schools and 70% of all mathematics teachers. 75% of the schools involved have experimented with the introduction of informatics in the mathematics course.

ANALYSIS OF THE TRAINING PROGRAMME

In this section we analyse part of the training programme in order to show the numerous and complex problems which have arisen in these types of initiatives (see also NUMI, 1987). We have based our work on the analysis of official documents and on materials provided in the training courses for trainers and teachers, together with interviews with teacher trainers and trained teachers.

The aspects which we consider to be of particular importance are:

a. training dissemination;
b. informatics content;
c. relationship between mathematics and informatics content;
d. pedagogical content.

a. Training dissemination. The organization of the training programme being considered has the advantage of reaching a large number of teachers, establishing a multiplier effect. Moreover, its original intention was to even up different levels of teacher competences throughout the country. The problem of teacher training in informatics has, from the early 70s, been met in an uncoordinated manner by means of private initiatives of groups of teachers, school headmasters or groups of researchers from universities or research centres. Obviously the levelling-up process can only be effective if there is adequate control of the global training programme.

<u>b. Informatics content.</u> The problem of the balance between knowledge of the discipline and pedagogical knowledge is crucial in the design of a teacher training course. With regard to informatics contents we consider that teacher trainers should have more knowlege of the discipline than can be acquired in a three week course, particularly since in this course other objectives have also been set - discussion of the insertion of the informatics content into the mathematics course, and discussion of pedagogical aspects. Figure 2 shows the topics and the related scheduled times of a prototype training course for teacher trainers which has been proposed in the training programme under discussion.

The time dedicated to informatics topics suggests that they are not completely developed, but are only hinted at and left to autonomous elaboration. As a consequence, these trainer courses generally do not modify the learner's pre-existing image of the discipline, which may be harmful if this image is poor or wrong. Thus, even if we do not consider

Informatics	h.	Software Tools	h.	Didactics	h.
Evolution and current trends of programming languages	8	Lotus	8	Innovation of the Italian school system	7
Close examination of Pascal elements (structured and modular programming)	8	Disciplinary or didactical software	4	Dynamics of work teams	4
Introduction to Prolog programming language	8			Leadership	4
Evolution of computers architecture	4			Learning theories	4
Close examination of: (a choice from) Pascal, Prolog, software tools	8			Learning evaluation	4
				New programmes of Mathematics and Physics and proposal of didactic units	8
				Analysis and proposal of didactic units	8
				Comparisons among given didactic units	24
				Epistemological analysis of the logic, mathematics and informatics area	4

Figure 2: Contents and scheduled times of a teacher trainers' training course

cases of trainers who start with an inadequate background in informatics, there is certainly a failure to achieve the main aim of the trainers' preparation, of getting them all to the same standard so as to obtain uniformity in the subsequent teachers' training courses. Those courses we have examined as case-studies appear to follow a common line in the informatics content proposed (top-down approach to problem solving; algorithms; logical-functional model of a computing system; introduction to Pascal; datastructures; recursion; applicative software; automata), but from interviews which we have carried out with both teachers and trainers, we have found differences at different centres on the emphasis given to the various topics and, consequently, different images of the discipline.

In one of the cases examined, the emphasis was given to problem solving and a top-down method as the first approach to informatics. The use of LOTUS spreadsheets was stressed in various didactic exercises; automata were introduced by means of elementary examples such as coin telephone boxes. The prevailing methodology followed appeared to be to use examples in the introduction of the various notions.

In a second case considered, the emphasis was more on attempts to formalize the introduced topics. The links with mathematics were stressed in various areas - logic, real number representation, numerical methods. Particular attention was given to Prolog language. In a third case, the major emphasis was on programming (in Pascal) and special consideration was given to various examples of didactic software tools.

c. Relationship between mathematics and informatics content. The different orientations stressed previously also suggest that there will be differences in the way the informatics content is put into the mathematics course (Bottino and Furinghetti, 1990a). On the one hand we saw an emphasis on problem solving and a top-down approach as a methodology common to the two disciplines, but on the other hand, subjects such as logic were stressed to highlight the links between the two disciplines; there were also cases in which computer science was developed as a self-contained subject with respect to mathematics. Moreover, there was a tendency to consider informatics as a service-subject with respect to mathematics, with the emphasis being on performing calculations and on using didactic software for the illustration of mathematical concepts. In general, we noted that the problems of the links with mathematics would need closer examination than that allowed in the short time available during the training courses.

d. Pedagogical content. From a pedagogical point of view, the problem is the presence of two distinct learning hierarchies (that of informatics and that of mathematics). This fact implies some priorities in training: firstly, it is important to work at the learning problems peculiar to the age under discussion; and secondly, it is important to analyse the abilities and skills required by mathematics and informatics learning. It seems to us that subjects such as dynamics of work teams and leadership in the course for trainers (see Figure 2), are of secondary importance when the shortage of time is taken into consideration. In the training courses for teachers, time dedicated to pedagogical considerations tended instead to be spent in elaborating didactic units.

CONCLUDING REMARKS

One point to consider when discussing innovations such as that dealt with in this paper concerns teachers' attitudes when faced with the restructuring of teaching. Generally speaking, the demand from in-service teachers is for immediate short-term gains, such as 'recipes' to transfer into the classroom. It is our opinion that changes in teacher education are a long and deliberate undertaking and that short-term solutions with immediate results may lead to unsatisfactory situations in classroom practice, since they modify the superficial aspects but do not touch the roots of the problem of curricula renovation.

The final point we would draw attention to is that, at any stage of the process illustrated in Figure 1, the people involved have to have confidence in what they are performing. From interviews, we learned of the case of a teacher trainer who had not experienced the new programmes, and continued her traditional way of teaching mathematics when she returned to school after two years spent as a teacher trainer. What conviction and confidence can be passed on to trained teachers by a trainer who does not trust the curriculum changes she is working with?

REFERENCES

Bottino, R.M. and Furinghetti, F.(1990a): Computer science and mathematics education in upper secondary school (age 14-16). Proceedings of the 41st CIEAEM's Meeting. To be published.

Bottino, R.M. and Furinghetti, F.(1990b): Computer science in the basic formation (age 14-16): curricular issues and school practice prospects. In, McDougall, A. and Dowling, C.(eds): Proceedings of the IFIP TC3 Fifth World Congress on Computers in Education. Elsevier Science Publisher, Amsterdam. (To be published)

House, P.A.(1988): Theme Group 1: the profession of teaching. In, Hirst, A. and Hirst, K.(eds): Proceedings of the Sixth International Congress on Mathematics Education. J.Bolyei Mathematical Society, Budapest.

Il Menabo(1987), Nouva serie, anno 1, nos.3-4.

NUMI (1987): Notiziario dell'Unione Matematica Italiana, Suppl. No.11.

NUMI (1989): Notiziario dell'Unione Matematica Italiana, Suppl. Nos.7/8

Wojciechowska, A.(1989): Curriculum reform in mathematics: beyond the impossible revolution? Journal of Curriculum Studies. 21, 2, pp.151-159.

Rosa Maria Bottino is a research scientist for the National Research Council (C.N.R.) of Italy. Her research interests include the use of computers in education and, in particular - the teaching of computer science and applications of computers to the teaching of different scholastic subjects, both at upper secondary school and university levels; - applications of artificial intelligence to education, in particular knowledge representation, logic programming and intelligent tutoring systems. On these topics, Dr. Bottino has organized experiments in classrooms and training courses for teachers, has presented papers and published articles at national and international level.

Paola Forcheri is a research scientist for the National Research Council (C.N.R.) of Italy. Her research interests are focused on the computer in education and on the introduction of computer science in school curricula. She is head of a research project on Computer Science Tools and Methods in Education, sponsored by the Institute of Applied Mathematics of C.N.R. and is the author of numerous papers in these and related fields.

Fulvia Furinghetti is associate Professor in the Department of Mathematics in the University of Genoa, Italy. She is responsible for the Research Group in Mathematics Education working at Genoa University with a grant from C.N.R. She has organized teacher training courses in mathematics and in computer sciences, and has authored or edited many books and papers in these and related fields.

Maria Teresa Molfino is a research scientist for C.N.R. Her research interests are in the application of artificial intelligence, including those involving the educational domain. She heads a research project on Knowledge Modelling: Programme Synthesis and Automated Learning, sponsored by the Institute of Applied Mathematics of C.N.R. She has written several papers in these and related fields.

Address for correspondence:
R.M.Bottino: P. Forcheri: M.T. Molfino,
Instituto per la Matematica Applicata del C.N.R.,
Via L.B. Alberti 4, 16132 Genova, Italy.

21. The 'Basic Maths Project': a CBL approach to basic mathematics and numeracy in further education

Peter J.Clare, Matthew Boulton College

Abstract: This paper outlines the background and a brief history of the **'Basic Maths Project'** that was set up in 1986 at Matthew Boulton College of Further Education, Birmingham, to create student-centred computer-based learning materials in basic mathematics and numeracy for use in further education. A statement of the aims and basic design criteria of the project is followed by a description of how these are implemented in the course structure and computer-based learning materials. Reference is made to a current proposal for a companion project to set up a computer-based skills diagnoser and profiler that will generate suitable study programmes and act as a 'front end' for the **basic maths project** materials.

INTRODUCTION

Background to setting up the project

Experiencing the wide range of mathematical abilities, histories, ages and levels of motivation in typical BTEC First Level classes, I was concerned to introduce a suitable learning system in basic mathematics that would cater for this diversity and match appropriate vocational needs. I was also aware of national trends and the need to develop 'Open' or 'Drop-in' learning materials that could be used for both remedial support and for flexible learning in basic mathematics and numeracy in further education.

I had some experience in developing computer-based learning packages, aimed at secondary level and I had found that by providing interactivity, colourful and animated text and graphics, greater motivation was created amongst students using the materials.

I would emphasize that I am concerned with students learning mathematics as a service subject, where skill acquisition and self-confidence in the use of those skills in real life is of first importance. The learning of maths skills and the application of those skills call for a mixture of practice and assignment. The **BMP** materials are primarily aimed at the learning and practice of mathematical skills and, where possible, relating these to real life and vocational situations.

A brief history of the project

With these concerns and considerations in mind, in the summer term of 1986, I successfully proposed the setting up of a pilot CBL project to develop a sample course design, its management system and two study packs in algebra. I drew up the relevant aims and design criteria and these with minor modifications apply to the project as it is at present.

Since 1986 I have succeeded in obtaining funding for each year, totalling about £20,000, which has covered the development of nine study packs in algebra and eight study packs in mensuration, of which all the algebra and most of the mensuration packs are in 'a' versions and are being used in courses at Matthew Boulton. I also got funding from Manpower Services Commission via a City ABE project to cover the development of a Basic Numeracy Study Pack aimed at catering students.

I am currently seeking Further Education Unit help to set up an evaluation exercise of the use of the materials and of the project as a whole, which I hope will produce a report and case study towards the end of next year.

THE AIMS OF THE PROJECT

Before going on to discuss the project and its materials, I think it essential to state its aims:

1. to provide a student centred learning course in basic mathematics that would cover the mathematics skills content of most Business Technical Education (BTEC) Level 1 (now First certificate) courses as well as the core of General Certificate of Secondary Education (GCSE). A recent addition to these is the use of the materials in Access to Higher Education courses being set up in the college;
2. to provide a subset that will cover basic numeracy needs of students on various courses;
3. to provide a course that is matchable to student vocational and course needs and individual mathematical background;
4. to provide a course that can be used in a variety of learning contexts, e.g., maths workshop, open learning, remedial support, infill learning and even, possibly, distance learning;
5. to provide a course that can be developed and extended in line with educational needs and technological advances.

It was not and is not an aim to provide a complete mathematics course and the aims do not include those skills of problem solving which are best learned in real or simulated problem situations via assignment.

THE DESIGN CRITERIA

There were two distinct sets of design criteria; those relating to the course as a whole and those providing a framework for the development of individual self study packages ('Study Packs').

The Course

The course should have:

* a comprehensive, effective and efficient learning management system;
* a well structured set of curriculum content units to which can be matched individual study packages;
* a diagnostic/skills profiling 'front end' that is matchable to user needs and which can generate appropriate course study programmes;
* add-on sub-curriculum content units that are directed at specific vocational needs;
* a reference system that allows for easy updating and extension of course content.

Expanding on these criteria in turn:

Learning management. At the heart of the learning management systems is, of course, the individual student data. These include course needs, initial skills profile, recommended course study programmes, exercise and test marks and profiles, dates of completed tasks, tutor and student comments. Such data is best handled by computer using a tailored database manager. I have devised such a system based on a BBC master for use on networked workstations but the hardware available to me has not enabled me to implement it: for the present we are using a paper-based system and Study Packs are being developed in 'non-monitored' versions.

Curriculum. The division of the curriculum content into 'bite-sized' lumps has to take into account that there will be a number of different learning routes through the course materials and, consequently, I decided first on a division into subject areas such as arithmetic, algebra, mensuration, etc., and then within those areas structured a directed net of content modules. The relationships between modules in different areas has yet to be determined.

Diagnostics. From the beginning, I have considered the development of an intelligent diagnostic 'front end' to the scheme as being of great importance. Recently a proposal has been made that links this development with that of providing a counselling and computer-based skills profiling package. It is planned that this can be used for language and information technology skills as well as basic mathematics and numeracy. I see that such a package should have the following features:

* it should be matchable to course/user needs;
* it should be intelligent, i.e. responsive to client input in its subsequent selection of test items;
* it should be friendly and encourage rather than discourage, and involve the client in the diagnosis;
* it should automatically generate a skills profile;
* it should automatically generate a recommended study programme for the individual client based on a diagnosis of her/his skills deficiencies related to vocational and course needs.

A simple version of what I have in mind is included in each study pack as the Self Assessment Module that each student is encouraged to use first. This selects questions based on how the student feels about her/his ability to do earlier questions. This approach has proved to be particularly well received by the students.

Such a 'front end' package should have a much greater range of application than just the users of the project materials and I anticipate that it can be tailored to different institutional needs and the learning resources available.

Add-on units. Initially I considered the creation of specific revision packs that were vocationally orientated, such as commercial, engineering, technician etc.. I am inclined now to think in terms of what I call 'bolt-on' vocation modules to individual study packs and I will describe these when I consider the design criteria for the individual study pack.

The reference system I have developed so far, is based on a two character curriculum area code, eg., AR for arithmetic, AL for algebra, etc., followed by a one-digit number.

The Study Pack:

Study packs should provide:

* a comprehensive and automatic monitoring of student progress that integrates with the course management system;
* for complete student control of learning;
* objective matched pre- and post-tests that generate study programme guidelines;
* a rich and varied array of teaching/learning modules, worked and guided/interactive examples and balanced progressive consolidation exercises that can be used flexibly to suit different learning styles and study programmes;
* motivation for effective learning;
* different versions for different learning contexts;
* for easy creation, adaptation and development of the study pack that takes into account extension or modification of content,

mode of presention and software and/or hardware improvements as well as portability;
* `bolt-on'vocational modules that relate the skills covered to realistic vocational contexts.

Again I will expand on these criteria and how they have been achieved or not as the case may be.

Monitoring. As indicated earlier, because of the lack of a reliable networked set of workstations at college I have been unable to provide the planned integration of progress monitoring I wished for. However, each study pack builds up its own progress data that can be accessed by the student or tutor and which can be printed out on request via a Progress Report Module at any time.

Student control.A considerable amount is provided via menu driven modules and the ability to escape to a menu at almost any point in a module. A map of the typical study pack is provided so that the students can see where they are.

Tests. Each content unit is broken down into learning objectives in a conventional way and this provides the basis for the design and creation of pre- and post-tests, teaching units, worked and guided examples and, of course, exercises. In the light of my experience of using a self-assessment approach to the pre-test, current study packs have been converted to this form of pre-test. I have already briefly described the approach above.

Variety. I think it important to provide more than enough learning material than would be necessary for the average student. I do not expect all students to work through all the material available. Some will need more of this and others of that. The Study Pack provides three distinct learning strategies:

* interactive teaching units which take as their model 'a teacher explains and discusses with the student';
* step by step worked examples selectable from a listed bank; and
* step by step interactive or guided examples.

Much use is made of colour, animated text and graphics as appropriate.

Consolidation of learning is effected by balanced and progressive exercises which are matched to objectives. If a question in an exercise is answered incorrectly the student is offered a sight of the correct working.

This rich variety of learning materials, with the student in control of his/her learning provides the flexibility so that a reasonably wide range of learning styles can be met.

Motivation. The provision of student control, self-assessment, and a mixture of learning resources, does seem to produce greater motivation for effective learning than I have experienced in many years using conventional schemes. However, where the study packs have been used with two or more students to a workstation, the resulting discussion and enthusiasm has been particularly encouraging.

Variety. It is intended that in the long term, versions of the Study Pack be provided for different learning contexts. RM Nimbus and IBM PC versions of the materials are being produced in addition to the original BBC Master versions.

Amendments. By using a modular approach and the authoring language Microtext upgrading can take place relatively easily. Already study packs have been updated and extended and the inclusion of interactive video (IV) can be taken care of, using the additional IV commands of Microtext.

Bolt-ons. Tailoring the project materials to vocational need is being addressed by attaching different vocational modules to the general course study pack stem. These `bolt-on' modules will consist of some teaching material, providing vocational context, worked and/or guided examples and an exercise.

CONCLUSION

I am hoping, as mentioned above, to obtain funding for an evaluation of both the project and its materials and prefer to await its outcomes before forming any definite conclusions.

Address for correspondence: **Peter J. Clare,**
Matthew Boulton College, Sherlock Street,
Birmingham B5 7DB, UK.

Section 4: Computers as aids to realizing potential

22. The role of computers in education and training

Noel Thompson, National Council for Educational Technology

Abstract: This paper looks at the roles computers have and might have in the implementation of NCET's purpose, to make beneficial changes in education and training through educational technology. Dr. Thompson emphasizes their present contributions to languages, data handling, modelling and simulation, design and technology and expert systems, and their potential contributions towards truly flexible and open learning systems. Major constraints he identifies as the use of the electron tube, the lack of really good programs which are powerful but simple to get into, user unfriendliness, and the time it takes to standardize systems.

The theme of this conference is very relevant to the National Council for Educational Technology, which was formed in April 1988 through the amalgamation of two other organizations. One was the Council for Educational Technology, which used to confuse people (and those of you who remember our history will recall that it was called the National Council for Educational Technology about ten years ago). The other partner was the Micro-Electronics Education Support Unit, which followed the Micro-Electronics Education Programme and which had a profound and lasting influence on the use of information technology in our schools.

So we had these two relatively small quangoes and Kenneth Baker (UK Secretary of State for Education at that time) was persuaded that the two together would be better than the sum of the two parts. We now are an organization with rather more than a hundred people - we are relocating to Coventry, though keeping our London office for very good reasons - and our mission statement is 'to plant beneficial change in the processes of learning, in education and training through the development and application of educational technology'. That still begs the question of what educational technology is about, but we do have a brief version which we use when we are trying to persuade people to give us some money, and the brief version says 'Supporting change in the ways we learn'.

I have to say that we are not in the high ground of cognitive science that is going to promise us, in twenty years time with a bit of luck, better understanding of the ways people learn. Our job is to implant beneficial change, which means that we're in the engine room; we are actually taking the best we have now and trying to spread it and develop it and apply it and implant it. We do very much watch with interest and indeed sit at the feet of cognitive scientists and others, and assess the point when they have something which is capable of being applied and implanted, but we are not ourselves engaged in basic research - we are applied people.

Derek Rowntree was of course right when he said in 1974, "Educational technology is not to be confused with electronic gadgets. It is concerned with the design and evaluation of curricula and learning experiences, and with the problems of implanting and renovating them."

Well, hear hear! The voice that was crying in the wilderness in 1974 still needs to be heard just as loudly today, because technology is too often in the driving seat and too often technology is about an idea looking for an application. I am a technologist; I am unashamed of that, and I still say it. But I have worries, for example, about the

European Community's Delta Programme, for it is the computer technologists that have been driving that programme, not the educators and trainers who know best of all what are the constraints and what are the opportunities for technology in improving the quality of learning.

Maybe this is changing. I sincerely hope so because the Delta Programme has great potential, but only for what it can deliver for learning and not what it can deliver for the computer manufacturers, important though they are to the economic benefit of the Community and individual member states.

So what are the roles for computers in education and training? Apart from research applications and some fairly straightforward administrative functions, there really is very little justification for having computers in schools and colleges, in training departments or wherever, except to the extent that they really do enhance the learning process. I say **learning**, not teaching. If I wanted to be provocative, I would say that teachers are logically and hierarchically like computers, in that they are means of facilitating effective learning - it is salutary to stop now and again and notice that very important distinction between teaching and learning.

When the chips are down, machines of any sort have to demonstrate either that they do conventional tasks better than any manual ways of doing them, or that they can do worthwhile things that cannot be done any other way. I emphasize 'worthwhile'. The computer salesman, like the car salesman, is always trying to persuade us that the one often esoteric feature of his product, which no other products have, is the one which above all else, we the client must surely value above all others, and of course it is nonsense -*caveat emptor*- and I think that as far as the schools in this country are concerned a great new problem is developing, for the simple reason that although the principles of local financial management are in many ways beneficial, it is now up to individual schools to decide what equipment they buy, and what staff they employ. There are going to be some very, very serious and costly mistakes made. Unless the schools have a way of drawing upon more expert advice, there is always going to be on a governing body some person who reckons to 'know about computers'. But the people who know about both computers and learning at the same time are much less common.

In education, and even in skills training, it is not at all easy to demonstrate that machines actually enhance learning. It's fairly easy to test the acquisition of knowledge, but to test whether that knowledge gain is more profound or more long lasting is much less straight forward.

When we turn to testing the acquisition of lateral thinking skills, the evaluation is very far from easy; controlled experiments in the field are extremely difficult to organize and often have to be of prolonged duration if they are to produce results of significance. Nevertheless, there is a growing body of evidence, and a growing consensus even, that machines can undertake tasks which are valuable to the learning process.

To quote just a few examples:

* they facilitate the use of language through experimentation. This is a very profound change. It is not a 'once or never task' now for children to write essays. It is not a punishment to ask children to revise an essay. The word processor and machine enables genuine experimentation, or refinement, to take place as a normal part of the use of language. This is a major change which of course applies not just in English, but in the use of word processors across the curriculum.

* they can help in the handling of data. This is still under-developed - it is already making a considerable impact, but the revolution is only just beginning - and the reason for that is we are only just getting machines of the magnitude and power to handle huge volumes of data. The 32 bit machines and the mass storage techniques of CD ROM offer already very considerable promise of opening up new capabilities, capabilities which are increasingly needed everywhere.
* modelling and simulations. Here it was the economic models that were in the van, but increasingly analogue simulations are being used to enable science to be undertaken, with machines which would otherwise be beyond the scope of normal education and training laboratories. The educational power of 'what if' tests again parallels what I have been saying about word processors, and you can with models genuinely experiment - so long as you have good programs - in ways which do away with the degree of artificiality normally present in the formalised traditional laboratory experiments.
* in design and technology. Here again, the new generation of fast micros is really necessary. But beyond design itself there are now real possiblities of testing for performance in simulation. There is a great deal that can be done in the design field by the use of sophisticated programs.

These programs take a great deal of investment, in time and money, but the schools in this country are used to buying programs for about £5 on a cassette. They are having to learn that these days it is not unreasonable to pay £100-150 for a program - hard going for schools that haven't got much money. But they have grown up in the culture of expecting a highly subsidized program that can be copied freely as many times as they want, and they still expect an educational software industry to be waiting there serving them, maintaining existing programs and writing new programs for new machines. So they are worried and surprised when program suppliers think they can make an honest buck in many other ways more profitably than by serving schools in the way mentioned above.

I would also mention expert systems applications, particularly the highly sophisticated guidance and counselling systems, using large data bases and involving a high degree of interactivity between the student and the machine. It is odd that something of such obvious importance as guiding and counselling has always been the cinderella in this country's education system: apart from the very powerful arguments that it is important that people get on the courses that are right for them, there is a very strong economic argument that if there are mismatches between peoples' needs and the courses provided, there will be immense waste of resources - a waste of peoples' lives, of teachers' lives and of vast sums of public money. These arguments don't seem to have prevailed yet in areas where they ought to have done. But there are very sophisticated programs now - there's at least one very good one being produced in this country called PROSPECT.

What is all this about anyway? Educators and trainers have long had as their ideal the creation of flexible learning systems - systems which can be adapted to the particular needs of each individual, whether a child in primary school, a trainee on a BTEC course, an undergraduate at university or an employee at any level in an enterprise, requiring new skills or the updating of existing skills.

What is really needed is for individuals to be able to study what they require; when they require it; when they are actually available to study; where it is convenient for them to study; starting at the level of competence which they've already reached; proceeding at the pace which their individual circumstances and abilities make right for them. That is, in my book, not just a definition of what open and flexible learning is about, but what in fact education is about. But just to state this ideal is to indicate how difficult it is to achieve in practise. Certainly our existing institutions and learning systems have a long way still to go.

The Open University, which I am sad to say is usually admired far more outside the UK than it is at home, cannot and does not pretend to be all that open or all that flexible. It has of course an open entry system: you don't need any prior qualifications to enter the Open University. But at the same time, if you look at the structure of its student body, it is geographically weighted towards the south-east. It is certainly socially structured towards the middle class, who (in Britain at any rate) pre-eminently respect the value of education. But the Open University has not really achieved one of the fundamental aims of its founders, namely to open university education to all sections of the community, to redress the excess numbers of the middle classes in higher education in the country.

It is not even of course very flexible. You can't start a course at any time. You have to start at the right point of the year, and to progress at a particular pace and a particular time train. Again one can see why. I mention this, not to knock the OU, but just to indicate how far we still have to go if we are to approach this ideal of true flexibility and the matching of particular educational or training offerings to the needs and opportunities and availability of individuals.

Certainly didactic teaching and chalk and talk were and still remain for many the best that can be done; a poor best for too many. Even in homogeneous study groups the lecturer in the seminar room and the teacher in the classroom have to pitch their offerings at the average ability, and inevitably because of that the most advanced and the most able are bored and lack stimulus, while the least able tend to be lost. The reality is that it has never been affordable to be able to provide for most people the individual tuition which might come nearer for them to the educational or training requirement that I have been talking about.

The need to break free of that mould, especially for adults with the constraints of jobs and family, has led to the development of open and flexible learning systems. Undoubtedly, the Open University is the most significant experiment in this area, though not the only one. But fundamentally the need for flexibility is very difficult to achieve other than via the effective teaching machine approach.

Up to now the sophisticated computing power required has resided only with very inflexible main frames, with the micro offering promise for the future, but there being very little in terms of practical possibilities today. We are now, just, approaching the stage where the micro has the power and the affordable price to make a really substantial contribution towards achieving the ideal of flexible learning. Some may feel that that is a slightly pessimistic view of advances in the applications of micro technology to education and training, but I think that in the generality of provision in universities and colleges in this country you will only very exceptionally and unusually see the micro-computer being used in the ways I have suggested it can and should be used.

I don't know why we should be expected to take a training course in understanding micro-computers before we can begin to use them effectively. There is still this idea that you have to get half way to a masters degree before you can actually start using a machine. That is now changing with the new machine user interfaces we are seeing that originally came out of Park in California and were then adopted by Apple in the Macintosh.

But it is only really the beginning. When you think about it, the machine has such advantages for trainers and for employers. If you are in a small firm - I run a small firm, that's what NCET is about in a way - it is very difficult to afford to release a key member of a management team or middle managers to go on a course. I've got several people doing OU courses in their business school. I am very easy about that - I don't lose their services. But the cost to employers of releasing people for a year or even a few days to study full time is too much.

So the machine has enormous advantages if (and that is a very big if) it can deliver training effectively. I'm perfectly happy to say to someone in my organization, "Yes, go down to the library and run that IV programme on whatever" because I know that if something happens where I've got to have that person, I ring up the library and say to them "Drop what you're doing, come back here, come and sort something out, a crisis has arisen". The machine is switched off, they come back, and half an hour later they say, "I don't know why the boss was getting so hysterical, it's all sorted out properly", but he goes back, switches the machine on, runs it back a few frames to pick up where he left off and away he goes again! You can't do that in the conventional system.

So there are enormous cost advantages, and the other advantage that I've touched upon to employers is the low risk. They feel comfortable, because it is a low risk strategy for them, but the big question is - is the technology capable of delivering? The answer is - sometimes. But we ought not, as educators and trainers, to be surprised at the attraction to employers of machine-based systems. We need to be critical about their quality and their effectiveness, but we needn't be surprised, because they have great advantages.

They do have to be user friendly and indeed that is increasingly happening now, and it is a trend that will have very profound implications. We will need of course to have machines that are maintained and operated and so forth, but we will no longer need to have lecturers and trainers who are experts in IT - they need to be experts in their own field, but we shouldn't expect more of them, and increasingly we won't need to.

We also require micro-computers to be able to handle in straight-forward language learning algorithms of considerable complexity and this is again beginning to happen. The good programmes, the really good programmes, have enormous power and sophistication; they have bells and whistles built into them to do anything that anyone could conceivably want them to do. I class Wordperfect in this category except that it does not network very well. It will do most things, so much so that most of the facilities are not actually used by any one person, but the great strength of that program is that it is very easy to do simple things on it. We have just rationalized,post merger, our word processing and we are adopting Wordperfect; the secretaries did a half day course and they then produced our medium term plan using Wordperfect. I don't pretend that the secretaries throughout the organization know all there is to know about Wordperfect, what I am saying is it is sufficienly logical in its design for people to be able to do normal, fairly sophisticated but routine operations, without more than an absolute minimum of training. That is actually difficult, you know: writing a programme of great sophistication with a large number of facilities, but which is very easy to get into to do the most common and important things with the minimum of training, is for me the mark of a really good piece of software. And those really good pieces of software are not written over a weekend by an amateur in BBC Basic - those days have gone.

Even so, we are only at the beginning because there are many more programs that you could quote that do not satisfy those criteria, thus my enthusiasm for Wordperfect. We have quite a way yet to go but there are new developments that are going to be very powerful; multi-media and hypertext applications certainly, and we are only really at the beginning of those.

We desperately need simple but powerful machines that are small and light enough to move around easily, yet with a screen that is capable of displaying high resolution colour and shades. We're not there yet. As long as we are prisoners of the electron tube, the VDU, that is the one thing that is really stopping massive and really flexible applications in schools, in homes, in colleges and probably in firms. The amount of space, the weight, the amount of energy that is dissipated as heat. In my organization we have got something like 1.9 systems for each of our employees, because we use them every day for routine work but we have to have lots more for experimental purposes, and when you have this density of machines, you realize the limitations of the VDU, the conventional cathode ray tube. And I think we are still four or five years away from being able to afford high resolution colour tubes that get over that difficulty.

Nevertheless, we are on the brink of massive steps forward towards the aim of flexible learning. They won't be done by machines alone: we are going to need a huge amount of human input. There are going to be vast implications of retraining educators into being managers of learning rather than purveyors of lectures, which is a huge task, and in terms of cost it is far greater than the cost of hardware or software or of the two together.

It is not an easy vision that I present you. It is actually a difficult and costly one. Nevertheless, I do believe that the world is changing very considerably in the direction of being able to realize human potential and of course it is important not only to be able to identify the technologies that can help - which we think is our role - but it is also equally important that we ensure that we do not lose sight of the elementary and obvious fact that the technology is a servant and not the master of what we are trying to do. There is one particular problem, certainly in most of education but perhaps less so in training, and that is you cannot afford to make investment mistakes. A school, certainly in this country, will buy a micro-computer and expect a life of six, seven, eight, nine years.

If you go into a typical British school you'll still find lots of BBC model B's around and they're not falling to pieces because they were well made! But a school cannot afford to invest in some particular machine and then find that it is not right for them. It is not like an industrial concern, perhaps investing in an interactive video where that investment can be amortized over quite a short period, and therefore standards don't matter too much. There, you have a system which you use intensively for 18 months - 2 years, and you can then say it doesn't owe you anything, you've had your value out of it. But that isn't so for schools; so one of the biggest impediments to the adoption of new technology in schools is the lack of standards. Only when a new technology has an established standard is it likely to make a case for widespread adoption in schools rather than pilot studies and so forth. We are more or less at that stage with CD ROM, but we are nowhere near that stage with interactive video. I would expect to see in the next year or so in this country's schools the adoption of CD ROM technology, which will be the first really major application of mass storage, but not to see massive implementation of interactive video. Until the bigger, wider market than education and training determines where interactive video is going you will not see too much in our schools.

AUDIENCE. One major area which you did not touch upon is the use of electronic mail, which in corporate America is the second form of communication which is paperless. Do you see a need for this within the educational industry?

THOMPSON. Yes. One of the major impediments in this country is that our electronic mail, the standard system, is awful. The growth of electronic mail in the UK has been severely handicapped by there not being a very easy user friendly system and whether anything is going to be done about it I don't know. It is very significant to me that the growth area has been in fax, and this is a nonsense technologically; to do something on the word processor in digital form, to de-digitize it and spew it out on a piece of paper which a secretary takes to the fax machine, feeds it in (which promtly digitizes it again) and then at the other end the digital data usually is de-digitized onto a piece of hard copy. But the reason why there is huge growth in that and relatively slight growth in electronic mail is because the former is simple - you don't need to become an expert, the only thing you have to remember about a fax machine is that you don't put the paper the wrong way up or else you get blank sheet coming out, but if you learn that there is nothing much more you need: they are very, very easy to use. And the growth in fax in this country and right across Europe has been explosive, with fax machines that are very cheap to use. I think this is very sad, and it is technological nonsense, but until we have really simple user friendly systems for electronic mail then people will use fax. I know incidently that fax doesn't have all the facilities, it doesn't have mail boxes and so forth, so it isn't an exact analogue or alternative but that's where the growth is here.

AUDIENCE. You mentioned the problem of cost and the fact that schools can't make wrong investments, and you also relate that to interactive videos. One of the frustrations I have found with interactive video is the interactive bit. When video disc players became linked with computers, that seems to be where they went wrong. The original video disc player, which was very cheap, is itself marvellously interactive. What we lack or have lacked all along is discs to play on them. I'm wondering if there are ways in which we can sponsor more material like that becoming available.

THOMPSON. Well, it is the usual chicken and egg situation with a new technology. It's not worth investing in the hardware until there's a decent range of software but until there's an installed base the software writers and software houses don't think it worth the investment in software. The reality, in my view, is that we are in the same position as we were with VCR standards about eight years ago, with no one knowing whether VHS or Betamax or even the V2000 system was going to win. Now it's easy; the market place has determined. Whatever the technological advantages of Betamax or V2000, and V2000 was the most advanced system of the lot, the reality is that VHS is the *de facto* standard. We don't know what the interactive situation is going to be in 3 or 4 years time in schools. So I hold fast to my view that the education system will wait to see what happens, and it would be right to do so. But what ought we to be doing in the mean time?

I think there are two main things that we ought to be doing. First of all we ought to be maintaining pilot studies so that we can understand what type of learning applications are really suited to interactive media. We haven't done much - we've done something, but we haven't done it very well in this country so far. We ought to be doing that in classrooms to see what density of machines are necessary for the technology to be really useful. We ought to be trying better to understand the implications for classroom teachers and lecturers in using the new technology. It does not use a lot of money to do that. For that purpose we need some software, and as you may know the National Curriculum Council and NCET have been engaged and are engaged in the production of mathematics discs for the national curriculum. That choice was made by the Prime Minister, so I'm told. I think also we shall see within the near future something which is even more logical and that is to use IV for updating purposes, for the training of teachers. The education business has enormous updating problems and we don't often make the analogue with other industries, though other industries have been using interactive video with quite high degrees of success. Certain criteria have to be satisfied of course, but when they are it is a very potent and effective medium and it is only now that the education business is saying, well perhaps we ought to be doing inservice training with interactive media. Why aren't we using interactive video for inservice training? You'd have thought that with the size of our industry that this would have been a natural idea five years ago. If the Woolwich Building Society can use interactive video effectively for training various levels of its staff, surely the unit costs of training for people in education with a much larger population ought actually to be even lower and it ought really to be very attractive. The spin off from that would be having an increasing core of teachers who are actually familiar with the medium and if it works, saying "Why aren't we using this in the classroom?"

AUDIENCE. Some of us envisage educational technology as being more closely related to operational research and systems rather than to hardware technology, and I'm wondering whether you are planning any initiatives in operational research related to innovation, or whether any specific operational research initiatives are under consideration.

THOMPSON. As far as my own organization is concerned we have a tradition of promoting open and flexible learning, and if you think that meets your definition and I'm not sure it does but it ought to, then the answer is yes. We start off not from the proposition of finding uses for machines but actually developing practical learning systems with the aim, as I said earlier on, of getting closer to the needs of the individual in learning terms and being able to address them in a variety of different circumstances. I do think indeed that is a major thrust of NCET. There still seems to me, though, to be a huge gap between the concepts of learning psychology for example, through to practical learning systems. One wants to get to the stage where you will be able as it were to diagnose the best sort of learning approach for a particular individual or a particular training need, and we're still a fair distance from that I feel.

Dr.Noel Thompson trained as a metallurgist, and taught that subject at university level before transferring to the Department of Education and Science. After some years there, he moved to his present post of Chief Executive at the National Council for Educational Technology.

23. Practical considerations on the introduction of CAL into university teaching

Stephen Fallows, Kathryn Huckbody and Terry King, University of Bradford

Abstract: The Electronic Learning-Package Factory (ELF) at Bradford University is researching ways of introducing computer-assisted learning (CAL) into university teaching. The aim of the workshop was, firstly, to introduce and give 'hands-on' experience of the ELF Starter Pack (a form based design system, incorporating the simple ELFsoft authoring system, which is being developed for academics with little or no computing experience). The workshop then introduced the ELF Transition Pack, which facilitates the progression of lecturers with a basic knowledge of CAL to the commercial authoring software, PROPI. Emphasis was placed on the practical problems associated with the appropriate use of authoring software and integrating CAL into the normal teaching environment.

BACKGROUND

The ELF project started in 1988 as a fundamental part of the computerization of Bradford University (CBU) to facilitate the introduction of CAL on a campus-wide basis. In keeping with the philosophy of CBU (Fallows, Radtke and Stonier, 1990), which aimed to bring a network of personal IBM PC type computers into the offices and rooms of every member of staff and student on the campus, it was decided that CAL would only be used widely if lecturers could be encouraged to prepare their own courseware rather than rely on a small team of professional courseware designers. Because the production of customized CAL courseware using a high-level language (like BASIC or Pascal) is extremely labour-intensive (often quoted as 100 hours development time to 20 mins of CAL), the ELF team looked for a commercial authoring package both to reduce this overhead and to make courseware construction possible for computer novices.

INITIAL DIFFICULTIES

ELF evaluated several commercial authoring systems and found that all of them presented problems in the University environment for academics with limited or no computer experience. They were complex to use, required professional CAL design and programming skills, could not deliver on the complete range of PCs at the University and often required the purchase of costly development and publishing licences (Fallows and King, 1989). Also, their educational approach was often geared more towards CAL at a secondary rather than tertiary level. It was considered important that CAL would only 'take-off' in a University environment if lecturers could make full use of existing teaching materials whether textual in the form of handouts or graphical (from existing pictures, slides or simulation programs). It seemed unrealistic to ask hard-pressed teaching staff to start re-creating ALL their teaching materials. However, on investigating various authoring packages we found that few were capable of incorporating existing text files or graphics or running external programs from inside the software. Also, as we were used to the Apple Macintosh environment we felt that hypertext would be useful at a university level in order to give the student the possibilty of extra references or extra work assignments or just pass some control over the work to the student with the ability to browse through linked hypertext screens. None of the commercial software we evaluated had any hypermedia facilities.

THE DEVELOPMENT OF THE ELF STARTER PACK

In view of the problems encountered with commercially available authoring software, we decided to write our own authoring system which would overcome all the difficulties discussed above. The result was the ELF Starter Pack incorporating the ELFsoft authoring software. The Starter Pack was designed to incorporate many features (like hypertext and the ability to run external programs from within a tutorial) (King and Fallows, 1990a) but its essential philosophy was very simple. Lecturers would be able to use the software from the base of knowing simply how to use a word processor and the associated limited range of MS-DOS commands associated with running that word processor. That, we would not expect a dramatic change in the teaching resources needed but rather existing materials could be converted into CAL using the computer as a new medium of delivery in the initial stages. We looked in the first instance towards the 'electronic handout' rather than the 'electronic book'! And finally by providing a comprehensive range of facilities in an inflexible format, we drastically reduced the number of design options available, reducing complexity for computer novices and allowing us to present pedagogically sound frame designs and unknowingly develop some good design awareness in our 'subjects'. For example, a question frame will display the question, then the student response and then an immediate evaluative reply all in the same frame.

FEATURES OF THE ELF STARTER PACK

The ELF Starter Pack comprises an extensive user manual containing a set of designs forms, which when completed and keyed into a word-processor, generate a text file which can be interpreted by the TEACH component of the ELFsoft authoring software to generate a CAL tutorial on a wide range of PCs. ELFsoft also provides an interactive route (WRITE) to the same text file as well as a tutorial note generator (NOTES) and a rudimentary computer managed learning facility (STATS) which will provide diagnostic reports on how a student has completed a tutorial. The Graphics version will also allow pictures in .PCX format to be called up directly or as hypertext. (For more details see King and Fallows, 1990b). By using this method, lecturers can take existing text handouts and convert them into CAL in just a few hours.

BEYOND THE STARTER PACK

The current development version of the Starter Pack will generate CAL containing a reasonable (if inflexible) range of features (for example, five question types). Once academics have experimented with this, we believe that there are likely to be two parallel developments. Firstly, changes to the ELFsoft software itself so that it is tailored for different subject areas and the development of such simple 'niche' authoring systems. And, secondly, a demand from lecturers themselves for access and training in more complex commercially available authoring software, so that more sophisticated CAL can be authored. It is to this end that ELF is now developing the ELF Transition Pack, which aims to aid the transition from the simple ELFsoft system to a more complex commercially available authoring system.

SELECTING THE COMMERCIAL AUTHORING SYSTEM

The first step in the development of the Transition Pack was to choose a suitable commercial authoring system. The final decision was made on the basis of several criteria:

* The system selected had to support a range of facilities that lecturers might wish to use, but which were not available in ELFsoft. These included the option of overlaying screens (to build up diagrams step by step), the ability to use a variety of fonts and characters from the extended ASCII character set, full use of colour, and facilities to produce graphics, animation and sound.
* The system had to be affordable within the University budgets (being free of recurrent authoring, runtime or publishing licences).
* It had to be easy to use by relatively computer-naive lecturers. Ideally, the main editors should be operated via pull down menus, with lecturers always being able to amend material using the same editors in which they created it. The main text, graphics, sound and animation editors should be "WYSIWYG" (What-You-See-Is-What-You-Get) in nature (allowing lecturers to create material directly on the screen as they want it to appear), but for absolute freedom, the system should ideally allow them to modify the lesson code directly if desired.
* ELFsoft produces lessons that are basically linear in nature (with the exception of hypertext references). It was therefore decided that the commercial authoring system should not only support branched lessons, but actually encourage lecturers to think in terms of creating different pathways through their lesson material.
* Bearing in mind the diversity of computer monitors which staff and students were likely to possess, we decided that the commercial system should also be capable of creating lesson material using a range of graphic standards (e.g. Hercules monochrome, CGA, EGA and VGA if possible).

The commercial authoring system that met the maximum number of our criteria was 'PROPI'. It is easy to use and offers a full range of pull down menu driven, WYSIWYG text, graphics, sound and animation editors, for the creation and modification of lesson material. The system has no associated recurrent or extra licensing costs, and supports a wide range of extra features. PROPI supports the production of material in CGA, EGA and VGA, but not in Hercules monochrome graphics mode. This problem can however be solved by the use of an emulator, which converts CGA material into a form that can be viewed on a Hercules monochrome monitor. One of the most powerful features of PROPI is that lessons are created via a menu-driven 'on screen' lesson map, (automatically drawn by the system). This should not only help lecturers think in terms of pathways through their lesson material, but also,(by linking diagrams of the lesson's structure to the actual content of individual screens) help reduce lesson development time.

PROBLEMS WITH THE USE OF PROPI

We anticipated that the transition from ELFsoft to PROPI was likely to cause lecturers problems in two main areas:

* Lecturers can use ELFsoft to produce sound CAL material without being familiar with any of the underlying principles of CAL. PROPI, however, gives lecturers free rein to develop practically any type of lesson or screen layout that that they can think of. Without a suitable background knowledge of CAL, most individuals will either stick to the ELFsoft style of screen with which they are familiar, or experiment with PROPI to produce their own style of material.

Unfortunately, experience in the CAL industry has found that educators without a basic knowledge of CAL tend to misuse many of the effects that authoring systems offer (for example, dribbling text onto the screen letter by letter; centring large quantities of text; producing screens with a variety of different foreground and background colour combinations). The quality and effectiveness of the resultant lesson is therefore reduced - even if the actual lesson material is educationally sound.

* The user manual is typical of most user manuals, in that it explains exactly how each part of the system works, but not how to use the system to create specific material. For example, the manual contains explanations of how to write information to an external file, how to register a student identification, and how to manipulate external variables, but does not explain how and why the lecturer must combine these facilities in order to produce a permanent record of a student's progress.

DEVELOPMENT OF THE ELF TRANSITION PACK

The Transition Pack will contain two main components.

The first is a basic introduction to CAL, designed specifically to meet the needs of relatively computer-naive lecturers. It will cover a wide range of material, from when and why CAL should be used, to guidelines for producing interesting (but sound) screen designs, and the creation of an effective student-computer dialogue. Due to the mainly text-based nature of this material, we decided to present it in booklet form. Although the material in the booklet has been designed primarily with the transition to PROPI in mind, much of the guidelines and principles are also applicable to the production of CAL using ELFsoft. The booklet will therefore eventually be made available to lecturers on receiving their first copy of ELFsoft.

The second component will take the form of a set of short CAL lessons. These do not aim to replace the manual, nor to provide general online tutorials on how to operate the system. Instead they aim either to complement or to extend the material covered in the manual, as applicable. Most of the material will fall into the latter category, with great emphasis being placed on how to create basic CAL materials using PROPI. However, after assessing the manual, we came to the conclusion that it would be a good idea to include some additional explanatory material in certain areas. (For example, we thought lecturers would find it very time consuming to work out how to create student records or produce certain screen overlay effects with sole reference to the manual). Unlike ELFsoft, PROPI places great emphasis on lecturers producing their own screen layouts and methods of interacting with students. A number of short PROPI lesson map sections (incorporating a variety of screen designs and types of student-computer interaction) will therefore be included in the form of map templates.

CONCLUSION

By introducing lecturers to CAL through the ELF Starter Pack and then encouraging them to develop their professional skills in the production of educationally sound, innovative CAL using the ELF Transition Pack, the ELF Team hope to generate a widespread and lasting commitment to CAL throughout Bradford University.

REFERENCES

Fallows, S.J. and King, T.R.(1989): ELFsoft: a simple route to CAL authoring in higher education. Educational and Training Technology International, 26, 4, pp.342-347.

Fallows, S.J., Radtke, A.L. and Stonier, T.(1990): Computerization of a UK University - the Bradford University Experience. 7th International Conference on Technology and Education, Brussels, March.

King, T.R. and Fallows, S.J.(1990a): The development of ELFsoft: a user-friendly CAL authoring system. 7th International Conference on Technology and Education, Brussels, March.

King, T.R. and Fallows, S.J.(1990b): ELFsoft: a simple but effective CAL authoring system. 7th International Conference on Technology and Education, Brussels, March.

Dr.Stephen Fallows is currently employed as project manager for the ELF Project. Since obtaining his PhD from the University of Bradford in 1981, his research interests have been wide ranging and have included reference to health education and training. He makes no claim to be a computing expert but rather aims to represent the interests of the non-specialist user of computing technology.

Kathryn Huckbody joined the ELF team in July 1989. After obtaining an MSc in Computing from the University of Bradford, she worked for the National Computing Centre as a Computer Based Training (CBT) designer. She is currently working towards a PhD by designing and researching materials which enable academics to make the transition to commercial CBT authoring software.

Terry King joined the ELF Project in October 1988 immediately after completing her MSc in Computing at Bradford. A qualified teacher, she worked for four years as a lecturer in Computer Studies and Information Processing after a career as a project analyst in the computer industry. She is currently working towards a PhD in the development and implementation of CAL authoring starter tools.

Address for correspondence: **S.Fallows, K.Huckbody** and **T.King**,
ELF Project, University of Bradford,
Bradford BD7 1DP, UK

24. Supporting learner strategies in CBT

Neville Stanton, University of Aston in Birmingham

Abstract: This investigation set out to examine learner strategies in a non-linear computer-based training (CBT) environment. It was proposed that as learning is an active process, CBT should allow learners to adapt the material to their own preferred learning strategy. Therefore a non-linear CBT package was developed: learners in this non-linear environment appeared to have sequenced the training modules in three main characteristic ways. These were classified as top down, sequential and elaborative. Overall it was concluded that the non-linear environment was able to support these different learning strategies.

INTRODUCTION

Computer-based training (CBT) is potentially the most exciting and flexible of all the training media, yet this potential has not been fully realized. The main failure is to account for individual differences and preferences. One solution to this problem is to allow the learner to decide how the information to be learnt is presented. An individualized approach has been called Self Directed Learning (SDL). The self-directed approach considers learning to be a personal individual act, and advocates that the learner should take the responsibility for learning. Decisions such as: determining goals, deciding on materials, structuring, grouping and allocating tasks, as well as evaluation, all come under the learner's remit for management in learner-centred methodologies (Dickinson, 1981). Dimensions of self-direction are: aims, method, pace, place, materials, monitoring and assessment. Each of these emphasizes the autonomy of the learner; as Dickinson argues, automy represents maximum self-direction on a scale ranging from directed to autonomous learning. Giving the learners autonomy assumes that they want it and that they are able to cope with it. This follows from the assumption that individuals can be self-motivated.

It is suggested that placing individuals in an environment allowing them to be self-directive will lead them to behave in a self-directive manner. Mager and Clarke (1969) proposed that learners may often enter the learning environment with a significant amount of relevant knowledge. Therefore, allowing the learners to judge and choose what they need to add to their current knowledge to meet the training objectives would reduce both training time and boredom.

SDL shares many terms with hypermedia, such as 'networks' and 'pathways'. Hypertext (Nelson, 1981) is the idea that knowledge (be it in the form of text or graphics) may be linked in many ways, providing no formal structure, allowing the individual to explore the knowledge domain at will. The hypertext approach may have certain advantages over linear training. For example, courseware authors do not have to concern themselves with structuring the information in any particular order. Trainees may approach the learning environment with a wealth of previous experience which can enable them to be directive in their own learning.

One further dimension that is worthy of consideration is the notion of 'self perception' and 'attribution'. If individuals are actively involved in deciding what is to be learnt, and in what order it is to be learnt, they are more likely to interpret personal (internal) attributes (such as quality of these attributes) as determining their success. This is likely to lead them to behave differently in the learning task to individuals who perceive tha situation as involving an external locus of control. The latter could arise if the computer is seen as responsible for deciding which training module is presented next. Luthans (1985) reports studies suggesting an internal locus of control leads to better performance. This may be due to more effort being exerted when the locus is perceived internally. The individuals may internalize the outcomes and goals as being their own. This increased commitment to the goals leads to increased motivation to see that they are realized. In addition, if the individuals perceive that they can have some influence on their surroundings, they are more likely to engage in activities that are able to achieve this (Shackleton and Fletcher, 1984). On the other hand, individuals who perceive the locus of control as external are less likely to be as successful. Linked to the notion of control is 'learned helplessness' (Rachlin, 1976) which suggests that failure can lead individuals to 'give up', or become passive recipients. Norman (1988) suggests calling this phenomenon 'taught helplessness', referring to the teaching (or training) failing to impart the information in one stage which then hinders further stages.

Learning strategy was considered to be as an important variable in this investigation. Allowing the learner to control the sequence of instruction provides great potential for examining individual differences in learning. Brooks, Simutis and O'Neil (1985) describe four general categories of individual differences that are related to learning strategies, namely: abilities, cognitive style, prior knowledge, and motivation.

METHOD

Twenty subjects were employed for this investigation. They were allowed to navigate freely between the training and practice modules as shown in Figure 1. When subjects elected to finish their training the

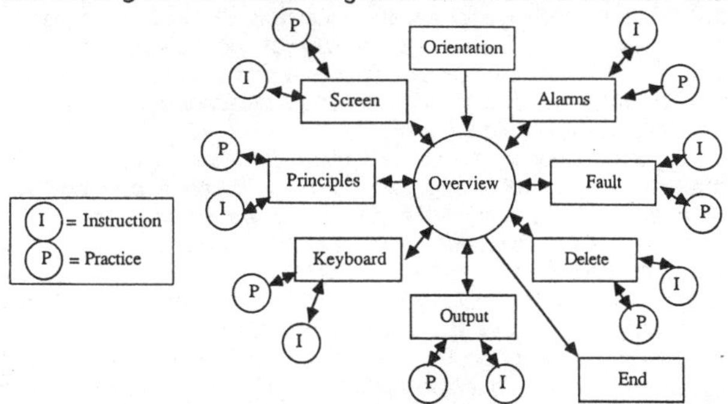

Figure 1: Navigation through non-linear training modules

effectiveness was assessed on a 'process plant'. The training modules can be split into prerequisites and tasks (for further details see Stanton, 1989).

RESULTS

To analyse the subjects' strategy, the training modules were arranged in a hierarchy of complexity. The subjects were divided into groups based on the order that they visited modules in their navigation around the non-linear training environment. Three groups were categorized by their characteristics: the Top-Down strategy group (n=6), Sequential strategy (n=9) and Elaborative strategy (n=5). The data were analysed based upon these three catgories. A summary of the results is as follows:

* there was a significant difference between all three groups for the mean number of modules compared (Mann-Whitney U, $p<0.01$);
* there was a significant difference between the sequential and the elaborative groups on the number of modules repeated (Mann-Whitney U, $p<0.05$);
* subjects in the top-down group accessed significantly less modules than subjects in the other two groups (Mann-Whitney U, $p<0.05$);
* subjects in the elaborative group spent on average less time in each module compared to the other two groups ($F_{2.17}=7.609$, $p<0.005$).

From the results the 'observed strategy' analysis accounted for the most variation in subject behaviour within the non-linear condition. Significant differences were found in the number of modules completed, repeated, not viewed, and the average time spent in training modules. Therefore the groups labelled top-down, sequential and elaborative were adopted in preference to the other analysis groups for further discussion. It should be noted that there was no significant difference between overall training time and transfer task (see Stanton, 1989).

DISCUSSION

Taken individually the strategies were quite different. The top-down group imposed its own structure on the otherwise relatively unstructured environment, to good effect as the results indicate. It is proposed that these subjects are able to deal with the ambiguity of the situation effectively and are able to structure it. Subjects in the sequential group however use the overview screen to provide structure; they appear unable to impose their own, and are possibly concerned that they may forget where they have been if a less explicitly structured approach is taken. It is possible that these subjects may have preferred to be in a linear training environment, with a predetermined sequence of modules, relieving them of the management function.

The elaborative subjects appear to be acting spontaneously (or with situated actions) in what outwardly appears to be movement around the modules in a random sequence, although it is supposed that this behaviour is intended to be structured, as a random strategy was not reported. It is proposed that subjects are linking modules that are important to building up their individual learning structures, filling in gaps in their knowledge. In order to make effective choices of modules to enter, a global knowledge of what is contained in each module is needed. This was provided for to some extent with the overview screen which informed subjects briefly of the content of each module. However it was reported that this facility was not used very often.

Intentions, goals, plans and actions

The non-linear condition allowed subjects to interact with the training modules in a freer manner than the linear subjects. It is necessary to consider therefore the intentions, plans and goals of subjects. Assuming that the subjects' goals were to operate the task simulator (it should be noted that from previous experience the majority of experimental subjects are extremely highly motivated, being in a novel situation, and very eager to please) current thinking on cognition would assume that they formulate some sort of plan to extract information from the system. Whilst the behaviour of the top-down and sequential subjects appears to fit neatly into this idea of plans, actions and goals, the behaviour of the elaborative subjects is a little harder to explain. Possible explanations suggested by Suchman (1987 - 'situated actions') and by Norman (1988 - 'opportunistic actions') are that purposeful behaviour may be ad hoc, rather than following a preplanned series of steps, depending upon the humans' intelligent adaptation to fluctuating circumstances. The non-linear environment did allow subjects to interact with the material in an ad hoc manner if they so wished. Therefore it could be inferred that CBT may need to support situated actions by allowing the learners to adapt and change their learning strategy throughout the training as required.

Hypermedia

A recent revival of self-directed environments has been heralded by the advent of hypermedia. The hypermedia environment is much freer than the non-linear condition reported in this investigation. It has potential to allow linkages and access between all parts of the knowledge domain. In this investigation, however, the choice between training modules was taken at the point of the overview screen, to which subjects were required to return. Despite the relatively simple network in this investigation, the two environments did have similarities. Hypermedia has been advocated for education and training because it gives control to the learner by encouraging exploration, but there are a number of potential drawbacks intrinsic to such systems that also apply to the non-linear condition.

The most often cited disadvantage is disorientation or 'getting lost' (Conklin, 1987; Hammond and Allison, 1989; Edwards and Hardman, 1989). The network in the non-linear condition was quite simple, and yet six subjects did report becoming lost at some point in the training session. Therefore disorientation is a problem even in relatively simple networks. The sheer size of a network may cause users greater navigational problems. Some research has proposed the use of navigational tools using the travel metaphor to assist the learner around the knowledge domain (Hammond and Allison, 1989). Mayes, Kibby and Anderson (1989) suggest that this may be inadequate for large networks as they do not help the learner navigate in conceptual space. They propose conceptual orientation of the material rather than spatial orientation of the nodes and links in the network, as the learner's goal is to become orientated conceptually rather than spatially. Mayes et al suggest that this will facilitate learning; learners are forced to concentrate on shared attributes between frames rather than the structure of the network. The relatively shallow nature of the non-linear condition should have helped subjects concentrate on the task, rather than the network, but problems associated with cognitive overhead, motivation, knowing content and learning to use the interface cannot be ruled out.

Cognitive overhead (Conklin, 1987; Doland, 1989) is the term given to describe degree of complexity in a non-linear environment such as: number of choices, task scheduling, tracking and navigating. This is related to the management function the subject was required to perform in the non-linear condition, including the decisions related to which modules to select and in which order to select them. As has already been suggested, the further through the training session, the better the decision probably is. This is undoubtedly linked to the subjects becoming aware of the content of the modules from implications of what has already been covered (Hammond, 1989; Doland, 1989). It is also a function of reduced numbers of choices making the decision easier.

Motivation of learners may be impaired if they become overwhelmed by the freedom allowed in the learning environment. Subjects who behaved in a sequential manner were able to get around the problem of freedom and ambiguity by using the overview screen to structure the task. However, in more complex networks where the structure is not so visible it might be necessary to provide some initial constraints, such as in the training wheels philosophy (Carroll, 1984) or guided exploration (Robertson, Koizumi and Marsella, 1988), to prevent the trainee becoming unmotivated and just rambling aimlessly through the network. Such interaction may lead to a situation of 'taught helplessness' (Norman, 1988).

The non-linear interface (like the hypermedia interface) is relatively new. None of the subjects in the experimental condition had ever encountered such an environment before, so subjects were required to learn this task on top of learning to use the interface and becoming self-directed. These additional tasks must have put extra load on the subjects. Mayes et al (1989) reported that with their system, subjects either learn to navigate in it or learn the instructional material, but they cannot do the two together, at least initially. The non-linear environment was relatively simple, and it is proposed that this initial problem was fairly short-lived as is shown by the change over time in performance differences.

Cognitive maps

Related to the notion of mental models is the idea of cognitive maps; the internal representation of external spatial information. Billingsley (1982) found that a pictorial representation of a menu structure assisted subjects in developing a mental model of the interrelationship of data. This proved to be significantly more effective than providing an index or no assistance at all. Subjects reported in this investigation were provided with a pictorial representation of the first level in the non-linear hierarchy, but not the second level. In addition the interrelationships were only visible at the point of the overview screen, and as soon as the subjects moved to another point in the system they were required to navigate by dialogue boxes. From Billingsley's work, it seems clear that users of non-linear environments need pictorial representations of their environment in order to alleviate navigational problems. Application of cognitive mapping to hypertext environments has suggested that readers form a spatial cognitive map (Edwards and Hardman, 1989). It appears that individuals attempt to create representations in the form of survey-type maps for orientating and navigating around hypertext. It is therefore suggested that the electronic environment supports the analogy of navigation based on the physical environment. Edwards and Hardman demonstrated that under certain conditions it was possible to disrupt the development (and therefore successful navigation) of cognitive maps, by not fully supporting the physical analogy.

Learning strategy

As Messick (1976) noted, cognitive styles differ from cognitive strategies. Styles are related to a predisposition of behaviour whereas strategies are the translation of the predisposition in combination with the multi-factorial environmental, situational and social variables. There does not appear to be one overriding strategy that can be used to provide guidelines for structuring training machines in one particular sequence. As Allinson and Hammond (1989) warn, the dangers of presenting material in a manner that suits one particular style is such that individuals that approach the material from another perspective may well be frustrated in their goal of assimilating the material into their own cognitive structures. Furthermore, it is just as likely that individuals do not operate solely from one particular style or strategy, but that they are capable of switching as factors change such as material familiarity, structure of material, motivation to learn, etc. Given this, it seems clear that any training environment must be designed to allow for different learning strategies. Unlike previous studies, this investigation directly compared linear and non-linear training environments. From the findings it is clear that a non-linear environment is superior. The advantages postulated are that it:

* allows for different levels of prior knowledge;
* encourages exploration;
* enables subjects to see a sub-task as part of the whole task;
* allows subjects to adapt to their own learning strategy.

This suggests that the non-linear environment is supportive of a wide range of strategies, whilst not actually biased towards one. The instructional material is passive, requiring the subjects to be active in response to their changing knowledge base. Brooks et al (1985) agree that the efforts of the researchers would be better directed at the relationship between the four general categories of individual learning strategies - they suggest that the four general categories of individual differences that relate to learning strategies are: abilities, cognitive style, prior knowledge and affect/motivation. These however cannot be considered in isolation, and research has to encompass the whole learning strategies framework for reliable advances to be made. A possible criticism of this investigation is its failure to account for the variables relating to abilities and prior knowledge. However all subjects were of undergraduate educational level, but some may have been more familiar with computing technology than others. These are rather minor criticisms given the size of the study and the tentative nature of the findings.

CONCLUSIONS

Whilst it is recognized that little is known about the learning process, this research has shown that progress can be made by providing an optimum environment within which learning can occur. This environment may be manipulated to improve the learning process. A 'goodness of fit' is required between the learner and the learning environment in order to maximize the uptake of the material to be learnt. In general, the hypothesis does appear to have been supported by this empirical study: learners in the non-linear environment appear to have sequenced the training modules in a manner that was congruent with their preferred learning strategy. These findings are presented cautiously, though they do underline the notion of learning as an active process. Therefore, the more pro-active the learner is, the more effective the learning process will be. Conversely, the more passive the learner is, the less effective the learning process will be. This is a rather gross overgeneralization. However, it indicates that the greater involvement learners have in their own learning, the better the subsequent transfer performance will be. The principle to emerge from this study is that the learning environment needs to be flexible enough to support the learner in a wide range of strategies. This may be necessary because actions in a particular situation may differ from the original course or plan, whilst being consistent with the overall goal.

REFERENCES

Allinson, L. and Hammond, N.(1989): Learner support environment: the hitch hiker's guide. In, McAleese, R.(ed), Hypertext: Theory into Practice. Intellect Books, Oxford. pp.62-74

Billingsley, P.A.(1982): Navigation through hierarchical menu structures: does it help to have a map? Proceedings of the Human Factors Society, 26th Annual Meeting, pp.103-107.

Brooks, L.W., Simutis, Z.M. and O'Neil, H.F.(1985): The role of individual differences in learning strategies. In, Dillon, R.F.(ed), Individual Differences in Cognition, Volume 2. Academic Press, U.S.A.

Carroll, J.M.(1984): Minimalist design for active users. Proceedings from Human Computer Interaction INTERACT'84, Volume 1, pp.219-224. Imperial College, London

Conklin, J.(1987): Hypertext: and introduction and survey. Computer, 29,9,pp.17-41

Dickinson, L.(1981): Self-directed learning. In, Carver, D. and Dickinson, L.(eds) Self-Directed Learning. Moray House College of Education, Edinburgh.

Doland, V.M.(1989): Hypermedia as an interpretive act. Hypermedia, 1, 1, pp.6-19

Edwards, D.M. and Hardman, L.(1989): 'Lost in hyperspace': cognitive mapping and navigation in a hypertext environment. In, McAleese, R.(ed), Hypertext: Theory into Practice. Intellect Books, Oxford.

Hammond, N. and Allinson, L.(1989): Extending hypertext for learning: an investigation of access and guidance tools. Proceedings of the Fifth Conference of the British Computer Soc. HCI Specialist Group: People and Computers V, pp.293-304

Luthans, F.(1985): Organizational Behaviour (3rd Edition). McGraw-Hill, Singapore.

Mager, R.F. and Clarke, C.(1969): Explorations in student-controlled instruction. In, Anderson, R.C. et al(eds), Current Research on Instruction. Prentice-Hall, Englewood Cliffs, N.J.

Mayes, T., Kibby, M. and Anderson, T.(1989): Signposts for conceptual orientation: some requirements for learning from hypertext. Proceedings of Hypertext, II. University of York, York.

Messick, S.(1976): Individuality in Learning. Jossey-Bass, San Francisco.

Nelson, T.(1981): Literary Machines. Published by the author.

Norman, D.A.(1988): The Psychology of Everyday Things. Basic Books, New York.

Rachlin, H.(1976): Behavior and Learning. Freeman, San Francisco.

Robertson, S.P., Koizumi, D. and Marsella, S.C.(1988): Constraints on training: informativeness and breadth in procedural skill learning. Proceedings of the Human Factors Society 32nd Annual Meeting, Volume 1, pp.377-380.

Shackleton,V. and Fletcher, C.(1984): Individual Differences: Theories and Applications. Methuen, London.

Stanton, N.A.(1989): Learner Centred Control in Computer Based Training. M.Phil. Thesis, Aston University, Birmingham.

Suchman, A.(1987): Plans and Situated Actions: a problem of human-machine communication. Cambridge University Press, Cambridge.

Neville Stanton is a Research Officer in Aston University's Applied Psychology Division. His research interests include CBT, Hypermedia and HCI. He has over 20 publications in these areas, and has recently been awarded an M.Phil. from Aston. He is now pursuing a Ph.D. and also works as an independent consultant within his areas of specialism.

Address for correspondence: N.Stanton,
Applied Psychology, Aston University,
Aston Triangle, Birmingham B4 7ET, UK

25. Some difficulties in describing human potential in educational and training technological systems using computers

W.Weston-Bartholomew, University of Warwick

Abstract: Uses of computers for information storage and exchange continue to grow rapidly, so that many more people are involved in using computers in many work and leisure environments. It is thus important to continue to investigate what types of relationships humans have with computers in the workplace. At the interface of e.g. educational and training technological systems involving computers and humans, all factors that affect delivery, consistency and continuity should be considered. This paper gives consideration to a suitable philosophy which is necessary when describing such relationships if we are not going to automate all functions or endeavours of work.

INTRODUCTION

At the interface where humans meet computers there are problems to be recognized. Investments in computer systems are for the purpose of performing certain tasks which are best done by human and computers working successfully together. However it is not always easy to get this perfect interaction at the human-computer interface.

There is therefore a need to look at all facets of computers and of humans realizing their potential as users, especially as naive and as non-naive users (Eason 1976). The task to which the computers will be put in this paper is for educational and training technologies using information technologies as a delivery mode.

The user can operate as an instructor or as a learner, and the system usability (Shackel, 1986) will determine use of the computer system. The International Standards Organization defines usability as:-

> the degree to which specific users can achieve specific goals within a particular environment effectively, efficiently, comfortably and in an accepted manner:

while a working definition of usability that has evolved is that the following are shown:

usefulness	effectiveness (ease of use)
learnability	attitude (likeability).

It is proposed in this paper that in educational and training technologies using computers the difference between the actual and the user-perceived job allocation between human and computer might be a factor that may restrict the full realization of human potential. The term Dynamic Job Allocation (DJA) will be used to indicate that the job allocation can change within a learning task between human and computer. Humans are better at small-scale complex tasks than are computers: as the tasks become larger in scale, whether complex or not, then the computer is better at present. There is however a 'grey area' where it is difficult to decide whether human or computer should be given the task (see Figure 1).

The decision on how to allocate jobs will be made from explicit and implicit data about naive and non-naive users; the proportion of the allocation may to some extent determine the type of person who will use the system. The dynamic job allocation relationship may not be perfect at all times, but a certain 'degree of perception' that it is so by the user could be 'built in' by designers in education and training technologies. The allocation may even be 'chaotic' in reality. Also, since users vary so considerably it may not be possible to design for

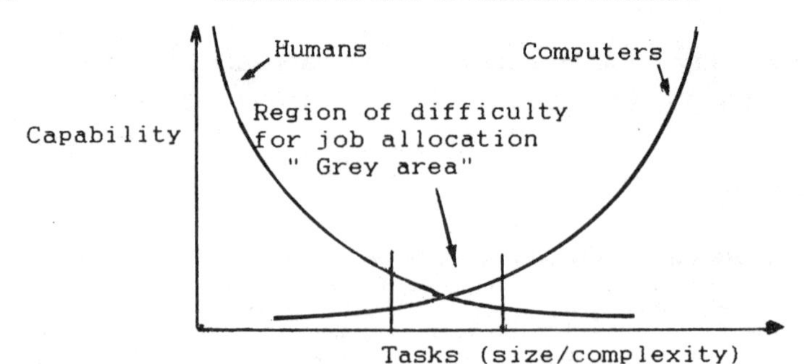

Figure 1: Simplified human-computer job allocation response curves.

all types of users, as is suggested for hardware design consistency at the human-computer interface (Grundin, 1989).

A PROBLEM FOR EDUCATIONAL AND TRAINING TECHNOLOGIES?

Microprocessors today can replace many high performance super computers, with considerable cost savings. Mass storage devices (magnetic disks) have been upgraded and flash memory solid state drives may soon be used as the most important storage media on PCs. Paralleling computing is now at an affordable price and computing power on a normal PC is increasing considerably. Users can demand processing power or intensive number crunching to do e.g. data base searches, 3D animation, complex financial projections, molecular modelling and finite element analysis.

However, while each secondary school in the UK has about 30 computers, primary schools have only 3; there is a problem of training tutors to use them. In Japan there are about 25 computers in each secondary school but only about 13% of the teachers believe that they can install or operate them: no doubt in many countries a similar belief is held.

Information in the 1990s will have a great impact on technology and the communication between people and computers and between people and people. It will expand the use of computers and many people will be trained on-line and off-line. It may be useful therefore to study the actuality and perception of dynamic job allocation (DJA) between user and computer in educational and training technologies for the 1990s. This is necessary because computer systems are becoming smarter and faster and the belief held by some humans about computers is difficult to define. It is recognized that this area is very complex to study but if it can be identified as important, it will not be neglected.

TOWARDS A POSSIBLE OR PARTIAL SOLUTION?

Methodology

The method used was:-
* to ask two questions which may affect DJA, viz.,
  a - As machines become smarter will instructors/learners become smarter;
  b - As machines become faster will instructors/learners learn faster?
* to hypothesize answers and attempt to interpret them for the 1990s;
* to look at studies on observed user differences, and the search for reasons for differences whilst interacting with computers, and use these to illustrate the problem; and
* to propose a description of users and a concept for possible DJA.

The two relevant questions

The answers to these questions may affect the design and use of educational and training systems using computers. Possible answers, accompanied by a comment as a possible interpretation (in brackets), are

a. Yes/Yes (ideal case) c. No/Yes (ambiguous)
b. No/No (inappropriate) d, Yes/No (ambiguous)

This paper will discuss only the ambiguous cases (c) and (d), as it is probably in these regions that it will be difficult to match the actual and the perceived DJA. It may be here where some users will interact in an inefficient manner with the computer: this might be misunderstood as being unable to interact with the technological training system.

The first question is similar to that asked in the 1970s about children and the impact of artificial intelligence (AI) in education (Goldstein and Papert, 1977). The MIT LOGO project (see Papert, 1972) was used to get children to grasp and manipulate concepts whilst programming a computer. Group work and discussions were used to improve vocabulary skills so as to articulate the strategies used in problem solving. The paradigm was for the learner to have knowledge and know what type of knowledge to use whilst being observed by the observer.

It is not certain as to how the concept of actual and perceived DJA can be extended to this model, but the concept is individual-based. Also the model might only represent part of the concept proposed for the 1990s.

The second question is time related. This is because increase in processor speed is only now beginning to trickle down to the desktop machine level. Future designers of educational and training technologies will have to consider its effects or non-effects.

User difference observed

User difference was observed in studies by Hughes (see Hughes 1986; 1987), in which a simplified form of LOGO was used for group problem-solving and mathematical discussions. The subjects were 6 year olds and differences were observed accidentally. The same researcher (1987) found sex stereotyping about using computers at the early age of 7 years.

It was said that a similar difference exists between girls and boys in the choice to study mathematics, science and technology (Whyte, 1986).

User difference was found when sixth form students interacted with a computer in an open system mode in two separate studies (Weston-Bartholomew, 1985). All were mathematics and science students. No attempts were made to classify them when analysing the data except as individual users interacting with the computer. Difficulties of some would-be users of computing are also reported by Dain (1989).

Search for reasons for user differences

The search for reasons for user differences is given in the discussion by Hughes (1989). No conclusive reasons were advanced but two types of explanation were considered, one based on cognitive difference and the other on attitudinal factors. Both reasons advanced however appeared to be clouded by social factors about working in groups with the computer. One idea he advanced, that perception of a task as being user orientated may inhibit engagement with the task seems interesting. This no doubt further adds to the difficulties in searching for an explanation for user differences.

In this paper it is argued that user difference is individual-based and might even be time-related and/or task-related for the purpose of study for the 1990s.

MAPPING CONCEPT FOR DYNAMIC JOB ALLOCATION - A TRAINING TECHNOLOGIES PHILOSOPHY FOR THE 1990s?

Basis for the concept

The concept is an attempt to allocate job functions to job-type persons. This, it is hoped, will make the human-computer interface more realistic and productive whilst being task orientated. It is not suggested that this will be an easy exercise, but with such a type of philosophy for the 1990s educational and training technologists using computers may be able to select and train all persons in need of training.

The mapping process

Firstly, known ideas and responses by humans to computers are used, in that there are some people who prefer to spend more time working with computers than others. It is suggested that users should be broadly classified as:

* computer-type user (CTU), and
* computer-user type (CUT

for the purpose of training and utilization of technological systems with computers.

Secondly, the user type is mapped into the ambiguous regions (No/Yes and Yes/No) shown previously. The results for the purposes of this paper are:

* computer-type user (CTU) - allocate to smarter (but not too fast) computer environments, and
* computer-user type (CUT) - allocate to faster (but not too smart) computer environments.

It is only to be expected there are many users classifiable in between these two types, so difficulties of identification will always be a problem in DJA between humans and computer in technological training.

DISCUSSION AND CONCLUSIONS

A suggestion has been made that computer programming should be taught differently in the 1990s, making it more derivation-based and using no predicative languages (Djikstra 1989). A further idea is to consider bringing computer programming closer to mathematics.

Another study reported that people who knew neither programming nor mathematics (i.e. most people) believe that programming is like mathematics. This belief is held even though students from other disciplines can program as well as mathematics students (van Emden, 1989).

If the idea of user classification and mapping users into dynamic job allocation spaces is accepted, trainers in technology using computers in the 1990s may have to consider the following problems:

* to determine the best way to obtain suitable descriptions of users. There should be an awareness of the difficulties in generating and accepting both self and observer descriptors. This is not a new problem but it may become more important in the 1990s;
* to recognize that each user-type is part of a continuum at the interface. If they are not perceived as such then there may be human

inefficiency and even inconsistency at the interfaces;

* ensuring that the actual DJA is perceived to be so by the users, and recognising that this can be time related.

For the 1990s it is hoped that educational and training technologies will be able to train most people using computers. It is suggested that computer-type user (CTU) will be concerned with system designs whilst the computer-user type (CUT) user will be using the information-based system to its fullest for the benefit of all.

REFERENCES

Dain, J.(1989): Getting women into computing.University Computing, 10,pp.154-157.

Djikstra, E.W.(1989): On the cruelty of teaching computer science. Communication of ACM, 32, 12, pp.1398-1404.

Eason, K.D.(1976): Understanding the naive computer user. The Computer Journal, 19, 1, pp.3-7.

Goldstein, I. and Papert, S.(1977): Knowledge and language in AI. Cognitive Science, 1, 1, p.84.

Grundin, J.(1989): The case against user interface consistency. Communication of ACM, 32, 10. pp.1164-1173.

Hughes, M.(1986): Children and Numbers. Blackwell, Oxford.

Hughes, M.(1987): Children and computers. In, Crook, C. and Rutkowska, J.(eds) The Child and the Computer. Wiley, London.

Hughes, M.(1989): Girls and computers. In, Hughes, C. (ed), Bedford Way Papers, 34. University of London Institute of Education, London.

Papert, I.(1972): Teaching children thinking. Journal of Structural Learning, 4, pp.219-229.

Shakel, B.(1986): Ergonomics design for usability. In, Hamson, M. and Monk, A.F. (eds), people and Computers,

van Emden, M.H.(1989): Reply to 'The cruelty of really teaching computing science'. Communication of ACM, 32, 12, pp.1398-1404.

Weston-Bartholomew, W.(1985): The electronic office - people work there too! Human-Computer Interaction: 1985 IERE Conference on Networks and Office Systems (neos '85). (Read paper).

Whyte, J.(1986): Girls into Science and Technology. Routledge and Kegan Paul, London.

Address for correspondence: **Dr.W.Weston-Bartholomew,**
Writer/Researcher, c/o Dept. of Engineering,
University of Warwick, Coventry.

26. Computer-mediated seminars: realizing the potential of both students and tutors through interactive distance education

Alexander J. Romiszowski, University of Syracuse

Abstract: Computer-mediated communication (CMC) has been used primarily as a conferencing system, but it also has great potential as an instructional system in both distance education and on-campus courses. For the latter, it has been demonstrated that using CMC systems for achieving specific educational outcomes needs careful design and implementation. Experience of the advantages and problems of student-initiated conversations in CMC are discussed, and several instructional strategies for dealing with problems are reported. Hypertext-based communication environments are described, and a model for the use of CMC within distance education systems is developed.

DISTANCE EDUCATION: INSTRUCTION OR CONVERSATION?

As an introduction to our discussion, it may be interesting to compare and contrast two paradigms of teaching that we shall refer to as **'instruction'** and **'conversation'**, (see Figure 1).

The instructional paradigm is that within which much of the educational technology has developed. This is the approach which designs teaching on the basis of particular pre-defined objectives that specify some post-learning performance and the expected standards to be attained. The teacher's role, apart from delivery of the message, is to match student behaviour against predetermined criteria and to furnish corrective feedback as and when required.

The conversational paradigm differs sharply in many aspects, as the compare/contrast table in Figure 1 seeks to illustrate. The objectives may be the result of an agreement between teacher and learner to explore a topic and may be more concerned with the topic itself, or the exploration process, than with specific pre-defined outcomes. The role of the teacher is to analyse and evaluate that important aspects of the content and its structure are being adequately addressed and, when necessary, to participate by means of constructive comments that challenge the participants to rethink their positions or restructure their ideas.

For Distance Education in Figure 1, one can see the contrast between the suitability of the most commonly used delivery media in relation to the two paradigms of teaching. Classical correspondence course assignments, with automatically marked objective tests, supported by the minimum of postal contact with the tutor, are good examples of the instructional paradigm in action. Audio and video teleconferencing, as most commonly practised, are examples of the conversational paradigm. Computer-mediated communication has been placed in the middle, to emphasize that it may be used in both manners: either to deliver computer-based instruction at a distance; or as computer-based teleconferencing (or indeed, as some combination of these).

There is no implication in the schema presented in Figure 1 that one is 'good' and the other 'bad'. On the contrary, most educational and training systems require the use to each of these teaching approaches in different parts of the total course.

PARADIGM	"INSTRUCTION" "CONVERSATION"
OBJECTIVES:(why?) (output)	specific--------------general
	pre-defined-----------negotiable
	products--------------processes
	standard--------------variable
MESSAGES:(what?) (input)	designed--------------created
(when?)	pre-prepared----------on-line
(who?)	instructor------------participants
(whom?)	one-to-many-----------many-to-many
INTERACTION:(focus) (process)	behaviours------------ideas
(analysis)	criterion-ref.--------content/structure
(feedback)	corrective------------constructive
(complexity)	one-layer-thick-------interwoven layers
DISTANCE EDUCATION (example)	CORRESPONDENCE COURSES \ TELECONFERENCING VIDEOCONFERENCING / \ COMPUTER-MEDIATED COMMUNICATION /

Figure 1: Two teaching paradigms.

CMC IN DISTANCE EDUCATION

The growth of electronic networking in education and training is being driven partly by educational goals and partly by economics. The educational thrust, especially in distance education, is to use electronic conferencing systems as a medium for discussions, between teacher and students and also between the students, thus injecting some elements of the collegial campus experience into basically 'instructional' correspondence courses (Harasim, 1986; Kaye, 1987). The economics are driving organizations to use more electronic communications for all purposes, including education and training (Chute, 1990).

There is a danger of inappropriate use of telecommunications media, just because they are available and are rapidly becoming cheaper. Can teleconferencing be effectively used for those parts of the curriculum where specific performance objectives are to be achieved by all students? Is there a danger that the simplicity of setting up an electronic network between students will reduce the attention paid to the design of effective teaching materials, on the grounds that the 'tutor at a distance can patch up any problems that students may have', just as he/she used to do (or rather was supposed to do) in the face-to-face classroom?

On the other hand, when the educational aim is to explore a topic in order to gain insights, rather than to master pre-defined tasks, are the techniques of effective discussion on a network the same as those used in a classroom-based group situation? Many early experiences suggest that they are not and that participants (both tutors and students) must learn to interact effectively in these new media (Hiltz, 1986; Mason, 1988). Some people tend to write their contributions in a more belligerent and abusive tone than they would ever use in a face-to-face conversation - this is so prevalent that it has gained the internationally accepted name of 'flaming'. Others, being free of the time constraints and group pressures present in a class meeting, develop long dissertation-like replies that clog up the network and make it more difficult to find other contributions hidden in their midst. Yet others lead the discussion away from the original topic and refuse to return (Romiszowski and Jost, 1989; Grabowski, 1990).

PROBLEMS OF STRUCTURE AND CONTROL IN CMC

The last mentioned issue can be seen as a combination of two problems which seem to be particularly prevalent in computer conferencing systems - of maintaining a clear picture of the **structure** of a complex discussion over time, and of **controlling** the direction of flow of conversation that involves a large group of participants (Romiszowski and Jost, 1989). Computer-based conversations take place over extended periods of time, in an asynchronous manner. Each participant logs on at convenient moments, reads what has been contributed since the last log-on and reacts to items of interest. The nature of such a discussion promotes greater and more thought-out participation than typically occurs in a group meeting, but on the other hand creates some problems for the participants in maintaining a clear memory of other related comments that were made some time earlier. Therefore,unless previous files are re-read and few do this - at the end of a computer-based conversation of this nature extending over a few weeks, participants may have quite different memories of the content and the structure of the topic that had been discussed (Romiszowski and DeHaas, 1989).

The related problem of **control** is a result of failure to maintain a structured picture of the discussion as it develops. When a participant logs on, some interesting and possibly strongly provocative message (see 'flaming' above) is read. This prompts an immediate response which in turn may generate several other responses. Soon the discussion has branched off onto a tangential issue, only loosely related to the original topic of conversation. Whereas in a classroonm a teacher may let such a 'red herring' run for a time and then, quite easily, revert the converastion to the main topic by a simple intervention, it is very much more difficult to reroute in CMC environments in that way (Romiszowski and Jost, 1989).

The commonly practised way of overcoming this tendency to drift is by means of a purpose-designed computer-conferencing system (such as CoSy or PARTIcipate), which allows for the creation of sub-conferences to the main theme, in separate files. As a potential 'red herring' appears, a moderator, who is pre-reading all messages as they come in, creates a sub-conference for this discussion, thus imposing a structure on the conference as a whole - open to criticism as, for clarity, one person is controlling (censoring?) the discussion and limiting the expression of minority views.

When the discussion is part of a course with certain clear (albeit not specifically predefined) goals, the moderating task is an essential part of the teaching function. It does, however, impose a very time-consuming and perhaps unwillingly taken burden on the teacher who is leading the discussion. As a consequence, CMC may be unnecessarily limited or ineffectively used in education due to inadequate moderation.

STRUCTURING AND CONTROLLING THE COMPUTER-MEDIATED SEMINAR

Over the last two years at Syracuse University, we have been developing a programme of research and development which is investigating the use of CMCs as a support medium to campus-based courses (Jost et al., 1990). Many of these follow the conversational paradigm in general, but do have clear objectives of a 'general skills' nature in mind, e.g. management decision-making skills, consulting skills, content analysis skills or heuristic design skills as used in management information systems design and, indeed, instructional design systems. Some conventional teaching methods which are particularly successful in such areas include: seminars (to research the relevant knowledge base, share experience and viewpoints); case study exercises (to develop the necessary heuristic skills of applying the knowledge base to real problem solving, under controlled conditions); and project work (to transfer and further develop these skills under real-life conditions).

Live audiographic or video teleconferencing would seem to have closest similarity to the classroom-based seminar or case discussion. Indeed, there are many successful implementations of these methodologies in both educational and training contexts (Chute 1990).
The use of CMC has revealed both advantages (greater, deeper and more participative discussion) when well moderated, and problems (structure and control) when less well moderated. It would seem appropriate to focus attention on how to overcome the problems and therefore make seminar and case methods more effective in CMC environments, and less dependent on the skills and dedication of the teacher/moderator.

1. Structuring the initial paper

One approach to overcoming the 'problem of structure' was to create a discussion environment that would automatically cluster all comments on a given issue, or interrelate them in some way, so that a reader accessing the discussion files may quickly and easily gain an overall impression of the conversation so far. The simplest approach to doing this was to somehow separate the issues in the original position paper, so that any later comment would be automatically related to that issue, by numbering or otherwise identifying the paragraphs of the original paper and requesting that comments on any paragraph are directed to files whose names correspond to the relevant paragraphs. A trial experiment in the summer of 1989 showed that this simple discipline did much to reduce both the structure and control problems which were observed in earlier attempts at running seminars on electronic mail systems (Romiszowski and Jost, 1990).

2. Structuring the discussion as Hypertext

An alternative approach to maintaining structure is to furnish some form of hypertext environment for group discussion. This was implemented in Hypercard, on a Macintosh computer cluster. The 'notecard' metaphor which Hypercard is based on is particularly useful in the present context, as the discipline of writing each issue of a seminar position paper on a separate card, followed by the linking of any comments by a button to that specific card, would automatically create clusters of related information in the growing discussion.

The implementation is illustrated in Figures 2 and 3. Each participating student has an individual 'stack' of cards as a workspace, and prepares a short seminar paper on some aspect of the topic under study, structuring it so that each issue addressed is placed on a separate card. Figure 2 shows the fifth card of a seminar paper dealing with the topic of expert systems. Though the student's paragraph is short, and is indeed completely visible in the top window of the card, this is a scrolling window so students are not unduly restricted in the

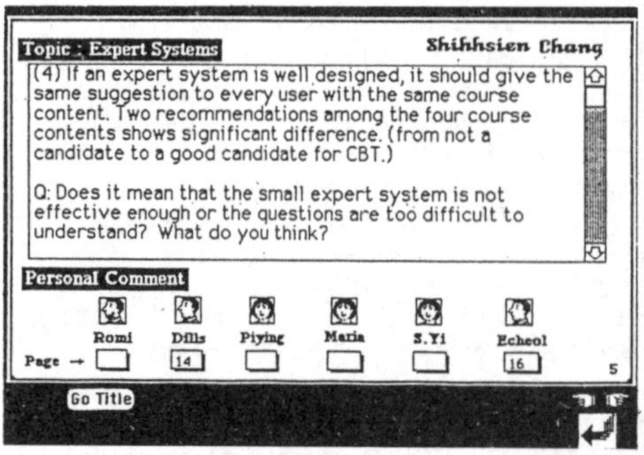

Figure 2: The 5th Card in a seminar paper on Expert Systems.

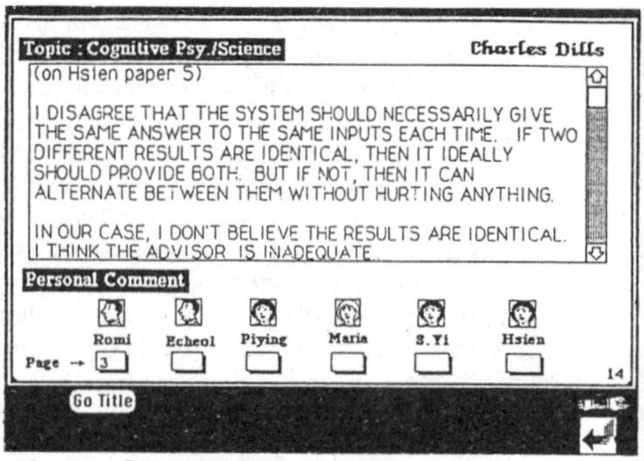

Figure 3: A comment card on the question posed in Fig.2

amount of text they may use. Below the text window, there are (in this use) six icons which act as gateways to the workspaces of the other seminar participants.

Two participants have, at this time, made comments on the issues presented. To see what, for example, 'Dills' has said, a reader clicks on that icon and, when requested, types in the card number which appears in the window below the icon (14 in this case). This takes the reader immediately to card 14 of Dills' stack, to read the comment shown (in part) in Figure 3. This comment has aroused a reaction from another participant, which has been cross-indexed to be found on card 3 of the 'Romi' stack. All initial comments are linked to a specific card in the position paper, but later, readers may make connections between comments from different clusters, eventually creating a complex network of cards that can be browsed along many different 'trails'.

3. Clustering related comments in a communal workspace

Yet another approach involves all the comments on a particular issue being placed by all participants in the same scrolling comment window on the same card. Each participant may make a comment on the original paper, or on some other participant's comments, or may reply to these comments. One can add comments to the end of the list, or insert them at the most appropriate point, as full word processing capability is available in the window. A reader will browse the discussion by scrolling the two windows on a given card, adding comments if desired, and then move to the next card and repeat the process.

This approach was also implemented in an IBM mainframe environment, under CMS. The screen design possibilities were more primitive, and the students had to learn a number of operating commands to get the paper and the comment space as two scrolling files on a split screen, but in terms of access to comments and the structure of the resultant textual records of the seminar discussion, the mainframe and Macintosh versions were identical. Students found the system equally acceptable on either machine. The initial learning curve to master the mainframe operating system was an inconvenience far outweighed by the greater availability of mainframe terminals, which eliminated queueing.

RESULTS SO FAR

The various methods described above were used systematically on several seminar-type courses during 1989-1990. Observations and tests were made to evaluate the effect of the different approaches on the problems of structure and control, and whether any other problems or advantages were observed. Student surveys were also applied. The results are summarized below (for a full account see Romiszowski and Jost, 1990; Grabowski, 1990; Chang, Corso and Romiszowski, in press).

1. All the approaches described were successful in considerably diminishing the problems of structure and control. A final 'test discussion' across all topics in a one semester long seminar-based course revealed that all students had a similar view of the topics that were discussed, and the relationships that existed between topics. They did not agree, however, on their viewpoints in relation to these topics. This is as should be: the structure of a complex domain was successfully communicated, without necessarily conditioning the participants to one set of opinions (the professor's) on how the domain should be interpreted and used.

2. The hypertext environments were rated as inferior to the split screen environment by most students, mainly because of the need to move back and forth between cards that were addressing the same issue, as opposed to seeing the issue and the earlier comments side by side on the screen. This objection may not have been present if a more sophisticated hypertext environment, with windowing capabilities had been used (e.g. as in the Intermedia system - Meyrovitz, 1986). However, as the split screen methodology was successful in overcoming the structure and control problems, and is easier to implement, there is some doubt about the need for more complex solutions.

3. Student preferences were 2:1 in favour of computer-based seminar discussions, over face-to-face seminars along more conventional lines. In particular, participants praised the discipline of having to think out a response carefully - "It not only records creative observations which would otherwise be forgotten, but actually encourages the generation of creative insights". They also tended to make a hardcopy printout of the discussion record, sometimes to study it at leisure and plan their own comments "in the comfort of my armchair before going to the computer to key them in", but also to keep a record for later use.

4. Prolonged use of the system over a series of seminars during a whole semester, led to an increase in effectiveness on a number of counts. Level of student participation increased, from a few short and rather superficial messages per student at the beginning, to a much richer and deeper discussion in later seminars. This is accompanied by significantly decreased teacher/moderator intervention as students become accustomed to the methodology; in one course, by a reduction in moderating messages from the tutor from twice the volume of student messages at the start of the course to 10% of them by late in the course, without recurrence of structure and content problems. The quantity and quality of participation of some foreign student groups (who, for reasons of language difficulties or cultural habit seldom participate actively in small group seminars) would grow to be almost indistinguishable from American students.

CONCLUDING COMMENTS

It appears that quite simple approaches to the design of a structured conversational environment may be enough to overcome some critical problems associated with less structured approaches to the use of CMC for goal-directed discussion. Furthermore, the use of such structured environments appears to facilitate student participation and student direction of the discussion process. This is important as, in contrast to moderator-based conferencing systems, it opens the possibility of quite intensive use of student-directed group discussion, with little moderator intervention. This extends the practical viability of CMC as a distance education methodology to that very large area of education which requires a conversational approach with respect to the learning process, but nevertheless has some relatively precise goals in mind as regards the outcome.

Further research is in progress, extending our inquiry to other effective group discussion methods which are yet to be efficiently implemented in CMC environments (e.g. the case-study method) and to other approaches to discussion-organization tools and environments that may help learners to interact intellectually in the 'deep processing of complex ideas'.

We are on the brink of the 'information age' in which most work left for humans will be concerned with the 'processing of knowledge to create wisdom' and to do this, most workers will be involved in a continuing process of self-development. At the same time, they will be ever more accustomed to do most of their communication and knowledge processing from their multipurpose electronic workstations. Self-educational 'conversations at a distance' may turn out to be one of the most important and most used methods of adult continuing education.

REFERENCES

Chang, E., Corso, M. and Romiszowski, A.(in press): Effects of interface variables on learning from computer-mediated seminars and case studies. IDD & E Working Party Paper, No. 27. Syracuse University School of Education, Syracuse, N.Y.

Chute, A.(1990): Teletraining. Educational and Training Technology International, 27, 3.

Grabowski, B.(1990): Social and intellectual exchange through electronic communications in a graduate community.
Educational and Training Technology International, 27, 3.

Harasim, L.(1986): Computer learning networks: educational applications of computer conferencing. Journal of Distance Education, 1, 1.

Hiltz, S.(1986): The 'virtual classroom': using computer-mediated communication for university teaching. Journal of Communication, Spring.

Jost, K. et al(1990): Computer mediated communication: developments and innovations. Instructional Developments - Journal of the School of Education, Syracuse University, 1, 1.

Kaye, A.(1987): Introducing computer-mediated communication into a distance education system. Canadian Journal of Educational Communications, 16, 2.

Mason, R.(1988): The use of computer-mediated communication for distance education at The Open University, 1988. Paper presented at the Open University International Conference on Computer Mediated Communication in Distance Education Milton Keynes, UK, 1988.

Meyrovitz, N.(1986): INTERMEDIA: the architecture and construction of an onject oriented hypermedia system and applications framework. Proceedings of the 1986 OR:OOPSLA Conference. Portland, Oregon.

Romiszowski, A. and DeHaas, J.(1989): Computer-mediated communication for instruction: using E-mail as a seminar. Educational Technology, October.

Romiszowski, A. and Jost, K.(1989): Computer conferencing and the distance learner: problems of strucure and control. Proceedings of the 1989 Conference on Distance Education, University of Wisconsin, August.

Romiszowski, A. and Jost, K.(1990): Computer-mediated communication: a hypertext approach to structuring distance seminars.
Proceedings of the 1990 International Symposium on Computer Mediated Communicatio University of Guelph, Canada.

Address for correspondence: Prof.A.J.Romiszowski,
School of Education, 330 Huntington Hall,
Syracuse, New York 13244-2340, U.S.A.

27. A CAI and CMI system considering student's achievement and consciousness

Yoshikazu Araki

Abstract: The author presents some of the problems of engineering education at university level and proposes a new solution using CAI and CMI together, taking into account the individual student's ability and attitude. The teaching system consists of three main parts: the conventional lecture, CAI and CMI. Courseware has been piloted on a module on semiconductors. The flexibility of the system allows it to be constantly improved.

INTRODUCTION

One of the reasons for the present success of Japanese industry is said to be the Japanese educational system. This system has functioned to create people who are homogeneous, diligent and patient. The graduates of Japan's educational system have taken Japan to the forefront in world business and industry. Although the Japanese educational system has been successful, it has some problems and the Japanese college entrance examinations have a harmful effect on the whole educational system.

In Japan, one's position in life is determined, not by ability, but by the ranking of the educational institution from which one graduated. So, naturally, high school students want to go to the most prestigious national, public and private universities. A student's scores on the college entrance examinations determine to which college or university he or she will be admitted. These are usually written tests which cover English, mathematics, Japanese, social studies and science. When high school students study for these tests they try to memorize the answers and solutions to questions and problems that might appear on these examinations. As a result, the students' concept of learning becomes rote memorization. On every level of the educational system, in all aspects, the goal is to get higher grades in the next examination in order to get into a better school. The students don't enjoy their education which is unfortunate because they don't realize their true potential and don't gain any real knowledge.

The author thinks that an interesting and stimulating environment is more conducive to the acquisition of knowledge than a stultifying one geared to rote memorization of facts. Japanese universities evaluate their teaching staff on the basis of research work rather than on their teaching ability. Because career advancement is based on research, the members of the faculty make no effort to improve their teaching techniques, or to focus on the student's needs.

Students and teachers think about higher education in different ways. Most students think of their university or college years as a time to enjoy themselves after having finished a hard, painful year studying for the university entrance examinations, a period often referred to as 'examination hell'. They have little motivation to study because once they have entered university, future success is pretty well guaranteed. The teachers complain that today's university students don't study hard enough. The teachers do not understand, or care to understand, the students' attitudes towards education and university life.

Q 1: What do you think about the teaching methods?		%
1	The course is too easy	0.8
2	The course is too hard	14.4
3	Teachers should check students' understanding	43.2
4	Lectures are unnecessary	3.4
5	No complaints about present method	9.3
6	Other	28.8
Q 2: How could university education be improved?		
1	The courses should be easier and the lectures more understandable	13.6
2	Teachers should make sure that students understand the basics	48.3
3	Practical things that will be useful in business should be taught	17.8
4	Teachers should keep the students up to date with current research and developments	20.3

Table 1: Results of questionnaires about university education (n=118)

Table 1 shows the results of questionnaires about university education that the author wrote and administered to students last year. The results clearly show that students think about university life in different ways.

In addition most teachers are not enthusistic about teaching and employ the traditional lecture method, supplemented with textbooks and handouts. Most students are bored in this type of passive environment. Some students don't bother to go to the class and then cheat on the final examination, knowing that the teachers usually award credits based only on the finals. The situation is not improving: despite the increasing numbers and diversity of university students, teachers are continuing to give lecture courses. Instead of treating the students as a group, teachers should try to meet their individual needs and interests.

SOLUTIONS

There are two solutions; long term and short term.

The first, an essential long-term solution, is to change the entire Japanese educational system. This includes a change in the entrance examination system. In order to achieve this, the attitude of university teachers towards education must change. As their attitude changes, the attitudes of high school and university students will follow. As far as university education is concerned, the concrete suggestions are as follows:

* Students should be evaluated according to their daily efforts and not only by the results of a final examination.
* Instructors' teaching techniques should be evaluated by both teachers and students, as is done in some other countries.
* Teachers should teach the fundamentals and then make efforts to stimulate the students' creativity and originality.
* Teachers should motivate the students and help them recognize the necessity of learning. To achieve this, teachers should be aware of the students' feelings about higher education, as in Table 1.

The second, a short-term solution which is one part of the long-term solution, is an experimental model to be used in universities. This model is intended to help a teacher improve his or her teaching technique. The author would like to take this opportunity to introduce a new teaching system currently being used in the instruction of 'semiconductors', part of the engineering curriculum. This method is applicable to other subjects.

THE NEW TEACHING METHOD

Most teachers do not consider their students' abilities and attitudes when they prepare and give lectures. The students' progress, creativity and ability to solve problems is directly related to their attitudes and motivation.

The author has done a study that revealed a strong relationship between a student's attitude and progress. The final examinations were used to evaluate progress, and the results of the questionnaire, 'What do you expect to achieve in college?', to evaluate the student's attitude.

The responses from the questionnaires were divided into three groups:

1. 'Will-type' - students with many interests and hobbies who are eager to improve themselves;
2. 'Duty-type' - students who study in order to pass the courses necessary for graduation;
3. 'Party-type'- students whose main interest is partying.

Approximately one hundred of these questionnaires were distributed and evaluated. The questions included those concerning the purpose of college, lectures, examinations and learning systems. The results showed that the 'Will-type' students progressed faster than the 'Duty-type', and were also engaged in outside activities in a positive way.

Another questionnaire, 'When do you most want to study' was also administered and evaluated. Results showed the 'Will-type' students want to study areas not related to their major, such as English: the other two types of student tend to study only for final examinations.

These results indicate that the students' individual personalities must be taken into account to maximize the effectiveness of education. Clearly it is beyond the capability of even the most dedicated teacher to be totally aware of each student all the time, therefore computers are necessary to cope with mass education. Flexibility in the modification of material is also necessary to keep abreast of the rapidly changing field of engineering.

To meet these needs, flexible computer-assisted instruction (CAI) and computer-managed instruction (CMI) are necessary. The CAI and CMI systems are flexible in that they are not fixed but are always being improved to adapt to new situations. This is possible because the whole system is authored by the teacher. The system consists of the CAI, including authoring system and courseware, and the CMI, which collects data on the students' progress and evaluates the results of the questionnaires. The system can immediately accommodate changes in response to suggestions about the lecture and the CAI courseware.

TEACHING SYSTEM AND PROCEDURE

The teaching system consists of three main parts: the conventional lecture, CAI and CMI. Figure 1 shows the whole system. The courseware includes a pre-CAI test, the main CAI and a final CAI test. The pre-test consists of quiz-type and questionnaire-type tests, both administered by computer. The quiz is given to check the student's basic knowledge of mathematics, electromagnetics and physics; knowledge necessary in order to understand semiconductors. There are ten problems on mathematics and five on each of the other two subjects. Each problem has two hints. The

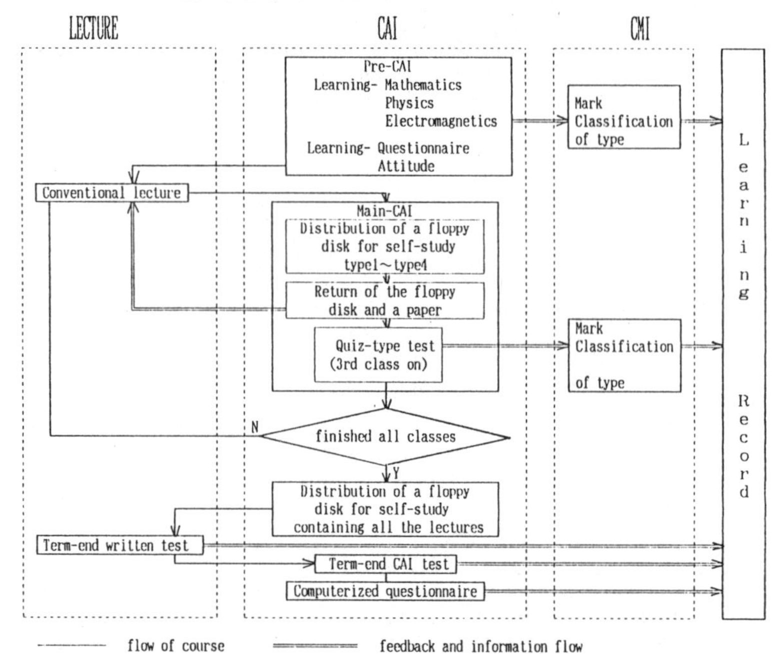

Figure 1: The teaching system

questionnaire investigates the student's attitude towards learning and college life and his or her academic interests. Also included are questions regarding the level of difficulty of the previously taken CAI quiz, the student's personality and which specific CAI the student would like to use.

The courseware for the main CAI consists of nine subjects, including semiconductor physics and applications. One subject is given per week. Each one week segment consists of four kinds of courseware for self-study and CAI quiz courseware for testing. The CAI final examination is taken from the weekly quizzes and the final questionnaire includes the questions from the questionnaire given before the course as well as some additional questions. The results of the questionnaire are used by the instructor to evaluate and improve the course. The students' test scores and the questionnaire results go into a data base.

The data recorded from the student's pre-CAI quiz are the following:

1. the student's ID number;
2. the number of problems in the quiz;
3. the random problem order number;
4. the random problem order variation number;
5. evaluation of the student's answers;
6. answers to the first questionnaire;
7. answers to the second questionnaire;
8. the time taken to answer each problem

The data recorded from the pre-CAI questionnaires are the following:

1. the degree of difficulty experienced on the quiz and the student's level of confidence;
2. the reasons for difficulty and lack of confidence;
3. student's questions concerning academic achievement and the system of gaining credit;
4. level of student's interest in lectures, i.e. does the student

listen and take notes;
5. student's problem-solving methods;
6. why the student attends class;
7. student's suggestions for improvement of teaching methods;
8. what the student mainly uses a personal computer for;
9. which the student is more interested in: hardware or software;
10. when the student is most likely to study hard;
11. what factors have a detrimental effect on the student's studying;
12. what aspects of education give the student satisfaction;
13. what the student hopes to get out of college;
14. student's requests for guidance or assistance;
15. student's interests, hobbies, etc.;
16. student's plans and hopes for the future, including employment;
17. personality evaluation;
18. what type of main CAI the student would like to use.

The questionnaire at the end of the course includes, besides the above, questions about the difficulty of the written examination and some designed to assist in the evaluation of the CAI system.

In addition to the computer-administered test, there is a written final examination which checks the student's writing and calculating skills. This test cannot be corrected by computer. Students who do well on the computerized tests usually also do well on the other test.

MONITORING THE STUDENTS' PROGRESS AND ATTITUDES

Computerized tests are given to monitor the students' academic progress. The results are available in printed form to both students and teachers. In order to monitor the students' attitudes, the questionnaires given at the beginning and the end of the course are used. The students also write a paper containing their impressions, opinions and suggestions concerning the lectures and the CAI courseware.

HOW THE SYSTEM FUNCTIONS

The pre-CAI test is given in the first class to determine the students' basic knowledge and attitudes. From the second class, a conventional lecture is given after which the appropriate courseware is handed out to the students. There are four types of courseware, including one on the basics and one on applications. These are selected using the CMI system. This is where the results of the pre-CAI test are used: the grade on that test, the student's attitude and his or her preferred type of main CAI are all considered. Each student's main CAI course is decided by the third class.

SYSTEM EVALUATION

The system was evaluated last year by dividing one hundred and twenty students into a control group and an experimental group. Although the experiment was not tightly controlled, the results were encouraging.

The main CAI for self-study had been decided beforehand for the control group while the main CAI courseware for the experimental group was selected as previously described. Figure 2 shows the grades for the control groups and the experimental groups.. The uppermost graph is the experimental group in the fifth class; the second graph represents the control group from the same class; the third graph is the experimental group from the ninth class; and the bottom graph is the control group from that class. Figure 3 shows the change in the average marks on the CAI test for the control group (solid line) and the experimental group

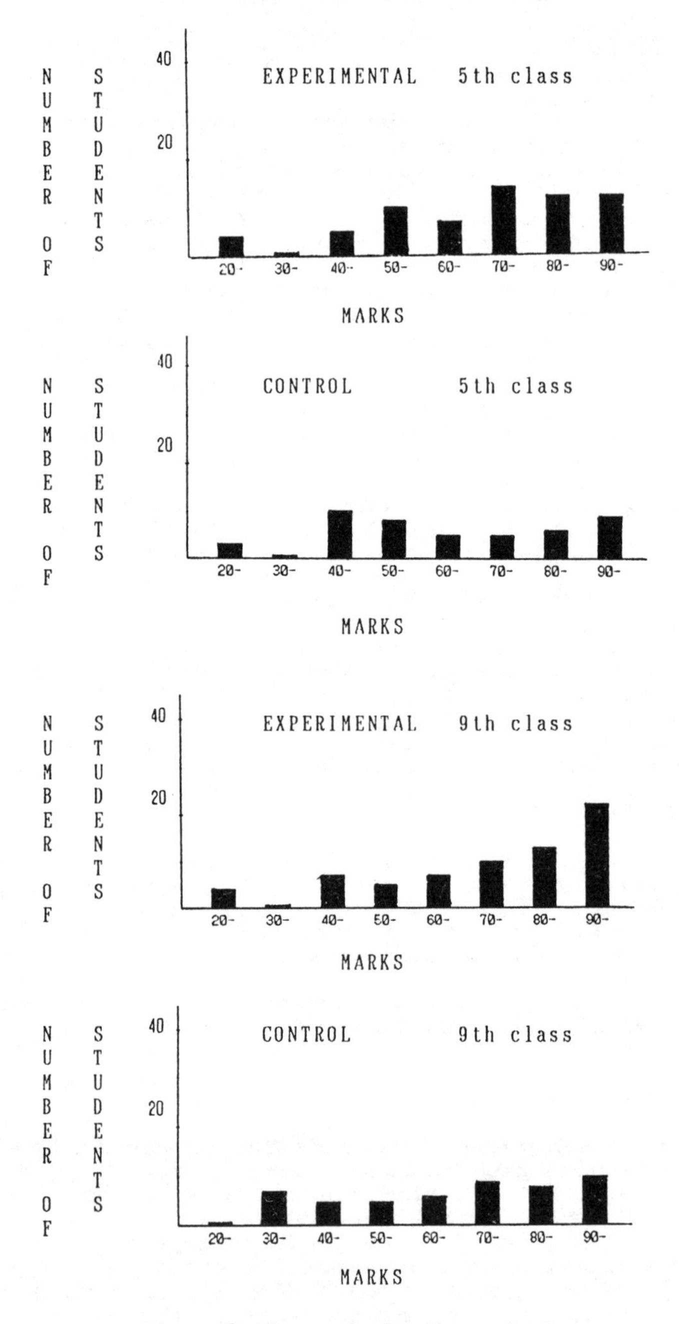

Figure 2: The grade for the control groups and experimental groups.

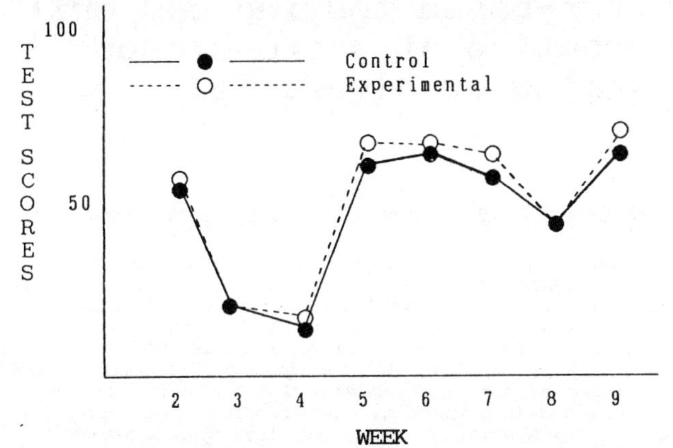

Figure 3: Change in average marks of the CAI test

(dotted line). From Figures 2 and 3 it is evident that the progress of the experimental group was more rapid than that of the control group.

SUMMARY AND PROSPECTS

The author has presented some of the problems of engineering education at university level and proposes a new solution using CAI and CMI together, taking into account the individual student's ability and attitude. The system is constantly being improved, a task rendered simple by the flexibility of the system. The following are some of the new features:

* currently the students' papers containing their impressions, requests and suggestions are hand written. In the new system this will be done on the computer so that the students' thoughts can be analysed quickly;
* the results of the pre-CAI and main CAI tests will be handed out in printed form to the students. The names of the outstanding students will be noted on the handouts. In this way the best students can serve as role models to their classmates and students who are having difficulty will know where they can go for help;
* the conventional lectures should be more persuasive and practical. A new system in which the theories presented will be verified using actual experimental data is now being developed.

ACKNOWLEDGEMENTS

The author wishes to thank Prof.A.Nakajima for his advice, Mr.Y.Takee and Mr.N.Yamazaki for their assistance. Also he would like to thank Ms.E.Chatillon and Mr.G.Emberley for correcting the English.

Yoshkazu Araki has B.E. and M.E. degrees in electrical engineering, and worked as a design engineer before joining Saitama Institute of Technology as a lecturer. His main research interests include reliability of insulators, hydrogen sensors and educational technology. He is a member of several Japanese learned societies.

Address for correspondence: **Yoshikazu Araki,**
1690, Fusaiji, Okabe, Saitama, Japan
Tel. 485 (85) 2521; Fax 485 (85) 2523

28. Computer-based testing and drill and practice at a crossroads: converging or diverging?

Clement Dassa and Jesus Vazquez-Abad, University of Montreal

Abstract: Among the various applications of computers in education and training, testing and drill and practice share some characteristics that make them appear very similar. Their surface look is indeed the same: the user is asked to respond to the items presented (typically requiring the use of previously acquired information) and a managing strategy takes into account this input in deciding the next events (which rarely include direct tutorial instruction). However, upon looking at their purposes one can readily realize that the basic difference between them is of an intrinsic instructional nature: while drill & practice aims at the acquisition or reinforcement of information, testing assesses whether information can be properly recalled by the learner. In spite of this, a common challenge for both is to devise more 'intelligent' management strategies. In this paper, the authors review the similarities and differences among these two applications and discuss the nature of the challenge. In particular, two approaches to tackle the development of more sophisticated courseware are discussed: adaptive testing and performance-responsive drill and practice.

INTRODUCTION

Among the various applications of computers in education and training, **testing** and **drill and practice** share some characteristics that make them appear very similar. Their surface look is indeed the same: the user is asked to respond to the items presented (typically requiring the use of previously acquired information) and a managing strategy takes this input into account in deciding the next events (which rarely include direct tutorial instruction). However, upon looking at their purposes one can readily realize that the basic difference between them is of an intrinsic instructional nature: while drill and practice aims at the acquisition or reinforcement of information, testing assesses whether information can be properly recalled by the student. In spite of this difference, a common challenge for both is to devise more 'intelligent' management strategies. In this paper, we review the similarities and differences among these two applications and discuss the nature of the challenge. In particular, two approaches to the development of more sophisticated courseware are discussed: **adaptive testing** and **performance-responsive drill and practice.**

Testing and drill practice are among the oldest applications of computers in education and training (Rushby, 1979; Suppes, 1966). Testing refers to an activity where the student is asked to demonstrate a particular knowledge or skill for diagnostic and/or evaluation purposes. Its most common form, the exam or quiz, is composed of **items** usually called questions. Drill and practice refers to an activity where the student is asked to apply a particular knowledge or skill for learning and/or reinforcement purposes. Its most common form, the D&P, is composed of **items** usually called problems or prompts.

Thus, at a first level both applications require the development of an **item structure strategy**, involving

* decisions about the stem (one or a collection of alternative phrasings);
* the user input (open answer or selection of choices);

* the support to this input (operational and instructional advice, hint or help available or not); and
* item feedback (elaborate, formative, response-sensitive or succinct, summative).

Whether items are developed as scripted or generative; whether they include parameters (e.g.,in terms of difficulty); and whether feedback is delayed or given immediately after student input, the item structure strategy refers to a local property directly affecting the item-creation or item-writing process, where good-design principles are instrumental in developing all the necessary information. In the actual process of student interaction with the application, however, management strategies as to what to present then become necessary.

Therefore, at a second level both applications require an **item presentation strategy**, involving decisions about the selection of practice or test items for presentation, scoring, banking and elimination purposes. (Although **estimation of learner's score** and **decision to end the session** are often considered third level strategies, we will include them within the **presentation strategy** level for the purpose of the present discussion.) It is mostly at this level that strategies have been sought for developing more sophisticated courseware. In particular, approaches to render item management responsive to the evolution of a student's interaction have been studied under the names of **adaptive testing** and **adaptive instruction.** Criticism of the latter term, mainly concerning the inappropriate use of the term adaptive (Vazquez-Abad and Larose, 1984), has led us to prefer the use of **performance-responsive** instead (Vazquez-Abad and LaFleur, 1990), highlighting the fact that the learner's actual performance is used to diagnose and prescribe what further immediate practice should take place. As for adaptive testing, it calls attention to the fact that a testing activity should always be accompanied by a diagnosis of student learning; and that, in principle, this diagnosis should be made **while,** and not **after,** the student is being tested, and the diagnosis then used to manage the actual composition of the test - e.g.,what (kind of) item to present next.

Thus both performance-responsive D&P, and adaptive testing call for diagnosing while the activity is taking place, and for using this diagnosis to regulate or manage the activity.

DIAGNOSIS DEFINED

The following operational definition of educational diagnosis was proposed in the context of a computerized diagnostic assessment within a classroom setting (Dassa, 1990). However, it may be used to further our understanding of the nature of the diagnostic information required in both computer-based testing and D&P in general. In order to carry out an educational diagnosis one needs to:

1. identify the error; that is, within the classroom, cohort or learning group context, what the instructor or the instructional developer identifies as an incorrect response;
2. describe the nature of the error;
3. describe the instructional context;
4. propose a cause or a set of probable causes for the error;
5. attempt to link the cause(s) to a learning paradigm.

The search for causality in such diagnostic procedures is intricately linked to the description of errors and misconceptions in a way that allows adequate assessment of declarative and procedural knowledge. In order to do so, "we need to identify cognitive procedures that facilitate or interfere with correct performance" (Lane, 1989, p.17).

If, in theory, the thorough analysis of cognitive tasks is a prerequisite to diagnosis, in practice such an approach needs to be constrained by the instructional environment, be it the classroom or the work place; no 'real' diagnosis takes place in a vacuum. Furthermore, depending on this context, diagnosis will focus on one level of information. At the **individual** level, diagnosis can range from the very specific, pertaining to the mastery of a given objective, to a global diagnosis relative to the mastery of abilities. At the **interaction** level between learner and instructor/instructional system, diagnosis may be centred on a variety of factors such as the effect of a particular teaching approach on a given student. Finally, at the **educational/ training system** level, the focus of diagnosis can range from the efficiency of a particular instructional strategy for a given objective to a global diagnosis centring on the characteristics of a whole curriculum - and for that matter, on the educational system which produced it. (It should be noted that the order of presentation of these levels is not indicative of their relative importance.)

In this paper we limit our discussion to the diagnosis of the individual learner. It follows then that the individual level of information prevails. The other two levels are important insofar as the errors made by the learners express, at least partially, the type of relationship to knowledge that the learner is gradually building with the aid of the teacher and the system. This is why any corrective measures, in order to be effective, need to be related to the dynamic description of errors as well as to their cognitive underpinnings.

DIAGNOSIS WITHIN D&P AND ADAPTIVE TESTING

Both testing and drill practice call for a management strategy that develops the actual application (a drill or test) as the student interaction progresses. It is clear that such a strategy will involve diagnosis at the individual level. Two general approaches can be envisaged for this, namely whether the application responds only to the immediate, most recent performance or collects and analyses performance over a period of time before making decisions. (This incidentally, can be used to differentiate between **traditional** and **intelligent** tutorial interventions as well.) Thus, for example, algorithms have been proposed to control drill and practice applications that take into consideration student's performance with a set of practice items before eliminating, scoring or replacing them (Atkinson, 1974; Vazquez-Abad and LaFleur, 1990). Because D&P is an instructional intervention where practice and reinforcement prevail, it is reasonable to define criteria for success in terms of an observed repeated performance. In the case of testing, decisions may be taken at shorter delays: after enough data has been gathered to estimate, say, the mastery of certain objectives, it is no longer necessary to have the learner persist in answering items belonging to the bank used. On the other hand, one may argue that the diagnostic nature of testing could very well justify this in order to collect more data, for the purpose, say, of better estimating the learner's ability. The problem here is to devise an optimal testing strategy, i.e., a strategy that allows the best possible diagnosis under the previously mentioned constraints. Computerized adaptive testing offers such potential; it may be defined as a strategy for the dynamic selection of tasks dependent on the learner's previous performance and orientated towards either formative or summative evaluations (Bunderson et al., 1989).

Because the longitudinal nature of the information collected is essential to its diagnostic interpretation, the strategies presiding over the actual selection of the basic components of an adaptive test (the items) are quite similar to the intervention strategies of drill and practice. In both cases, the rules to build the test or select the problem are dependent not only on the learner's immediate response but also on:

* the learner profile over a period of time, ranging from a specific sequence of responses to a multidimensional description of the individual skills and abilities;
* the direct use of the basic characteristics of the population from which the learner originates in the form of statistical indices contributing to the estimation of certain parameters (e.g.,the difficulty of a given item or task);
* the indirect influence of such information through the perceptions of the developer of the system regarding the way to structure the domain of study, the cognitive prequisites as well as the decision rules controlling the regulatory processes.

More specifically, adaptive testing seems to lend itself to the same two general approaches to a management strategy and point towards either a **traditional** or an **intelligent** adaptive testing session. The more a testing system uses information concerning an individual's performance and difficulties over time, the more 'intelligent' the strategy and the more adequate it is in the context of classroom-based or group-based diagnostic evaluation.

The current dominant procedures for adaptive testing are based on item banks calibrated using Item Response Theory (IRT) models to provide estimates of a learner's ability. The individual score obtained is independent of the particular set of items given. The criteria used in item selection procedures "has as its goal the administration of the most informative item in the item pool at the most recent estimate of ability" (Reckase, 1989, p.13). This means that even though a learner's ability estimation is based on a **profile** of responses to a tailored string of items, the dynamic nature of the information is essentially limited to the learner's most recent performance **during a testing session.**

Thus, in the development of more sophisticated applications one finds a potential point for divergence between testing and drill and practice in whether the learners' most recent performances or their repeated performance should be used to manage the application. Rather than considering this as an indication of a fundamental difference between them, it seems that adaptive testing - at least in the context of diagnostic evaluation - could be conceived of as an intrinsic part of instructional interventions. It would then naturally provide the necessary input to corrective procedures in complex instructional environments such as intelligent tutoring systems. However, it remains to be seen whether computer-based testing and drill and practice could be so reconciled at a conceptual level thereby allowing for concurrent general development efforts.

REFERENCES

Atkinson, R.C.(1974): Teaching children to read using a computer. American Psychologist, March, pp.169-178.

Auger, R., Blais, J-G. and Dassa, C.(1990): In search of an adaptive testing strategy in the context of classroom based diagnostic evaluation. Paper to be presented at the XVIII CSSE Annual Conference, Vancouver, B.C., Canada, June.

Bunderson, C.V., Inouye, D.K. and Olsen, J.B.(1989): The four generations of computerized educational measurement. In, Linn, R.L. (ed), Educational Measurement. Macmillan, London.

Dassa, C.(1988): L'intégration du diagnostic pédagogique aux apprentissages scolaires: de la théorie à la voie informatique. Mesure et evaluation en education, 11, 1, pp.5-24.
Dassa, C.(1990): From a horizontal to a vertical method of integrating educational diagnosis with classroom assessment. The Alberta Journal of Educational Research, 36, 1, pp35-44.
Lane, S.(1989): Implications of cognitive psychology for measurement and testing: diagnosis of procedural errors. Educational Measurement, 8, 4, pp.17-20.
Reckase, M.D.(1989): Adaptive testing: the evolution of a good idea. Educational Measurement, 8, 3, pp.11-15.
Rushby, N.J.(1979): Introduction to Educational Computing. Croom Helm, London.
Suppes, P.(1966): The uses of computers in education. Scientific American, 215, pp.206-220.
Vazquez-Abad, J. and LaFleur, M.(1990): Design of a performance-responsive drill and practice algorithm for computer-based training. Computers and Education, 14, 1, pp.43-52.
Vazquez-Abad, J. and Larose, R.(1984): Computers, adaptive teaching, and operational learning systems. Computers and Education, 8, 1, pp.27-29

Clement Dassa is an Associate Professor in the Départment d'études en éducation et d'administration at the Université de Montréal. His research and teaching interests centre on measurement and evaluation in education, more specifically on classroom assessment and computerized testing. He is currently conducting research, funded by the Social Sciences and Humanities Research Council of Canada, on the integration of diagnostic evaluation in the classroom setting.

Jesus Vazquez-Abad is an Assistant Professor in Science and Technology Education at the Université de Montréal; he is also affiliated with the Canadian Workplace Automation Research Centre of the Department of Communications. His main areas of interest are AI applications in instruction, instructional design, CBT production and educational research methods. He is currently conducting research on the application of intelligent training systems in the Canadian public service.

Address for correspondence: **Prof.C.Dassa** and **Prof.J.Vasquez-Abad**,
Faculte des sciences de l'education,
Universite de Montreal, C.P.6128, Succ 'A',
Montreal, Quebec, Canada H3C 3J7

29. Developmental reading and writing disorders: courseware as a remedial tool

Camillo Gibelli and Michela Ott, Institute of Educational Technology, CNR Italy

Abstract: Many children, irrespective of language or nationality, show difficulties in the reading and writing areas (for dyslexia as a deficit reported in many different orthographies, see Aaron 1989a). As far as these deficits are concerned, the use of computers as a remedial tool is now taking off and there are a number of computer programs devoted to their treatment. The choice of suitable computer programs is undoubtedly very important in the setting up of effective remedial treatments. From data obtained from a long-term experiment held at an Italian Junior High School involving children with severe reading and writing problems who have been undergoing computer-based remedial treatment, we attempt here to draw some conclusions about the main criteria for evaluating software products suitable for the treatment of such problems. We will also attempt to show that if correctly chosen and adequately used, courseware can be considered an effective remedial tool in the realization of the human potential of children considered impaired in the field of reading and writing.

INTRODUCTION

A relatively high total number of children in their first years of school have difficulties with reading and writing. In many cases these difficulties represent a considerable obstacle to these children accepting school itself, leading them to refuse to apply themselves at school; they are also at times a real barrier to continuing with school.

This is also true for the Italian language, despite the fact that it can be considered a relatively 'shallow' or 'transparent' language (regarding the transparency of Italian, see Miceli, Silveri and Caramazza, 1985); that is, there is a fairly regular correspondence between grapheme and phoneme (for details of the characteristics of Italian, see Morchio, Ott and Pesenti, 1989).

The aim of this paper is to report on a long-term experiment which we have been conducting with Italian children who have specific difficulties in the areas of reading and writing and for whom remedial therapies have been adopted which focus on the use of computers and in particular of specific courseware. The promising results obtained with these programmes have encouraged us to try to determine how computer-aided remediation can contribute to the solution of these problems, paying special attention to the characteristics the software has, or should have, for it to represent an effective treatment of these disorders.

WHICH READING AND WRITING DIFFICULTIES?

The term 'reading and writing difficulties' commonly means a series of problems which are typologically and aetiologically very different but which all relate to the ability to both interpret and produce written texts autonomously.

Below we shall deal exclusively with the problems of coding and decoding written language, as these have been the focus of our diagnostic and remediation experiments. We shall deliberately leave aside those disorders which relate to reading comprehension, linguistic expression, lexical richness and the correct interpretation and production of syntatic links.

Within this area - the problems of coding and decoding written language - we shall be referring exclusively to those problems which can be defined as 'specific' to reading and writing (otherwise defined as dyslexia and dysgraphia), i.e. those which are not present at the same time as other cognitive, emotive, behavioural or attentional disorders (for definition of specific as opposed to non-specific problems, see Aaron 1989b).

Our decision to limit remediation to subjects who have specific problems in coding and decoding written language was made according to, on the one hand the need for a very accurate functional diagnosis of the type and the extent of the disorder, and, on the other the need for effective tools. Only on these premises is it possible, in our opinion, to set up a remediation experiment capable of allowing the generalization of the problem and the subsequent definition of strategies which can be generalized and used on a large scale.

WHICH TOOLS?

Computers in remediation

The use of the computer as a remedial tool presents many advantages, particularly compared with traditional tools, which are in general based on the constant presence of a teacher next to the impaired child.

The use of the computer in the remedial process is in itself a source of numerous advantages: it permits resource saving; it allows for greater flexibility; it provides a guarantee of uniformity while at the same time permitting the individualization of the work path; it makes it possible to obtain a detailed analysis of performance and to store it for the purposes of a comparative assessment of the various levels of ability acquisition. In some cases, and for some specific disorders, computers can even be seen as indispensable tools (on the advantages of the use of computers in this field, see Morchio and Ott, 1989).

Generally, when one speaks of the advantages of the use of computers compared to traditional methods, one tends to put particular emphasis on the element of 'motivation'. For it seems that the mere fact of working with a computer makes the activity of recovery agreeable to the child, whereas otherwise it would be laborious, monotonous and demotivating. Certainly in some respects this is true, but it is definitely not the computer alone, *per se*, which guarantees success in a field as special as that of remediation, where the tasks to be completed are by their very nature difficult and the activities to be carried out are often repetitive.

In order to capture the child's attention and consequently to obtain the best results possible, the computer on its own is not enough; it is also the quality and the specific characteristics of the work which the computer enables one to do which play the most important role.

The key elements in computer-aided remediation (as a whole already advantageous) is, therefore, the software. It is this which can qualitatively change the work (and consequently the results which can be obtained); its functional characteristics, its specific nature, its appropriateness to the problem, the degree of interaction it achieves, its capacity to involve and not to tire the user, and to make the work as varied, as lively and as interesting as possible.

Software in Remediation

Criteria of choice

The choice of the software to be used in the context of remediation is one of fundamental importance, on which the result of the entire re-educational process can to a large degree depend.

The parameters on which to base the choice of software may be various. It is particularly important to have a clear understanding of existing products so as to make a correct evaluation of the individual products, in particular with regard to the quality of communication and usability (regarding software evaluation criteria, see Olimpo and Ott, 1989).

The quality of communication has to do mainly with the features of facility and simplicity of interaction between user and machine; the capacity of the product to avoid repetitiveness and thus not tire the user; to provide feedback and both appropriate and effective reinforcement. Basically, one can speak of good-quality communication if the software is capable of initiating a dialogue in which the user is motivated to work, is sufficiently autonomous in carrying out the activities and at the same time is given the right kind of guidance to complete the task at hand.

Usability is a question primarily of the features of ease of use of the product, its flexibility, its adaptability to various situations, and the possibility of modifying its contents in such a way as to present exercises which are of the same type but are still new and varied.

In order to make a functional choice, however, it seems to us to be of fundamental importance that the exercises proposed by the software are interpreted and used in accordance with a theoretical interpretative model (of the normal processes of reading and writing and of the specific disorders). The software should also be effectively integrated into a global remediation program.

Existing products

There are many products at present available on the market which can be used as tools of recovery in the case of specific reading and writing problems. However, they are not always designed specifically to treat these disorders but are often simply programs conceived for linguistic education and are sometimes aimed at the lowest school levels.

There is a basic lack of specific products conceived according to an exemplary theoretical model. As we have seen, it seems always necessary to operate with precise cognitive models and to try to assess the effective value of each individual product on the basis of a theoretical model, in order to insert it into the appropriate remediation procedure.

The existing programs are often very different from each other in terms of content but they can be distinguished typologically into two broad categories on the basis of the instructional strategy they use:

* drill and practice;
* word processing environments for the free production of texts.

Drill and practice exercises are often presented in the form of a game. The most sophisticated use graphics and sounds in a pleasant and fascinating way, but all of them, by their very nature, maintain a structure which is relatively rigid. The standard procedure consists of a question followed by a reply and subsequently possible feedback on the correctness of the reply. These drill and practice programs are in general quite rigidly directive and often place drastic constraints on the type of reading and/or writing modality. This means on the one hand that they are not very attractive for the young user, but on the other they are very functional in terms of the specificity of the recovery program.

The types of possible exercises are varied, ranging from recognizing letters, to cloze tests, to text reconstruction, to games such as crossword puzzles and the putting together and splitting up of words.

One rarely finds relatively complete products comprising exercises of various types which would thus make it possible to alternate and combine the various activities. Often, another limit of these products is the unalterability of the contents, which, of course, drastically limits their usability. The free environments for the writing of texts, on the other hand, are much more flexible and make it possible to carry out more than one activity at the same time and in the same environment (free composition, summary, reconstruction exercises, etc.). In a certain way, therefore,they are much more 'plastic' and seem to be better adapted to various types of demands and, on the whole, to remediation which is composite and varied in content.

The major limit of these programmes lies in the total lack of interaction, i.e. in the absence of any possible feedback or correction, elements which are of fundamental educational importance.

OUR REMEDIAL EXPERIMENT

The context and the activities

The experiment which we report here took place in close collaboration with the Don Milani Scuola Media (Junior High School), an experimental school in Genoa whose organizational structure provides remedial facilities expressly reserved for pupils who are pathologically late in acquiring the use of written language.

The subjects in question are identified at the moment of starting the school in two successive phases. The first round of tests provides quantative data on the levels of speed and precision in reading and on orthographic correctness. The sample which diverges from the norm is subsequently subjected to further investigations aimed at ascertaining whether or not there are specific functional deficits, at the same time as excluding subjects with affective, behavioural or cognitive problems.

The characteristics of the activity towards which the pupils thus chosen are directed can be summarized as follows:

* attention is concentrated on the physical aspects of the linguistic code, on the signifier;
* reading and writing abilities are exercised outside a significant context and are not tied to the learning of contents; the activity is thus aimed at instrumental linguistic competence;
* the exercises are to be seen as ends in themselves, i.e. with no aim other than learning to improve performance in the exercise.

These characteristics give the activity a necessarily repetitive, fragmented character and make it,as it were, 'unnatural' in that it is far removed from the usual methods of exploitation of reading and use of writing. In this sense, the proposed exercises bear the same relation to reading and writing as exercises to strengthen muscles do to practising a sport. The success of the remediation procedure relies on the factors of quantity and intensity, as well as precision of aim. Timed reading, reading from right to left, reading unspaced or incorrectly spaced texts, anagrams, the reading of phrases with words or letters missing, together with the relevant writing tasks, are all situations which are reproducible with varying degrees of accuracy in paper media, but the modalities and operational possibilities which are exercised using such materials are by no means comparable with those exercised by means of a computer and appropriately chosen software. The replies or the manipulation of words and texts repeated several times in a graphically clear way, the immediate comparison between the starting datum proposed by the program and the solution offered by the user, the possibility of seeing the original writing corrected in actual time as the result of one's own actions - these are some of the conditions which increase the efficiency of the exercises. To resort once again to the metaphor of physical education, using such instruments in remedial programmes rather than other more traditional ones is like using specific, corrective gymnastic equipment rather than doing free exercises. If one then also thinks of the possibility of spreading the use of such instruments in schools, and not only on an experimental basis, efficiency should be seen in terms of the facility with which the exercised material can be prepared in advance and adapted to the operators.

The instruments

The experiment we conducted was focused on the use of the computer and makes use primarily of educational software. Obviously, in the choice of the products to use we wanted to ensure that the material used fulfilled the criteria of theoretical and practical functionality referred to above. The software used always permits the contents to be altered in the sense that different exercises can be created on the model of the basic exercise, and those products were chosen which would respond to both types - open environments and drill and practice - since they have both demonstrated different types of value and adaptability. Fundamentally, however, the products were set within an exemplary theoretical model in such a way as to make possible a differential analysis of performances and a functional remediation program.

We based our experiment on the theoretical interpretive model of 'two routes' (Figure 1: for details of the model, see Marshall,J.C. 1984). This model states that there are two possible routes for the decoding of written language: the visual route, which operates in a global fashion, analysing words as whole units; and the phonological route, which works in a sequential way on the basis of the system of grapheme-phoneme conversion and vice versa.

The software used in our experiment was reorganized on the basis of

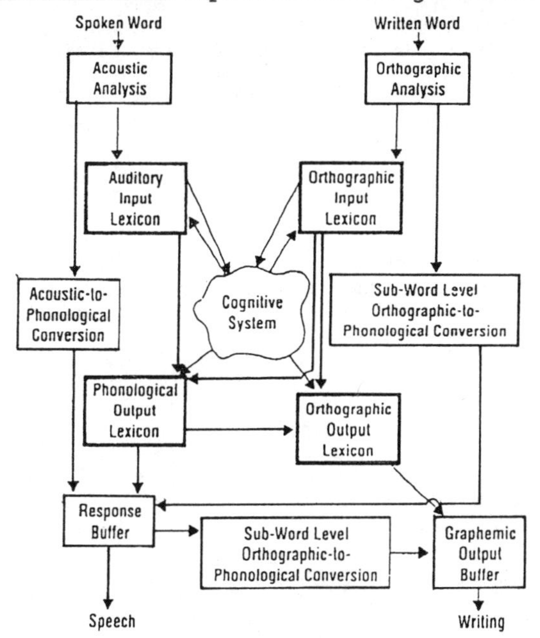

Figure 1: The 'two-route' model for decoding written language.

the theoretical model so as to make it conform to our approach to the problem of 'reading and writing difficulties'. Specifically, we used both programs designed expressly for remedial purposes and programs mainly focused on other tasks, such as comprehension. Because of their flexibility, these last could usefully be employed to prepare exercises centred on the processes of coding and decoding.

These are the characteristics common to the programs used:

* interweaving of reading and writing: the initial stimulus is always given by the suggestion to decodify, followed by a task to be completed in writing;
* possibility of grading and diversifying the activity and/or content by personalizing the remedial procedure and making it progressive;
* providing immediate feedback, by showing the error or rejecting the wrong solutions and, in parallel, providing suggestions about how to proceed;
* registering and quantifying (with various levels of precision) the results of the performances and the 'behaviour' of the user.

Normally, in the time available, (about an hour and a half a week) the pupils alternate between the different working environments proposed. This is a further guarantee that their motivation and consequently attention is maintained and that they therefore do not become tired and too familiar with the exercises.

As the subjects are about 11-13 years old and because the activity is structured in an extremely individual way, we have tried very carefully to avoid generating the sensation of isolation with regard to the machine (its requests, its pace) and of rendering the activity passive. The close and intimate presence of the teacher (in a one-to-three relationship with the pupils) in this sense helps to minimize this problem, as well as to expedite the activation of knowledge processes (meta-cognition) regarding the nature and the specific object of the activity being carried out, the difficulties encountered, and the procedures set in motion by the subject. The experiment has shown that this type of involvement, while not actually resolving the problem, plays a very important part in the success of remediation. The teacher also has the task of regulating the intensity and duration of the commitment required. The direct contact with the pupils permits the analytical observation of the work and provides data for the programming of the following phases of the treatment.

CONCLUSIONS

The computer-aided remedial treatment of developmental reading and writing impairments seems to give on the whole very good results, at least as far as our experiment is concerned.

One of the main problems of such a treatment appears to be the choice of the most fitting software products. We suggest therefore to evaluate first of all the different available products on the basis of their usability and of their quality of communication.

We must however stress that the most important factor appears to be to use products designed or reorganized on the basis of a theoretical model, thus allowing a specific, not generalized, functional remedial treatment for each impairment.

REFERENCES

Aaron, P.G.(1989a): Orthographic systems and developmental dyslexia: a reformulation of the syndrome. In, Aaron, P.G. and Malatesha Joshi, R.(eds), Reading and Writing Disorders in Different Orthographic Systems.Kluwer Academic Publishers, Dordrecht.

Aaron, P.G.(1989b): Dyslexia and Hyperlexia: Diagnosis and Management of Developmental Reading Disabilities. Kluwer Academic Publishers, Dordrecht.

Marshall, J.C.(1984): Toward a rational taxonomy of developmental dyslexias. In, Malateshi Joshi, R. and Whitaker, H.A. (eds), Dyslexia: a Global Issue. Martinus Nijhoff, The Hague.

Miceli, G., Silveri, C. and Caramazza, A.(1985): Cognitive analysis of a case of pure dysgraphia. Brain and Language, 25, pp.187-212.

Morchio, B. and Ott, M.(1989): Using computers in the diagnosis and remediation of developmental dyslexia. In, Bell, C., Davies, J. and Winders, R., Aspects of Educational and Training Technology XXII. Kogan Page, London

Morchio, B., Ott, M. and Pesenti, E.(1989): The Italian language: developmental reading and writing problems. In, Aaron, P.G. and Malateshi Joshi, R.(eds), Reading and Writing Disorders in Different Orthographic Systems. Kluwer Academic Publishers, Dordrecht.

Olimpo, G. and Ott, M.(1989): Guida all'analisi di software didattico: una raccolta di esempi. Instituto Geografico De Agostini, Novara.

Patterson, K.(1986): Lexical but non-semantic spelling. Cognitive Neuropsychology, 3, pp.341-367.

Camillo Gibelli is a teacher in an experimental junior high school, directly involved in the recovery of children who have reading and writing impairments; in this field he collaborates with the Institute of Educational Technology of the National Research Institute (CNR).

Michela Ott is a researcher at CNR, working in the field of educational technology and computational linguistics.

The two authors are presently working on the project: 'Developmental Dyslexia and Computers', supported by CNR.

Address for correspondence: **Dr. C.Gibelli and Dr.M.Ott,**
Instituto Tecnologie Didattiche (CNR),
Via all'Opera Pia, 11,
16145 Genoa, Italy.

30. Developing informational technology skills for nurse teachers

Helen J. Betts, Wessex CAL Project, Winchester

Abstract: The paper outlines the experiences of a five day workshop, with a distance learning component, which nine nurse-teachers attended. There was initially a three day workshop covering wordprocessing, databases, spreadsheets and other content-free software; there were four main facilitators and four co-facilitators who contributed as part of their own staff development. The participants then undertook a work-based study of one piece of software from the workshop. After ten weeks they returned for a further two days and presented their projects and various experiences. The sessions were organized so that participants could work at their own pace and receive help when required. The ethos of the workshop valued the previous experiences of the participants.

INTRODUCTION

The aim of this paper is to share the experiences of a five day workshop, with a distance learning component, on 'PCs in midwifery and nurse education' organized by the Wessex Regional Health Authority's Computer-Assisted Learning (CAL) Project.

The Project

The Wessex CAL Project was originally conceived in 1985 as a major staff development initiative by Wessex Regional Health Authority, in collaboration with King Alfred's College, Winchester. A non-nurse Teacher Fellow was appointed to King Alfred's as the project tutor.

As the project's work developed a senior nurse teacher was appointed as a second Teacher Fellow. These two full time project tutors complemented each other in their innovative work within the Wessex Region, facilitating workshops for teachers in eight schools of nursing and one midwifery school. They were responsible to a steering group which was chaired by the Regional Nursing Advisor.

For the work of the project to have any impact a minimal computer resource was required initially by each school of nursing. One BBC Model B computer, monitor, disk drive and printer was provided by Education Advisory Group money and this was supplemented over the following two years by local funding.

The workshops organized by the project tutors were on two levels. Level One was a basic computer awareness course over a five day period, held several times a year with a maximum of fifteen participants each time. Three schools of nursing were eventually able to take over running these courses, so freeing the project tutors to run Level Two courses.

A prerequisite for attending a Level Two course was to have completed a Level One course. Level Two took the form of a small school-based action research study on one piece of software. This lasted nine weeks, starting with a three day workshop and then eight weeks' school-based study, with visits and support from the project tutors, and then a review day. Three courses were run which eighteen tutors completed. This initial phase of the project ended in September 1987: the project then had a period of reflection and considered its future.

THE WORKSHOP

Introduction

I was appointed as Project Tutor in February 1989. An early task was to plan and implement a national course on computers in nurse education, as part of the ENB Teacher Refresher Course programme. Since the conception of the project in 1985 there have been developments in computers and information technology (IT) both in Wessex and nationally. It was thus decided to base this course/workshop on MS-DOS personal computer (PC) machines, to give nurse education compatibility with the Open University and other commercial bodies who have made MS-DOS their standard.

Most schools of nursing in Wessex have bought hard disk PC machines to supplement their BBC computers. Resource management in the Health Service is currently developing rapidly and computers are being installed in the wards; these are mainly PC compatible machines. PCs may be installed in schools of nursing for students to learn the hospital system in a safe environment.

Planning

Planning for the workshop began in early 1988 when a small working party was convened to propose a course outline and consider the role of a new project tutor. With my subsequent appointment planning began in earnest.

The initial programme contained about 25% MS-DOS compatible software and 75% BBC computer software, but the local and general changes in computing over the intervening year made the planning team decide to make the whole workshop content MS-DOS compatible.

A meeting was then arranged for all the Level Two course participants and other Tutors within the Region, known to have an active interest in computers. The programme was outlined and volunteers requested (four offered, and learned as part of their own staff development) to co-facilitate the workshop with four main facilitators. The co-facilitators received software training and because this was mainly 'Shareware' they were able to take copies back to their Schools to gain more experience. Twelve people were accepted for the workshop, on the understanding that they had access to a MS-DOS compatible computer.

Part 1

Eventually nine participants arrived at King Alfred's College in late September for the first, three day part of the workshop. Most of the first day was spent familiarizing the participants with the MS-DOS operating system for the PC, some of its useful commands and menu systems. A few participants already had some knowledge of MS-DOS and were eager to help those who were struggling. There were several facilitators also available such that the participants had 1:2 help. The individuals soon became a group and were interacting well by the end of the first day.

The second morning was spent looking at a wordprocessing package, a skill thought necessary by most teachers, while in the afternoon and the following morning three options were available - desk-top publishing (DTP), databases and electronic book systems, then DTP, spreadsheets and expert systems. There were two facilitators to each option and the participants divided themselves evenly between the groups. This arrangement of options permitted a wider range of experiences for the participants so making the workshop more personal.

During the third afternoon the learning contracts for the distance learning part of the course were negotiated and written and verbal evaluations held. The nine participants all appeared to enjoy the first part of the course and were very enthusiastic when they left. One of the strong points was that there were always several facilitators around so no participant ever had to wait long for help.

Everything suggested that it had been a success, but its true value would be demonstrated in the distance learning part of the course.

Part 2

Back in their schools of nursing the participants undertook a study of one piece of software chosen from among those used in the workshops. Most chose to investigate a 'Shareware' package so they could take a copy away with them (budgets in nursing schools are small!). Those who chose to study a different (inexpensive) package were given the address of the supplier, but delivery took time from the ten week study period. During Part 2, I acted as a 'Hotline' for the participants, but had very few telephone calls, although I did call them to make sure all was going to plan. Some of the participants had few problems, others overcame extreme difficulties to complete their projects, others still had hardware problems which meant that they did not complete their projects, but all demonstrated the commitment that any distance learning needs.

Part 3

In early December eight of the participants returned to Winchester, and one sent apologies, for the final part of the course. Each participant was invited to recount his/her experiences during the ten weeks. Those who completed their projects produced some excellent work and were congratulated.

* One participant produced a school newsletter using a desk-top publisher on floppy disc only (eight disks which constantly needed changing). His school has now placed an order for a hard disk PC computer as a direct result of his work.
* A second participant used a spreadsheet to look at student sickness in his school. He was able to demonstrate that one unit had a higher sickness level than the others. The spreadsheet he created is now being used as a standard in the school.
* A third compiled a database of journal articles for the department in which she works, first reformatting the hard disk of the computer!
* A fourth compiled a database of references for a course she is studying; this will become a valuable resource for her school.

The other four participants all came from the same school. The computer they had originally hoped to use was not available, so they had ordered two PCs on returning from the workshop, which took seven weeks to arrive.

Their motivation to complete their learning contract was high and so the group agreed to give them another eight weeks to complete their study and a follow-up day was arranged at their school. This has not yet taken place but I am to visit them shortly.

The afternoon was spent in two groups with one looking at a hypertext facility and the other at communications networks. On the last morning, following group negotiations, everyone looked at a program with obvious use for all of them, which constructs and marks objective questions. Databases and expert systems were also offered as options later in the morning. Following lunch we had a 'trouble-shooting' session where we tried to solve any of the participants' immediate problems relating to their projects and how to take them forward.

To close the workshop we had a group discussion on the way forward for them and IT in their schools. This is a time of change in nurse education; new courses are being developed in which IT must be integrated into the curriculum. The participants now felt they had some knowledge on which to base this integration.

REALIZING HUMAN POTENTIAL?

How does the above account of a workshop for nurse-teachers in IT encompass the ethos of the conference theme?

On a personal level, for me as Project Tutor, I feel I realized my potential, or as Maslow says, "self-actualized". I had a 'peak experience' - a rare event - I wanted to share.

The planning of the workshop was hard work, and I had the organizing role, so it could have all gone very wrong. The 'peak experience' was working alongside three colleagues whom I respect tremendously. We all have different skills which complement each other well and we worked as a real team, which was obviously to the benefit of the participants. It was a joy to be part of the sharing of knowledge, the team spirit and the cooperation which fostered the experience for the participants.

The participants quickly worked through the group dynamics and also became a team, helping each other and working with the facilitators. We became a group working towards a common goal, sharing and helping each other. This facet of the workshop has most personal meaning for me. I have been in contact with several of the participants this year and regard them as friends as well as colleagues.

For my three colleagues, I cannot say if it was a 'peak experience', but I know they all enjoyed the experience of working together. The fact that the workshop was a success must at least have satisfied their 'esteem needs'! (One level down on Maslow's hierarchy).

All learning should be fun. I believe that the participants experienced this through the facilitative learning environment of the workshop. They did learn information technology skills, as was demonstrated in their projects and the continuing work in their schools. But more than this I hope they learned that computers are not frightening; that given time they could learn to apply their skills to their workplace and integrate IT effectively into the curriculum; and above all that they can do it! They each have a potential which was sparked in the workshop, if not brought to fruition and each one of them can 'self-actualize' and realize their own potential.

Miss Helen Betts took a degree in Nursing at Newcastle upon Tyne Polytechnic, then trained as a midwife in Cardiff. After gaining the Advanced Diploma in Midwifery, working for 3 years as a midwifery Sister, and then obtaining the PGCEA, she took a teaching post in the Midwifery School in Basingstoke. Miss Betts is currently on a two year secondment from Basingstoke to the Wessex CAL Project.

Address for correspondence: **Miss H.Betts,**
Wessex CAL Project Tutor,
Royal Hampshire County Hospital,
Winchester, Hampshire SO22 5DG, UK

31. Tools for hyper-media authoring

Philip Barker, Teesside Polytechnic

Abstract: Within education the effective realization of human potential depends critically upon our ability to provide pedagogic environments that are motivating, efficient and cost-effective. This paper outlines the hyper-media paradigm and the way in which it can be used to achieve these requirements - both for users and producers of instructional resources.

INTRODUCTION

The evolution of the human species has been accompanied by the creation of a wide range of tools and machines and a variety of prosthetic aids and devices. Some examples of the various generic classes of artificial aid now in common use include: the clock; the typewriter; the motor car; and the computer. Undoubtedly, computers are one of the most versatile types of machine that the human species has ever invented. Indeed, when describing the human interface to computer systems Roosen-Runge (1989) has used the term 'universal prosthesis'.

The various types of artificial aid upon which we have all now become so dependent have each been designed in order to enhance or augment some aspect of human activity. Indeed, many of these aids can now be used to develop and extend both physical and cognitive performance. Currently, there is much interest in the area of human performance engineering (Bailey, 1982). An important aspect of work in this area is the design of performance aids that will facilitate the complete realization of human potential within any given domain of activity. Naturally, the full realization of a human's educational potential is of paramount importance both to society and to that person's well-being.

In the context of performance aid production, the concept of the 'science of text engineering', was suggested by Balajthy (1989): "the flexibility of text presented on a computer monitor holds tremendous potential for the improvement of education. Words can be highlighted in text, questions interspersed, definitions of unknown vocabulary requested, more or less complex explanations provided, and so forth, all at the command of the reader or under the control of software authors."

Indirectly, in the above quotation, Balajthy is referring to the ability of the new information storage and processing technologies to allow us to organize a text corpus in a reactive, non-linear way. The result of such an exercise is often referred to as hyper-text. This paper discusses a broader issue; it describes how knowledge (independent of its containing medium) can be organized in a non-linear fashion. Such an arrangement is often referred to by the term hyper-media.

Education is undoubtedly the vehicle by which the realization of human potential will be achieved. Because of its importance within educational settings this paper briefly describes the hyper-media paradigm. It then goes on to review some tools for authoring instructional resources based upon this approach. Finally, we present some hints as to how hyper-media (and intelligent hyper-media) might be used to achieve the more effective realization of human potential.

THE HYPER-MEDIA PARADIGM

Human performance within any given task domain varies quite considerably. Furthermore, this performance is invariably influenced by the quality of the tools that are available for executing tasks within the chosen domain. Therefore, within education we should be particularly concerned with the production of high quality tools and aids that will facilitate pedagogic processes. Two basic types of tools are envisaged. First, those that will facilitate the cognitive and motor skill development of students. Second, tools that will allow the facile creation of learning and training resources. In other words, we should be designing performance aids both for students and for producers of resources (authors and designers).

Unfortunately, most approaches to instruction suffer from many inherent limitations; alas, there is no universal pedagogic panacea. The limitations of many of the conventional tools that we use to effect learning and training processes have been extensively discussed and debated. They are well documented in the literature. In the past, many of the short-comings of computer-assisted learning (CAL) and computer-based training (CBT) have originated from the need to impose a linear or quasi-linear structure on knowledge. This is very unnatural. Because of this 'historical' limitation we anticipate the future widespread use of the hyper-media paradigm as a 'way forward' towards the creation of better learning and training aids. The essential difference between linear and non-linear arrangements of knowledge is illustrated in Fig.1. Hypermedia, then, is a generic term used to describe non-linear arrangements of information and knowledge. As can be seen from Figure 1 the paradigm allows the creation of complex net- or web-like structures analogous in shape and form to a 'fishing net' (McAleese, 1989). A major

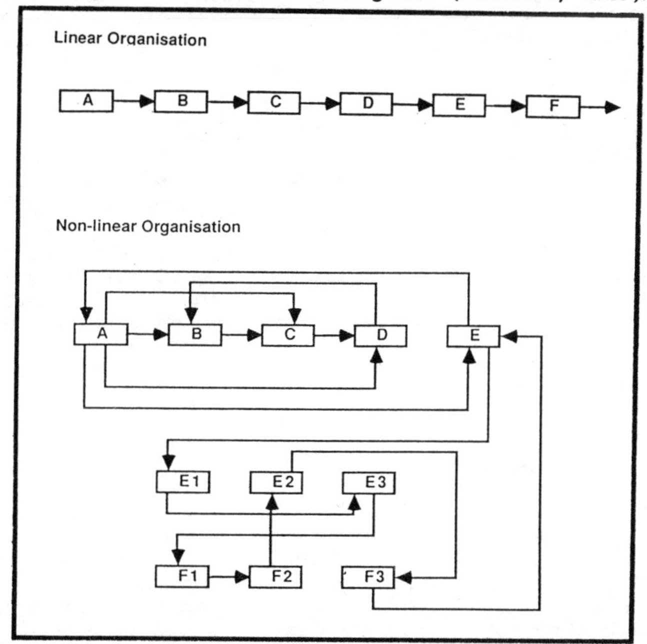

Figure 1: Linear and non-linear arrangements of knowledge.

attraction of the hyper-media approach to knowledge handling is the tremendous flexibility it offers to the ways in which knowledge can be structured, accessed and displayed. The simplicity with which knowledge units can be inter-linked (through multiple linkages) also enables different user-views of stored knowledge to be achieved (Barker, 1987).

The implementation of the hyper-media paradigm depends basically on two types of technology - one hardware and one software. The first important requirement is the availability of high-resolution graphic displays that support windows and pointing operations (Barker, 1989). The second is the availability of software that will allow:

* the incorporation of 'buttons' or 'hot-spots' within a knowledge unit;
* the facile linking of a button to other units of knowledge.

This latter facility allows the hyper-media author to build up the type of network structure that is illustrated in Figure 1. Software tools that facilitate this process are often referred to as hyper-media authoring tools: examples are presented in the following section.

Currently, the commonest form of hyper-media is hyper-text. However, hyper-imagery is gaining rapid popularity. Other possibilities (such as hyper-sound, hyper-animation, hyper-reality and hyper-surrogation) are not yet widely used although there is much scope for them in a large number of educational contexts (Barker, 1990a).

HYPER-MEDIA AUTHORING TOOLS

Two broad types of tools are commonly used for hyper-media authoring: conventional tools and media orientated tools. The latter class usually offers specialist 'services' for use with particular media - for example, CD-ASSIST for authoring CD-ROM based resources. In this paper we shall be concerned only with examples of general purpose tools. Four examples of such tools are briefly considered: HyperCard; LinkWay; Guide; and KnowledgePro.

HyperCard

HyperCard was one of the first widely available (and low cost) hyper-media authoring tools. Examples of its use are well-documented in the literature (Raper and Green, 1989; Barden, 1989). As its name implies, the system implements a 'notecard' metaphor. That is, each screenful of information is likened to a notecard. Screens (or cards) are built up from four basic types of entity: backgrounds; text fields; pictures; and buttons. Collections of cards are referred to as stacks. Using HyperCard buttons it is possible to link cards together in virtually limitless ways - thereby creating non-linear structures similar to that depicted in Figure 1. HyperCard does not support colour and only limited animation is possible. However, materials produced outside of the system can be easily 'imported'. HyperCard is easy to use and embeds the 'standard' Macintosh WIMP interface.

LinkWay

LinkWay is a more recent hyper-media tool that runs on PCs and compatibles. In many ways it is very similar to HyperCard. As its name suggests it provides a tool that enables units of multimedia knowledge to be linked together in various ways so as to produce a hyper-media network. LinkWay uses a 'page' metaphor that requires users to think of a screen of information as being analogous to a page of material in a conventional book. Pages may contain text, pictures and buttons. Colour is supported and provided suitable hardware is available it is also possible to create windows in which moving images (from a video disc) can be displayed. Collections of pages are referred to as folders. The base page within a folder can be used to hold material that is common to other pagers in that folder. The base page can be cloned and other pages can be copied, cut and pasted. A page can be linked to any other page - either in the same folder or within another folder. Like HyperCard, LinkWay employs an easy to use WIMP interface.

Guide

Guide is probably one of the most sophisticated hyper-media authoring tools in current use. Versions of the system are available for both Macintosh and IBM-PC environments. Although primarily not intended as a CAL/CBT authoring tool it could, in principle, be used as such. Two essential features of Guide are its embedded text-processing and graphics facilities. It is, therefore, ideally suited for the creation of 'interactive documents' containing text and pictures (Brown, 1986; Ritchie, 1989). The text can be cross-referenced using standard hyper-text conventions. Buttons may also be embedded within graphics so that it becomes easy to create hyper-image networks analogous in form to that illustrated in Figure 1. Guide is a very powerful tool. It contains many useful features such as an online help system, a backtrack icon and a glossary facility. The power of Guide is reflected in its more difficult to use WIMP-based end-user interface. However, once mastered Guide provides many of the facilities needed for online authoring in a very flexible fashion.

KnowledgePro

All of the systems described above are fairly 'standard' examples of hyper-media authoring tools. Unfortunately, none of these tools embeds any mechanisms that allow substantial degrees of 'intelligence' to be built into the nodes of a hyper-media network. In contrast, KnowledgePro (which is an example of a knowledge processing environment) can function both as a hyper-media authoring tool and as an expert system shell (Barker, 1990b). It is therefore extremely useful for implementing 'intelligent hyper-media' networks that can show some degree of adaptivity to the needs of different users. KnowledgePro is a PC-based tool that provides an 'easy to use' authoring environment which enables quite complex applications to be created using a minimal subset of commands. These applications may embed hyper-text, hyper-images (based on static pictures), video disc pictures and material taken from CD-ROM. Because of the sophisticated range of facilities that it offers, KnowledgePro is gaining widespread popularity as a professional hyper-media authoring tool.

CONCLUSION

We have been using the authoring tools described above for the creation of a number of different types of 'electronic book' (Barker, 1990c). This work has given us invaluable experience with respect to assessing the relative utilities of these tools. We have also gained much useful design experience with respect to the production of interactive documents for the support of learning and training activities.

Undoubtedly, the hyper-media approach has a great deal to offer those involved in instructional resource production. Two major attractions are the flexibility and adaptability that it can be used to achieve. For example, resources can be designed in such a way that they can embed multiple parallel learning pathways. Each of these pathways can be designed for a different type of learner. Learners can then 'flip' from one learning route to another - depending upon their mood, preference, ability or learning style. Similarly, through the incorporation of simple artificial intelligence techniques it would be possible to monitor student performance and then make these transitions automatically - thereby allowing a document dynamically to adapt its presentation and content to the particular needs of individual students. We are currently exploring these possibilities in the work that we are undertaking into the fabrication of 'intelligent electronic books' (Barker, 1990d).

ACKNOWLEDGEMENTS

The work described in this paper has been partly funded by the United Kingdom's Training Agency under contract T89/23H/189. The support of Intellisoft (UK) Ltd. is also gratefully acknowledged.

REFERENCES

Bailey, R.W.(1982): Human Performance Engineering: A Guide-for Systems Designers. Prentice-Hall, Englewood Cliffs, N.J.

Balajthy, E.(1989): Computers and Reading - Lessons From the Past and Technologies of the Future. Prentice-Hall, Englewood Cliffs, N.J.

Barden, R.(1989): Developing a HyperCard-based intelligent training system. Educational and Training Technology International, 26, 4, pp.361-367.

Barker, P.G. and Proud, A.(1987): A practical introduction to computer-assisted instruction. Part 10: Knowledge-based CAL. British Journal of Educational Technology, 18, 2, pp.140-160.

Barker, P.G.(1989): Basic Principles of Human-Computer Interface Design. Century-Hutchinson, London.

Barker, P.G.(1990a): Hyper-Media and Beyond. Paper presented at CBT Update, CBT seminar organised by the National Computing Centre, Connaught Rooms, London, 25th January.

Barker, P.G.(1990b): KnowledgePro: a review and assessment. Engineering Applications of Artificial Intelligence, in press.

Barker, P.G.(1990c): Human-computer interface design for electronic books. Paper submitted to INTERACT '90, IFIP Conference on Human-Computer Interaction, Cambridge, 27-31 August.

Barker, P.G.(1990d): Intelligent electronic books. Paper submitted to Journal of Artificial Intelligence in Education.

Brown, P.J.(1986): Viewing documents on a screen. In Lambert, S. and Ropiequet, S. (Eds): CD-ROM The New Papyrus, pp.175-184. Microsoft Press, Redmond,WA.

McAleese, R.(1989): Hypertext: Theory into Practice. Blackwell Scientific Publications, Oxford, UK.

Raper, J. and Green, N.(1989): The development of a Hypertext-based tutor for geographical information systems. British Journal of Educational Technology, 20, 3, pp.164-172.

Ritchie, I.(1989): HYPERTEXT - moving towards large volumes. The Computer Journal, 32, 6, pp.516-523.

Roosen-Runge, P.H.(1989): The interface as universal prosthesis. Paper presented at NATO Advanced Research Workshop on Multi-Media Interface Design in Education, Il Ciocco, Italy, 21-24 September.

Dr.Philip Barker is a member of the Interactive Systems Research Group in the School of Information Engineering at Teesside Polytechnic. He has written widely on the use of computers and of authoring systems and the contribution they can make to improved teaching and learning.

Address for correspondence: **Dr.P.Barker,**
Interactive Systems Research Group,
School of Information Engineering,
Teesside Polytechnic, Middlesbrough,
Cleveland TS1 3BA, UK

Section 5: The use of technology

32. Bridging the gap between seeing and doing

Andy Finney MultiMedia Corporation

Abstract: A consideration of the purposes of, and some examples of the use of multimedia applications.

The first chapter of Ecclesiastes, always a good place for a quote or a song lyric, includes this bit:

> **All things are full of labour; man cannot utter it: the eye is not satisfied with seeing, not the ear filled with hearing.**

Which, for the purposes of this argument, I take to mean that just talking about, looking at, or hearing about something is not enough. The verse also goes on to say that there is nothing new under the sun, which brings us on to the subject of educational - and informational - technology and how it might just be able to bridge that gap between the talking, the seeing, hearing... and the labour...the doing.

You don't get a user guide for life. Your mother was not given a manual showing how to operate, maintain and, when necessary, upgrade the baby. Growing up is one of the things that you can't really be taught about ... and you wouldn't believe it if anybody tried to teach you!

I don't want to get into a discussion about learning styles because that is out of my competence, but some things can provide a guide to using technology for teaching:

* Firstly people learn best when they don't think they are being taught.
* Secondly **tell me and I forget, show me and I remember.**
* Thirdly ... you always think <u>you</u> are moving even though it is really the train next to you.

Couple all this with a suspension of disbelief and you get a fairly straightforward set of reasons why <u>**flight simulators**</u> are useful. I have even been told that one computer flight simulator is so effective that it counts towards your pilot's licence!

Simulations ... and surrogates ... are the buzzwords here. Pragmatically a simulator is a good way of letting a pilot shear his wings on one of those blocks of flats alongside the Hong Kong flightpath without making too much mess. It is 'safer' and, above all, more cost effective to use a simulator than to train airline pilots on real aircraft with real passengers. And it keeps the computer graphics people in business.

So simulators can provide a good way of training people without the risks, and costs, associated with letting them learn on the job.

The <u>**Ecodisc,**</u> produced by Peter Bratt when he was at the BBC, uses a simulation as a part of process-led learning. The aim is to learn about the environment but it is disguised as a management simulation where you have to manage a nature reserve. In the course of this you have to learn about the environment you will manage and you do this by studying the plants and animals in the reserve. In Ecodisc you can set remote cameras to see what wild life lurks in the undergrowth overnight and check the cameras next morning; on the original version you can even put a radio collar on an animal and follow its movements, you can sample the fish in the lake and count the plants in an area of land ... just as you would in the real world.

In the Ecodisc you can walk, and even fly, around the nature reserve you are learning about, by using **surrogate travel** techniques. Surrogate travel developed from research done at Massachusetts Institute of Technology for the American military. The first surrogate travel videodisc let you move around the town of Aspen in Colorado. On **Domesday** we had a group of surrogate walks (sounding friendlier than **travel**) around different houses and a couple of towns ...to let you explore from your armchair. Surrogate walks enable the user to move at will through an environment to explore it. The walks on Domesday show various types of British housing, ranging from a flat in a tall tower block to a stone-built rural cottage. Besides the houses there are walks around a town centre, an area of urban housing, a farm and a forestry plantation.

The walks are built up of thousands of still photographs which are taken according to a computer algorithm to enable the appropriate image to be selected following the appropriate action by the user. Here is a small walk example based around eight photographs taken at every viewpoint:

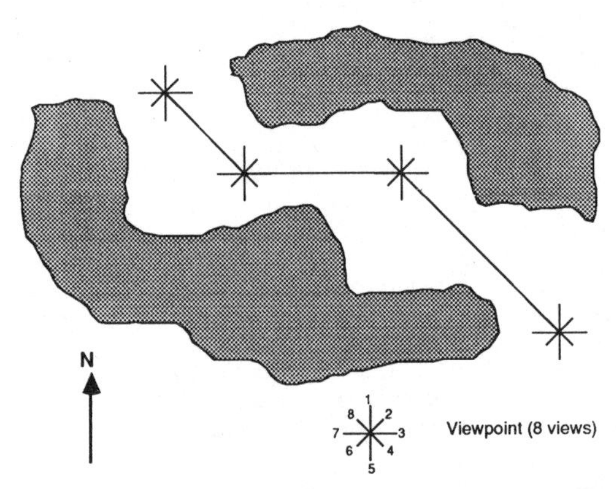

The photographs are all taken in groups of eight at 45 degrees to each other, so they complete a circle. With a lens of about 28mm on a 35mm still camera you get an overlap between adjacent shots. These eight shots always rotate in the same sense - in the case of Domesday this was going to the right, clockwise from above.

Every individual photograph has associated with it two sets of data, called vectors - the direction vector and the detail vector. The former holds the frame number of the shot you get by moving forwards. If there is no shot this vector is empty. The detail vector holds a pointer into a data table where the software can find information relating to things in that shot. In the case of Domesday that information is always a pointer to a series of photographs showing close-ups of things in the shot, hence calling it a detail vector. On the final disc output the software puts a magnifying glass icon on the screen to indicate the presence of detail. The menu bar indicates whether you can move in a particular direction. You can always turn on the spot to rotate your viewpoint around.

There is one rather innovative use of a surrogate walk on Domesday which is the **Gallery**. This is the entry level of the National Disc and is a computer-generated art gallery. The images were generated professionally on a Bosch FGS-4000 computer graphics system. It is an art gallery in which hang pictures that iconically represent the picture sets available on the National Disc. The user can walk around the gallery and point and click on a picture and so access the group of pictures 'behind' it. By walking around the Gallery the user is browsing in the database in a way that would be difficult by any other means.

This method is not the only way of doing a walk. Many implementations use a technique more akin to making a movie, where stepping forwards and backwards are the only actions allowed; and some add occasional places where you can turn around. A walk shot for the DVI (Digital video interactive) demonstrator on the Palenque archaeological site in Mexico shot the 'look around' points with a fish-eye lens pointing upwards. All the horizon was then captured around the rim of the frame and it could be unwrapped by computer to produce a continuous strip of the horizon view. Like this:

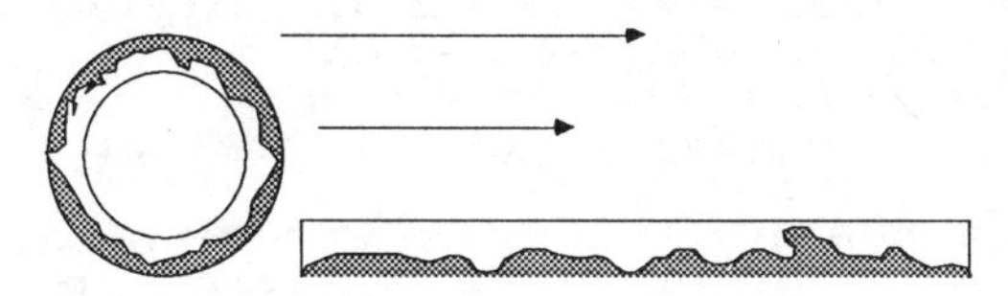

One of the problems with shooting eight stills at a point, as on Domesday, was that time elapses between the shots and things move. With the Palenque approach the whole horizon is captured at one time.

The techniques of surrogate travel are all, in essence, related to the flight simulator but with simpler technology, and as such should prove very useful.

Another project that combines elements of surrogacy and simulation is for television training. It is part of a series called **Action!** which David Allen at the BBC (and later the MultiMedia Corporation) devised and which use interactive video simulations. In the case of the **EastEnders Gallery**, again from the comfort of your armchair, you can explore the Queen Vic pub and vision mix some scenes from EastEnders (a top-rated British soap opera made by the BBC). This package puts you in the role of vision mixer, in the TV control gallery. You can walk around the control set, look at the scripts and plans, and finally mix three cameras in real time during scenes from the programme.

How is this done? Well, several interleaved recordings,each covering a camera,are played with the videodisc player playing only the segments that relate to a particular camera at any one time. This relies on the ability of some videodisc players to jump around on the disc very quickly and looks something like this:

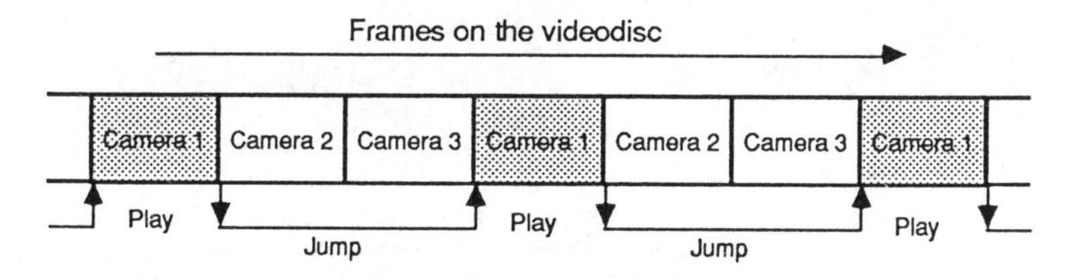

Surrogate travel can be taken a stage further. **Virtual reality** is where a computer tracks your actions and allows you to move through an environment that only exists in the computer. The Domesday Gallery is a very simple example of this. (This raises whole issues of identity and self awareness that are covered by Douglas R.Hofstadter and Daniel C.

Dennett in their book 'The Mind's I'. Here a remote body is controlled by a person in much the same way as in virtual reality. It's an essay called 'Where am I' by Dennett). NASA are behind the main research in this area as virtual reality has applications in space travel. In a virtual reality the voyager is wired up to a computer that can sense his body position and is wearing three dimensional glasses which show the world image generated by the computer. When he puts his hand up in front of his face he sees a computer generated hand there. When he reaches up and picks up a book from a computer generated shelf he can seem to be actually picking it up.

We can also make the experience of interacting with the computer more like the real world. **The real world model** is a good way of analysing functionality. However ... beware that one man's clear, normative real world is another man's fantasy. It is often easily seen with door handles. The classic is where you are asked to push on a handle (rather than pull on it). This confuses people so often that I wonder how an architect can bear to specify it. I suspect it is a triumph of form over function.

The standard road sign for roadworks is a triangle with an icon of a man bending down using a shovel. But Viv Stanshall proposed another subject for that icon with the title of his album **Men Opening Umbrellas Ahead**(think about it) and similar thoughts apply to the Batman film logo. It shows the bat symbol, but could equally be seen as an open mouth with fangs and tonsils! Two different mechanisms here. One is simply a misunderstanding whereas the other is a perceptual ambiguity rather like the two faces making a vase.

In the opposite case I offer an example of an icon which has no function. It is a windmill which exists as a mosaic icon on a pavement in the Azores. A shot of such a pavement is also shown. Perhaps the ancient Egyptian hieroglyphs were an early attempt at a WIMP interface!

Andy Finney was one of the founders of the BBC Domesday Project and the BBC Interactive TV Unit. He is currently a producer, and Technical Manager, with the MultiMedia Corporation in London (Tel.+44 71 722 7595, Fax +44 71 722 7027).

33. The utilization of media in the lecture from a didactical perspective

C.J.Nel, Rand Afrikaans University

Abstract: This paper examines the problem of perceiving media as mere supplements to the teaching process. This situation is possibly the result of a 'short circuit' in the relationship between media experts and teaching experts. The advice given to educators by media experts is usually not in the form of didactic guidelines. If lecturers use media as the point of departure and then seek applications in the teaching situation, it may arouse avoidance and possible resistance among lecturers, since media will then not be an intrinsic component of the teaching process. The categorical forming theory, as put forward by Klafki, offers a possible solution to the problem. In applying this theory, the media expert can advise the lecturer on the utilization of media in the lecture.

INTRODUCTION

The question can be asked if there has been any improvement in education since the (South African) Human Science Research Council's (1981) comprehensive investigation into the provision of education, and if the role of educational technology, as spelt out in the investigation, has subsequently been treated on its merits.

With regard to the latter question, there are serious doubts. Verification of this statement can possibly be found from reports on investigations in other countries concerning media utilization, that concluded that very little had been done. For Example, Coombs (1985) shows that the report made in the sixties by the International Institute for Educational Planning on the effect of instructional television, affirms twenty years later that no real significant results have been achieved.

One of the problems that has arisen is that educational media, after twenty years, still functions as a mere supplement to instruction, with the exception that it now extends over a broader spectrum. As a possible cause of this problem, the assumption can be made that there is probably a didactic short circuit in the media-educational relationship.

When looking for possible solutions it may be inadvisable to begin with media and then look for areas of application. This will only arouse avoidance and possibly resistance among lecturers. The use of media for media's sake implies that media is merely a supplement to education.

THE LECTURE AS AN APPLICATION AREA

The utilization of media is part and parcel of viable didactical practice. This means, as in the presentation of a lesson at school, that the lecture proceeds in episodes and in each episode different media can be used. The function of the media varies according to the different stages or procedural moments of the lecture. (The acid test for media utilization will thus not only refer to the lecture as a whole, but to the effectiveness of media application in each episodal phase.)
The model of Heimann and Schulz (Figure 1) as quoted by Heidt (1976, p.48) serves as an example to illustrate the episodic development of the lecture. It is probable that, depending on the learning goal, a lecture may be successful without the use of any media whatsoever.

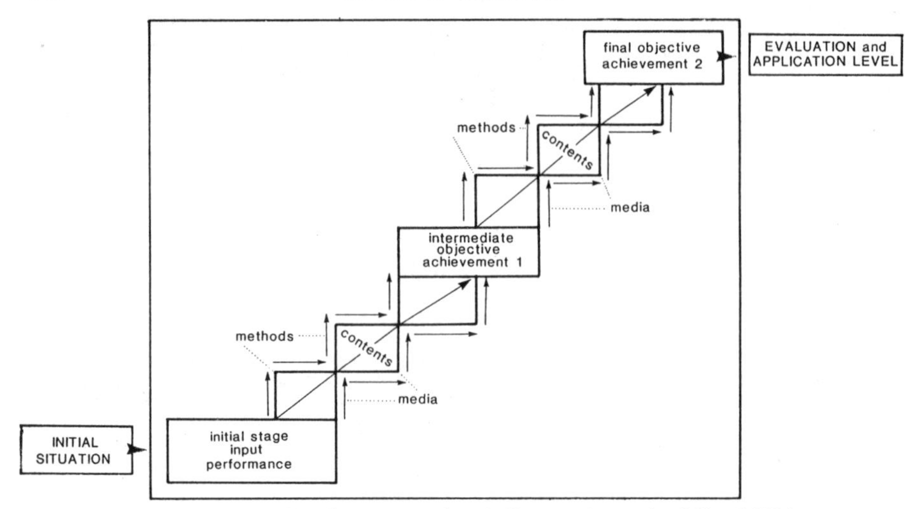

Figure 1: Episodic development of the lecture (Heidt, 1978)

Although a considerable amount of research has been published, certain observations of Brown (1978,p.41) are applicable: "Lectures are for the benefit of students. They are predominantly oral methods of giving information, generating understanding and creating interest." Note that Brown implies a hierarchy, namely the giving of information (low cognitive activity), the promotion of concepts and the arousal of interest (high cognitive activity). Brown (1978,p.44-45) shows how a student can learn with the help of a lecture, namely through listening, observing, summarizing and note-taking. The hidden variable, 'understanding,' is often 'discovered' during a lecture or when own notes are being perused.

The students' attention fluctuates during the presentation of a lecture, and after 20 minutes there is an observable decrease in the concentration span of the student. One way in which this decrease in concentration can be avoided, is by aligning media to the set of lecture goals - such as the presentation of information, concept promotion, arousal of interest and verification of knowledge. Information is initially 'stored' in the short-term memory but after 30 seconds it is forgotten if it has not been transferred to the long-term memory. Information associated with and similar to existing concepts and facts is assimilated in the long-term memory. The long-term memory will also accommodate knowledge that is loosely connected to existing knowledge, while meaningless messages will be forgotten (Brown, pp.44-45).

The optimal lecture requires conscientious attention and deliberate structuring by the student. Brown concludes that "...... If one wants students to learn from lectures and to take good notes one has to structure one's presentation so that it is meaningful and interesting, one has to ensure that their attention is gained and sustained and that the ideas and facts presented may be readily assimilated into their existing store of knowledge and skills" (1978,p.45).

THE STRUCTURE OF THE LECTURE

If the lecture, including its content, is properly structured the lecturer assists the student to learn effectively, implying that the learner understands and assimilates the learning content so thoroughly and effectively that it eventually becomes part of his personal lifestyle (BUE 1984, p.3). The nature and quality of the learning activity therefore largely depends on the nature and the quality of the teaching.

The two concepts 'teaching' (Unterricht) and 'forming' (Bildung) are seen to be largely identical by German didacticians. The word 'Bildung' indicates both an event (taking place continually in the life of the learner) and a condition (indicating a certain level of formedness or educatedness). The deduction can thus be made that the aim of teaching and lecturing *per se* is to reflect a change in the life of a learner, - a change in his level of formedness. This is not merely a change in behaviour, as is shown later on. (Van der Stoep and Louw 1990, p.34).

Various theories of forming can be categorized into two main groups: the theory of formal education on the one hand, and material forming on the other hand. According to Van der Stoep and Louw "... these theories are directly opposed to each other in that formal forming emphasizes the unlocking of human intellectual powers or capacities, while material forming accepts that content in itself possesses an intrinsic quality which can effectively change and shape the human spirit" (1990, p.35). It is furthermore of importance to note that the idea of forming cannot be fully understood, unless the concept of man as a totality is taken as the point of departure (Van der Stoep and Louw 1990, p.37).

The categorical forming theory, as put forward by Klafki (1954), offers a possible solution to the problem of forming by postulating the perspective or concept of totality in a new synthesis. Three aspects are of importance (Van der Stoep and Louw 1990, pp.38-39) :

The learning content involved in the forming is in direct relationship to the reality which surrounds the learner. This reality is assumed to have a clear order and consists of certain categories. In their coherence they form the totality of reality. Reality has a categorical structure and forming can only take place if the whole forms the forming content in the instructional situation. The more fundamental and basic the structural concepts of the content are, the more the multitude of differentiated concepts becomes meaningful and connected.

Access to the different categories is not self-evident as the scope of learning content is so wide that it is impossible for the student to gain all-encompassing knowledge. For successful teaching to take place it is the task of the lecturer to study these categories of knowledge intensely in order to determine the so-called elemental, that is, the content must be reduced to its essentials. (Elemental : German [das Elementare] didactic terminology to indicate the essence or categories of the content of a specific subject.)

Authentic grasp, understanding and command of the content are conditions for effective learning in each subject. Where elementals are ignored in the teaching situation, the teaching is incidental, haphazard and therefore non-authentic. Should the student manage to understand the underlying elements and make them part of his own lifestyle, these elementals are then transferred to fundamentals.

[Fundamentals : German (das Fundamentale) didactical terminology which means that the learner, by means of insight into elementals, has given his own meaning to the reality represented by the basic content. The concept 'fundamental' indicates the expected dividend which accrues from progressive lecturing. Fundamentals pose the question ,"What is the learner going to do with the content?"

Teaching is an important aspect in this theory of categorical forming. The categorical structure of reality (represented in selected content) which confronts the student, is so complex that someone is needed to unfold this complex reality meaningfully to the student. Teaching therefore supposes a pre-planned and systematic attempt to do this.

The learner must be prepared and willing to be open to this reality (the learning content). Entering the reality means that the student is prepared to answer the demands and appeals made by both the content and the lecturer.

The lecturer's focal point in presenting the subject content to the student is the elementals. "The elementals form the field of concentration of didactic endeavour, or the concentration point in the lesson" (Kruger and Muller 1988, p.61). The transition of the elementals to fundamentals is schematically presented in Figure 2. The reduced learning content assists the student in eventually controlling and commanding the learning content. Through the elementals as a port of entry, the student is led to knowledge (knowing), understanding (insight), application and integration into everyday living (life content) (Kruger and Muller, 1988, p.60). The elemental-fundamental transition or thrust does not conform to a hard-and-fast causal rule. The student still has a free choice in access to and functionalization of the learning content, accepting or rejecting meaning as wished.

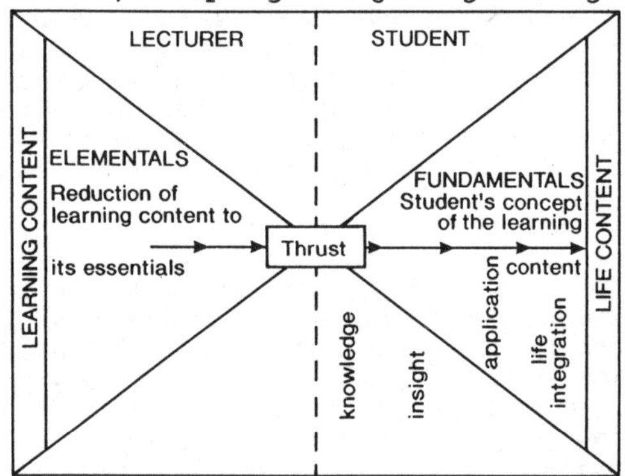

Figure 2: The elemental-fundamental transition (adapted from Kruger and Muller, 1988, p.61)

In conclusion, the subject matter must be presented in its most fundamental and essential structure, that is, where the elemental is realized as a fundamental.

It must be borne in mind that the fundamental structure of the subject matter is not always self-evident. The lecturer must therefore think of ways and means to reduce the subject matter to the level where it is readily accessible to the student. 'Difficult' subject matter should thus be reduced to its fundamental structure, which is introduced to the student as the elemental of the lecture. In this manner it becomes possible for the student to build fundamental concepts and relationships or to acquire factual knowledge in a coherent structure from the elemental concepts.

UTILIZATION OF MEDIA IN THE LECTURE

In the preceding explanation, the problem of the didactical partnership between media and education is raised. To give advice and guidance on the utilization of media in the lecture, the media expert must be aware of the didactical point of departure. At present, a medium is used without responsible reflection of the role it is to play - it is usually selected on the grounds of its availability and, in some instances because of its diversity. The actual role played by media in teaching and learning is secondary by nature. The media expert can, with the aid of the categorical formation theory, advise the lecturer in the following when media is to be selected for a particular lecture content.

In the initial choice (transparency, chalkboard, etc.) the medium is selected by the lecturer with the view that the student must be open to the learning content, and through the lecture, the learning content becomes accessible to the learner (the so-called double unlocking - see Figure 3). The lecturer must endeavour, with the help of the selected medium, to present the learning content in the form of a **problem** or **question.** Through questioning and instructional conversation, alternated with group discussion, a questioning attitude has to develop around the essentials or elementals of the content (Kruger and Muller, 1988, p.62). The student must start wondering about the learning content (Green, 1971, p.198). The questioning attitude which is created in such a way in the learner forms the ideal basis for arousing the student's interest and is the first directing of the **learning intention** towards the objective (Kruger and Muller, 1988, p.62; Freysen et al, 1989, pp.34-37). After this, the same or another medium can be applied in the introduction of the student's learning activity to the learning material. Through listening to explanations, through asking questions and reflecting on the answers, the student gradually gets a **grip** on the content, which has now become meaningful to her/him.

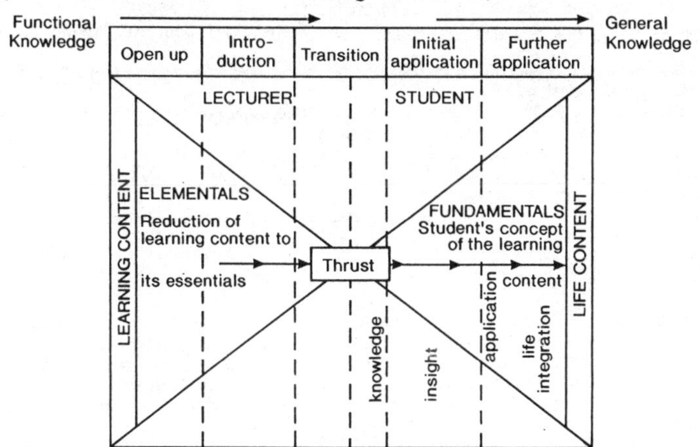

Figure 3: Utilization of media in the lecture.

Subsequently, the same or an alternative medium can be selected to help with the actual transition of the elemental to the fundamental - the merging or unification between subject (learner) and object (learning content) and the establishment of a new insight into the learning content. This phase is sometimes referred to, if the student has already obtained a general knowledge about the elemental, as the attainment of an interim goal. The newly acquired content enables the student to make a variety of applications.

Through the unlocking of learning content, the student has added new knowledge (i.e. categories of knowledge) to existing knowledge. A further medium can now be utilized in the lecture to ensure that the newly gained insight is utilized in an initial application, after which, during a further application phase, it is integrated into the frame of reference of the student in a more permanent manner. Kruger and Muller conclude, "The learner should be given the opportunity to apply his knowledge and insight functionally. Therefore, evaluation should not be limited to facts **(short-term memory)**, but has to account for learning experience in which application and creativity play a role **(long-term memory)**. In this way, every lesson becomes a function of attaining adulthood" (1988, p.63).

CONCLUSION

The learning events that occur during lecturing do not happen in such a simple way as is implied in the previous paragraphs. The relationships that function in didactics are more complex than these causalities that can be reproduced. Nevertheless, Pear, as quoted by Brown (1978, p.75), stresses that ".... the techniques of imparting knowledge in the special way called lecturing can be learned and improved upon".

REFERENCES

Bureau for University Education (1984):The Lecture. Rand Africaans University, mimeograph.
Brown, G.(1978): Lecturing and Explaining. Methuen, London.
Coombs, P.H.(1985): The World Crises in Education. Oxford University Press, Oxford.
Freysen, J.B. et al.(1989): Media Science. Audio Visual Aids, Kempton Park.
Green, T.F.(1971): The Activities of Teaching. McGraw-Hill, Tokyo.
Heidt, E.U.(1976): Instructional Media and the Individual Learner. Kogan Page, London.
Human Science Research Council, (1981): Principles for the Provision of Education in the RSA. HSRC, Pretoria.
Klafki, W.(1954): Das Padagogische Problem des Elementaren und die Theorie der Kategorialen Bildung. Julius Beltz, Weinheim.
Kruger, R.A.(1980): Principles and Criteria for Curriculum Design. HAUM, Pretoria.
Kruger, R.A. and Muller, E.C.C.(1988): Lesson Structure and Teaching Success. Rand Africaans University, Johannesburg.
Van der Stoep, F. and Louw, W.J.(1990): Didactics. Academica, Pretoria

Professor C.J.Nel is deputy head of the Bureau for University Education at the Rand Afrikaans University. He is responsible for the teaching of Media Science at postgraduate level (B.Ed., M.Ed., D.Ed.). He was initially involved in the training of teachers at Goustad Teachers' Training College and RAU. Before starting his career at RAU he was for 14 years a geography teacher at various secondary schools in Johannesburg.

Address for correspondence: **Professor, C.J.Nel,**
Rand Afrikaans University, P.O.Box 524,
Johannesburg 2000, RSA

34. Students: they also can tell us something about the new technologies

Antonio Bartolome, University of Barcelona

Abstract: The first aim of this study was to evaluate the efficiency of new media in higher education. Some revisions and meta-analysis have defined the limits of this evaluation. We chose the acceptance of video by students as an indicator of interest in its use. A questionnaire was given to 1,568 students of Barcelona University. For students, videos worked as learning facilitators and this was as a result of their capacity to help memory and intuitive presentation, but was not related to technical quality or implication in other learning activities. However, video is not a habitual resource in this university. Other results are presented in more detail.

INTRODUCTION

This work tries to evaluate the use of media in higher education. Generally, distinct media like video or computers have been studied, particularly the specific use or programmes of fixed media (as can be seen in Zuber-Skerrit, 1985). The work reported here is restricted to video and, specifically, to the use of instructional videotapes.

A look at history

Media research was first orientated towards proving the benefits of a certain medium. This research concentrated on hardware, supposing that the medium's potential was so strong that differences between programmes and applications were irrelevant (Salomon, 1979). This comparative research used any programme; e.g., someone studied the medium of television by means of programmes based on a talking bust (cited by Mielke, 1968). Lumsdaine (1963) has given the philosophy of this viewpoint: "The effects of an instructional instrument's use can usually be established only through measurements made in connection with the controlled administration of that instrument. By 'controlled' we mean, basically, that the instructional instrument is administered arbitrarily to a given group of students, in order to reveal the effects it produces" (p.592).

Regrettably, Clark (1983) showed that "most current summaries and meta-analyses of media comparison studies clearly suggest that media do not influence learning under any conditions" (p.445). He adds that "the most common sources of confounding in media research seem to be the uncontrolled effects of (a) instructional method or content differences between treatments that are compared, and (b) a novelty effect for newer media, which tends to disappear over time" (p. 448). In the same way, Kulik and others (1980) found in a meta-analysis of computer-based instruction (CBI) versus conventional courses an effect size of 0.51, but this effect was reduced to 0.13 when the same instructor planned and taught both experimental and control courses.

A new approach was taken to media research in the 1970s: the study of the attributes of media and their influence on the way that information is processed in learning. For example: does the vision of motion help comprehension? The aim was to understand how brain and technology interact (Salomon and Gardner, 1986).

A third and more recent technique in media research is to study these in the context of classroom and teacher thinking, reflecting the present interest in qualitative methods (see Cook and Reichardt, 1986).

However, educational institutions have to justify the large capital investments needed to produce video programmes. How should and do they respond to this need for media benefit evaluation?

The aim of this work

We have studied the benefits of the use of video in higher education by considering the level of acceptance of programmes by students. This acceptance level can reflect the motivation level and the efficiency of programmes as perceived by subject. Furthermore, we presume this also reflects the suitability of the medium to encourage cognitive processes of learning, because unsuitability provokes a lack of close communicational links between viewer and programme, with a consequent lower acceptance level. These assumptions are not regarded as hypotheses needing to be proved by us, because this research is merely of a descriptive kind, trying to describe the acceptance level of videotape programmes by the students of Barcelona University.

METHOD

The instrument used was a questionnaire containing 28 items, specifically designed for this investigation. The questionnaire was previously validated in a group of 100 students. Every item was multiple choice, generally including four steps or levels from the more positive to the more negative opinion.

The subjects

The questionnaire was applied to 1568 students from different Faculties (see Table 1).

BAR	ELEMENT	COUNT	PER CENT
1	Chemistry	401	25.57
2	Biology	360	22.96
3	Pharmacy	326	20.79
4	Educational Science	229	14.60
5	Law	252	16.07

Table 1: Faculties doing the questionnaire.

The groups of subjects were selected from courses in which instructional videotapes were systematically used. Other uses of video were not considered, e.g., the use of films in the History of Cinema, and the use of recorded observations in Social Psychology. A description of use of these instructional videotapes can be found in Tosi (1984).

The subjects had attended classes for at least two years in the faculty (see Figure 1).The answers were analysed by descriptive and some inferential techniques.

THE RESULTS

The main question was to know if students thought that videotape programmes facilitated their learning. The answer was highly positive: 65% of them considered that videos assisted their learning either quite well or very well (see Figure 2).

A later analysis showed that the students related this answer with the

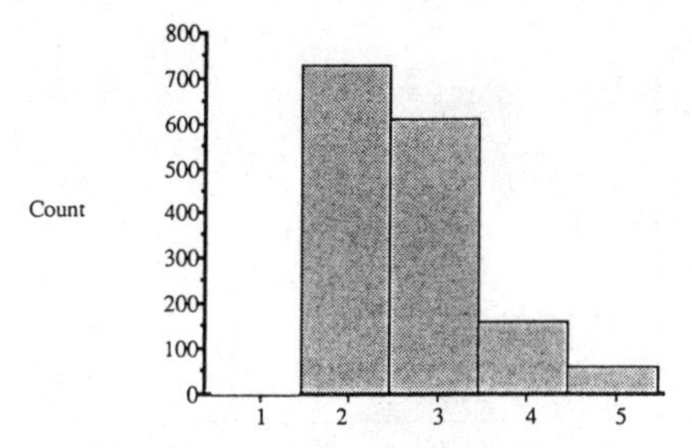

Figure 1: How many years have you studied in this university?

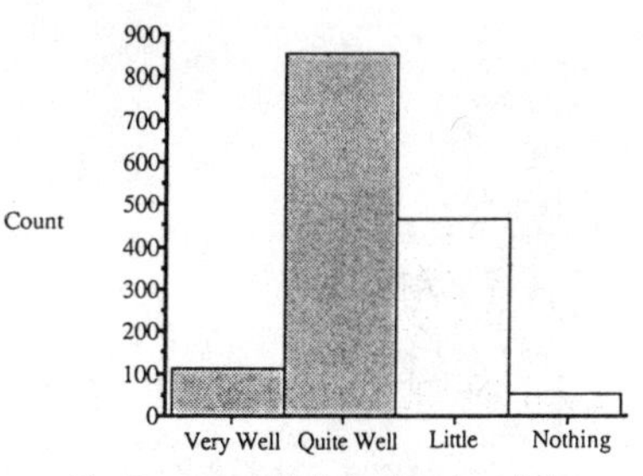

Figure 2: Do you think that videos facilitated your learning?

fact that instructional videos helped to understand notions (r=0.53) and motivated them to study (r=0.56). However, this answer was not related to technical quality (r=0.17) nor to any connection between the video projection and other learning activities.

More than half of the subjects thought that videos motivated studying (55%) and 75% thought that they helped to settle doubts and to understand notions. Furthermore, 69% also thought that they helped them to memorize. And, finally, 85% considered videos overall to have a positive effect on their education (see Figure 3).

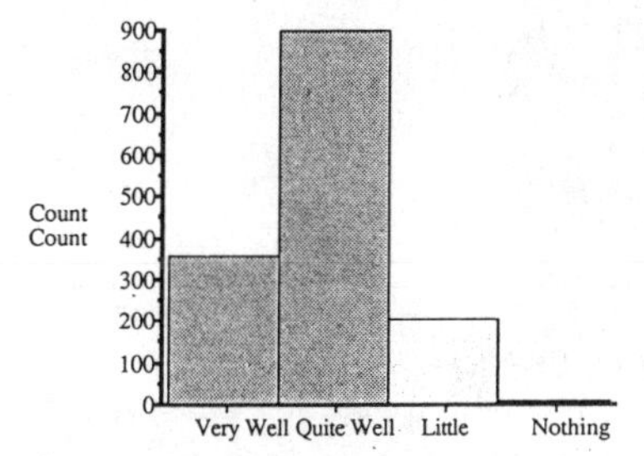

Figure 3: Do you think that the videos helped you memorize?

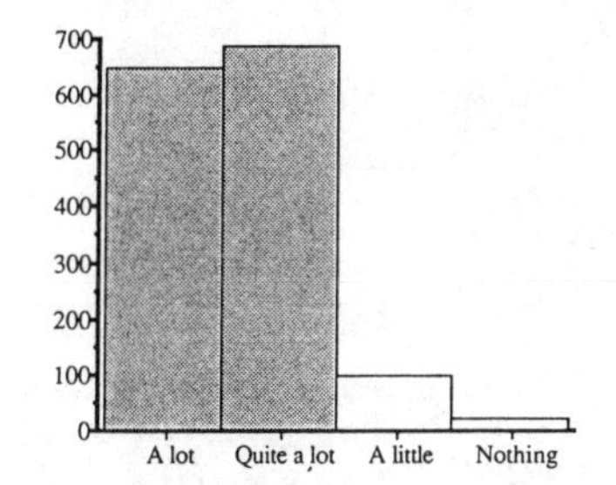

Figure 4: Do you suggest using the videos again during the next year?

Consequently, 93% of subjects suggested using the videos again during the following year (see Figure 4). Similar results were found in each Faculty, with the best being in Pharmacy and Chemistry. Curiously, their videotapes had been produced in the University of Barcelona, at U-Matic level, whereas in the other cases broadcast programmes had been used. This result was congruent with the low correlations between the question about videos helping learning and their technical quality ($0.10<r<0.22$).

Instructional videos were mostly integrated into other learning activities (89%) and overall quality was considered good or very good (83%). The duration of programmes was suitable (97%) and they were generally interesting.

An interesting finding was that 88% asked for individual use of programmes (see Figure 5). A video library is at present still a need of the old library in the university.

But, do we use video?

Our experimental sample was selected from groups where video programmes were systematically used. Figure 6 shows the number of programmes seen in this course. However, a typical student at Barcelona

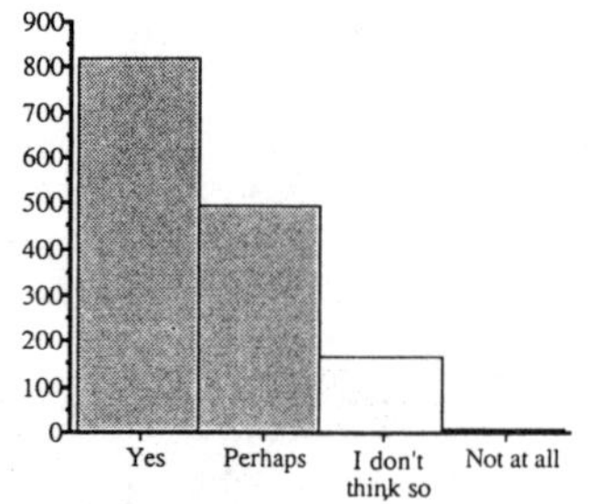

Figure 5: What about access for individual use of programmes?

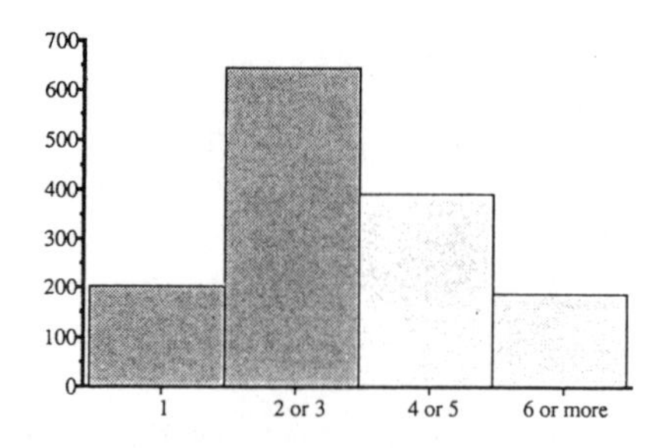

Figure 6: How many programmes have you seen this year, in this subject?

University studies five subjects every year. Had they seen video programmes in any one of the other subjects during this year? For 75% of the students the answer was "No" (see Figure 7), nor was the result any better when they were asked about seeing videos in previous years at the university (Figure 8).

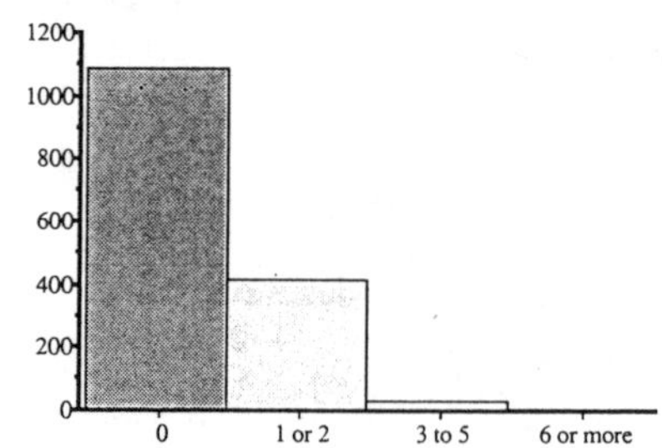

Figure 7: How many programmes have you seen this year, in other subjects?

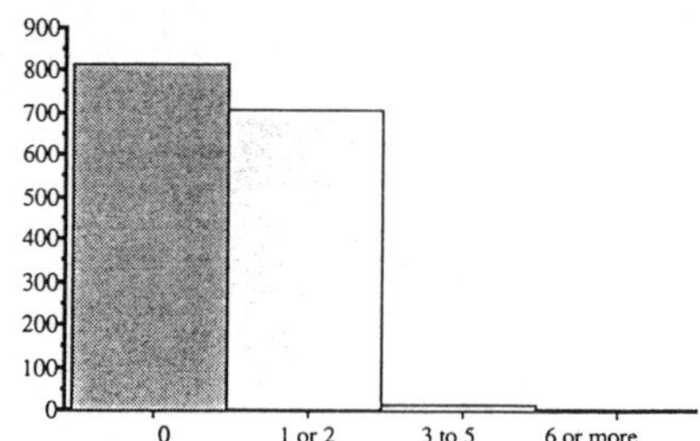

Figure 8: How many programmes have you seen prior to this year?

The technical conditions

This part of the study was particularly relevant to the management team of the university, but we include only a brief resume in this report.

In most cases, a special projection room was used, sometimes with a video projector and a large screen, and other times with a TV monitor (see Figure 9). No differences in quality of sound and vision were found between these two kinds of devices but differences were found between models.

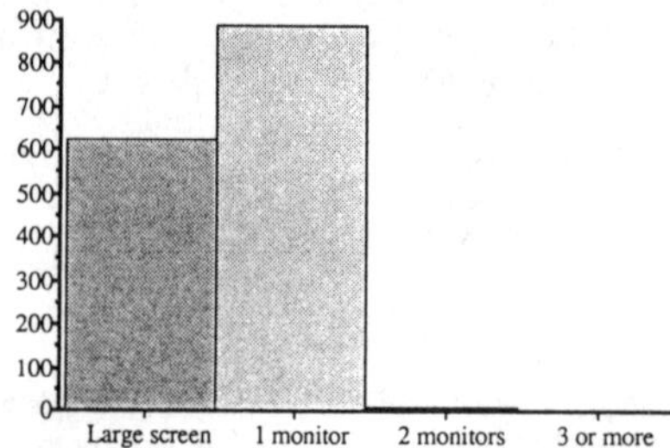

Figure 9: Video viewing system used.

The programmes and the students' attitudes

Among other results not included in this paper, we have selected one that shows how students' interest affects their attitudes to media. The same instructional videotapes were used in Chemistry and Pharmacy. In both faculties, they were applied in a course of Chemistry but the same videos seemed both significantly longer and also less entertaining to the pharmacy students than they did to the Chemistry students.

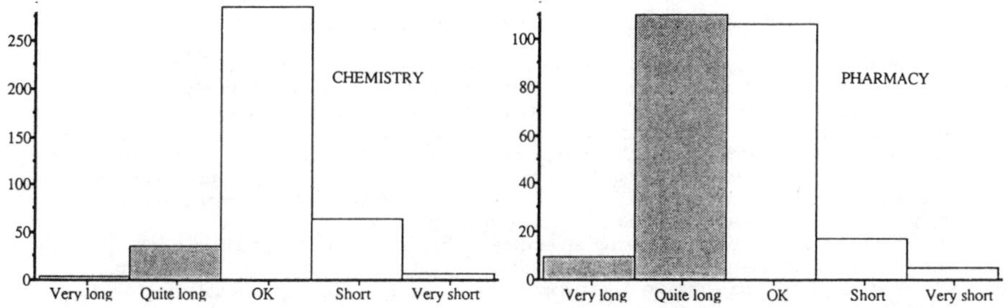

Figure 10: What did you feel about the length of programmes?

CONCLUSION

We would draw attention to five results of this experiment:

* students assess the use of video very positively;
* the videotapes produced in the university were comparable with broadcast productions, for the purposes of improving learning;
* video libraries can be a powerful help to individual study;
* quality of vision and sound is not related to the kind of screen but to the suitability of the models and rooms;
* instructional videos are not much used in the University of Barcelona.

REFERENCES

Clark, R.E.(1983): Reconsidering research on learning from media. Review of Educational Research, 53, 4, pp.445-459.

Cook, T.D. and Reichardt, C.S.(1986): Qualitative and Quantitative Methods in Educational Research.

Kulik, C., et al.(1980): Effects of computer based teaching on secondary school students. Journal of Educational Psychology, 75, pp.19-26.

Lumsdaine, A.A.(1963): Instruments and media of instruction. In Gage, N.L.(Ed), Handbook of Research on Teaching (pp.583-682). Rand McNally and Co., Chicago.

Meilke, K.W.(1968): Questioning the questions of E.T.V. research. Educational Broadcasting Review, 2, pp.6-15

Salomon, G.(1979): Interaction of Media, Cognition and Learning. Jossey-Bass, San Francisco.

Salomon, G. and Gardner, H.(1986): The computer as educator: lessons from television research. Educational Researcher, 13, 1, pp.13-19.

Tosi, V.(1984): How to Make Scientific AV for Research, Teaching, Popularization. UNESCO, Paris.

Zuber-Skerrit, O.(1985): Video in Higher Education. Kogan Page, London.

Antonio R.Bartolome is Professor of Educational Technology at the University of Barcelona, and coordinator of the 'New Technologies Work Group'. He previously worked in educational audiovisual production. He has published a number of books on educational technology, and is currently working in two interactive videodisk projects: his research is centred on educational media evaluation and on interactive video.

Address for correspondence: **Prof.A.R.Bartolome,**
Amadeu Vives, 8,
08320 El Masnou (Barcelona), Spain.

35. Intellectual enrichment and cooperative learning through interactive video in a whole-class situation

Pedro Hernandez Hernandez, University of La Laguna

Abstract: Two principal drawbacks have been attributed to computer-assisted instruction: (1) an impersonal, cold type of learning; (2) a markedly 'reproductive' education. To overcome these problems, we have developed a system of collective teaching in class through interactive video which we call AULAICAI. The hardware consists of a video-computer system with access for each pupil through simple individual terminals, while the group coordinator pupil controls the central terminal. The software allows pupil-videocomputer interaction and stimulates interaction between pupils within the group.
This system shows the following advantages: high motivation; audiovisual attraction; personal involvement; continual change of activities; enjoyable, entertaining and cooperative learning; intellectual enrichment; individual and collective feedback.

INTRODUCTION

There are a number of reasons for using technologically advanced equipment in education, e.g.

* they offer exceptional material that can reproduce and truly represent the reality that one wishes to teach (video, film, slides). This material is available without restrictions of time, is made by experts and applied to different teaching/learning situations;
* some of these advances permit the possibility of choosing from different types of information and of offering feedback (e.g. by computer).

The advantages, on the other hand, do not guarantee that technological media for teaching are superior to the direct and personal work of the teacher. Among the possible reasons for this are two main drawbacks which have been attributed to educational technology and, especially, to computer-assisted instruction (CAI):

* an impersonal, cold and individualistic type of learning;
* a markedly 'reproductive' education.

In order to overcome these problems, we have developed a system of collective teaching in class, which we call AULAICAI.

AULAICAI is a sophisticated technological system of teaching based on video, assisted by computer and in a group learning situation. In this way learning is more constructive, cooperative and motivating.

This idea was born from observing how pupils' motivation and creative thinking increased by asking them to do their own elaboration on the contents of some videos. These advantages were not observed when the videos were merely shown without the interaction of the pupils.

We therefore thought of using interactive video in a group situation to emphasize two aims:

1. to foster active and creative learning, rather than passive reproductive learning;
2. to create the conditions for cooperative and interactive learning in a group.

In the later stages of our research, and after having already obtained interesting results, we came upon a similar project (CAVI, see

Noell and Douglas, 1989), which differed from our system mainly in their software.

We believe that AULAICAI, unlike CAVI, focuses less on the evaluation of the results and more on the creative and social aspects. These latter give greater emphasis to the opportunity for alternative options, the display of problems, creating cognitive dissonances, cooperative learning, stimulation and control of participation, checking the feedback given by the system and the evaluation of open-ended questions.

THE HARDWARE

The hardware consists of a video-computer system with the possibility of access by every pupil through simple individual terminals, while the group coordinator pupil controls the central terminal.

For this, the Canarian Astrophysics Institute built individual terminals, to allow connection between each pupil and the system, and the interface to connect the computer with the U-matic video system, using tape instead of videodisc.

The hardware of AULAICAI has the following components (see Figure 1):

* a computer designed specifically for processing images;
* a reading magnetoscope for a U-matic videocassette;
* a television monitor;
* an interface to connect the computer and magnetoscope;
* twelve small terminals for connections between the pupils and the computer;

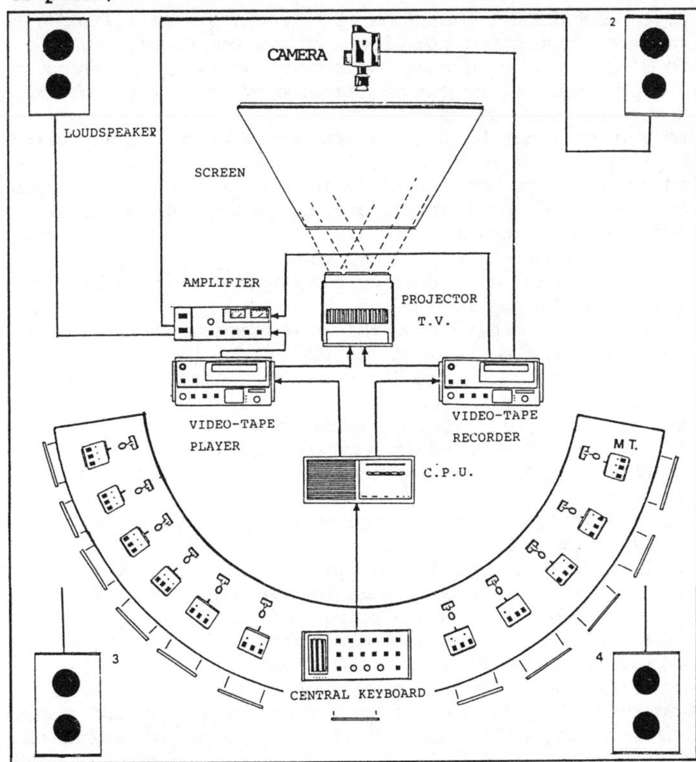

Figure 1: Hardware of the AULAICAI system.

* optionally, a videocamera and recording magnetoscope to record the behaviour of the pupils as feedback for them according to the types of work performed, and as material for research.

THE SOFTWARE

The software of AULAICAI consists of five main reference points:
* the audiovisual material on video (this can be edited material or material of one's own design);
* the psychoeducational programme, when different didactic functions and requirements (e.g. overview, group discussion, evaluation, feedback, etc.) are used in programming material sequentially;
* the author programme. This can be used to produce complementary instructional material by computer (titles, graphics, feedback, etc.) and to structure all instructional material according to the sequences and functions. It can be used by professionals in education, even if they have only little knowledge of computers;
* the users' programme. This controls the working and running of the system when it is used by pupils in class;
* the analysis programme, which is used to analyse data on the pupil/system interactions.

THE PSYCHOEDUCATIONAL FUNCTIONS

The psychoeducational functions of AULAICAI are as follows:
* to give information via video and via computer;
* to generate constructive thinking by means of dissonant questions and problems, which can be answered by using the work-book, keyboards or by group discussion;
* to give optional information and tasks which clarify, revise and amplify the information shown;
* to evaluate the answers of individual pupils or groups during and at the end of the learning process, using both multiple choice and open-ended questions;
* to offer feedback on the answers;
* to show quantitative data or percentages of the achievement levels of the pupils;
* to indicate the direction that the learning should follow, depending on the previous results of the group;
* to signal any member of the group to explain to other members a question that is unclear;
* to encourage participation in group discussion;
* to give positive reinforcement or praise;
* to obtain statistical information during and after the learning process;
* to be able to record and reproduce the performances of the subjects on video;
* to be able to integrate the opinions and contributions of the pupils for future programmes, so that they can be used by other groups, providing new and richer material;
* to be able to modify and improve instructional programmes in accordance with the results obtained.

The main conclusion we have been able to come to from this investigation is that AULAICAI is not only a good teaching system but also an interesting medium for educational and psychological research.

ASPECTS OF THE EVALUATION

The values that we attribute to this system have been inferred observing its working in different groups. We used several points of view to evaluate this system of teaching, such as the achievement, the attention level,the participation and elaboration of ideas in the group discussion, the elaboration of written material and the pupils' own evaluation. As yet though, we have not done a comparative evaluation of this with other systems.

EVALUATION OF A SPECIFIC CASE

We show below the specific case of a session dedicated to General Aspects of Energy. This session corresponded to the first of four modules developed in the Institute of Educational Sciences of the University of La Laguna.

The subjects

The group is formed of twelve subjects, boys and girls, between thirteen and fourteen years old taken from a class in the final year of elementary school.

The contents

The contents of the module are:

1. Energy in the Universe.
2. The Energy Cycle.
3. Energy and Material.
4. Energy and Work.
5. Transformation of Energy.
6. Potential and kinetic energy.
7. Potential Energy of Position.
8. Potential Energy of Composition.
9. The Changes of Energy: Physical, Chemical, Electrical, Temperature, etc.

The structure

As an example of the structure of the module, we list the first sequences in Table 1. It is easy to see the different functions and

	TOPICS AND TASKS	INSTRUCTIONAL FUNCTIONS	TIME
1	Kisses	Motivating information	4 mins
2	What is energy? (group discussion)	Motivation and intellectual enrichment	15 mins
3	Table of choices	Information guide	1 min
4	Sketch (detective searching for Energy)	Motivation	1 min 30 secs
5	The Universe	Specific information	1 min 30 secs
6	Test: the importance of the sun as a source of energy	Evaluation	8 mins
7	as 6	Feedback	9 mins
8	The biological cycle	Specific information	5 min 10 secs
9	Label a diagram	Evaluation	5 mins
10	Group discussion	Activation of thought processes	5 mins
11	as 10	Feedback	1 min

Table 1: First sequence in the structure of the module.

The structure

As an example of the structure of the module, we list the first sequences in Table 1. It is easy to see the different functions and varied changes. The time spent on each function is as shown in Table 2:

	FUNCTIONS AND TASKS	TIME
1	Motivating information	10 mins
2	Group discussion	20
3	Specific information	20
	(Revision or amplification)	5
4	Information guide	6
5	Evaluation and individual elaboration	50
6	Contrast of opinions on pupils' own answers	13
7	Feedback	30
8	Data about group or individual results (scoring)	1
	TOTAL	2 hrs 35 mins

Table 2: Timetable of functions and tasks in the module.

The conditions

The conditions under which we did this research were as follows:

* the session was recorded on video;
* there were three observers during the session;
* the session had the following sequence:
  an initial part of 1 and 1/2 hrs; 30 mins break; then the second part lasting 1 hour.
* the results were considered according to different criteria.

The outcomes

Knowledge

* **First phase** of the group search - the pupils showed erratic behaviour. They gave the impression, by their body language, of having had some idea of energy, but they had difficulty in expressing these ideas. Words mentioned relating to energy were 'strong' and 'power', although these had previously been indicated in the presentation of the theme.
* **Second phase** - the pupils gave an anthropomorphic description of energy, limiting it to the idea of power and physical force of the human body.
* **Third phase** - the pupils remembered some information they had learned: one mentioned theory of conservation of energy and another, the idea of energy and work.
* **Fourth phase** -the pupils were capable of defining energy in a broader sense as in power or energy that exists in everything.

Achievement in the evaluation test during the process

* **Specific instruction** - the questions that were directly inferred by the information shown were answered adequately by a high number of pupils (between 80 and 100% of the subjects).
* **Constructive information** - it was more difficult to answer this type of test (50% correct answers), as the questions needed new work and special thought.

Examples - to complete, in diagram form, the biological cycle.
- to match the energy phases of a machine and of a man.

* **Dissonant information tests** - completion of this type of test is also difficult (50% correct answers) because it generates doubts and contradictions. For example - Does a piece of glass have energy? (The uncertainties do not arise if we refer to a piece of wood "because you can burn it" or a piece of iron "because you can lift things with it".) In the comparison of opinions in the group afterwards, some interesting ideas came up. One pupil pointed out that glass has energy "because by using glass you can make fire". This led on to useful thought as to whether that was because of the glass or the sun.

Difficult concept tests - some questions, such as potential energy are difficult, and were answered by only 42%; also, such topics may not be explained very well.

Achievement in the final evaluative test

The results indicated that the main aims of this module were achieved by 90% of the subjects.

Level of attention

Two and a half hours of learning were completed without any signs of tiredness or loss of attention being noticed in any of the subjects.

Pupils' evaluation of the system

All of the subjects said that they had enjoyed the class, that they had learned a lot and that the questions posed had been stimulating and had forced them to think in a different way. 17% added that some points needed further explanation.

CONCLUSIONS

The properties demonstrated by this system, as in the data shown, suggest that AULAICAI is an unusual method of teaching. It is a system which has a potential for being constantly improved and which stimulates the enrichment of the mind and favours cooperative work between pupils. In addition, this system gives an enjoyable way of learning, because it offers the pupils a high level of personal involvement and a continual change of activities.

We think that many schools could have this collective system of teaching, because of its high effectiveness and low cost. The most important objective at the moment, though, is to have an adequate supply of programmes for the system.

REFERENCES

Noell, J. and Douglas, C.(1989): Group and individual computer assisted video instruction. Educational Technology, January, pp.36-37.

Pedro Hernandez Hernandez is the Professor of Educational Psychology at the University of La Laguna, Tenerife. He has taught at all levels in the educational system, from primary schools onwards, and has been President of the Canarian School Council. He has published many books and articles, principally on schoolchildren, teachers, and psychology.

Address for correspondence: **Prof.B.Hernandez Hernandez,**
Instituto de Ciencias de la Educacion,
San Agustin, 30, University of La Laguna,
Tenerife, Spain.

36. Electronic audience response

Stephen C.Day, Mid-Kent College

Abstract: This records a session which reviewed the experience of one college of higher education in applying electronic audience response to the assessment and development of interpersonal skills and competences, and explored the direction of future development.

COMPUTERS AND MICRO-TRAINING

The assessment and development of interpersonal skills and competences normally relies on observers' impressions and verbally-articulated criticisms. It is notoriously difficult to ensure that such criticism is

* constructive;
* sufficiently specific to be actionable; and
* sufficiently objective to be acceptable.

Attempts to systematize personal judgement by the use of multivariate rating scales have proved themselves prone to revert to the reporting of subjective overall ratings.

In applying computer-assisted learning to the assessment and development of interpersonal skills and competences, the focus has been on:

* providing immediate, graphic and specific feedbacks to learners;
* rating the performance in a precise and objective manner.

THE CONCEPT OF ELECTRONIC AUDIENCE RESPONSE

The system operates with the help of a microcomputer linking audience keypads to a video recording being made of the performance. As an expert panel and/or a group of observers watches the learner's performance, each observer continuously registers a rating by using individual keypads and actively responding to the performance by logging a real-time good/bad rating. These are recorded against time on computer disk.

Feedback to the learner is normally in the form of a moving graph showing performance against time; this graph is usually overlaid over a video recording of the performance. This feedback tells the learner precisely which behaviours are well received and which require correction, providing a solid factual foundation for the tutor's coaching intervention.

Observers are categorized according to their salient characteristics such as status (customer/colleague etc), and are briefed to observe particular dimensions (such as entertainment/persuasiveness). The resultant feedback may display graphically overall acceptability, persuasiveness to customers, etc.

Observers are not required to articulate their observations, and remain anonymous. Any inhibitions to the expression of frank criticisms are thus largely removed.

CURRENT DEVELOPMENTS IN ELECTRONIC AUDIENCE RESPONSE

Roleplay training and assessment centres are currently the main areas of application; electronic audience response has been used in combination with traditional open-ended feedback techniques.

The established process for interviewing skills training for professional and managerial staff is to run the studies and tutorial workshops back-to-back: the learner conducts an interview, and is then handed the videotape of it (with feedback in the form of the audience reaction overlay). The learner then views the videotape with a tutor, typically concentrating on the high and low spots, agrees suitable development action, then rejoins the group as an observer.

Presentation and influencing skills for public speakers and sales people are treated in much the same way; in the case of more mature and robust performers, feedback includes a group review of selected examples of individual performances.

Assessment centres have made use of electronic audience response to record the incidence of specific behaviours (such as proposing; disagreeing; etc., in a group discussion) to create a behavioural analysis profile. Using a video-recording, it has been possible to aggregate the judgements of experts at different times, and of employers at a different location.

Other possibilities could include audience participation and balloting in meetings; interactive teleconferencing; evaluation of audio-visual materials such as recorded performances or new productions; and so on.

ANTICIPATED TRENDS AND DEVELOPMENTS

The meeting focused on the following issues when discussing the presentation:

* the collection of responses where a whole group (rather than just individuals) needs to respond to multi-choice questions, either in a quiz or a computer-based training context;
* current technological developments, including the measurement of involuntary physiological reactions to stimuli, in addition to cognitive responses as at present;
* the need for rapport and understanding where closed-circuit TV and associated techniques are used;
* the use of electronic audience response for psychometric profiling by analysing response to a trigger video.

The advantages in involving observers in role-play, without them needing to articulate their opinions and create any confrontation, and in seeming to have the effect of making them more perceptive and alert, was welcomed. Considerable advantages were also felt to accrue for trainers in that their role became that of adviser and resource rather than judge and teacher; the task of identifying performance shortfall is largely complete, and the trainer is free to concentrate on the constructive phase of building more appropriate behaviour.

Address for correspondence: **Stephen C.Day,**
Mid-Kent College, Maidstone Road,
Chatham, Kent ME5 9UQ, UK.

37. Using training technology requires more than money!

Ted Hutchin, Tangent Technology Design Associates

Abstract: In addressing skill shortages many companies are turning to computer-based training (CBT), distance and open learning, interactive media and so on. This paper raises the problems associated with rushing into this 'technological fix' approach without careful thought and planning, linking the training requirements to business objectives and sound application. Based on recent experience in the East Midlands of the UK and current thinking within industry, it is intended to be provocative.

INTRODUCTION

It is becoming almost old hat these days to question the spending of money on the development of training materials using any of the current technologies. Given that training as an exercise has been given a very low priority in the last ten to twenty years, those of us involved in the development of training material, and its presentation, should be pleased that what we have been saying for so long has now come to fruition. Training is a vital function in the development and continued growth of our manufacturing base. This is equally true in areas such as health, transport, commerce and so on. Indeed the list is endless. What we are seeing now is the resurgence of training as an activity and the use of training technology is I feel a major part in that new growth. The cynic might argue that as there are so many computers lying around offices these days, all looking for a use, it is not surprising that they are being put to such new uses!

As more and more companies are using personal computers (PCs) for business applications, so the opportunity to use that same technology for training is not to be missed. With all this technology it isn't surprising that not only can they be used for real work but also practice. With the new computer-based training (CBT) software that is available it is possible to practice and make mistakes, thus learning without being seen to fail. There is also the feeling that because training now uses the latest technology it is in some mystical way better than what had gone before; that it is now a fit subject for investment.

I find it strange that when the process of training changes, the content remaining largely the same, it is in some ways 'better'. But I don't want to sound carping: the central fact is that training is now being given due recognition in the boardrooms of our manufacturing industry, and in many other industries. So what is the problem?

PROBLEM, WHAT PROBLEM?

In some ways it is really the same old problem but in new clothes. In the past the major problem in creating training programmes was that the customer rarely knew just what was wanted and relied on the training professionals within the company to suggest the proper and most effective methods. While the range of presentation methods and the nature of most training programmes were still linked essentially to chalk and talk, with the odd book or workbook to take home, the task of suggesting appropriate methods was fairly straightforward.

Today the situation is completely changed. The technology being used in the workplace is appreciably more complex and difficult to understand. There are considerable fears in the minds of many that the new technology will lead to deskilling, to redundancy, to loss of status, to loss of power and so on. Equally, the methods used to train have changed. No longer are the old methods enough. Through the use of the training technologies such as interactive video, CBT and CAL, open and distance learning, group working and experiential learning, the range of techniques now available to training professionals is wide and, for many, bewildering. To present a course now requires the individual tasked with the job to have an understanding of how all these various methods interact, which are the best for any given situation, for any given group, and for any given subject. This requires a new approach to the development of courses, and leads to the concept of instructional design. This term implies much more than the old concept of 'course development'. It is in essence an holistic approach to training which encompasses all aspects and tries to be systemic in nature.

SO WHERE DO I START?

For any given group of people in a company there will be training needs. The first step is easy - carry out a training needs analysis to identify what training is required, by whom, when and then to consider how. This is not new, there are no secrets here. I am sure that many readers will have used the standard approach to training needs analysis (TNA), based on knowledge, skills and attitudes of both the individual and the job role. This is not the place to cover these techniques in any detail as I am sure that they are well known. What does require flagging up is that, even now, many companies still do not do this activity at all and therefore leave themselves open to all kinds of problems. Perhaps even worse are those who only pay lip service to this activity and wonder why their training fails to meet the basic needs of their staff. But let us assume that they have done this.

There is still the central problem of how do I as a manager, either a training manager or a line manager, ensure that the knowledge and skills that I have just spent a fair amount of time investigating and describing are catered for. It seems to me to be a foolhardy exercise to invest in the analysis and then not invest in the required training. Once the content of the training has been identified, it is necessary to consider the means, the process by which the training will be given. There is, sitting on the shelf, a whole range of methods that can be used, there are the requirements of each individual that requires the training and there is the need to develop the learning environment and a learning contract such that the training is optimized and not wasted. This forms the crux of the paper.

DELIVERING THE TRAINING: meeting the need, the equation from the supply side

Meeting the need of training requires a careful and systemic approach which means that there has to be a structure to the way in which the whole is developed. Currently the following outline is used for the analysis of projects at Tangent:

1 Description of Business and Training Needs
- 1.1 The Business
- 1.2 The Training Need
- 1.3 The Benefits

2 Existing Training Arrangements

3 Nature of the Training Innovation
- 3.1 Aim
- 3.2 Objectives
- 3.3 Outcomes

4 Project Activities
- 4.1 Work Programme
- 4.2 Project Management
- 4.3 Project Roles

5 Costs
- 5.1 Cost Summary
- 5.2 Contributions

6 Assessment/Evaluation
- 6.1 Short Term
- 6.2 Longer Term
- 6.3 Assessment Methods

7 Dissemination
- 7.1 In-Company
- 7.2 External

The main task of this approach is to develop the objectives of the training that is determined by the analysis, and from that, the tasks of the training programme can be developed and that is where the use of the training technology comes in. Given the normal practice of just buying solutions rather than spending the time analysing problems, following an outline such as that above has the advantage of giving structure to the development of training solutions. But it is possible to fall into the trap of analysis by paralysis. Equally it is essential that the providers are set up ready to meet the demand.

SUPPLY SIDE

The main point about this whole area is that there is a need for the development of new ideas within education, particularly Continuing Education/Adult Education as practised within our current FE/HE institutions. This implies that the current methods of looking at such activities, i.e. on the margin of activities, is not enough and that the whole area requires to become mainstream sooner rather than later. Whether this will actually happen depends greatly on the way demand through industry is focused over the next two to three years and also how the demographic effects that the country is about to experience, cut into the way in which organizations recruit, and from that, retain their present staff. It is not going to be enough, in this new environment, to rely on the old practices as they are already outdated and will become ever more so.

What is required is a new dimension to training and development which initiatives such as the Management Charter Initiative and Business Growth training schemes from the Training Agency have shown. Relate this to the need to develop more managers with the equivalent technical skill within our manufacturing industry and it is easy to see why there is likely to be a major explosion in the provision of continuing education in these fields through the nineties.

The challenge is quite clearly with both sides of the equation. Industry must realize that it will have to train itself out of any further recession, and the providers will have to develop much more flexible responses to the needs of industry. This will require both flexible approaches to delivery and also flexible approaches to the recognition of training needs within these companies. Trainers will have to develop the necessary business skills to match their human resource skills, this being a feature of recent Training Club meetings in the East Midlands of England. There the focus has been to place training onto the boardroom agenda and ensure that the whole subject is given proper discussion and investment within the company.

CONCLUSIONS

Training today is an expensive business. There are many people around who will develop training material, but they are in this as a business and need to make money at it. The creation of training material is not cheap. Therefore it is important that once created it can be used many times, that it allows for the development of repeat business for the company creating the material, and that it allows the degree of flexibility that the purchaser requires. This means a close association with both supplier and customer. I have called this the 'JIT' approach to training; hardly original but neatly summing up my view of the way in which training development has to go to be cost effective and provide a service that ensures repeat business. The link in terms of supplier-customer is vital if the end product is to meet the required standards. This has been recognized by the Japanese for some time. Only through such close association can a real service be provided and long-term work developed. It is through the development of quality in the product and not through price that the real benefits are to be made.

Ted Hutchin is a Senior Associate in the firm of Tangent Technology Design Associates.

Address for correspondence: C.E.Hutchin,
Tangent Technology Design Associates,
44, Baxter Gate, Loughborough,
Leicestershire LE11 1TQ, UK

38. The hidden technology: societal mechanisms now hampering realizing human potential

EM Buter, formerly University of Amsterdam

Abstract: Schooling, training, career guidance and personnel selection are being more and more influenced by interaction with the Structured Habitat - that interdependent mix of modern bureaucracy and the furnished environment. It is maintained that, despite many positive influences, the tendency is for human potential not to get sufficient recognition and opportunity. Negative influences show in the ways training methods, selection modes and personal guidance systems are used, and appears as a focus on lower cognitive levels and in the filtering out of the affective. In many cases norm reversal shows itself, in that the artificial environment becomes the norm and humans conform to that. It is maintained that the negative effects of these Hidden Technologies can be counteracted by the careful inclusion of interaction between humans in assessment, metacognitive and affective learning-orientated training and education.

WESTERN SOCIETY AS AN ARTIFICIAL ENVIRONMENT FOR HUMAN BEINGS

The Western habitat, mainly as a result of an all-pervading and mushrooming technology, has become highly constructed and artificial. This habitat is a mixture of **modern bureaucracy** (with manifold and abundant rules, restrictions, laws etc.) and the **furnished landscape** (the structured material environment with houses, schools, hospitals, institutes, transport systems etc). Both are highly interdependent, combining into the **structured habitat.** Routes through life are more and more geared to our interactions with this structured habitat. Part and parcel of it is the way it influences and directs school and career paths.

HIDDEN TECHNOLOGY: INTRINSIC TO THE STRUCTURED HABITAT

Interaction with the structured habitat is important for Realizing Human Potential. The effect of some aspects of interaction is however a growing reduction and limitation of human operation - **The Hidden Technology.** In training, schooling and career guidance, these reductive aspects are hidden in the training approaches, the modes of selection and assessment, the gearing of decision models to function- and task-analysis, the interpretation of the possibilities of technological aids to training, and the friction between training and working conditions.

MULTI-DIMENSIONAL AND FUNCTIONAL BEHAVIOUR POTENTIAL IN HUMANS

Humans are, to a high degree, potentially **multi-dimensional** in behaviour (given the chance and the right training facilities) on different levels of cognition (or digital behaviour), of emotional and affective (or analogue) behaviour and of psychomotor levels.

In my own work I have found that new teachers are often very able in using their multi-dimensional potential in a high degree of multifunctionality. I have observed the same in the working situation, provided that latitude is given for teamwork, responsibility etc. (Buter, 1988).

Really, this is just what is wanted. We want people who reflect on their behaviour (in context), analyse, synthesize, decide and act accordingly; with motivation and affect geared to continue or to develop such behaviour, **even** in situations where job analysis seems to indicate that only routine and stereotype activities are involved. It is this potential I am talking about, that must be optimalized and used. **Environments should be geared to do just that. Do they really?**

ANALYSIS OF ENVIRONMENTS DIRECTED TO BEHAVIOUR MODIFICATION

Only some of the items will be dealt with, i.e. those which are relevant to schooling, training and career paths. Schwartz and Jansma (1989) give an excellent review of the technological culture in general.

Reduction of learning in the cognitive or digital areas

The general tendency is to focus only on the lower levels of cognition in learning, then to gear all learning activities to these levels. **The situation is amplified or intensified by the use of many interactive media.** Such devices are capable of being interactive only at lower levels. Their coding system does not allow for more, and the control on the modes of learning cannot reach beyond simple external control of choice responses. While in traditional training and teaching **level reduction** has already become a dominant feature (Van Hiele, 1957), technological implementation seems to amplify this reduction **(and sometimes seems to become the norm).** Criticisms of mathematics teaching, under the influence of information-processing models illustrate the observation: (1) "Emphasis on the purely cognitive, and..... de-emphasis of affect, context and culture". (2) "A narrow view of cognitive activity as mere symbol manipulating, with a related lack of attention to meaning" (Searle, 1984). (3) "Concentration on precision....., resulting in a devaluation of knowledge...that cannot be represented symbolically and precisely" (Cobb, 1987)

Reductive decision tables and algorithms for training

In educational technology decision tables are used to develop satisfactory learning situations (Romiszowski, 1988). Many aids are geared mainly to the analysis of specific functions and specific tasks, leading to neglect of areas not explicitly mentioned in the task description.

Reductive aspects of structured habitats

Workplace, schooling and training positions are governed by rules and codes of behaviour based on efficiency and maximization of output. These seldom take into account the multi-dimensional potential of human beings so **basic personal experiences** become zero (Mole, 1988). Response ranges elicited, and the variety allowed for in response quality is small. In my training work I often find apparatus and software with immense possibilities but which are not used to their maximum potential, because stress on the shopfloor hinders full development in practice. Wordprocessors are a case. See also the description of such analogue situations by Romiszowski and Atherton (1979).

The technological attribution model for personality (TAMP)

Modern bureaucracy uses assessment categories that seem easy to measure, count or define and which are very easily inputted into databases. It is assumed that every aspect of (wanted) human behaviour - in a function, a job, a school career, or even a family - can be put into specific formulations or definitions. Thus the database profile becomes the person - and can thus be the basis for manipulation (to TAMPer with people).

In this way individuals are translated into sets of categories for intelligence, motivation, performance, emotional stability, authority, etc., mostly given by indications on a scale. TAMPS are of varied character; many are used as selection tests for specific jobs. [it is very easy to be trained for parts of such tests, hence the secrecy around them. In Holland a debate is now raging around the acceptability of providing such training. One professional tester has been expelled from the psychologists' professional association for doing just that].

The selection syndrome and the growth of TAMPs

There is mushrooming growth of organizations that select people for e.g. new schooling projects, reintegration projects, assistant to the manager, etc. Hence many people nowadays are tested frequently.

It is more Parsonian than ever, using matching and trait psychology - successfully - even if these had already in the twenties been proved to be based on non-valid assumptions (Wiegersma, 1990, in his farewell lecture on career guidance). But they 'work' within the framework of industry as it now functions.

For selection purposes humans are evaluated according to their position in a group.

This was normal procedure long before automation. We do this intuitively all the time, and create categories such as 'over 50', 'under 15', senior, jobless, immigrant, 'has experience', married, junkies, yuppies, very biased indeed.

Much automation thrives on such categorized personality inventories. Individuals are often measured against such statistical clusters of categories, but 'statistical' humans do not exist in reality.

Teulings in an interview on Human Resource Management warns specifically of the fact that information from the informal circuit cannot be stored in the database. "A new kind of personnel management - created for such use on a terminal screen - but with its back to the personnel, could be a danger" (Robroek, 1990).
Van Gelderen, in an introduction to the database program JOB CONSULTANT for personnel guidance and selection, warns of "the danger that such programs are developed only with the screen in mind. The danger being that people are placed in the shade of the computer, and are judged on dry facts" (Van Gelderen, 1990).
The more elaborate assessment procedures are, at least in the Netherlands, used for middle and higher levels of the vocational or professional population (Wiergersma, 1990). This makes the observations of Robroek and Van Gelderen even more relevant.

Marginal effect and optimalizing human potential

Selection instruments - whether purely mechanical, or based on interaction between humans, or a mixture - tend to relate relatively high rewards to marginal selection differences. Very often this leads to over-valuing the persons selected, and under-valuing, and often non-use, of those not selected.

According to Meehl (1954) the clinical psychologist will always be worse than the statistical clerk. The same holds for the psychologist advising on career selection. The reason: most instruments are based on an empirical effective model. (Wiegersma, 1990).

The computer as a model for learning

The computer now plays an important role in our thinking about human learning. It influences our interpretation of interactive learning, our intelligence and reasoning, and the whole field of cognitive psychology. In the development of psychology it seems sometimes that conditioned and affective learning have only a relatively unimportant place (Sanders, 1989).

Computer-related mechanisms structure our habitat more and more in the direction of more abstract levels of cognitive behaviour. The handling of a complex coded world seems to become the major characteristic of many jobs, often replacing the real world, and psychological theory now partly shapes itself accordingly (see Anderson, 1985).

It is noteworthy that mankind has always tried to replace reality with the artificial. The so-called 'panoramas' - the invention by Robert Barker in 1787 - were an example, attracting many people, particularly from the larger towns. The autonomous development of technology now takes us in the direction of replacing many of our 'natural' environments with artificial ones. It seems Jaron Lanier is the successor to Barker, wanting to create a complete 'artificial reality' in which even touching and manipulating of objects is done in a computer governed induced space (Zachary, 1990).

By its very nature such a coded world is limited compared with reality, **filtering out non-cognitive aspects of behaviour**. Roszak (1986) warns us not to construct our interpretation of important and valuable modes of thinking along the lines automation is now drawing. Yet this happens, good intentions notwithstanding. (For other illustrations, see McLeod 1990; Fischbein 1990: Cobb 1990). Experiential learning, multi-dimensional by its very nature, becomes a smaller slice of the package every year; even such practical items as gardening and cooking are now modelled on the computer. **The structured habitat has a tendency to reverse normative approaches: the**

technology gives the norm, the human has to conform (Kuitenbrouwer, 1989).

A striking example: the passport was developed in the service of individuals to allow them to cross many frontiers quickly, but is now a device that has a mainly controlling and restrictive function. The technological revolution combining copying, printing and registration invited this control and made it possible on a large scale (Baudet, 1986).
The invention of the mechanical clock is another. It reversed our way of appreciating time: the clock controlled our time, synchronized our behaviour. This is not in accordance with our time perception (Houten, 1989).

Devices, instrumentation, learning aids in general

What has been said can be applied to many other examples, both isolated devices and more systemic combinations. Programmes, no matter what their technical sophistication seems to suggest, seldom do more than remain on the lower levels of digital thinking. They transfer information, or induce low level argument. Distance learning applications are a case in kind (unless implemented with teachers(!) [Holberg, 1990; Fox, 1989]). By focusing mainly on verbal knowledge, examination guides invite the use of computers for the indoctrination of knowledge on a very low level (IVIO, 1989).

This shows how traditional approaches and the use of devices are intricately linked, the device strengthening traditional approaches instead of breaking new ground.

HOW TO COUNTERACT REDUCTION, BUT USE TECHNOLOGICAL POTENTIAL

For reasons of simplicity, I generalize diagrammatically about some stereotypes of present training and/or teaching. Roughly speaking, in training/teaching situations human potential can be addressed in three ways:

The factual level

Sometimes in training the learner is addressed on the more or less **factual** level, with a strong emphasis on the learning of facts, training in (simple) skills, and an implicit stressing of acceptive attitudes. Interactions between teacher and learner are simple, with a considerable amount of external control. Thus effective negative feedback based on a small response range (e.g. reduced choice level) is possible, and human-machine interaction allowed for (F in the diagrams).

The argumentative level

Sometimes the trainee is addressed on the more **argumentative level**, with emphasis on reasoning, training in more elaborate skills, needing good interactional skills on the part of the teacher and the student, and geared to positive attitudes to communication and motivation. Internal control (i.e. more dependence on self-control and autonomous learning) is needed; external control is faced with greater response ranges, and so is less easy to impose. (Simple question and answer interactions are no longer adequate, though we are still dealing with a relatively closed loop learning system.) Human-human interaction to encourage further learning is very important. (A in the diagrams).

The reflective level

At other times the student is addressed on a more **reflective level**, with stress on metacognitive thinking, e.g. the learner reflects on cognitive and on other forms of learning. This requires, in the affective area, a highly critical approach to one's own learning and thinking. Response modes extend over a wide range and are impossible to control by simple external means, and negative feedback is difficult to obtain in standard teaching/learning situations. We have essentially an open-loop learning system. Human-human interaction is important, but so also are activities initiated by the student, such as **consulting** expert systems (R in the diagrams).

The traditional forms of schooling and training: FA-schools

Many schools and training systems, especially those dealing with the basics, are in the F sector. This is understandable, as external control is easy and learning products are measurable; also, we have only recently become aware that a sponge-type teaching/learning could be detrimental to learning in general. Programmed instruction was successful in this type of school, and post-school, distance learning packages were based on the same premises. In the good old sixties the delicate matter of sex 'education' was delegated to programmed instruction (guess why?). Figure 1 characterizes the situation.

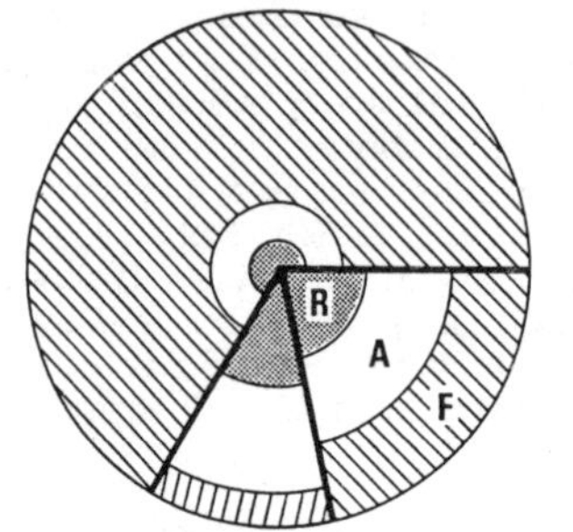

Nearly every session consists of a combination of learning facts (F),using them to reason with (A) and reflecting on them (R). In traditional training the combination with a high focus on transfer of facts and on argument - and the implicit interactional mode (see text) - is dominant.

(The meanings of the grids used in each diagram's sectors are: the argumentative element in training; the reflective element in training; the factual element in training)

Figure 1: Traditional training (the FA-mode)

Schools under technological pressure: the F-school

In the F-school stereotype we see the effect of technological implementation on teaching and training. It is understandable that the FA school can become an easy victim to this approach, as it already has a large F segment and barriers to implementing technology are low. The A part of the sector can be reduced to mainly low-level argument, which is easy to programme - something that happens when technologists want to make teaching programs.

The conversion from FA to F often takes place on the sly, because most scientists and technologists have been conditioned to transform all messages to the transfer of information. The F approach is easy to hide in often beautifully designed presentations, using sophisticated technical modes of interaction with the machine. Figure 2 typefies this situation.

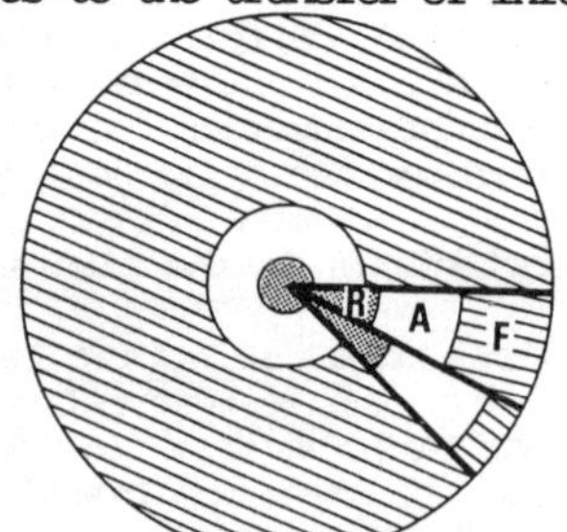

Nearly every session presents a combination of facts, reasoning and reflection, but in this mode the combination with a very high focus on facts - and the related mode of interaction (see text) - is more dominant.

Figure 2: Technology dependent training (the F-mode)

The idealized school: FAR-schools

Sometimes we find training situations which give balanced attention to all three sections, such as is found in e.g. modern Montessori schools, in intensive kinds of management training, and in some kinds of sports such as ski training. Schools with a high regard for outdoor project work sometimes fall under the heading; ballet schools; practical work in the laboratory often seems to fit the model, particularly when students and staff are not rushed for time. Figure 3 shows the approach.

Every session presents a combination of facts, argument and reflection. Generally, over a longer period of time we find a balance in the teaching between accentuating each of the factual, argumentative and reflective modes.

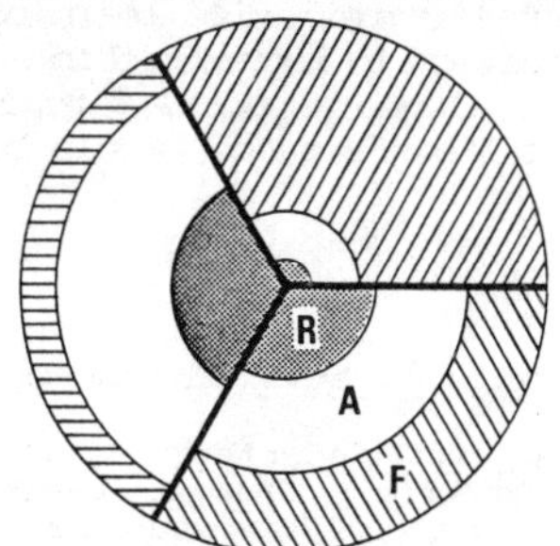

Figure 3: The ideal training mode (the FAR-mode)

It might be added that there are other diagrams, which might illustrate greater emphasis on the reflexive, and with a gradually reducing part of the teaching focus on the factual and the argumentative, and which can be classified as AR and R schools respectively. In the late sixties we found tendencies to use these types, with the R approaches doing much harm in situations where factual and argumentative learning was asked for (this might have been a factor in the rise of the back-to-basics movement in the eighties).

And now for the good news. The FAR stereotype is the ideal reference for those who construct teaching, training and career guidance situations, particularly when there is a high dependence on technological implementation. The F parts and the lower cognitive levels of the A parts in the FAR diagram can be done by essentially technologically dependent training. Every trained educational technologist can blueprint these situations and help them be effective. However, this means pushing many teachers out of their comfortable positions of being transferers of information, and get them to work more in the important - but often neglected - sectors of the argumentative (higher levels) and the reflective level.

The dynamics of the diagrams suggest:

To counteract the influences of hidden technology we have to push back the F sector clockwise and decompress the A sector and the R sector systematically within the formal context of the structured habitat.

Only by doing this can we get optimal learning, use human potential to the full and profit from the immense potential of technology, all at the same time. (The reader can probably guess why I call this ideal situation the 1:1:1 approach).

TO SUM UP

* Elements of the structured habitat, related to training and career paths, are assessed for their possible influence on the range of human behaviour considered.
* It is maintained that there exists a hidden technology that exercises a restrictive influence on the behaviour of humans in their training and career paths.
* This hidden technology is an intrinsic part of our structured habitat. Humans living in the structured habitat tend or are forced to adapt to the limiting influences of the hidden technology.
* The remedy offered is to counteract the negative influences which accompany the mainly beneficial implementation of technological

training and guidance aids. A balanced distribution of training over three described areas of behaviour and learning seems indicated. These differ in the amount of factual:argumentative:reflexive learning and hence in the ratio of human/human interaction to human/machine interaction. In this way the affective/analogue aspects of training, and the higher levels of cognitive/digital performance, would be encouraged.

REFERENCES

Anderson, J.R.(1985): Cognitive Psychology and its Implications. Freeman and Co., New York.

Baudet, H.(1986): Een vertrouwde wereld. 100 jaar innovatie in Nederland (A trusted world. 100 years of innovation in the Netherlands). Bakker, Amsterdam.

Buter, E.M.(1988): Design: scope and limits in the light of human sciences. In Mathias, H., Rushby, N., and Budgett, R.(eds): Aspects of Educational Technology XXI. Kogan Page, London.

Cobb, P.(1987): Information-processing psychology and mathematics education - a constructivist perspective. Journal of Mathematical Behaviour, 6, pp.3-40.

Cobb, P.(1990): A constructivist perspective on information-processing theories of mathematical activity. International Journal of Educational Research, 14, 67.

Fischbein, E.(1990): Intuition and information processing in mathematical activity International Journal of Educational Research, 14, 31.

Fox, D.(1989): The production and distribution of knowledge through open and distance learning. Educational and Training Technology International, 26, 3.

Gelderen, R.van (1990): Selectie van personeel per floppy. (Selection of personnel with floppy disc). PW, Magazine voor personeelsmanagement, 14, p.39

Hiele, P.M.van (1957): De Problematiek van het Inzicht (Problems of Insight). Meulenhoff, Amsterdam.

Holberg, B.(1990): Reply: knowledge produced as commodity versus humanism. Educational and Training Technology International, 27, 110.

Houten, H.J.van (1989: Timescapes and chronoclasms based on the power of ten in time. Delphi Consults, Amsterdam,

Houten, H.J.van and Meijenfeld, F.von (1989): Pleidooi voor een temporele ecologie (Plea for a temporal ecology). Science and Society, 41, 29 (Thematic number on tyranny of time).

IVIO (1989): Examengids Biologie, Schiekunde. (Examination Guide Biology, Chemistry). Hema BV, Amsterdam.

Kuitenbrouwer, F.(1989): De kwetsbaarheid van de technological burger. (The vulnerability of the technological citizen). In, Schwartz, F.(ed), De technologische cultuur. De Balie, Amsterdam.

McLeod, D.B.(1990): Information-processing theories and mathematics learning: the role of affect. International Journal of Educational Research, 14, 13.

Mole, J.(1988): Management Mole. Corgi, Berkshire.

Robroek, F.(1990): Human resource management by computer. PW, magazine voor personeelsmanagement, 14, p.8.

Romiszowski, A.(1988): Designing Instructional Systems: Decisionmaking in Course Planning and Curriculum Design. Kogan Page, London.

Romiszowski, A. and Atherton, B.(1979): Creativity and control - neglected factors within self-instruction programme design. In Terry Page, G. and Whitlock, Q.(eds): Aspects of Educational Technology XIII, p.45. Kogan Page, London.

Roszak, T.(1986): The Cult of Information: The Folklore of Computers and the True Art Of Thinking. Pantheon Books, New York.

Sanders, H.F., de Wit, H.F. and Looren de Jong, H.(1989): De cognitieve revolutie (The Cognitive Revolution), Kok Agora, Kampen.

Schwartz, M. and Jansma, R.(eds).(1989): De Technologische Cultuur. De Balie, Amsterdam.

Searle, J.(1984): Minds, Brains and Science. BBC, London.

Wiegersma, S.(1990: De geschiedenis van het beroepskeuzewerk. (The history of career selection guidance). Intermediair, 22, 45.

Zachary, G.P.(1990): Electronic LSD. Intermediair, 26, 10a, 11. (thematic special number: Automation in the nineties).

Address for correspondence: Dr.E.M.Buter,
Stadionweg 222-2, 1077 TE Amsterdam, The Netherlands.

Section 6: Human aspects of educational technology

39. Achieving potential

Tony Buzan, Consultant

Abstract: Each of us has available a superb instrument of almost infinite capacity - our brain By using a series of tests and illustrations, some ideas, concepts and misconceptions about the brain and our use of it are conveyed. Problems are shown to be universal rather than individual, but the possibilities for their solution are with everyone, as this presentation starts to show.

What I would like to do to begin with is to do a little check on the way in which the intelligences in this room are functioning at the moment. I would like you if you have a piece of paper to write down the title 'Creativity Test Number 1' - this is all in pursuit of realizing human potential - and then write down as fast as you can in any language you choose as many uses as you can think of for a paperclip, starting now.

(Pause of about one minute)

Okay, stop. I'd like you to add up your total number of ideas, which will be your score. Circle your best, your most creative, your most brilliant use, and then I'd like you in groups of three or four to exchange your ideas with your neighbours, to explain your best one and point out why you thought it was your best. Starting now.

(Pause of about one minute)

Round those discussions off now, please. The last major stretch of your intellect this morning is going to be, in fact maybe it won't, it will be the penultimate stretch, is 'Creativity Test Number 2'. Very similar to the first one, but this time I would like you to write down as fast as you can, again in any language you choose, all those things for which you cannot in any way use a paperclip, starting now. Simply the reverse, the negative of the first test.

(Pause of about one minute)

Again stop, again total your score and again circle your most brilliant, your most creative non-use and again in the same groups discuss your ideas, including your best one, and again why you chose that as your best: starting now.

(Pause of about one minute)

Finally a little memory test. It is fundamentally a long-term memory test, about some information that we estimate you have been confronted with for approximately 5 hours to 5 days of your life. Do this exercise without consulting with your neighbour - such consultation has been found to reduce your score. I want you to imagine that the sun is positioned here (diagram) and then I want you to write down, in order, closest orbit first, next orbit second, next orbit third, the planets of our solar system. Number these so the number one will be the planet nearest the sun, number two the next, three the next and so on. Make sure you have the numbers because you get a mark for the planet next to its correct number.

(Pause of about one minute)

You've had time to write down 25 planets by now, which should have been adequate for most. So could you now exchange papers with your neighbour.

The way in which you are going to mark this is to give 1 mark for the planet, wherever it is. If a planet has only been named, give a mark for that, as long as it is one of the planets, and then another mark if the planet is in the correct location. The possible total here is going to be 18 because there are, according to modern astronomy, 9 planets. The first is Mercury - if they have it in the correct place that's 2 marks - number 2 Venus, 3 Earth, 4 Mars, 5 Jupiter, 6 Saturn, 7 Uranus, 8 Neptune, 9 Pluto, which means 18 possible marks. If they have them all in the correct you can give them 2 extra stars. Extra stars also for the following: if they have the asteroid belt in between Mars and Jupiter give them a little star; if they have it in between Earth and Mars give them a negative star; if they have Pluto inside Neptune, and knew that at this particular juncture in solar system history Pluto has just gone inside the orbit of Neptune for a moment of time, give an extra star for that. So you can hand it back to your neighbour now, marked out of 18 plus stars.

Let's check these tests in reverse order, in other words we'll check the memory one now. Could I have a show of hands for how many people here get 18 or 18 plus stars? Very good, 4 of us: 17? 16? (etc). You'll be interested to see that normally in these situations there is a direct correlation between the number right and the height of the hand. The average on that test is very, very low; it's between about 4 and 7 average around the world.

Second check on this test: how many people in here really like the planets, and by that I mean find it exciting when they hear news of a new space probe, can't wait to see the photographs coming in, and are really involved in the planets? How many of you don't like the planets - bunch of rocks, waste of time, shouldn't send space ships, waste of money and so on? Finally, how many people don't care about the planets, basically couldn't give a damn? Okay, by far the majority, and I would like to point out at this juncture that indifference is far worse than hatred. We will discuss memory in relation to one's motivation, and why one can learn and then, so to speak, unlearn a little bit later in the paper.

I want now though to turn to the first two creativity tests. I'm going to discuss these theoretically and statistically.

The topic here is creativity. This is a standard, roughly normal curve with a slight skew (Gaussian curve drawn), of the distribution of the scores on the first test you did this morning. Those scores range from 0 (and that is with effort), to an average of 3 to 4, to an excellent of 8 to a superb of 12 to a one in a million of 16, and if you leave people and just say, "Carry on until you've finished", how many do you think they get before they complete? About twenty-four tends to be the average to completion.

These tests are after a man called Torrence, for those of you are interested in pursuing this and I recommend it. The tests are valid, or have been up to recently, and are reliable, which is a pleasant way of saying that you are stuck with your score. In other words, the test measures what it is supposed to measure, which is the quantity and the quality of your creativity. So if we give this group or any individual the same type of test over time the scores will be the same.

Let us check this group against the world averages for the first and second tests. How many people had a lower score on the second, the negative test? How many people had the same score? How many people had a higher score on the negative test, which is the one I want to focus on for a moment.

Quite a number of people had a higher score on that test. Why would that be? Ignorance suggested! Someone said practice, in other words the first test was a warm up that allowed it. Any other suggestions? It was a fantasy which helped them break the frame of reference? A larger number of alternatives? How many people would confirm that practice would have helped these individuals get a higher score on that second test? Right, so nearly half of us. It's all right to agree with that, as long as you recognize that when you do agree with it you disagree with and contradict 30 years of reliable research, so to speak, which says that practice, training, warm up has no effect on the result.

How many people would agree our list of the alternatives is larger, in other words the universe of ideas for which you cannot in any way use a paperclip is obviously larger than that arena of ideas for which you can use a paperclip? Right, that is in fact the majority of us who agree with this one, which is all right if you can explain why it is that in this group over 50% got a lower score on this test? Does it mean that they are suffering from creativity test burnout at 9.25 on the 10th April 1990? So we notice from an apparently simple test that there is a diversity, a divergence of results and that the explanations for those results are different as well. In other words, there are a number of questions surrounding these two little tests. We may be able to resolve those by looking at quantity/quality.

When you circled your best idea in the first test you circled it because it was what? What were the defining characteristics for that best idea? 'Humorous'; what was yours? 'Holding your nose while wiping your bottom' - that's a good one. In fact, in the 20 years that I've been doing this test nobody has come up with that before. Good; any others? 'Far away from tradition' - what was yours? 'Getting out of the bathroom'. This is a very interesting group! Any others? 'Useful in a new way' - what was yours? 'The transport of heat to an area that was not accessible by other means'. Excellent: you'll be pleased to know that you are actually dead on with Torrence's main impetus vector of creativity, and he said that the quality of creativity can be judged by its degree of removal from the norm. In other words, how far away from the norm is the idea, and the further away it is the greater the probability that it will hold the seeds of some brilliant, creative possibility within it. And that is almost a definition of the great thinkers, who were great partly because of the fact that they leapt away from the norm and forged new mental arenas for the human race.

That raises the question of what happens to this quality as quantity goes up. As quantity goes up what happens to quality? Let's have a little show of hands on that then to clarify things - how many people say as quantity goes up quality goes down? That's about 30. How many people say as quantity goes up there is no relationship with quality? About 40 of us. And how many people would say that as quantity goes up quality goes up? Six. That means we have a major series of disagreement here as well. Now this is where what might seem like an innocent discussion becomes deadly, and I mean it seriously, deadly serious. One of the major things we have discovered about the brain, and as you'll know from my work the brain is my field, is that the human brain works synergetically; in other words, the people you train and yourselves and your family work synergetically. The key word is synergetic. Synergetic, meaning in mathematical terms that one plus one equals two plus, towards infinity. In other words, it is a system which self-generates. So we can say that the brain self-generates - that is, on an informational level, it self-creates. And when you are in education and training as we all are, that is the organ which is the prime focus of our attention. There is a little computer acronym GIGO which is the way it has been thought the brain functions. GIGO, standing for garbage in, garbage out. We now know that is not the way the brain functions. It is for a computer, but not for the brain. For the brain, it is GIGG - garbage in, garbage grows. It finds a nice little nesting place and multiplies. And really multiplies. That is where it is serious, because if that is the case then the brain is also self-destructive, and all you have to do is look around in society, the world at the moment to see that.

The good aspect of that somewhat disturbing news is that the brain is only self-destructive in one instance and one instance only, which is when it has the wrong formula and believes it to be true. That's the only instance in which the brain will self-destruct. The irony within that is that the more intelligent, honest, loving, compassionate, marvellous, brilliant, dedicated, determined and wonderful human being you are, the faster you self-destruct, because you put all that phenomenal energy into the wrong formula and down you go like a person in quicksand struggling harder and harder to get out, and the harder you struggle the faster you go down. For example, if you teach or believe that as quantity goes up quality goes down, and you are correct, then the more you and the people you teach eliminate the quantity and search for those gems, the more you'll find them. If you believe and teach that as quantity goes up quality goes down and you're wrong, the more you try, the less you get, and because you believe in that formula and you're not getting any results, you will try harder applying it and the less you will get, and the less you will get, and you will end up fundamentally getting no quality at all, if the formula is wrong. So it is essential in our field that we start to search for the appropriate formula. Whatever we give out to people who are receiving from us has the potential to help them self-create on an infinite and positive spiral or self-destruct similarly. The responsibility we have, from my point of view, is the ultimate one. It is literally the life and death of intelligence and it is in our hands, hearts and minds. So I want to address that for the remainder of my paper and then give some indication of what the answers are on this.

I'd like you very briefly to jot down what are, for you, your two main problem areas using your own brain. The main problem areas, the main difficulties in the mental arena that you have. Just your two highest ones. And then again in your paperclip groups, have a quick discussion about what those were. Starting now.

(Pause of about one minute)

Can we now have a machine gun compilation of these: what kind of problems do we have? (Suggestions from the audience were) memory, maths, handling value judgements, choosing, historic time scale, specific code, concentration, creativity, communication, priorities, hangovers!, more than one idea at once, validity of what is taught, separating things, co-ordination. How many people here have a problem with communication - public speaking, writing, receiving communication, in other words, communicating in and out? The majority of us. How many people have a problem with creativity - we found that out earlier! How many people have a problem with mathematics, would have a hard time getting a degree at university in mathematics? Again the majority. How many people have a problem with memory? 100%! How many people have a problem with concentration? That's interesting, I've been doing this survey for more than 20 years now and on concentration it's nearly always about 95% of the audience put their hand up for it. The 5% who don't put their hand up aren't keeping them down because they haven't got the problem, they're keeping them down because they weren't paying attention when I was asking the question!

Now what is intriguing is that, if you look at this list of problems, it is the same list as you would have gathered had you asked what problems could the human brain have. In a sense we have the lot and most of us have most of them. It means you can change your curriculum vitae: normally we have name, sex, date of birth, first school, second school, third school, graduate work and so on, career, all by date, and all your accomplishments, awards, hobbies, so on and so forth. You can now add personal problems - "My memory is rather weak, in addition to which I can't calculate too well and get confused in terms of the handling of value judgements; can't choose very well between alternatives and really, in conjunction with having a bad memory, that also relates to the fact that I don't really know what history is about. I find specific codes difficult to understand and focus on. My concentration is pretty awful, added to which I am not a very creative individual, which doesn't particularly matter because I can't communicate anyway, and as you can imagine I am a somewhat fearful character with all these growing incapacities. In those rare instances where I do get things in front of me I can't decide on the priorities anyway. One of the reasons for many of these problems maybe the fact that I regularly have hangovers. Ideas more than one at once, you know, I can't handle that, and it may surprise you but I actually have taught, but I don't really believe in what I've taught anyway. I've already said that I have trouble choosing value judgements, which confirms the 'separating things' problem that I have, and in addition to all this I am physically unco-ordinated. Would you please employ me as I want to teach."

It's humorous, but it's true. And just so that you feel comfortable with these areas, here are a group of others. I have a pile in my studio literally over a foot high of these problems gathered from around the world in my travels. Who do you think these are? (Examples of results from a number of other groups displayed.) So we see, around the world at all levels of education, wealth, class, race, and so on, the problems are basically the same. What is interesting is the explanation commonly given, which is the same in every language and is a deep-seated belief about what we are as human beings.

This has to do with the title of this whole conference: basically, here we're talking about human potential. What we interpret by that, I've been told, is helping people to realize, ie bring out their potential. I want to take a different tack on this title and talk about realizing what that potential is and then helping people realize it. So you must realize what it is first and then help them realize, i.e. grow, into that potential. It has a lot to do with the way we think about it.

I want you to imagine that you have done a job and it is a disaster, and people are starting to point the finger and say, "It's your responsibility". You are going through the standard excuse routine, you're saying, "I didn't get the facts on time, your instructions, the phone didn't ring, the computer broke down, I had a bad knee on Thursday", and all the other wriggles, but in the end you are trapped and you have to admit that the whole catastrophe is your fault. What people in all languages and countries say is something like this: "All right, all right, it was my fault, but what do you expect, I'm only human. Just a pathetic, slow thinking, unintelligent, standard model human being, and for that reason forgive me this catalogue of catastrophes."

The reverse happens. People are saying to you that you've done a job and that it's amazing, unbelievable, and you're going through the other denying routine saying, "Oh no, I couldn't possibly take the credit for that, it was the team not me, I can't take the credit". But in the end you have to, because you're getting awards and so on. How many people do you see get up and say, "Do you know something? You are absolutely correct. I am a genius, it was an astounding job and the reason why it was astounding - and by the way it was so astounding that it astounded even me: I richly deserve the accolades and awards you're so appropriately giving me and for which I thank you - and the reason why it was so astounding and why I am so incredible is because I am a human being"? Basically never, except perhaps in the heyday of Mohammed Ali. And yet in terms of realizing human potential, the first is wrong and the second is correct.

The reasons why we have these problems is nothing to do with being only human. It is to do with where we are evolutionarily. If you consider, for example, your own academic career: how many hours you spent learning about mathematics and numbers - was it tens, hundreds or thousands? About language and literature? Hundreds, thousands. About geography, history and the sciences? Hundreds, thousands. About how your memory works as time goes on while your brain assimilates information, how many hours? About the nature of your perception and how you can change it to your particular needs in terms of focus, concentration, comprehension and understanding. How many hours about the nature of creativity and its relationship to memory? How many hours about the nature of memory itself, and forgetting, and what you can do about that? To put it another way, if you go into a shop and you buy a steam iron you get a twenty page book on how it was made, how to use it, how to look after it and how to fix it if it goes wrong. You buy a megabyte computer which is 10,000 times less intelligent than one of your students and you get a 200 page book. What do you get for using your brain, which is in fact incredible in terms of realizing human potential? The organ that we are dealing with is arguably the most miraculous thing around. And I want to, very briefly, introduce you to what we have done with and to it and what we can do about that.

Apart from the fact that the brain is synergetic, we have over the last twenty years, through the work of many researchers, recognized the left/right brain theory, for want of a better phase. How many people have heard of that - left/right brain? How many people know the distinction between the left and the right in terms of function? On the left side, logic, words, numbers, lists, lines, linearity; these are called the academic or the business side activities. On the right side, rhythm, colour, imagination - being your ability to generate image - daydreaming, space. Do you daydream? You'll be pleased to know that research, both medical and psychological, has recently confirmed that you have to do night dreaming and daydreaming or die. I mean that it is that necessary for your continued existence, so if anybody comes into your office and sees you with your feet up on the desk, dozing away, and accuses you of being lazy and goofing off on the job, you can just open one eye and say "Survival training". What are these activities called? Artistic, creative. Now in terms of realizing potential I want you to consider for a moment first of all the fact that this is not the creative side. Lots of people are doing brain dominance testing and they come out and they are happy when they are dominant right brain. They come out saying "I did those tests and I'm right brained". You know the kind of person - creative, artistic, sensitive, a real nineties human being. Anyone who tells you that they are right brained is telling you that they're less than a half-wit. Because all of these processes combine all of these skills. All these processes: creativity is all over the brain, art all over the brain, academic business, all over the brain, and that brain itself in terms of realizing its potential is staggering. Everything we ever thought we couldn't do we now know we can. Each individual could get a degree in mathematics, could get a degree in art, could get a degree in music as long as you were taught to learn how to learn in the appropriate way. By the way, what happens to your brain cells as you get older? They die, they drop off, they rot, they disintegrate? What's the point of training anybody if they're losing a thousand to ten thousand brain cells a day? The delightful news is they don't: you do not lose brain cells as you grow older. It's a myth made up in the early 1920s by a student in a London hospital medical school who was told brains weighed so much, weighed some slightly older brains in jars, found they didn't come quite up to par, so he said they must lose brain cells as they get older. People said "Yes, sounds good, pass it on". No medical evidence. So as you get older and if you continue to learn and train, your brain cells, your million million brain cells, get more complex, more integrated.

If we could get in there, which we can't yet, we would see a Niagara of intelligence. Realizing human potential means realizing that we are fundamentally infinitely capable of creativity, that our memories are fundamentally perfect, That the storage system can take in everything we experience in a lifetime and feed it back - as long as we know how to operate the equipment that we have.

On the paperclip exercise, I just leave you with the challenge: how is it that an organ so phenomenal can think of three to four uses for a paperclip in a minute and run out at twentyfour. Something is wrong somewhere and it stems partly from school - when we were in school what did we have to be good at in order to be good in school? Reading, writing, arithmetic - left brain. If, instead, we exercised those right cortical areas, if we showed we were good at things such as banging rhythms on the desk, if we were excellent at making imaginative comments in class, we were good in the playground and top of the form in daydreaming, what were we called? Lazy, trouble, dunce, unintelligent, non-university material, suffering from a tension deficit disability syndrome, disobedient, morons - and yet we were demonstrating half of the qualities of genius.

When we were babies, what side of our brain developed first and fastest? Yes, people normally say right. I'm a baby; you've just given me a piece of paper, so you know it's not going to last long in this situation. Do I attack it like this? (Tear) Or do I do it like this? (Crumple) Which one? Using which side of my brain? The whole of it. What kind of musical instruments can I make; what's the sociological, psychological, economic exchange value of this piece of paper; does anybody want some? Test the engineering, mechanical, tensile strength of the material, stick it in a chemical laboratory (mouth), announce your verdict, review your musical instruments and then move on to the next learning experience. And we take that little Leonardo da Vinci, that little genius, out to explore the third planet, (and by the way, da Vinci said that everything connects to everything else. How many people would agree with that? If you agree that everything connects with everything else, and you are interested in one thing, then you are interested in what? Everything. Nice to know that you are all interested in the planets).

So we take the baby out to explore the third planet: we take it out in the pram, and to prepare it we put on nice big woolly shoes; we put on nice, big, thick trousers over hip locking nappies: a really big, woolly overcoat and a nice big, woolly hat that goes over the hearing apparatus and comes down over the eyes; gloves with no fingers, and then we lie it down in the pram. Then we think, it could fall out, so we strap it in around the hips - if you buy a pram from Harrods you can get two straps so you can get them around the chest as well - and then we think, 'Light could damage the eyes', so over the top we put a nice hood - early training in tunnel vision - and then we think, 'Got to develop the linguistic capacity' so into the mouth goes a dummy; then we must develop the eyes so from the roof we take a piece of string, we dangle a little plastic toy and it goes hypnotically back and forwards, back and forwards - and then we wonder where all the da Vincis have gone!

I suggest to you that those da Vincis are yourselves, myself and everyone with whom we work. That realizing what human potential is, is one of the most glorious things we can do, and then to follow that through in allowing our students to realize it is the other most glorious thing that we can do. Those of us who are in training and education have arguably the greatest privilege the world has ever known.

AUDIENCE: How would you account for the effect of environment?

BUZAN: The environment is incredibly important. The brain is so sensitive to everything that goes on around it: there is a simple check for the environment in which you teach individuals, and that is simply to ask yourself, 'Am I nurturing and supporting, caring for the entire cortex and the physical needs.' Is there colour in the room? Is there form? Are there plants? Is there light, natural light? If you are teaching people, natural light is far better, they actually learn better, see better, feel better, think better. Food is important which is also, in my definition, part of the environment. Lots of coffee, sugar, milk, cookies, cakes and so on are nice as treats, but they're a real disaster in terms of the brain actually getting down to work on thinking. It is also important when people are, for example, studying in the office or studying at home, to make sure that the place where they study is one of the most beautiful places in the house or in the building. It should be a place you recognize as your brain's learning home. It should be like one of the great thinker's studies - telescopes, maps, whatever they want.

AUDIENCE: You make the point very powerfully that we're very good at narrowing down people's perceptions. Where everything is linked to everything else, where the situation is essentially infinite in complexity, can you see any need to create a balance using the power in the idea that certain patterns seem to have an effect and that it is useful to make people aware of those patterns?

BUZAN: Yes I do, very much so. In fact mind mapping, which as you know is my child and truelove, is a device which allows you to access intelligence, it allows you to explore the infinite range of associative ideas, but by the method of focusing your main thought in the centre and then branching out where the main branches are, so to speak the chapter headings of your thought, you put order on that infinite complexity. So it allows you to focus on a central image - a mind map is, if you like, a somewhat detailed answer to your question. It explains how you can use your entire cortex by mind mapping out your thoughts and the ways in which you can analyse, categorize, note take, plan and so on and so forth, and I personally feel that it is as important to go infinitely complex as it is to organize and construct from that infinite complexity. The first thing I suggest one needs to realize is that it <u>is</u> infinite and that your brain can handle that, then you start to organize, integrate, pluck from it the structures and systems you want.

AUDIENCE: You're talking about me, and you talk about my brain; if the brain is there and I'm not using it, where am I?

BUZAN: It has to do with the potential of what we are and I'll answer it by asking the group what percentage of what we are do we think we use?

Of the conscious capacity of the brain's intellect to learn, remember, create, what percentage on average is it now estimated we use? It has gone down every decade. It used to be 50% in the fifties and then it was 40%, and the more we realized about the brain's amazing potential the more we realized that of that potential we're using less and less in comparison to what we're discovering it is. So what you are and I am and we are, if you like, are phenomenal potentials, with the capacity to use all kinds of skills. We are just a waiting explosion of creativity, memory, love, science, all those things.

AUDIENCE: Do you think we might in fact develop and use more of our brain?

BUZAN: That's a question on which I would happily conclude and, if you like, lead into the future. One of the things that has often been said is, if the brain is so amazing, then why has evolution given so much of it to us when we're only using 1% of it? Two reasons. One, it is the ultimate survival organ, and we are designed to survive. That organ has to be as infinitely flexible as it can possibly be, to be able to deal with any kind of eventuality. But in addition to that, the brain that each one of us has in this room today is only 45,000 years old. We are the latest model. Even if you take homo sapiens, the human race back to 2 or 3 million years ago, in evolutionary terms we are a baby less than an hour old. Now again in terms of your question, a baby is what? A baby is potential: it is this glorious creature wide open to the universe, learning. If we consider the human race in evolutionary terms to be a one hour old baby, we are a prodigy in terms of what we've done and what we've explored and where we are at the moment and where we're going and the concerns we have. And you don't stand over the crib and say to a baby, "You've got two feet, two legs, two arms, a mouth - why don't you speak, walk, run, dance, create". You say, "Let me help you", and you start to talk, coach, teach them. It's the same with us; we are a one hour old baby and in my opinion we are doing really, really well, and in the future we're going to do even better.

Tony Buzan is the originator of Mind Maps and various other practical techniques and concepts in brain functioning. He has published nine books on the brain ('Use Your Head' may be the best-known) and one of poetry; has featured in, presented and co-produced many television, video and radio programmes, and is adviser to royalty, governments, to many multi-national organizations and to international Olympic coaches and athletes and to the British Olympic Rowing Squad.

Address for correspondence: **Tony Buzan,**
The Harleyford Manor Estate,
Marlow, Buckinghamshire SL7 2DX

40. Concept mapping as an adjunct study technique for unlocking human potential

P. David Mitchell and Stephen G. Taylor, Concordia University

Abstract: Concept mapping is a term that embraces several techniques for representing knowledge in a visual expression of concepts and relationships believed to model some subject matter. Such visual representations occasionally appear in text books but few students seem to prepare their own. We hypothesized that making a concept map of one's study material would benefit the student. Students were instructed in procedures of concept mapping and given a print-based biology module to study. They were asked to prepare a concept map of the contents. A control group studied the same material but concept mapping was never mentioned. The depth of understanding of both groups was then assessed using a Hypercard-based structural communications module. Students who made a concept map had much higher scores (mean=82) than those who did not map (mean=64). This difference was statistically significant ($P<0.01$).

CONVERSATION THEORY

The rationale for this paper lies in formal descriptions of Conversation Theory (Pask, 1975; 1976; 1984; Pask, Scott and Kallikourdis, 1973). Unfortunately this comprehensive and potentially valuable theory of human learning and communication is not explained sufficiently clearly for most readers to understand it fully. One of its key tenets, as a theory of human learning, is the need to conceive, analyse and evaluate learning as occurring not in one person but in a system composed of two interacting subsystems, teacher (live or mediated) and learner.

In the context of Conversation Theory, learning is less a process of (more or less) passive receiving of context-free information than an active, goal-directed though context-determined search for concepts that one may link to others. This involves the construction of relationships amongst topics within a knowledge structure where agreements on concept meaning (between the participants) lead to understanding on the part of the learner.

Learning may be viewed as a conversation, between these two systems' representations of knowledge, which occurs when they share goals. Such a conversational system may include private knowledge structures but what the observer sees is an agreement (or series of agreements) by the participants that they share the same understanding of some topic. These agreements constitute the hard data which provide evidence of learning.

In Conversation Theory, understanding is a synthetic process that depends on the ability to reconstruct a concept by applying cognitive operations to topics already understood by the learner. Expressed differently, an instructional communication only comes into existence when it is received and understood by the learner - who brings to the symbol exchange an idiosyncratic repertoire. In addition, the learner is postulated to consist of at least two sub-systems, learner and self-teacher, that function to produce internal agreements about what one understands. Therefore instructional messages are functionally different for each learner, depending on the information flow and the knowledge resources and self-educational strategies available internally and externally. The comprehension of spoken or written discourse about some system of concrete or abstract concepts requires a mix of phonemic/graphemic representation, propositional representation and a conceptual or mental model of the relevant world. The trouble is, we have no simple procedure for identifying these in our students.

CONCEPT MAPPING

Insofar as the subject matter expert qua tutor must have a comprehensive knowledge of the knowledge domain and the learner is expected to develop his own, we can assume that each has a mental map of the subject matter (albeit one that changes). Although our concern with abstract knowledge structures is consistent with much of the work on schema theory, our research is driven primarily by work in cybernetics and systems theory, especially Conversation Theory. It is animated by problems encountered in attempting to develop an intelligent conversational hypermedia tutoring system (Mitchell, 1987; 1988; 1990). For simplicity we state that both schemata and conceptual systems are representations that can model knowledge, have variables, can be embedded, may be active processes and may be used to compare and evaluate their goodness of fit to perceived events or experiences.

A defect in such representations is that only verbalized parts which appear in instructional materials or in the discussion are publicly observable. Textbook illustrations and diagrams, like discourse, may be thought of as partial representations of the expert's knowledge while students' notes may serve a similar purpose.

Several writers have advocated the use of various kinds of concept mapping techniques to represent key concepts and the relationships between them, whether for:

* conducting research on learning (Pask, 1976);
* course development for self-instructional systems (Rowntree, 1981);
* CAL authoring (Mitchell, 1982; 1984);
* teaching (Novak & Gowin, 1984); or
* learning and remembering (Neil, 1970; Buzan, 1974).

It may be advantageous to provide both participants with an external representation of the subject matter to guide their discussion (Pask, 1976). However despite the finding that a shared representation might facilitate learning, it is arguable that the learner should construct his own concept map as an exteriorization of his mental model.

STRUCTURAL COMMUNICATION AND ASSESSMENT OF UNDERSTANDING

In normal tutorial conversation, understanding of a topic may be demonstrated if a learner can explain it to the teacher. In most computer-aided learning lessons, such 'How?' and 'Why?' questions cannot be answered except in the most limited fashion (typically a multiple choice or constructed response). Indeed, 'What?' questions seem more common.

How can we detect the occurrence of an understanding in a computer-mediated conversation? Recall that learning (in Conversation Theory) occurs through the construction of relationships amongst topics within a knowledge structure where agreements on concept meaning (between participants) lead to, or demonstrate, understanding on the part of the learner. Thus learning is viewed as an observable, active process in which the learner must 'do' something to operationalize understanding; he must not only be able to describe the concept but also must be able to use the underlying relationships to explain relationships. To understand implies that one can structure and extend that knowledge meaningfully.

Using the technique of structural communication (Hodgson,1974; Romiszowski, 1986),we permit a student to study written discourse and, in response to a problem posed by the tutor, to produce a knowledge representation to be shared with the tutor. This is accomplished by selecting, from a large pool of concepts, several symbols or statements that cohere to form a bundle of related concepts which outline a response to the tutor's challenge. The student's model is compared to the expert's in order to provide agreement or tutorial conversation intended to extend, explain, query, etc. The student is encouraged to speculate or to go beyond the discourse just studied rather than simply to recall. To operationalize the degree of shared understanding we used an index that shows the degree of coherence between the two models.

THE RESEARCH QUESTION

Would it be advantageous for both participants to use an external representation of the subject matter to guide their discussion? In this way, either might identify topics for discussion. In particular, will students benefit from being instructed in procedures of concept mapping when they engage in a structured dialogue using such a system?

We hypothesized that students who employ recommended concept mapping techniques while studying will have a higher degree of understanding (i.e. agreement with an expert when attempting to solve a problem) than those who do not use concept mapping.

METHOD

One group of students was instructed in procedures of concept mapping (in the manner of Novak and Gowin rather than Buzan or Neil) and given a print-based biology lesson to study. They were instructed to prepare a concept map of the contents. A control group studied the same material but concept mapping was never mentioned.

The depth of understanding of both groups was then assessed using a Hypercard-based structural communication module developed to simulate a tutorial conversation. This includes a pool of concepts used by the student as a source of topics that may be linked together and presented to the computer tutor to promote dialogue. In addition a discourse control scheme is incorporated to analyse the student's model and respond to it.

An illustrative problem posed to the students is, "If you consume a protein rich food like steak or eggs, what does your body do with it?" Students then composed an outline or structure of their response by selecting a group of concepts intended to cohere together and communicate an answer. This knowledge representation was compared with that of a subject matter expert both for assessment of the student's understanding and for discourse control for conversation about the student's conceptualization.

UNDERSTANDING

Each response pattern representing a student's knowledge was evaluated using an index that represents the coherence of this model with that of the expert. Individual items in the pool were assigned values related to the significance of those items to the problem posed (i.e. essential, subsidiary, inappropriate, etc.). The coherence index is the sum of all values in the vector representing the student's response. An index of +100 represents total coherence, 0 represents some confusion and -100 represents total failure to comprehend.

SAMPLE

The sample consisted of college students in their final year, randomly distributed across groups.

RESULTS

The mean coherence index (of understanding) for the control group was 63.8 and that of the concept mapping group was 81.6. This large difference in favour of the treatment group is highly significant ($p<0.01$, Scheffe test).

Table 1 contains a summary of the data accumulated by recording the score of each user of the programme as they completed the Protein Module.

	No Map	Made Map
Highest score	84	100
Lowest score	40	60
Group mean	63.8	81.6
Standard deviation	11.9	11.4

Table 1: Comparison of coherence index scores across treatment groups

DISCUSSION AND CONCLUSION

Though both groups evidenced a high degree of understanding in this text plus conversational tutorial,the concept mapping group scored much higher than the non-mapping group. This supports the hypothesis that this approach is beneficial to students. (It is not certain that the explanation lies in the knowledge representation process; it may be that this group spent more time on the module. This could be tested by comparison with other strategies that require extra time, e.g. note-taking, outlining.)

We conclude that concept mapping provides a valuable addition to the structural communication approach in developing computer mediated tutorial conversations. In addition it would appear that students might benefit from the use of concept mapping in studying other instructional materials as well.

REFERENCES

Buzan, T.(1974): Use Your Head. British Broadcasting Corporation, London.

Hodgson, A.M.(1974): Structural communication in practice. In, Yearbook of Educational and Training Technology. Kogan Page, London.

Mitchell, P.D. (1982): Representation of knowledge in CAL courseware. Computers and Education, 6, pp.61-66.

Mitchell, P.D.(1984): Conceptual systems analysis, knowledge structures and learning: towards a conversational system. In, Smith, A.W.(ed): Proceedings of the Society for General System Research. Intersystems, Seaside, California.

Mitchell, P.D.(1987): ACME* A prototype system for tutorial development and evaluation of understanding. In, Proceedings of the 1987 IEEE International Conference on Systems, Man and Cybernetics, pp.811-817. IEEE, New York.

Mitchell, P.D.(1988): C/CASTE: an intelligent, multimedia, knowledge-based interactive system. In, Proceedings of the Sixth Conference on Interactive Instructional Delivery. Society for Applied Learning Technology, Warrenton, VA.
Mitchell, P.D.(1990): Problems in developing and using an intelligent hypermedia tutoring system: a test of conversation theory. Presented to the Seventh International Conference on Technology and Education, Brussels.
Neil, M.W.(1970): The nature, roles and construction of conceptual models in higher education. In, Bajpai, A.C. and Leedham, J.F.(eds): Aspects of Educational Technology IV. Pitman, London.
Novak, J.D. and Gowin, D.B.(1984): Learning How to Learn. Cambridge University Press, Cambridge.
Pask, G.(1975): Conversation, Cognition and Learning. Elsevier, Amsterdam.
Pask, G.(1976): Conversation Theory: Applications in Education and Epistemiology. Elsevier Science Publishers, New York.
Pask, G.(1984): Review of conversation theory and protologic (or protolanguage). Educational Communication and Technology Journal. 32, 1, pp.3-40.
Pask, G., Scott, B.C.E. and Kallikourdis, D.(1973): A theory of conversations and individuals. International Journal for Man-Machine Studies, 5, pp.17-52.
Romiszowski, A.(1986): Instructional Development 2: Developing Auto-Instructional Materials: From Programmed Texts to CAL and Interactive Video. Kogan Page London.
Rowntree, D.(1981): Developing Courses for Students. McGraw-Hill, London.

Address for correspondence: **Prof.P.D.Mitchell and S.G.Taylor,**
Centre for System Research and Knowledge Engineering,
Graduate Programme in Educational Technology, Concordia University,
1455 boulevard de Maisonneuve West, Montreal, Quebec, Canada H3G 1M8

41. A systems approach to the evaluation of a University's teaching, research and community service programme in a post-apartheid society

W.S.H.du Randt, University of Port Elizabeth

Abstract: The Republic of South Africa is in 1990 embarking on processes of radical reform which will (hopefully) lead to a democratic society in which all forms of discrimination, racism and racialism will be eliminated. The integrity of this programme will, apart from the broad constitutional procedures, to a large extent be highlighted by and assessed in terms of the form and content of a new functional and democratic educational and university policy and programme in which the systems approach to a coordinated university programme, applying the principle of synergy, will play a fundamental role, viz., to identify forces which will integrate existing resources into an open, equal, functional and dynamic structure.

Racialism, one of the bitterest fruits of imperialism, has been a curse to South Africa. What energies, physical and moral, needed for the upbuilding of our State, have been fruitlessly dissipated upon reciprocal demolition? What would these energies have accomplished if, instead of being thus deliberately devoted to cancelling each other out by mutual counteraction, they had been added together for common service. C.J.Langenhoven, 1927

SECTION ONE

Post-modernism in general and post-structuralism in particular have convincingly demonstrated that literary and other social texts are **evasive** in the sense that they do not 'contain' a fixed core of objective meaning and that each reading of a text is relative and incomplete. Some critics maintain that **deconstruction** - which is closely related to post-structuralism - has not taken root in the Anglo-Saxon world and is generally treated with suspicion outside France because it threatens the modernistic complacency with an existing order of capitalistic society structures and norms as well as the certainty with which we apply structuralistic (Hawkes, 1978) assumptions and criteria about language and meaning.

It is within this tradition which questions rather than confirms that Jacques Derrida postulates his theory that the word, sign or text can no longer be seen as a reflection of reality but that words (texts) play an active part in **creating** 'reality' (Brink, 1985). The application of deconstruction, according to Brink, is not a destruction of reality but rather a deconstruction: meaning is posited as referential and changing and not as non-existent. Words and ideas (meaning) are - in accordance with the precepts of structuralism - defined in terms of their differences with other words. Derrida, however, uses the term 'differance' to demonstrate that meaning is indefinitely extended or deferred. He rejects the logocentric premise of Western metaphysics that language (a text) refers to the 'pre-sence' of an external, objective reality and truth. In short, deconstruction has made it possible for us to radically question the 'pride and prejudice' that underlie the values and structures of an 'existing' order, particularly those pertaining to political, social and educational 'texts'. In this sense post-modernism has become one of the most valuable critical tools in our creative search for 'meaning' and 'truth' and consequently, for the purpose of this paper, a new, equitable society and its institutions.

It is from a post-modern perspective then that I want to interpret the 'text' of 'Education in South Africa' (South Africa Year Book 1988-89). Firstly, I shall project it firmly within the established, perhaps even immovable, metaphysical and historical socio-political context with its myriad of cultural codes and conventions. I reject at the outset as naive a prevailing South African belief that the 'outside world' under the influence of the Anti-Apartheid Movement has deliberately and maliciously politicized 'neutral' elements of our society for the sole purpose of undermining 'our' (the 'White' group's) claim to 'self-determination'. In other words: I accept that a social text is never 'neutral' or 'objective' but that its 'meaning' is inevitably determined by and committed to preselected ideological values and norms - in this case the doctrine of apartheid. Moreover, I acknowledge that 'meaning' is not only generated by what a text reveals but by what it consciously or unconsciously conceals.

Secondly I want to illustrate that 'educational technology', and particularly the 'systems approach' as its central theme (CET, 1974), through its intrinsic potential to integrate disparate and contradictory elements into a functional unitary structure, displays an inherent 'ideological' competence to expose the process of segregating or isolating parts from the whole as being 'unsystematic' and, in terms of a social 'text-grammar', (Malan, 1985) ungrammatical and unproductive. I shall assess the possibility that the so-called unassimilable parts can in fact, be integrated **synergetically** into a functional and productive whole, if one could but discover a unifying principle or theme.

Afrikaner-nationalism was initially inspired by the positive ideals of the Reformation as well as the French and American revolutions but later, understandably but counterproductively, influenced by anti-British sentiments in the decades following the inglorious Anglo-Boer War. It reached its climax in 1948 when the National Party came to power. One cannot deny that Afrikaner-nationalism was in the late thirties to a large extent contaminated by an admiration by some Afrikaners for elements of Hitler's national-socialistic ideology.

Since his succession to the leadership of the National Party Mr.F.W.de Klerk has created a new climate of realism and hope with his courageous and imaginative reforms and the release of Mr.Nelson Mandela and the unbanning of the A.N.C. However in a recent testimony before a Committee of the President's Council I reiterated my long-held belief that the continued adherence to a policy based upon 'group rights' at the first level of government will only continue to frustrate the process of liberation for all the parties. Moreover, I hold the firm conviction that Mr. Mandela will be able to make a fundamental contribution to create a climate of reconciliation and liberation for all in our country and provide Black aspirations with a unique and genuine leadership potential which is vital for negotiating the new apartheid-free South Africa. The integrity of his leadership role could therefore only be undermined by any overt or covert effort to co-opt him into the existing order.

Finally, I cannot but accept personal responsibility and express my heartfelt regret as a Christian, an Afrikaner and a supporter of the National Party for every conscious or unconscious act of identification with or support for apartheid ideology which inflicted such degradation, pain and suffering on its victims.

SECTION TWO

That the apology for apartheid policies and structures deconstructs its own 'message' becomes patently clear when we compare the recent enthusiastic endorsement of the De Lange Commission's report in the official Government text: Education in South Africa (South Africa, 1988-89) with the initial negative response to the Commission's moderate and even status-quo-orientated recommendations as reflected in its White Paper on the Provision of Education in the Republic of South Africa (1983), particularly in regard to a unitary education system for our country:

In 1980 the Government requested the Human Sciences Research Council (HRSC), an autonomous research institution, to conduct an in-depth investigation into education in South Africa .....The Committee's report, described by many as the most thorough and penetrating analysis ever to be made of education in South Africa, was published in 1981, and the Government's first White Paper was released in November 1983. Some of the most striking recommendations were a new educational structure, greater emphasis on technical and vocational education, a strong desire for an acceleration in the rate at which parity in education is to be achieved, more effective coordinating mechanisms at national level, and a management structure that would be acceptable to everybody involved in education in South Africa.

In addition to these, recommendations were made to promote the use of educational technology (in particular the computer) in education **(sic!)** and to bring about a more scientific approach in the development of curricula and syllabuses.

A new education dispensation was established based on the HSRC inquiry, the White Paper on the Provision of Education, and the new Constitution of the RSA. One of the first steps was the acceptance of the **National Policy for Educational Affairs Act**, 1984 (Act 76).

Education is an own affair for each population group in terms of the new Constitution .... However, provision is made for the rendering of services by one group to another.

Education of Whites is controlled by the Department of Education and Culture (House of Assembly) and administered by the provincial education departments of the Cape Province, Natal, the Orange Free State and Transvaal; while for Coloured and Indians the education is controlled and administered by the Departments of Education and Culture, House of Representatives and House of Delegates respectively. Education for Blacks (in the areas under direct control of the central government) is controlled and administered by the Ministry of Education and Training and for Blacks in the six Black self-governing territories and four independent Black republics by their own autonomous departments.

The majority of pupils in South Africa attend government schools which are administered by either a provincial or a national education department. However, private schools run by church denominations or private enterprise are an important feature of the education system. Private school pupils follow the same syllabuses as their fellow pupils in government schools. Educational standards, especially with regard to syllabuses and examinations, are the same for all departmental schools **(sic!)**. Furthermore, the same nationally recognized certificates are issued for trade training and advanced technical education (pp.85/86).

In its White Paper the Government confirmed its acceptance in October 1981 of the principles for the provision of education as proposed in paragraph 2.3 of the HSRC (De Lange report). I quote only the first three:

Principle 1: Equal opportunities for education, including equal standards in education, for every inhabitant, irrespective of race, colour, creed or sex, shall be the purposeful endeavour of the State.
Principle 2: Education shall afford positive recognition of what is common as well as of what is diverse in the religious and cultural way of life and the languages of the inhabitants.
Principle 3: Education shall give positive recognition to the freedom of choice of the individual, parents and organizations in society.

The real significance of the acceptance of these principles can, however, only be understood when we consider them within the context of the Government's absolute and categorical adherence to the apartheid doctrine:

The Government reaffirms that, in terms of its policy that each population group should have its own schools, it is essential that each population group should also have its own education authority/department. The need for coordination is recognized, but this policy will have to be duly taken into account in any proposals relating to structures for central coordination and cooperation between the educational structures of the various population groups, and also in any proposals relating to educational structures at the regional or local levels. Education departments of their own are also essential to do justice to the right to self-determination which is recognized by Government policy for each population group. (White Paper, p.4)

The Government's apparent agreement with and acceptance of the Commission's recommendations must be assessed in terms of its commitment to segregated or group structures. So for example its fear that unrealistic expectations to eliminate the backlogs and inequalities in education could lead to a lowering of existing educational standards and, consequently, frustrate the aims of economic progress and national stability appears to be the most ironic when one considers the privileged status of white institutions which has caused serious discrepancies between standards of, broadly speaking, the 'White' and 'Non-White'education departments and particularly the standards of 'Black' and 'White' universities (White Paper, p.29). One can assume that affirmative action programmes could have been an appropriate strategy to counter the effects of inferior education for the disadvantaged 'non-White' pupils. The lack of foresight to provide Blacks with technical and other vocational training can only be attributed to a mythical belief that Blacks should and could not be accommodated in South Africa's White environment and ultimately the obsession that they would have to be resettled in the 'homelands'.

It is also the Government's ideological adherence to the principle of group rights and its insistence that Afrikaans should be a compulsory school subject for Black pupils which precipitated the violence in Soweto in 1976. It is for this reason that not only Blacks but we, supporters of the system, share the blame for the white:black political dispensation and the extreme polarization which has become institutionalized in our political history. The references to equity must accordingly - as so many times in the past - be exposed from within the 'system' as a transparent effort to camouflage a policy of 'divide and rule'.

It is specifically on this point then that one has to question the moral integrity of an educational system which cannot and will not be able to contribute to the renewal and radical transformation of a society predestined to produce first, second, third and even fourth class citizens. It is also against this background that one has to assess the unproductive efforts to 'open' white universities to all population groups. The present measures are generally hollow gestures of tokenism which will remain cosmetic unless comprehensive and aggressive affirmation action programmes are introduced to reinforce the position of disadvantaged students. The new criterion of academic merit and external entrance qualification can only prolong the agony when, in 'an unwilling suspension of disbelief', we have to read "....that today there are ten residential universities originally established for whites. However, as pointed out earlier, all now accept both undergraduate and post-graduate non-white students" **(sic!)** (This is South Africa, p.88).

To summarize: to the same extent that the Government itself has recognized the bankruptcy of apartheid policies in respect of constitutional matters, it must now act to rid our country of a morally indefensible and economically unaffordable educational system. One can only marvel, then, that the continuing closure of white colleges and schools and the retrenchment of fully trained white teachers should continue in the present spiral of a dramatically decreasing number of white pupils. Moreover, it is a strange contradiction that in an era of 'rationalization' the established universities are, financially speaking, bleeding to death whilst a new apartheid institution such as Vista should be developed on six urban campuses without any apparent financial restraints.

SECTION THREE

The Republic of South Africa is in 1990, God willing, embarking upon processes of radical reform which will hopefully lead to a democratic society in which all forms of discrimination, racism and racialism will have been eradicated. The integrity of this process will, apart from the broad constitutional procedures, to a large extent be highlighted by and assessed in terms of the form and content of a new functional and democratic educational policy and programme. In this programme the systems' approach applying the principle of **synergism** will play a fundamental role, viz. to identify forces and strategies which will integrate existing resources into an open, equal, functional and dynamic structure.

It is perhaps symptomatic of our cultural isolation that the theory and practice of educational technology has not been understood by educationalists in South Africa. It is revealing that the De Lange Commission's recommendations on educational technology were rejected clearly as a result of the Government's inability to distinguish between educational technology as a modern, sophisticated educational **system** and 'educational technology **services**' as "... one of the modern and potentially extremely valuable **aids** in education": "The Government is of the opinion that the obvious benefits that can be achieved through the use of modern technology in education should be pursued in a sensible and systematic manner and that hasty action should be avoided **(sic!)** (White Paper, p.40). It is therefore not surprising that this decision is reflected as follows in the current edition of the booklet: **This is South Africa**: "... In addition to these, recommendations were made to **promote** the use of education **(sic!)** technology (in particular the computer) in education ..."(p.86).

This then, is the context in which educational technology offers solutions for the critical realities of South Africa in the nineties. The De Lange Commission recommended that :

> educational technology should be accepted from a policy point of view as a fundamental factor in the planning, development and implementation of the provision of education at all levels and in both the formal and non-formal sectors (White Paper, p.39).

In the first place, one has to expose the fallacy that educational technology as such is orientated towards a preference for the application of computers or any other hardware. In their **Bibliography on Educational Technology** the British Council for Educational Technology describes the concept as follows:

> educational technologists are primarily concerned with the design and development of curricula and materials, and with the problem of introducing them. In this development process, two complementary approaches can be used. Where educational research provides firm evidence about learning and teaching, these findings can be used as a basis for the design of courses. If, however, no such evidence is available, an empirical, developmental approach can be used in which materials are evaluated and modified before - and after - they are put into use. Both these approaches have in common the attempt to make teaching somewhat more systematic than it has been in the past; hence the use of the word 'technology' which, in its root sense, means 'something between an art and a craft'. Technology, then is being used here not to refer to machines or equipment but to describe a way of tackling the practical problems of teaching and learning...(p. 14).

In the second place, educational technology is through its intrinsic insistence on comprehensive strategies admirably equipped to analyse learning requirements from a unitary, non-discriminatory perspective. It is a fundamental force in the continuous process of defining and redefining objectives; planning flexible and socially relevant curricula; devising interchangeable short courses or modules and selecting appropriate learning and research methods and strategies. It offers a critical self-reflection on the form and content of its decisions and actions, the emphasis is inevitably placed on functionality and productivity - yet it provides adequately for self-paced and tempo acceleration programmes, self-motivation, cooperation and reinforcement. Experience has proved that its record of managing resources and devising appropriate strategies and instruments for scientifically accountable processes of evaluation and assessment is impeccable. Another vital factor here is that scarce top-level management and teaching skills can by definition be duplicated and integrated into the system in terms of educational technological procedures.

Thirdly, my own experience at various levels of a university's learning and research programmes led to the discovery that I could fulfil my teaching, research and community service commitments more productively by replacing my role as teacher with that of a 'systems' manager'. This provided new opportunities to devise a model for each unique situation or project. I was inevitably converted to the creative and innovative challenges that the systems' approach and its natural application of the principle of synergy offered to realizing human potential. The most important gain, however, was the discovery that students were not enemies or stumbling blocks but that they represented a vital resource and a source of cooperation and control.

In short, the 'system' - once operational - to a large extent became self-sufficient and allowed me to share and even transfer responsibilities to colleagues, assistants and students. In this way, for the first time, I became involved in criticizing and changing existing policies and structures at the local and national level. I could actively participate in decision-making processes and institutions. It is for this reason that I see myself as an enthusiastic apostle of this innovative concept.

SECTION FOUR

The ultimate questions, then, are: How can a viable unitary educational order, despite the diversity of groups and cultures, be achieved in South Africa? In what way can we escape the frustrations that Black societies themselves experience with Western, capitalistic societies and their educational systems?

Would it not be ironic - and in view of recent American and UK experience not an altogether unrealistic option - if Africa itself and Third World minority groups in Western societies from the predominantly disadvantaged classes or castes should ultimately respond to Western capitalistic ideological practices such as **competition** in school, commerce and society by creating 'self-imposed structures of apartheid'?

Will a deconstructive reading of the Western Establishment's fierce rejection of 'self-imposed apartheid structures' by minority groups within the context of the African insistence on an educational system reorientated to the social and economic needs of the groups or countries involved not precipitate a reassessment of Western capitalistic norms regarding education and the educational 'intertext'? And would it not be the height of irony if South Africa's claim regarding the relevance of its educational policies for diverse cultures should prove to have an ultimate validity? In this context Western-liberal rejection of Third World political realities and educational aspirations could, in spite of the 'co-option' of members of privileged classes or castes into the system for the purpose of *de facto* endorsement, to be exposed as a continuation of neo-colonialistic and imperialistic practices.

Does an 'Africanized' educational system offer solutions to the dilemma of multi-cultural societies? Is it just to expect people with a distinct and proud but repressed culture to adapt naturally to established traditions of Western values and systems? What contribution can African socialism and/or People's Education really make to the dilemma in Africa and Southern Africa? Is it possible to eliminate the predominance of one or more ideology in an educational system? Should learners be exposed to all expressions of ideology in an eclectic manner or should society indicate or dictate a preference?

I must confess that the above scenario - even if constructed hypothetically - has as much relevance for 'Blacks' as it has for any other minority group having to adapt to the norms of a dominant 'alien' cultural environment in which the learner not only has to survive but of which he has to become a useful and responsible citizen. Would a more feasible approach not lie in a critical assessment of Western education to provide a stimulating and inspiring environment for the challenge to realize human potential adequately in a radically changing society with its cross-fertilization of traditions, cultures and values?

I want to proffer a few recommendations which I hope could assist in laying the foundations for a completely new and dynamic educational policy in my country:

1. An equitable new social order in South Africa can only be achieved if we accept the 'checks and balances' inherent in our society, reject group or racial policies on the first level of government and introduce a unitary system of education to achieve the goal of an equitable social order.
2. The economic realities of 1990 dictate that the duplicated structures at the primary and secondary levels and the ethnic or group-based teachers' training colleges, universities and technikons at the tertiary level be redefined as soon as possible. An example is the possible consolidation of all tertiary institutions in the Eastern Cape into our first comprehensive and technologically orientated university.
3. A vital factor in creating parity will be the compulsory introduction of English as the medium of instruction from at least the last phase of secondary school and at tertiary level.
4. The Government should immediately suspend the incomprehensible extension of Vista University - particularly in view of the need to look very critically at contemporary definitions of university education in relation to the demand for highly trained technological and technical (wo)manpower.
5. Educational technology should be implemented as a matter of urgency and it is of vital importance that the confusion regarding educational technology's true definition be corrected as soon as possible.
6. The university must be rehabilitated as an independent autonomous institution of excellence which can be trusted to establish and maintain its own standards and to control its own budget in terms of academic performance. Productivity as assessed by a new generation of creative managers who would be accountable to a National Council for University Education would become a vital criterion. In this regard the establishment of structures to administer voluntary procedures of accreditation and evaluation is long overdue.
7. All centralized programmes by Government institutions and agencies - particularly pertaining to the financing of research - must be terminated. The HSRC and CSIR will in accordance with this measure be placed in a position where they can more consistently fulfil their primary function of undertaking community service or, as it is also defined 'contract research', in partnership with tertiary and other specialized research institutions. We must stop the process of the indiscriminate expansion of power structures and bureaucracies in our country.

I conclude by repeating an earlier reference to Derrida: "Words (texts) play an active role in creating 'reality'". In the Bushman legend 'The song of the rain' **(Dwaalstories)** it is specifically such a reality which primitive man with his still intact mystical senses has preserved for the more sophisticated but far less intuitive sensibilities of modern 'scientific' man. In his 'dwaalstorie' (dwaal= to lead someone astray) the primitive poet gives expression to man's inner longing to be liberated from all forms of oppression. It is the story of the great drought at Das-se-kant and the injustices and oppression which the ordinary Bushman folk have to endure at the hands of Jacob Makding (literally and ironically: the tamed thing in juxtaposition with 'Jacob' signifying deceiver).

Makding, the tyrant, has proclaimed himself Strongman of the Berry

Trees, and whilst everybody in this microcosmic Bushmanworld literally changes colour as a result of famine and thirst and looks up in vain to the Great Council (of politicians) to offer solutions and provide relief the diminutive hunch-back artist, Joggom Konterdans (Joe Counterdance) is diligently working on his Bushman violin. The old woman, the prophetic Nasi Tgam, then 'takes up the word' and reminds them of the law of the Berry Trees: the Strongman is chosen and the Strongman has to be just. If the rain stays away, water and food must be shared. When Konterdans plays the mystical song of the rain the tyrant capitulates and the Old Order is restored. This is the sacred moment for Nasi Tgam to recite the Law of the Berry Trees. She entrusts the symbols of authority to the heroic musician. The story ends: it was Krom Joggom Konterdans who divided the water among the people of every settlement. Only now is the great heavenly rain released upon the dry, scorched earth and is the scene set for the triumphant dance of the rain.

O the dance of our sister!
First o'er the mountaintop she slyly glances
And her eyes are shy.
She laughs softly
And from afar she beckons with one hand.
Her bangles glitter and her beadstrings glow.
Softly she calls out,
She tells the winds of the dance,
She invites them gladly, for the weddingplace is wide
And the wedding feast great.

The big game charge across the dry plains,
They mill around the hilltop;
They open their nostrils widely as they gulp the wind
And they kneel humbly when they see her footprints in the sand.

The small folk deep under the ground
Hear the patter of her feet
They crawl closer and sing softly:
"Our sister! Our sister! You have come! You have come!"
Her beadstrings rattle
And her earrings glitter in the setting of the sun.
She steps down from her high place.
She opens the vaal karos* with outspread hands.
The wind is left breathless:
O, the dance of our sister!

*literally: grey blanket made from animal hides.

REFERENCES

Brink, A.(1985): Transgressions: a quantum approach to literary deconstruction. Journal of Literary Studies, 1, 3, pp.10-26.

Cloete, T.T. et al(1985): Gids by the literatuurstudie. HAUM, Pretoria.

Council for Educational Technology(1974): Bibliography on Educational Technology CET, London.

De Beer, C.S.(1985): Representasie en disseminasie. Journal of Literary Studies, 1, 3 pp.1-9.

Grove, A.P.(1988): Letterkundige sakwoordeboek vir Afrikaans. Nasou Beperk, Kaapstad.

Hawkes, T.(1978): Structuralism and Semiotics. Methuen, London.

Malan, C.(1985): In, Cloete, T.T. et al, Gids by the literatuurstudie, HAUM, Pretoria. p. 60

Republic of South Africa(1983):
White Paper on the Provision of Education in South Africa.
South Africa 1988-1989: Yearbook of the Republic of South Africa.

Address for correspondence: **Prof.W.S.H.du Randt,**
University of Port Elizabeth,
P.O.Box 1600, Republic of South Africa.

42. Improving managerial productivity through information technology

Clive Holtham

Abstract: Many managers are sceptical that their own productivity can be improved, particularly through the use of information technology. This is particularly so at the very top levels of management. This paper outlines research that has been carried out at City University Business School into alternative ways that managers can improve their productivity through the use of IT, and also into the pre-conditions for successful use. It also discusses techniques developed at the Business School for overcoming the fears and resistance to the direct use of IT by senior managers in particular. It concludes with a discussion of the implications of these findings for management education and teaching, and areas for further research.

The use of computers by top managers has been something of a Cinderella area of information technology. Research into the nature of top managerial work has shown that the top manager is often addressing many issues simultaneously (Mumford, 1988), is often highly mobile geographically (ROMTEC, 1988), and has relatively short periods of time available for focusing on specific issues. There is also evidence of some resistance to the idea of 'training' for top managers, particularly in the area of information technology (IT) (Martin, 1988). The nature of top management work is also very diverse between different organizations and depends on ownership, size, structure and style (Donaldson and Lorsch, 1983).

Recent research data support the idea that top management use of computers is in reality a limited activity at present (Eosys, 1986; Business Intelligence, 1989). There does appear to be active reluctance on behalf of many British managers to use computer systems personally to improve their own efficiency and effectiveness. It is very common to hear managers arguing that the actual direct use of IT is much more appropriate for middle and junior managers, and for secretarial and administrative staff.

A number of barriers revealed by these attitudes have been identified in our research at the City University Business School:

Fear of Personal Innovation. Even managers who are remarkably innovative in mainstream business thinking may be reluctant or even fearful about innovating in their own personal style of working.

Learning Curve. Top managers have reached where they have by a process of steady learning, usually by experience and observation. Unfortunately learning to use IT tends to require more basic learning styles including reading manuals and learning from mistakes. Top managers who see themselves as self-assured experts in their own area are often exceptionally reluctant to have to ask a junior member of staff, "But exactly where did you say the ENTER key was?".

Human-Computer Interface. The conventional keyboard, operating systems and applications packages are often geared to regular users of IT. Top managers are normally occasional users, so touch screens, mouse and infra-red keypad are all advocated to get round the 'keyboard barrier', and for output simple but elegant colour displays are the norm. But just as significant as input/output technology is likely to be the overall system design, data structure, updating philosophy and response time.

Nature of Output. Paper-based output has enormous advantages for top managers. It is very light - not unimportant for a group which travels a lot. Layout is almost infinitely flexible. It is easy to annotate, redirect and cut up. It is supremely flexible. Screen-based outputs tend to tie the user to particular geographical locations where the screens are, and to fairly structured formats for layout. Most portable PCs have problems of cost, size and obtrusiveness, although the Psion Organizer is perhaps an exception to this.

Nature of Data. Whereas for operational and middle management decisions the data needed is often relatively highly structured, and thus ideal for computerization, top managers also need judgements about the data, and they need 'soft' data too - hints, rumours, feelings, opinions, ideas. Most conventional IT systems are not geared to the latter area, although there are now products that do so.

Beliefs about the Top Management Role. Top managers often describe their roles in very abstract ways e.g. as about 'chemistry', 'intuition', 'applying personal skills and judgements' and 'creating the right climate'. All these are undoubtedly important, but studies of the actual use of management time often show that significant amounts of time are actually spent on more mundane and mechanical tasks.

Lack of Input by Top Managers in Systems Design. Most 'management information systems' are specified by and for middle managers or specialist support staff. The particular needs of top managers are rarely sought (or given) directly. Middle managers often have a highly idealized model of the top managers' role; in particular they often regard it as rational and decision orientated. Yet Kotter (1982) found that in practice top managers were not strategic, reflective, proactive or well organized. He explained this by on-the-job demands of top managers allocating resources in relation to competing claims and problem solving.

Perceived Cost. Top managers who correctly identify that they will not make very intensive use of a computer may well be reluctant to be seen to incur costs for relatively low usage.

Most hardware and software is not designed with top managers in mind, so it is perhaps not surprising that as a group they perceive it as having little relevance to them. But there is some evidence that general purpose software in particular can be adapted or customized to meet some of the IT needs of top managers. These needs tend to be of a 'niche' nature. For example in the case of spreadsheets and word processing, two factors relevant for top managers are urgency and confidentiality. A finance director involved in late night negotiations may be working without support staff, and would benefit from being able to test assumptions personally, although he or she would be unlikely to have actually created the spreadsheet itself. For confidential matters such as salary reviews the director might well wish to input to create the spreadsheet itself.

One approach to examining the scope for impact of IT on the top manager is to identify some widely available packages that could be of potential value to them, and then analyse the reaction of managers to examples created specifically for their type of work. This is one approach we are taking. For example, the package Sidekick Plus is aimed at providing many of the desktop or diary tools that a manager might need to draw on.

The main modules of the package are set out in Figure 1. In discussion with managers, many of them see little scope for a package of this type assisting them in their work, because so many of them rely on secretaries to do this type of work. However, there is some scope for managerial use of this type of software in very small companies or those

File manager	Notepad
Outliner	Phonebook and autodialler
Calculator	Time planner and alarm
Vogon Poetry	Clipboard (edit,cut,paste)

Figure 1: Modules of 'Sidekick Plus' (Borland International)

with very lean administrative structures or lack of conventional offices e.g. where the senior managers are in effect peripatetic.

In my own research into top management use of IT, I am very struck with how often directors and partners say they would like to be able to keep unstructured notes and jottings, and then retrieve them flexibly. Examples of packages that meet this need are Memorymate, Lotus Agenda and the various hypertext systems.

The only types of software explicitly designed with top managers in mind are 'Executive Information Systems'. These typically involve colour displays, high resolution graphics, easy user interfaces and options for touch screen and mouse. EIS software is based on a pyramid-style model of both the organization and its data: it enables high-level summaries and analyses of the data to be made, and also in some versions at least enables 'drill down' into the basic supporting databases. The ease of use and graphical style of presentation are far in excess of that found, for example, in conventional management accounting software.

Advanced telephone	Telephone software for micros
Memory	Auto dial
Redial	Modem
Displays caller's number	Answering machine

Electronic mail and messaging

Computerized information services

Figure 2: Managerial productivity - communications

Another area of great potential relevance for the top manager is networking and communications technology. Figure 2 summarizes a number of areas of possible use, several of them strongly geared towards the telephone.

Of these areas, electronic mail (EM) is a promising area for top management use, but some EM systems have been far too complex and cumbersome for ad hoc users. They also suffer from the problem of building up a sufficiently large user base quickly enough that top managers do not lose interest in the system. It is probably fair to say that in only a few organizations has EM really made a major impact, including at top levels; in most organizations it has not as yet.

DEVISING MATERIAL TO DEVELOP THE TOP MANAGER

Given the constraints on management time, and managers' lack of inclination or experience in the use of IT, the Business School secured funding under the Training Agency's 'Applications of Technology to Learning' programme. It is contracted to research the area and then to produce courseware specifically geared to the director and senior managers. The Business School is working in a consortium with the Institute of Directors and the software house ICUC Ltd to produce this material.

The programme is known as 'Director and senior manager awareness of IT for business success', and it has three interrelated objectives:

* to inform, stimulate and even excite senior managers and company directors about the possibilities and potential of IT for their businesses;
* to promote with this key group of decision-makers the whole concept of computerized training and information, through their own hands-on use of IT;
* to evaluate alternative methods of delivery to the senior manager. It is well established that this group has in general problems with or aversions to use of conventional personal computers (PCs), and part of the project will explicitly evaluate some new and innovative technologies, both for their relevance in course delivery to this group and to their acceptability to participants.

In order to meet these objectives and to overcome the identified problems, the central core of the project is the design and production of PC-based courseware which is explicitly orientated to the needs of top managers and to the effective use of IT in business. The courseware is being designed to be used both on a desktop PC and also on a portable laptop PC which the top manager can use at home or during the course of travels.

The use of the laptop is significant for several reasons:

* as already indicated, the top manager is often highly mobile geographically and such a machine could be utilized for training purposes in 'slack time' while on the move;
* perhaps even more significantly, there is considerable anecdotal evidence that top managers are somewhat resistant to learning IT in a conventional classroom, laboratory or office environment. For this reason it is believed that much of the training will in fact be done at home. Previous work with top managers carried out in this field by one of the members of the project team suggests that top managers are also willing to make mistakes in front of, and learn from, children and relations in a home environment to a degree they would not feel comfortable with in an office or conventional training environment.

The Business School has already based a formal two day short course for directors and senior managers around the use of laptop computers, and this has proved to be a very popular approach.

RESEARCH INTO TOP MANAGEMENT AWARENESS

This research has been a critical early component of the project. It has been carried out by:

* identifying the key barriers to top management awareness of IT;
* investigating particular features of top management training and learning;
* interviewing top managers who have become successfully aware of IT, and who either use it or promote its use;
* interviewing top managers who are currently unaware of IT.

IMPLICATIONS

Actually achieving effective top management use of IT requires considerable effort. Training is a major issue which needs careful planning. The implications affect not only the manager personally, but also secretarial, support and advisory staff, who may well themselves feel threatened by direct top management use.

There needs to be much closer linkage between the research being carried out by social scientists into the nature of managerial work, and those responsible for designing, or advising on the design of, computerized systems targetted at top managers. Mintzberg (1980) devised a statement of ten managerial roles, summarized in Figure 3, and these are a useful basis to start making the linkage.

Interpersonal Roles	Informational Roles	Decisional Roles
Figurehead	Monitor	Entrepreneur
Leader	Disseminator	Disturbance handler
Liaison	Spokesman	Resource allocator
		Negotiator

Figure 3: Managerial Roles (Mintzberg, 1980)

CONCLUSION

There is little doubt that over the next few years an increasing number of organizations will encourage or persuade their top managers to use IT directly. And while it is unlikely to transform many organizations overnight, it does offer another route to encouraging innovative thinking and creativity, which must be at the heart of developing strategies for survival and growth.

SELECTED REFERENCES

Business Intelligence (1989): The EIS Report (2nd Edition). Business Intelligence, London.
Donaldson, G. and Lorsch, J.W.(1983): Decision Making at the Top. Basic Books, New York.
EOSYS (1986): Top Executives and Information Technology - Disappointed Expectations. EOSYS, Slough.
Kotter, J.P.(1982): The General Managers. Free Press, New York.
Martin, C.(1988): Computers and Senior Managers. National Computing Centre, Manchester.
Mintzberg, H.(1980): The Nature of Managerial Work. Prentice-Hall, Englewood Cliffs, New Jersey.
Mumford, A.(1988): Developing Top Managers. Gower, Aldershot.
Rajan, A.(1988): Information Technology and Managers: Some good practices. Institute of Manpower Studies, Report No. 146, Brighton.
Rockart, J.F. and Delong, D.W.(1988): Executive Support Systems. Dow Jones Irwin, Homewood, Illinois.
ROMTEC (1988): An Assessment of the Use and Awareness of Executive Information Systems. ROMTEC, Maidenhead, for Comshare.

Clive Holtham is Bull HN Professor of Information Management at the City University Business School. An accountant by background he was a finance director immediately prior to joining the Business School, with extensive experience in managing and using information technology. His research is centred around the top management use of IT, and the application of IT for strategic advantage. He consults and lectures widely, both in the UK and abroad. Research areas include: the relationship between information technology and competitive advantage in the financial services sector; Executive Information Systems; top management awareness of IT.

Address for correspondence: **Prof.C.Holtham,**
City University Business School,
Frobisher Crescent, Barbican, London EC

43. The new enfranchisement: who types the text?

Roslyn Petelin, Queensland University of Technology

Abstract: Two growing trends at opposite ends of the Australian corporate ladder have the potential for enormous benefits for both individuals and industry: 1. Executives, who are experienced at writing but generally inexperienced at word processing, are increasingly generating the text of their letters, memos, reports, and proposals on the PCs on their desks - thereby giving themselves much greater power and control over their writing and cutting down on the substantial costs incurred as documents 'loop' their way through a cycle of editing and reprinting; 2. Typists, who are experienced at word processing but generally regarded as being so inexperienced at writing that they are relegated to transcribing for 100% of their working time, are increasingly being encouraged to spend a certain proportion of their time 'composing' documents. Because the activity of writing is such a powerful means of developing important intellectual abilities, and because writing skill is directly proportional to employability, enfranchisement of typists is of great value to them. And because research has indicated that the word processor dramatically increases the productivity, accuracy, quality and efficiency of written communication, executives are increasingly recognizing the value of their new capability to their corporation. This paper gives a rationale, based on educational research, for these two trends, and concludes that wide spread adoption of these practices would transform the quality of work life within the corporate culture.

INTRODUCTION

Although commercial applications of word processing have been available in the workplace since the early 1950s, for much of that time this activity has been restricted to its use as a secretarial tool for transcribing and revising text generated by managers via dictation or 'scribble and throw'. This model is changing as new Australian Federal Government legislation moves in alongside the Affirmative Action policies which the government has been committed to since 1985. Award restructuring, which has been in place since 1988, arose out of the recognition, by government and industry, that changes in work practices and organization through the encouragement of 'multiskilling' would realize inherent capacities in the work force.

At one end of the corporate ladder, white-collar workers in the Australian Federal Public Service need now spend no more than 50% of their working day merely transcribing. At the top end of that ladder many chief executives are reluctant to relinquish the status and trappings they have enjoyed for so long and become competent at keyboarding their own communications. As students who have word processed their way through school and university join the work force, the power structure will alter, and it is highly likely that in future it will be necessary to master the keyboard to hold an executive job.

Developing technology will doubtless make it easier for the pockets of resistance to overcome their cyberphobia. Andera (1989) suggests that, by the end of the 90s, voice-operated, continuous speech word processors with 40,000 word vocabularies will be in general use. Secretarial transcribing jobs will certainly be reduced, as dictating executives who have disdained to use a keyboard will surely not baulk at automated voice input, or using the 'keyboardless computer' such as that which the Sony Corporation has recently introduced, whereby users will automated voice input, or using the 'keyboardless computer' such as that which the Sony Corporation has recently introduced, whereby users will enter data onto a liquid crystal screen with a special pen.

There is no doubt that a major restructuring of traditional work-roles will take place and that "people will perform tasks previously done by their bosses" (Strassmann, 1985). With the elimination of 'immutable jobs with a finite scope' will come the reality of a "service-based society that maximizes its people's skills" (Strassmann).

Can a training programme teach communicative and cognitive dimensions of writing to someone whose traditional role has been widely perceived as that of a keyboard operator? I would argue that such an objective would have been impossible given the rigidity and linearity of traditional typewriters, but that composing on computers allows writers to achieve writing quality far higher than using any other medium. My evidence for this comes from the large research base established in the U.S.A., along with results of a project which I carried out at the Queensland University of Technology.

BACKGROUND TO THE PROJECT

Implementation of word processing in most educational institutions was not viable until the early 1980s, when personal computers (PCs) became available. Since then PCs have become increasingly prevalent - ubiquitous in some institutions - particularly at the tertiary level.

Committed to the value of word processing, many universities and colleges in the U.S., the U.K. and Australia either provide or require their students to provide their own computers. For the last six years students enrolled in the Communication degree course in the Faculty of Business at the Queensland University of Technology have done all their writing on computers. These students have access to over one hundred and fifty computers, some of which are available twenty-four hours a day, seven days a week. More recently, an electronic publishing component has been included in their course.

Personal testimony about the value of word processing has always been enthusiastic. Hammond (1984) stated that "the computer is the most powerful tool ever developed for writers, offering greater control over words, increased production, and superb research capabilities". In a survey of writers published as a supplement to The Listener in 1985 Richard Gilbert claims that "most are infatuated once they've mastered the system". He quotes Marge Piercy, the American novelist and poet, as saying that: "If I had to give up writing on my computer, I would feel that I had returned to scraping letters in cuneiform on clay tablets".

But while anecdotal praise of personal word processing has been readily and immediately forthcoming since it became accessible to individuals, research reports - on writing in the classroom as well as in the corporation - did not appear in the literature until the early eighties. Since then, a proliferation of journal articles, editorials, conference papers, essays, research reports, bibliographies, newsletters, specially designed software, and new journals, books and conferences devoted entirely to computers and writing has reflected the exponential upsurge of interest and practice in all aspects of the computers+writing phenomenon by writers at all levels of development.

The following claims express overwhelming support for word processing:

* I now believe that word processing may well be the most important single advance in the teaching of composition since the Analytic and Rhetoric of Aristotle (Forseth, 1985).
* The new technology for writers offers such strong advantages over the old as to make eventual dominance certain (Danielson, 1985).

* The most powerful and versatile writing instrument ever designed. It can be compared to the printing press in impact (Noble, 1984).
* If it were only writing teachers who were enthusiastic about word processing, this would surely be enough....But students, who are usually beginning writers unconcerned with pedagogy, are enthusiastic. And teachers as writers, other professional and technical writers, researchers, collaborators, novelists and poets are equally enthusiastic (Gardner and McGinnis, 1988).

The anecdotal evidence about the efficacy of computers for writing is monumental, and there have been some empirical studies, but the testimonials and many of the research results have conflicted. Furthermore, most of the case studies reported in the literature in the mid-80s examined whether students revised more, rather than whether the quality of their writing improved.

THE NEED FOR CONTROLLED RESEARCH

The contradictory findings by many earlier researchers about the word processor's effect have been based mainly on small samples or anecdotal surveys, and have resulted in a clamour for conclusive empirical research findings on the qualitative effects of computers on writing, particularly at tertiary level. This prompted me to undertake a research project in 1988 with first year students enrolled in the Bachelor of Business (Communication) degree at the Queensland University

THE PURPOSE, SUBJECTS AND CONDUCT OF THE STUDY

The purpose of the study was to investigate whether students who used word processing to produce text would produce higher quality prose than those who used longhand.

The subjects in this study were one hundred students who enrolled in a course which prepares students for careers in Journalism, Public Relations and Advertising. Because of the emphasis in these professions on writing, and because employers' expectations of these graduates' ability to write effective and mechanically-correct prose are so high, writing features strongly in many of the subjects in the course.

Coordinating and teaching a core writing subject taken by both full- and part-time students in their first semester in the course enabled me to set up a quasi-experimental research design to ascertain whether word processing in a particular pedagogical environment - the problem-solving approach advocated by Flower (1985) - would enhance the quality of students' writing.

It was impossible to make random groups and thus carry out a true experimental design, because part-time students are not introduced to computers until the second semester of their course. They formed the control group, while the full-time students, who learn to type and to word process in their first semester, formed the experimental group. The use of intact rather than randomly assigned groups meant that there was a need to control statistically for initial differences in the group. This was done with an analysis of covariance, using the pretest mean scores as the covariate.

Because the cut-off point for entry into the course was slightly higher for full-time students than for part-time students, and their respective mean Tertiary Entrance Scores were 960 and 924 (the top 4% and 7.6% of students in the State), it was necessary to investigate whether this and other factors such as their secondary school exiting English score (presumably but not necessarily an accurate indication of their ability to write), age and previous tertiary experience were significant. Twenty percent of the total intake of students already had university degrees.

The semester started with eighty students in each group - all of whom did the two pretest writing tasks in longhand in fifty-minute tutorial sessions in weeks one and two of the semester. There was some attrition during the semester, but at least fifty students in each group were present for the two pretests and for the two posttests which were done in the final two weeks of the semester, some three months later. The control group used longhand for posttest, while the experimental group used computers for the posttest.

The preparation for the experiment consisted of pre-trialling the writing tasks, teaching the experimental group to use the word-processing software, and training the three markers who holistically assessed the quality of the writing samples.

The two writing tasks which the students completed required quite different skills. The first task was to write the body of a job application letter, for which they were given a number of essential and inessential details in a more or less coherent order. The results for this were not significantly different between the groups, perhaps as no major restructuring of the material was needed. However, the second test necessitated their classifying, organizing and synthesizing information which they had previously received in arbitrary order - this is where the computer proved to be of great advantage to the experimental group.

When four factors were tested - age, Grade 12 exiting English score, Tertiary Entrance (TE) Score and group membership - two factors were found to be significant: TE score and group membership. Further analysis of these two significant factors revealed that there was no evidence of a strong relationship between the Job posttest result and any of the three variables (covariates) - the job pretest, their T.E. Score and group membership. However, in an analysis of the second posttest, the Refectory Report,the TE Score was negative at .02, whereas the membership of the computer group was a positive factor, resulting in a highly significant gain of 2.01 points on an 18-point scale. Thus the use of computers for composing enhanced the quality of the writing produced by these able students.

WRITERS IN THE WORKPLACE

Zinsser (1985) contends that writers using a word processor sit down far more willingly, and gain motivation, immediacy, interaction, time, energy, enthusiasm, output and control of a further stage of the publishing process - and in 1985, when he wrote this, he could not have forseen how quickly electronic publishing software would become affordable, user-friendly and give even more control to the individual.

The benefits of electronic writing - widely accepted by converts to it - should be enjoyed by all writers in the workplace. However, massive training programmes will need to be implemented to introduce untrained writers to the strategies for and principles of computer-mediated composition that will allow them to write 'more, faster, better!'

Because computers are intrinsically motivating, they can break through writer's block and concentrate the writer's mind on getting text into the machine. Writing on a word processor enables writers to compose more quickly and freely, focusing on what they want to say rather than worrying about making an error, because they know that editing changes can be incorporated automatically and painlessly.

The computer short-circuits the linear approach to writing. The writer can start at any point in a text - particularly a daunting one - without worrying whether the first sentence is the right one, Words, sentences and paragraphs can be added, deleted and reshuffled like cards. Text can be inserted in spurts and fragments. Notes and jottings can be stored in a database and later recalled, reordered and filled out.

Rewriting is the essence of writing because most writers do not say in a first draft what they want to say, or say it as well or as succinctly as they could. The computer dissolves the distinctions between writing and rewriting, taking away all the drudgery of rewriting, so writers are more willing to follow suggestions such as "Let words talk to words!" (Elbow, 1973).

Documents can be used again and again with minor alterations. The information and/or format of these 'boilerplates' can be customized from material stored on line. The computer also facilitates collaborative writing - for so long a standard practice in corporate writing.

Once they have mastered the software, computer users tend to feel in control of the writing process. They are instructing a powerful machine to carry out massive and tedious editing tasks instantly, for example, global search and replace. Many writers derive much comfort from the immediacy of the computer as a helpmate - in the form of a spelling checker (great psychological benefit to all poor spellers), thesaurus, automatic text aligner, 'idea processor' and invention heuristic. Style-analysis software cannot compensate for incompetent writing but, "For the harried business person with too much to write and not enough time to write carefully... these programs could be helpful" (Matzkin, 1989).

CONCLUSION

Recent research in writing has revealed that word processors, long recognized as incomparable transcribing and revising tools, may well provide their most valuable benefits in 'online' composing. No one writing at present actually learnt to write online: however, this should not prevent all writers at all levels of the 'knowledge industry' from taking advantage of the radical transformation that this quantum leap in writing technology can have on the processes and products of their written communication.

REFERENCES

Andera, F.(1989): Voice input to computers: how will it affect the teaching of business communication? The Bulletin of the Association for Business Communication, 52, 4, pp.18-20.

Danielson, W.A.(1985): The writer and the computer. Computers and the Humanities, 19, pp.85-88.

Elbow, P.(1973): Writing Without Teachers. Oxford University Press, New York.

Flower, L.(1985): Problem-Solving Strategies for Writing. Harcourt Brace Jovanovich, New York.

Forseth, R.(1985): Converting freshman English to word processing: a case history. Paper at Meeting of the UCLA Conference on Computers and Writing, May.

Gardner, R. and McGinnis, J.(1987): Word processing in college writing labs: what the experience at ten American universities is telling us. Research in Word Processing Newsletter, Dec, pp.4-10.

Gilbert, R.(1985): Word processing supplement. The Listener, 25th April

Hammond, R.(1984): The Writer and the Wordprocessor. Coronet Books, London.

Matzkin, J.(1989): Grammatik III, Right-Writer 3.0: grammar checkers get smarter, but not by much. PC Magazine, February, p.14.

Noble, D.F. and Noble, V.(1984): Improve Your Writing With Word Processing. Que Corporation, Indianapolis, Indiana.

Zinsser, W.(1983): Writing with a Word Processor. Harper and Row, New York.

Roslyn Petelin is the Director of Organizational Studies at Queensland University of Technology. Her particular research interest is the application of computers to the composing process of tertiary students and corporate writers.

Address for correspondence: Faculty of Business,
Queensland University of Technology,
GPO Box 2434, Brisbane 4001, Australia.

44. Streamlining computer-based training production: improving communication between commissioners and contractors

Elaine England, Lloyd's Bank Distance Learning Centre

Abstract: In computer-based training (CBT), production problems occur between commissioning companies and contractors in specifying in print what is intended on screen. Some of the difficulties arise because of the interdisciplinary mix of people involved in the projects and their different methods of description. Other problems stem from design and programming revisions to materials during production. The development time and cost of CBT increase because of the re-negotiations around these problems. This paper investigates the difficulties in specification for CBT projects from both sides. It reports on practices that have evolved to counteract the communication gap by reference to case studies and structured interviews, and pin-points areas which still need addressing.

DEFINING THE SCOPE OF THE PROBLEM

From the experience of Lloyds Bank Distance Learning Centre (DLC),the central difficulty during CBT development appeared to relate to the scripting of the projects. After investigation, this proved to be only one part of the communication issues which needed addressing.

The investigation was based on structured interviews with twenty-two people covering both in-house and outside management, training analysts, training consultants, designers and programmers. The questions focused on the historical evolvement of work practices, the different perceptions of the problems encountered during CBT production, and speculation on some trends which could emerge. The difficulties encountered by the project teams during production will be the main focus here.

The work environment of the Distance Learning Centre

The variety of work practices at the centre in the development of CBT needs to be taken into account as it affects the designers' role and the types of skill that they need to develop projects. As it is a young centre for CBT, the designers tend to be inexperienced so may be paired with a consultant. They may be involved in projects which are being developed completely or partly in-house, or co-ordinating and monitoring projects analysed, designed and produced completely by contractors. Within the centre there is a hierarchy of Project Manager, Analyst, and Designer: for the purposes of this description analysts, consultants and designers are merged into one category of 'designer'.

There was a tendency for new projects to build on the style of previous documentation. An implicit 'house style' was becoming evident which reflected a systematic approach to learning and text biased, paper-based documentation.

Features of existing scripts

Separate sheets of A4 paper were used for text and graphics, with numbers used to reference between them. The text sheet began with a statement of the function or screen overview and then described the sequence of events which were to happen on the screen. These included: what was displayed; a text description of graphics and the position it was to be displayed on the screen; a description of the instructions to the user; any instructions to the programmer on feedback to the user; a description of the keys which were active and links forward or backward in the program.

The graphics sheet was A4 landscape, with space for notes on the left, a grid representing the screen and the position of the graphics on the right, and the reference number at the top.

This type of documentation assumed that the content had a beginning and an end - i.e. was linear. This is similar to many formats used in CBT particularly in the early 1980s, with the locus of control being computer driven, not student driven. However, as CBT becomes more complex and the learning approach changes - particularly if it becomes student centred - the linear approach embodied in the traditional paper-based design needs to change. More sophisticated computer programs need not be linear, but offer a range of access points to the information to allow users to describe the way they want to work.

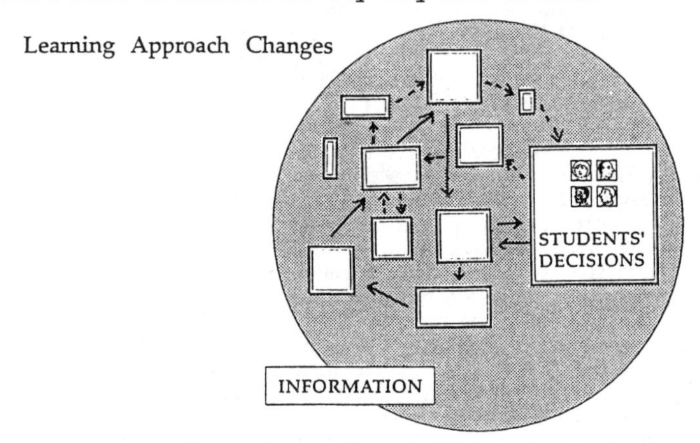

Figure 1: A problem-solving representation

It becomes increasingly difficult to use text - a static medium - to explain a dynamic interaction, especially when some of the readers involved in the projects may have very limited understanding of the capabilities of the computer and equally limited understanding of the less prescriptive teaching approaches.

Inexperienced designers of CBT are similarly limited, since they can only present information in forms they have experienced. They need to be trained up to the point that they have enough of a repertoire to mix and match teaching approaches with the capabilities of the system they use and the nature of the content they need to communicate. The equivalent situation would be giving a map of a town to people who have never been there and ask them if it is correct.

What does each person need from the documentation?

* The designer/consultant designer needs enough information to convey the content, learning approach, look and feel of the screens and the computer interaction between the content and the learner.
* The programmer needs enough information to have a clear overview of how the program is expected to work. This enables him/her to set up a structure to contain the content and for it to react as the designer expects. It should be noted that the experience and training of the programmer is as important as that of the designer.
* The subject matter expert (SME) and the people involved in sign-off agreements (up to four other departments can be involved) need to

check the accuracy and adequacy of the content, and if it conforms to company policy.

* The quality controller needs to check if the project documentation is adhering to any delivery system constraints and if it is taking shape to conform to fitness for purpose.

Each person therefore needs to relate to the documentation in different ways. If the documentation tries to be all things to all people it will cause confusion.

Putting the documentation in context

It is necessary to consider the whole cycle of CBT development to pin-point exactly where and how each stage is affected by communication difficulties rather than concentrating on documentation in isolation.

There are four broad areas contained in development: the training requirement study or needs analysis; the content agreement both by the SME and the sign-off departments; the coding phase of the software including the revision and testing of the code; and the trialling and evaluation of the project.

Each stage will be addressed and a summary of the main difficulties involved stated from each of the perspectives.

THE REQUIREMENT STUDY OR NEEDS ANALYSIS

The management perspective

Management representing the contractors said that most often, if they were asked to work from a requirement done by the company, they found that the real training need had not been established. They also said that different people in the organization had different perceptions of what the project was to achieve.

The Distance Learning Centre management found that if an external needs analysis was done by contractors, it was very often done poorly and the training was not identified clearly.

The designers' perspective

The consultants all agreed that the analysis stage was the most important but that this was rarely recognized and too little time was allocated for it. There was pressure to get results quickly but if the analysis was inadequate, the project suffered.

The in-house designers found it difficult to change the requirements into the detailed design necessary for a script. They wanted clearer links made between training definition and actual program shape.

The programmers' perspective

To make informed decisions on which routines were to be standardized and set up, they needed clear understanding of the overall structure. They recognized that it took a long time for the analysis to gell to the point that the designer could convey to them the complete picture of what was required. If decisions had to be made from inadequate knowledge, the project suffered.

If the programmers were being required to use standardized routines and programming tools, these could provoke problems if they did not fit the training need exactly. Time was wasted fighting against the system to try and make adjustments.

STAGE 2: ESTABLISHING AGREEMENT ON THE CONTENT

The management perspective

All agreed that problems of access to the SME held the project up. In-house management realized that inexperienced designers did not ask the SME the right questions at the right time to elicit all the content.

Generally the contractors found that the different sign-off sections had different expectations of the project and that company politics interfered, particularly when extra people began taking an interest and it became unclear who had ultimate sign-off responsibility. However, they had also experienced sign-offs being done without complete understanding so that clients reacted against the project when it was produced.

The Distance Learning Centre had experienced problems with the non-CBT personnel making comments on programming instructions and learning approaches instead of confining their comments to the content. They had also found that very often the expectations built up of what the program would look and feel like from reading the script did not match up to the program when viewed on the screen and this caused dissent.

The designers' perspective

The consultant designers found that from experience the project content, the people involved and their relative experience dictated the type and amount of documentation needed, in whatever form - there was no standard way of documenting, only some common components.

When they had to adjust to an existing house style, whether explicit or implicit, it affected the design - programs might be produced faster and were more uniform but lacked impact and creativity. But if many programs similar in approach and content were to be produced, then a common style and documentation, established and agreed by all involved, would assist.

The in-house designers found problems controlling the people involved to reach consensus and get sign-off. If the documentation was produced by the contractors, it was too programmer-orientated and difficult to understand. They also experienced the conflict in expectation of what was specified on paper and what appeared on the screen.

STAGE 3: CODING

The management perspective

The contractors found that if a company produced the script it often did not have enough information for programmers on routing through the program, help, or options for the learners to use. The scripts overall were not well thought out.

The in-house management complained that the code was not set up to facilitate changes. The monitoring and recording of changes to the script whilst the program was being developed and the control of which version of the program was under scrutiny, caused difficulty. There appeared to be poor communication between designer and programmer when the programmer worked off-site. This caused more re-writing of code.

The designers' perspective

The consultants realized the need for tight control over contractors to ensure that scheduling and standards are kept and that only agreed sub-contracting occurred. They considered the relationship built up with the programmer as very important in the development process. It looked as if they had knowledge of the tools the programmers used.

In-house designers found that programmers tended to code too much without confirmation and that re-coding became necessary. They found it easier to control the flow of work when the programmer was on site. Conflict arose because of changes to the script. Co-ordinating comments and keeping records of the changes was problematic. If the programmer worked on site, then changes were usually made around the screen and these slipped through the documentation process.

They were uneasy when a programmer said that something in the design was not possible because sometimes they thought the programmers were avoiding work. On occasions, the programmers spent too long achieving an effect which had little instructional purpose but had gimmick impact and which was not strictly in the script.

The programmers' perspective

Fast prototyping was essential to establish look and feel for all involved. Screen layout and presentation accounted for many of the changes during a project so that if these were established early, the project ran more smoothly. A graphic designer was invaluable.

If a project was large and one section was programmed before the whole analysis was complete, it was difficult to make effective decisions on standard routines and common coding. When more than one programmer was working on a project, they needed to understand each other's approach to avoid over-coding or counter-coding.

More experienced programmers wanted involvement at the design stage to enable them to make clear decisions about coding earlier and to let them work from looser guidelines, since they would have picked up a feel for the project and be able to offer more creative solutions.

STAGE 4: TRIALLING AND EVALUATING PROGRAMS

This stage is often neglected in training circles. Software producers often ask for feedback on their products but little is co-ordinated and recorded. The DLC is moving towards more evaluation and had tried various methods including usability labs, questionnaires, structured interviews, structured observation and a combination of these. The main difficulties encountered are finding the time and freeing the staff to perform the studies. There are also problems co-ordinating the information so that the unit benefits from the insights which emerge.

TOWARDS SOLUTIONS

Training analysis weaknesses

There was complete consensus on the importance of the initial training analysis which leads to the decision to produce CBT.

1. More time should be allocated to this stage to facilitate a smoother running project.
2. The analysis must result in a clear definition of the task, its components and its scope so that a designer can begin detailed design from a sound basis.
3. Inexperienced designers need training in understanding the different CBT approaches that can be applied, the possibilities that exist and which approach suits which type of training task so they can make better decisions on the approach.
4. It would be good practice for a project to be reviewed at the

completion of its analysis stage by independent observers.

Subject matter expert

1. Access was the prime consideration. The projects would save time and development in the long term if the SME could be seconded to the project for an initial period particularly for major projects.
2. The SME's expertise needed to be used efficiently. Presenting scripts to the SME without the distracting technical information would give little opportunity for them to comment outside their brief. They would need an overview of how the program would work to relate the content to the structure: a prototype section would give them enough understanding of how the program would operate.

Interdepartmental sign-off

1. Provide the same documentation of the content to these people as to the SME. They also need enough information to understand how the program will work and a viewing of a sample section. This would ensure understanding of the project without encouraging comments on areas which should not concern them.
2. Ensure the departments which need to approve the program provide representative who have direct responsibility for sign-off to avoid duplication of effort, difference of opinion and undue time lags.
3. Training for designers is needed in understanding how to judge the complexity of a project, what components will be needed to ease communication between people and the need to establish consistency across contributors when a number of programs belong to a similar group with a similar purpose. A job performance aid in decision making would guide them in using the right mind set.
4. The company needs to realize that its own culture and practices may leave them less open to suggestions of new approaches from contractors/consultants. The company needs to monitor its culture and recognize strengths and weaknesses.

The programmer's perspective

1. Experienced programmers wished to be involved in the design stage to facilitate decisions of effective coding and scheduling of projects.
2. If they are made aware that changes will be necessary and are trained efficiently, they will be able to code for changes. Bringing programmers to work on-site whenever possible would speed up the development and help communication between designer and programmer.
3. The designers and programmers need to be more aware of the difficulties they both face so that they can appreciate and predict danger points before they occur.
4. Projects can be coded to allow a final print-out of the script as a definitive record of the project. One contractor offered this full storyboard facility.
5. The contractors should be encouraged to train their programmers in internal documenting of code, script control, and the dangers of many programmers working on one project.

Address for correspondence: Dr.E.England,
Distance Learning Centre, Lloyds bank Plc,
The Beacon, Hindhead, Surrey GU26 6QZ, UK

45. The human elements of introducing a new computerized system to the workplace

Jacqueline Jeynes

Abstract: As a trainer involved with the introduction of a Management Information System in industry, a challenge was presented by both the 'resistance to change' and by differences in the level of prior information technology (IT) knowledge in the staff to be trained. This paper considers how these issues were addressed, and the outcome of training so far, with particular reference to: (1) attitudes beforehand (up to manager level) to the new system and to learning new IT skills; (2) level of experience to date, and any different attitudes to computer training evident from different age groups; (3) outcome of the initial training programme, and subsequent attitudes to further IT training. The training programme made use of various methods and materials, which are reviewed in this paper.

INTRODUCTION

This case study will look at the human aspects of introducing a new Management Information System (MIS) in an industrial company. The system is an integrated MIS Package running on UNIX multi-user basis rather than a network, using a Micro 386 system. There are eight terminals and four printers at one site, dealing with Stock Control. It will be shortly linked to Sales Order Processing and Accounts. There are two printers and terminals in the warehouse, one printer and terminal in Administration and one printer and five terminals in the Sales Office used to refer to current stock levels.

The system will gradually be added to and built on with :

a. Purchase Order Control;
b. Ledgers and Estimating;
c. Fixed Assets and Marketing;
d. Work in Progress tracking;
e. Job Costing;

all by the end of 1990, and

f. Materials Requirement Planning and
g. Capacity Requirement Planning

by Spring 1991.

The capacity will expand as the system does, with an estimated minimum cost of £200K over two years.

Background to the company

The company is part of a larger group within the plastics industry. Attempts have been made before to find an acceptable programme to cover the planning and production process, but these have never successfully overcome the problems of rapid changes in production requirements (for example, the dependence on the weather for the number of fresh produce bags needed), differing quality needs of clients, and a host of variables related to materials and environmental conditions. The introduction of a new MIS does, therefore, follow on the heels of statements such as "it just won't work with computers", considerable scepticism, and the added complication of the company being taken over by an international concern.

The company has no full time Training or Personnel function, using instead myself as Training Consultant on an agreed days-per-year basis.

Although originally brought in to develop a Management Training Programme in-house, my remit has broadened to answer the varying training requirements that arise. Hence my involvement with training related to the MIS.

While still being in the early stages of the MIS introduction, several issues have arisen which are worth considering more closely. These are:

* Some departments are more enthusiastic about computerization than others, as of course are individual members of staff. Does this relate to age? To job function? To the sex of the staff member?
* Levels of previous experience with computers are very broad, ranging from none, to a little with a home computer and games, to daily use of a keyboard/VDU.
* Using an Open Learning (OL) Package to support specific system training: which package? Would there be problems with an OL format?

In fact the number of staff using the new system at this stage is very small, with Amstrad PCs still being used in the Accounts and Sales Office, so emphasis is to be placed on the prior attitudes and experience of staff, and the use of OL to provide some Information Technology (IT) training.

ATTITUDES AND EXPERIENCE

Since the early 1980s there has been a general feeling that the public are very wary about the widespread use of IT in the work-place - hence 1982 being designed IT Year to reassure the British public (The Times, 1982), and this was the expectation here. However, reluctance to accept a MIS, or scepticism about its likely success were primarily due to the failed previous attempts already mentioned, and the fact that the system had been promised for two years but no-one believed it would actually materialize.

Results of individual interviews, group discussions and short questionnaires (see Figure 1) did not support a relationship between age

COMPUTER TRAINING QUESTIONNAIRE

This questionnaire has been prepared to give me some information early on in the training programme about your prior knowledge and attitudes to computers. It is anonymous, but I do need the information on age, sex and job function for statistical purposes. Please answer as honestly as you can! Thank you for your time.

1) JOB TITLE OR FUNCTION:
2) AGE: 3) SEX:
4) What experience have you had with computers prior to this course? Please mark on the scale from 1 (none) to 10 (regular user).

	1 none	hardly any	5 quite a lot	10 regular user
	I-----------------------------I			
home computer	I-----------------------------I			
word processor	I-----------------------------I			
micro computer	I-----------------------------I			
mini computer	I-----------------------------I			
main-frame computer	I-----------------------------I			
Network systems	I-----------------------------I			
Computer-aided manufacture	I-----------------------------I			

Figure 1: Part of the sample questionnaire.

and resistance to the new system. Any resistance was more likely to be related to skill level of job, and the extent to which the job involves fully-defined, repetitive, mathematical-based tasks rather than variable, decision-making skills based on experience and judgement. There certainly appears to be a general feeling that a MIS would be good for the organization and for their jobs.

One of the most significant points to emerge from the investigation was that no-one actually knows what the MIS is, what it is capable of, or the full implications of setting up such a scheme. This does seem to be an area where a little communication might go a long way!

As a company, there is a broad spread of age groups across different levels of staff, with a fairly high proportion in the 35+ group. Where age does seem to have a significant relationship is with the willingness to take advantage of training offered. Despite the general comments seeming to be, "I'm sure I am too old, but I'll have a go"; "You will need to go over everything at least twenty times before I get the hang of it"; and, "Well my children know all about them so I suppose I ought to have a go", about two-thirds of those volunteering were aged between 35 and 54 years. There was no evidence of sex-related bias, with a fairly even distribution of male/female participants.

Question 11 on the questionnaire (see Figure 2) was interesting in that responses seemed to align more closely with job function than with previous experience. For example, several people from Accounts and Planning are included, and envisage few problems with binary maths, but the vast majority of people not involved regularly with written work anticipated problems in this area. Using OL methods relates to previous training experience, and as most people do not have OL experience, responses were clustered around 5-7 on the ratings scale.

```
 11) How do you think you will cope with the following aspects
     of the course? Please mark on the scale from 1 (with
     difficulty, will need a lot of help/guidance) to 10 (very
     well, will need little help/guidance).
                                  1-----------5--------------10
  using open learning methods    I----------------------------I
  using a keyboard               I----------------------------I
  practical work on computer     I----------------------------I
  written work/answers           I----------------------------I
  maths section e.g. binary      I----------------------------I
  how the computer works         I----------------------------I
  taught sessions with Tutors    I----------------------------I
```

Figure 2: Question 11 from the questionnaire.

CHOOSING A TRAINING PACKAGE

With a diverse range of skills and abilities throughout the company; with only a small number of people using the system as yet (and even when they do in the future all will be using different functions); and with the absence of full-time training provision, an OL package could be ideal. Staff could work through at their own pace, depending on their prior skills and knowledge, and build up an IT awareness before using the system.

As no-one, not even those already using computers, had any formal qualifications, we decided to start with a very basic level open learning package, 'Office Automation', leading to City and Guilds 424, 'Basic Competence in Information Technology'. Figure 3 shows the modular

Module BC1	Introduction to computing
Module BC2	Computing hardware
Module BC3	Computer software
Module BC4	Software sources
Module AM1	Office micro application

Figure 3: Outline of modules covered in the open learning package.

outline. It was piloted with two Estimator/Cost clerks who used PCs frequently in their work, to identify:

* whether the level was suitable for diversity of user experience;
* how much time was involved;
* how effective the format was.

The result was that even with some keyboard skills, the theoretical basis of the modules was interesting and relevant, with very short practical exercises at the end of each of the five modules. We were also able to identify:

* parts of the text which confused the reader;
* topics which needed further back-up information in order fully to grasp the issues covered;
* sections which needed additional exercises and questions for students to check their understanding.

OFFERING THE QUESTIONNAIRE

So, having agreed that this would be appropriate, training for the City and Guilds certificate was offered to staff as an open learning package with tutor support (myself). A session was arranged to introduce the package to everyone, tell them what it involved, what the study format would be, and that there was certification for those who wanted it.

The response was overwhelming! The number of people expected to take up the opportunity was about fifteen, but in fact fiftyfour volunteered. Even after explaining that it was not all practical keyboard work, but involved reading workbooks and answering self-assessment questions, everyone still wished to continue and all were duly issued with copies of the first module.

Why such a massive response?

Responses to this question on the questionnaire (see Figure 4) ranged widely, from:

"it's free", and
"the company has never offered anything before", to
"the certificate", and

9) Why did you choose to start this C&G 424 course? (The REAL reason!)

10) What do you expect to gain from the course apart from a certificate on completion?

Figure 4: Why such a massive response? Q9 on the questionnaire.

"recognition that I have some competence in the use of computers" Not everyone who has taken up this course will be directly involved with the MIS; some of them are shop floor, others in direct sales or Health and Safety, yet they have all identified for themselves a requirement to develop their own skills and knowledge in this area.

Using the open learning format

Having identified a somewhat larger group than anticipated, using an OL format is obviously the most feasible, and is itself what has attracted many of the participants to the course.

As stated earlier, several parts of the text appeared to require some tutor back-up, using additional material and tutor-led sessions to go over specific points. Five groups were formed, each to attend a session where materials were distributed and topics such as binary maths covered until everyone in the group was happy with the concept.

A section of the notice board is now allocated for notices about tutor availability, practical sessions, and extra topics to be covered in face-to-face situations. Two days a week are currently made available for students to contact me, with regular 'study skills' sessions.

OUTCOMES OF THE INITIAL TRAINING PROGRAMME

1. We are now officially registered as a Test Centre to administer and assess the C&G 424 course.
2. Participants are forming small self-help groups, either within departments (such as Accounts), or even as families (such as the four shop floor workers who are related).
3. Additional practical work using the computer has been developed by the tutor, to maintain interest and motivation, as the one formal practical session at the end of each module is not enough.
4. Not all of those who originally showed an interest have continued, with numbers currently around twentyfive.

REALIZING HUMAN POTENTIAL - SUMMARY

Although no longer directly related to the installation of a Management Information System, this paper has looked briefly at the needs of an organization to utilize fully the skills and abilities of its human resource; has considered whether resistance to new technology is either sex- or age-related; and has identified several outcomes of the introduction of an OL training programme in IT. As the previous section illustrates, several of the actual outcomes are directly related to any realization of human potential.

In this case study, I see this realization in the following areas:

1. by offering the OL facility to ALL staff, not just a specified group, the company has been seen to value its staff and their development, thereby encouraging them to take an opportunity they might otherwise not have done;
2. although numbers of participants have fallen (as expected), the final number of students is still higher than originally anticipated, and has raised awareness levels of all staff to training;
3. by using an OL format, staff are obliged to take some responsibility for their own learning; to develop self-discipline and self-direction, and to plan and use their own time more effectively;
4. self-help groups have been formed without the intervention of the tutor, so leadership, teambuilding and target-setting skills certainly seem to have been gained;

5. groups have used the extra practical sessions, especially on spreadsheets, to develop their own relevant material that will enhance their effectiveness as employees;
6. their confidence has grown visibly as they have progressed through even the early modules, so that the fear of computers has now gone, and exploration of their capabilities can now take place. This is particularly relevant to a group of four men aged 35-48, who have set up their own working Health and Safety statistics file, but who were frightened to touch the keyboard at first;
7. I must include myself, as tutor, as my expertise both with OL and IT has necessarily developed as the course has progressed.

CONCLUSION

The unforseen delay in introducing the planned MIS to this company has provided the opportunity to develop an IT awareness amongst staff that was not previously evident, and has served to reduce anxieties and resistance to the new system.

This is a significant element in the success or failure of such a wide-ranging technological system, as has been witnessed by the far-from-successful first stage implementation. There are many aspects of introducing change to the workplace that are sometimes totally ignored by senior management - notably using and developing the human resource effectively. While there are other issues that need to be addressed in this instance, the current IT training programme has proved to give significantly greater rewards than merely a C&G 424 certificate.

Jacqueline Jeynes is an independent Training Consultant, providing a range of training courses forindustrial managers, She has been a manager herself in several training companies, and is currently developing Health and Safety, Equal Opportunities and Women's courses, as well as doing a part-time MBA.

Address for correspondence: **J.Jeynes,**
12, Knight Street, St.John's, Worcester WR2 5DB, UK

46. The potential takeup of mass training

Alison Fuller and Murray Saunders, The University of Lancaster

Abstract It has become fashionable to suggest that training and human resource development can meet the major economic and demographic challenges facing the UK in the 1990s. This paper explores why some sections of the workforce seem to resist 'formal' training and are therefore likely to limit the progress of the 'mass training' movement.

The data on which the discussion is based have been collected from primarily unskilled and semi-skilled employees working for a wide range of private sector firms. Our analysis suggests a number of personal, interactional and organizational factors which contribute to individuals' resistance to training, and concludes that a 'mass training' policy will need to conceptualize the concerns, preoccupations and priorities of the main participants and suggests that mass training will be constrained unless more general changes occur in the way work is organized and human potential is perceived.

INTRODUCTION

In recent years a head of steam has been building behind the idea that more-and-better vocational education and training will significantly increase the UK's chances of competing successfully in the global market place. The government and employers' organizations have published documents which argue the case for investment in human resources as a positive response to economic and demographic pressures (e.g. Department of Employment, 1988; Confederation of British Industry, 1989). In 1986 the National Council for Vocational Qualifications was set up by the government to provide a framework for the development of national vocational qualifications and to help increase the number of workers with qualifications by introducing awards founded on work-based competencies.

Many companies from a range of sectors have invested heavily in new training initiatives, notably in open learning and in computer-based training. In turn, work by researchers and consultants on all aspects of human resource development is burgeoning. However, we have collected data from a wide variety of industrial and commercial contexts which indicate that a significant proportion of adult workers do not share governmental and 'official' enthusiasm for training, a finding confirmed by the Department of Employment (1989). In the face of training's currently high and positive profile we explore in this paper why many employees are resistant to formal training (as opposed to sitting-by-Nellie training). We would argue that individual take-up of training will not increase significantly until the reasons for this attitude are more fully understood: until then mass take-up of training will remain a pipe dream.

The discussion provides a brief outline of the range of private concerns where data have been collected and characterizes the sorts of workers who seem most reluctant to engage in formal training. It then explores whether our cases can offer some explanation for employees' resistance. Finally, we ask if current training policies are addressing the emerging issues.

THE PROJECTS

The focus of this paper emerged from three diverse projects. The first was a year-long evaluation (1988) of the open learning training strategy of a major UK retailer. Notable features of the company were its rapid growth (at one stage, a new store was opened every week), long opening hours, shift work and high labour turnover. We used a questionnaire survey together with semi-structured interviews to investigate employees' perceptions and experiences of training and qualifications. Those interviewed ranged from shopfloor workers and store managers to training officers and senior managers.

The second study was commissioned by the National Council for Vocational Qualifications (NCVQ). The Council asked us to explore the factors which might mediate the uptake of NVQs among small and medium sized firms and to establish the incentives and disincentives which might influence the decisions of employers and employees to become involved in NVQs. We visited 13 companies from a variety of manufacturing and service sectors, interviewing general managers, training/personnel managers, general workers and supervisors. Vocational qualifications were common in some of the sites, particularly engineering. The discussions centred on current training practices and perceptions, allowing us to deduce the implications for NCVQ (Saunders, Fuller and Lobley, 1989).

The third project is current. We have been asked by a large distilling firm to provide an independent, formative evaluation of the vocational training and qualifications strategy being introduced. Data are being derived from discussions with general workers and first line supervisors in blending and bottling plants, grain and malt distilleries, and by large scale questionnaire surveys. In contrast with the first case, the workforce is stable, many workers having more than 10 years' service. In common with retailing, though, the distilling industry has not (in the past) been regulated by external vocational qualifications and therefore provides a good testbed for the implementation of new policies towards training and qualifications.

WHO SEEMS MOST RESISTANT?

The following categorization identifies three groups of workers that tend to resist formal training. The explanations proposed are tentative still. In general, the employees we refer to left school at 16 with few educational qualifications, and most have no vocational qualifications.

Unskilled Workers

Unskilled employees find it difficult to relate their perception of training (classroom-based learning, off-the-job courses, etc) with the sorts of jobs they do - labouring, cleaning, etc. They feel that 'unskilled' work does not warrant any formal instruction and would view any attempt to 'train' them as patronizing and insulting: "Anybody can do a job like this". They judge their job performance by whether they are criticized - no adverse reaction implies satisfaction. At present there is no convincing rationale for introducing formal training at the unskilled level.

Semi-skilled Workers

Whilst 'semi-skilled' duties require a number of skills and qualities (e.g. speed, dexterity, accuracy), many workers are still disinclined to seek formal training because they do not associate it with helping them to do their job better or gaining promotion. This group tends to be steeped in a learning-on-the-job, 'proven ability' culture. Job satisfaction is apparently gained from being confident that you 'know' the job and can answer the queries of less experienced workers. Some associate formal training with testing procedures and unwanted additional responsibilities (in particular supervisory duties).

Within the above two groups female and older are likely to predominate. Limited space and the current interest in women workers and 'returners' has encouraged us to concentrate on the former.

Female Workers (Unskilled and Semi-Skilled)

Female employees provide several reasons for being disinclined to seek training or qualifications, including:

- lack of self-confidence;
- low job expectations and aspirations;
- concern about 'causing' marital disharmony;
- anxiety about supervising others; and
- feeling satisfied with their current job performance.

Three underlying issues emerge which further explain their professed reluctance.

First: many women, particularly married women bringing in a second wage, do not perceive themselves as having careers or making a vital contribution to the domestic budget. They report going to work to boost the family income, 'pay for treats', for social reasons, and to gain the status associated with employment outside the home. Interestingly, women's perception of what their wages fund may conflict with reality. There is some evidence that in actuality their income is spent on crucial items such as the mortgage. Single women in our sample who are supporting themselves have a much more positive attitude towards qualifications, believing that their position in the labour market would be more secure if they held nationally recognized certificates.

Second: the majority of these women have the sorts of jobs which traditionally have not been regulated by external qualifications, e.g. production/assembly work and retailing. Formal training leading to qualifications has never been a part of their experience but is associated with 'careers' (e.g. professional and 'skilled').

Third: as pointed out above many women go to work in order to bring in a second wage. Typically, full-time female operatives earn £6000 (or less) per annum; not enough to count as a breadwinner's wage. Perhaps it is not surprising that many women are reluctant to spend time in formal training when experience tells them they will be under-rewarded.

CEILINGS AND BARRIERS TO MOBILITY

One of the most important disincentives to train seems to be the uneven connection between training, qualifications and career progression. We have identified three sorts of barriers to mobility. The first affects a group of people who are reluctant to seek formal training and qualifications because they anticipate consequences of increased responsibility and commitment. In other words, a ceiling on 'career' progress is self-imposed, the perceived outcomes of training not fitting with their (working) self-image or with the position of work in their overall lives. We found evidence of this attitude particularly in some of the firms in the NCVQ project where employees were resistant to formal supervisory training.

Paradoxically, a second group is disinterested precisely because its members do not anticipate that training and qualifications will help them achieve promotion. In this case, the informal rules of 'getting on' appear to be much more connected with 'proven ability' and a willingness to 'put in the hours'. For example, opportunities in the expanding retail company are high, it has a policy of internal promotion and there is ample evidence of employees reaching senior positions with few educational or vocational qualifications. Firms such as this, organized on the basis of a flexible, internal labour market (Marsden, 1986) can offer employees a high degree of hierarchical mobility provided they understand and are prepared to conform to the informal promotion processes. In this case barriers to mobility are more likely to operate in the open labour market where workers may find that the exchange value of experience is less certain than the possession of an externally recognizable qualification.

A third group displays a reluctant attitude towards training for very different reasons. These employees, particularly unskilled and semi-skilled, tend to work for firms organized on a rigid hierarchical basis where there is very little chance of rising beyond a certain level - a 'wooden ceiling'. For example, some parts of the distilling company have a legacy of autocratic management practices combined with the availability of few promotion opportunities (dead man's shoes syndrome). As a result employees experience a kind of hierarchical insularity which the introduction of vocational qualifications may help to break down, always providing that those gaining the awards are prepared to wait for promotion chances to arise.

OPERATIONAL CONSTRAINTS

On another level employees are often deterred from training by what they see as practical constraints but what we have characterized elsewhere (Fuller and Saunders, 1988) as an inherent tension between operations and training. Typically, work practices are organized to meet the imperatives of the production process or operating priority (e.g. weekly sales targets). Commonly, employees report a lack of time within work schedules for training, while tight staffing makes it difficult to provide cover while others train. In addition, they perceive inadequate support with little preparation or follow-up of training experiences. These constraints are all compounded in the case of part-time or temporary workers who feel that the company is unlikely to invest in them, partly because of their low status and partly because they tend to be brought in to cover peak periods (manufacturing, distilling and retailing) and so cannot be released from their purpose, which is to do the job.

PEER GROUP CULTURE

An important feature of the responses of workers to training is the role of 'peer group pressure'. To some extent the idea of peer group is an extension of the culture of 'solidarity' which characterizes work of any kind. Essentially, solidarity refers to the relative strength of the beliefs, attitudes and informal practices which bind a group of workers together. If the culture is what the sociologists call 'solidaristic' then the binding is strong and secure. Traditionally, 'solidarity' has been associated with working class jobs (often dirty, dangerous work) in which work place norms amongst a particular working group have been very strong. A corollary is that peer group pressure to conform to these norms is also strong. One effect may be to confirm insiders (members of the group) and accentuate outsiders such as supervisors, office staff, etc. This has a clear impact on training: we found that where this sort of tendency exists, e.g. in unionized factories, a negative training culture can develop because to engage in training is tantamount to breaking ranks. To appear enthusiastic about a management initiative is seen at worst as 'sucking up' to management or at best simply 'standing out'. As one machine operator commented: "We have a few problems with cattiness, some thinking that you are getting above yourself wanting to be better than the rest of them. This puts some off doing extra, like training."

THE ISSUE OF 'QUALIFICATION'

It might be argued that take-up of training may be enhanced if the training could be accredited or that a 'qualification structure' existed in which training could be undertaken and competence developed, in a systematic way. Our research has pointed to a complex set of factors associated with 'qualification' which has relevance to government policy on national vocational qualifications. Our intention here is to identify just one key feature. Qualification refers to an individual's capacity to display **suitable** qualities or characteristics. This suitability may be signified by a 'qualification', i.e. a symbol or representation like a certificate, usually associated with the successful completion of an externally accredited course. It may also refer to accumulated experiential knowledge. Now, qualifications need to represent both **use value** (accurately indicate an individual's competence) and **exchange value** (have wide currency in order that a holder can exchange it for better jobs, training, etc). There may be an important difference of emphasis between employers and employees on this issue - employers stressing use value while employees insist on exchange value. We are not, of course, arguing that these categories are mutually exclusive. However we look at this, if there is to be mass training take-up, a new qualification structure will need to bring together both use and exchange value in order for employees and employers to back it.

IMPLICATIONS FOR TRAINING POLICY

The thrust of our arguments is that a mass training policy needs to look far beyond a crude functionalization for a rationale and an implementation strategy. It needs to conceptualize the concerns, preoccupations and priorities that will shape the main participants' responses to training policy. With more apparently 'trainee-centred' approaches currently being developed - handy 'can do' statements of competence, on-the-job internal assessments and the accreditation of prior experience - some of these concerns are being addressed. However, while some trainee-centred gains are being made, the development of mass training in the work place will be constrained unless more general changes also occur in the way 'work' is organized and the way human potential is perceived.

REFERENCES

Confederation of British Industry (1989): Towards a Skills Revolution. CBI, London.
Department of Employment (1988): Employment for the 1990s. HMSO, London.
Department of Employment (1989): Training in Britain. HMSO, London.
Fuller,A. and Saunders,M.(1989): Open learning in action: a case study of open learning training in a large retail company. In Farmer,B., Eastcott,D. and Lantz,B.(Eds), Aspects of Educational and Training Technology XXIII: Making Learning Systems Work. Kogan Page, London.

Marsden,D.(1986): The End of Economic Man? Custom and Competition in Labour Markets. Wheatsheaf Books, Brighton.
Saunders,M., Fuller,A. and Lobley,D.(1989): Emerging Issues in the Utilisation of NVQs. NCVQ, London.

Alison Fuller is a researcher in the Educational Research Department at the University of Lancaster. She has extensive experience in the evaluation of education/industry links, training and open learning. Recently she has been focusing on the evaluation of training in the private sector and has co-directed (with Murray Saunders) a study for the National Council for Vocational Qualifications.

Dr. Murray Saunders is a Senior Fellow in the Educational Research Department at the University of Lancaster. He has directed projects in the areas of vocational education and training for the past ten years. He has recently directed a Training Agency sponsored evaluation of computer-based training practice in the UK, and is currently concentrating on the evaluation of training in the private sector and the relationship between the National Curriculum and the Technical and Vocational Education Initiative in the educational sector.

Address for correspondence: **A.Fuller and Dr.M.Saunders,**
Institute for Research and Development in Post-Compulsory Education,
Lancaster University, Lancaster LA1 4YL, UK

47. Realizing the potential of disabled people by promoting mainstream educational opportunities: a case study

Peter Funnell, Suffolk College

Abstract: this paper suggests that the potential of disabled people can be more fully realized by promoting access to mainstream educational provision and offers a case-study of a scheme seeking to achieve this at the Suffolk College, Ipswich. It offers two justifications for enhanced provision for disabled people based on humanistic and economic arguments, and discusses the policy and practice of the Suffolk College which offers an action-orientated approach strengthened by the adoption of a 'whole college' approach.

INTRODUCTION

This paper offers a case-study of policy and practice designed to promote enhanced education and training opportunities for disabled people through mainstream educational provision. The case-study is derived from experience at the Suffolk College, a large 'mixed economy' college offering higher, further and adult educational provision. As such this paper is concerned solely with 'post-16' education and training provision and not that provided within the compulsory education system. The intention of this paper is to suggest that:

* the promotion of learning opportunities for people with a physical or sensory disability can be justified on both humanistic and economic grounds;
* the labelling of disabled people as having 'special educational needs' is unhelpful, and the most effective means of realizing the potential of disabled people is by the application of a more sensitive form of categorization which distinguishes between the disabled and those with learning difficulties;
* within this more sensitive categorization effective learning opportunities for disabled people can be promoted through mainstream education provision if that provision (and the individual students therein) is adequately supported.

PROMOTING EDUCATIONAL OPPORTUNITIES FOR DISABLED PEOPLE

For many practitioners the presentation of a set of justifications for promoting enhanced learning opportunities for disabled people is an anathema. However, research (see for example National Advisory Body, 1988) consistently demonstrates that despite examples of innovative and effective practice there is an under-provision of opportunities for disabled people and a significant set of barriers facing the individual seeking access to that provision which is available. The reasons for this are likely to be attitudinal, founded either on lack of understanding or awareness of the needs and capabilities of disabled people, or based on a perception that the integration of disabled people onto mainstream programmes will affect the quality of the learning experience of the 'able-bodied' student. The findings of the Warnock Report (1978), and subsequently the 1981 Education Act, have created the legislative context within which it is possible to overcome both the attitudinal and perceptual barriers to enhanced educational and training opportunities for disabled people.

The Warnock Report is seen by many as a watershed in this respect.

Certainly it produced a coherent set of arguments supporting a more sensitive response to those it identified with 'special educational needs' and clearly identified the relatively slow progress being made in the UK to integrating disabled people into mainstream education as compared to Scandinavia and the USA. Following Warnock, the 1981 Education Act stressed the mutual benefit and increased understanding that both disabled and able-bodied people gain from interaction in a mainstream educational setting.

Access to post-16 mainstream educational provision clearly enhances the disabled person's ability to benefit from vocational and indeed pre-vocational training leading to the acquisition of qualifications and, it is to be hoped, subsequent employment. Equally, access to mainstream provision enhances the individual's choice and autonomy. It demonstrates a respect for that individual which is likely to contribute to the promotion of self-motivated learning with a positive impact on the individual's quality of life. Such humanistic concerns are the bedrock of educational practice. They offer a powerful rationale for positive, yet sensitive action to overcome the barriers to access experienced by disabled people. However, in the increasingly entrepreneurial education and training culture of the 1990s the concern has been expressed that the support of disabled people on mainstream provision is uneconomic, particularly given current concerns for efficiency as measured by quantifiable performance indicators, and in a context wherein institutions hold greater than ever budgetary and planning control of their service portfolios. This need not be the case, but it does offer a significant challenge and opportunity for educational institutions and their managers.

The challenge is for each educational institution to integrate through planning and prioritizing mechanisms its educational response to disabled people. The opportunity is created by the 'demographic time-bomb' which is currently reducing the numbers of 16-24 year olds both in the UK, and even more significantly amongst our European partners. Educational institutions planning now for the mid and late 1990s will be giving careful consideration to the recruitment of so-called non-traditional groups both to maintain and to expand levels of provision in the increasingly competitive market created by the Education Reform Act. The disabled as a client group provide a fresh and stimulating opportunity for educational institutions seeking to respond to changing market conditions.

However, the economic issues go beyond the immediate financial considerations of educational institutions. It has been generally acknowledged that the economic prosperity of the UK is being significantly constrained by major areas of skills shortage. This difficulty will be intensified by the structural changes being introduced by the Single European Market. It is in this context that the accessing of so-called non-traditional groups into educational opportunities takes on major economic significance.

It is suggested then that on both humanistic and economic grounds the promotion of educational opportunities for disabled students makes sense. The rest of this paper explores one example of such promotion through a 'Policy for the Provision of Mainstream Opportunities for Disabled People' (Jolliffe, Impey and Johnston, 1988).

IMPLEMENTING MAINSTREAM OPPORTUNITIES FOR DISABLED PEOPLE: THE SUFFOLK COLLEGE CASE-STUDY

The Suffolk College in Ipswich is one of the country's maintained 'mixed economy' colleges with some 29,000 student enrolments during the 1989/90 session. The college offers a wide range of higher (including degree and post-graduate) provision, further and adult educational opportunities, the majority of which are offered in part-time mode. The Academic Board of the college passed its policy for the provision of mainstream opportunities for disabled people in 1988. The policy document was itself a product of a small, committed group of colleagues, working with the support of senior institutional managers. As such it was a 'bottom up policy' informed by an understanding of the needs of disabled people and the pragmatic concerns of college lecturers. "The policy aims actively to encourage and support the functional integration of disabled students across the full range of mainstream college provision. The policy distinguishes persons with physical and sensory disabilities from the overly broad and unhelpful category of 'those with special educational needs'. It also stresses the importance of a task approach which enables disabled students to gain access to the curricular activities of their choice. Its approach is strengthened by the adoption of a 'whole college approach', one which identifies the provision of educational and training facilities for disabled students as being a shared responsibility of all staff of the college" (Funnell and Johnston, 1989).

The implementation of the policy began in September 1988 by a team seconded to the Research and Development Unit of the college - that part of the college structure with responsibility for cross-college curriculum and staff development, academic and commercial research and consultancy, and the provision of external conference activities. During the 1988/89 session the team consisted of a coordinator, an admissions support tutor, and three colleagues with briefs across the college's Faculty and Unit structures. All team members were seconded from substantive academic posts in the college on a part-time basis - the coordinator being seconded on a 0.5 basis (50% contact and non-contact time). In total the team constituted 1.5 full-time equivalent staff members.

The initial focus of activity for the team was:

* encouraging access through improved marketing and pre-admissions counselling;
* student support, guidance and counselling;
* staff development activities, principally awareness raising and helping colleagues understand disability;
* initial work to encourage curriculum review, to promote physical access and to find out more about needs and aspirations of disabled people in the communities the college serves.

Of these, student support took the greatest share of the team's time. However, the ability to recognize and articulate specific student need through a continuous dialogue with the student resulted in a more sensitive use of available resources and, during the year, to a negotiated increase in the budgetary allocation. Increased marketing and pre-admissions counselling, through the offer of a guaranteed interview to any disabled applicant, led to a twelve-fold increase in student numbers from this client group, albeit from a relatively small base. The use of press advertisements generated substantial interest from the disabled and also highlighted certain attitudinal barriers to integration amongst some disabled people. For example, a number of telephone respondents to advertisements asked what 'special courses' were being planned. Improvements to the physical access of the college buildings were also identified and acted upon.

The major successes of the first year of activity can best be judged in terms of the new prominence given to the needs of the disabled and drawing together of the disabled community of Suffolk and the college itself, with consequent spin-offs. The initiative also proved to be a stimulus for the development of other policies promoting equal opportunities. Those concerned with black and other ethnic minority groups and gender issues were passed by the Academic Board in 1989, whilst a policy for those with learning difficulties is being actively developed. The decision to differentiate those with a physical or sensory disability from the broader category of 'special educational needs' caused considerable debate at the time, and continues so to do. However the spirit of the policy for disabled people is clear:

> ...the attributions made of disabled persons are invariably in a direction that grossly underestimates their abilities and capabilities. The categorization of children, young persons, and more recently adults with 'special educational needs' is both unhelpful and misleading, and serves to perpetuate the existence of stereotypes towards disabled persons. The range of students covered by this umbrella label includes the severely mentally handicapped, those with mild or moderate learning difficulties, persons with emotional and behavioural disorders, as well as the physically and sensory impaired. In order to avoid the perpetuation of such damaging attributions, and to provide a clearer framework for the analysis of educational requirements and provisions this policy document is specifically targetted at those students with physical and sensory impairments who could benefit from mainstream college (provision). (Jolliffe, Impey and Johnston, 1988).

During the 1989/90 session the policy initiative has been incorporated into a larger equal opportunities initiative again housed in the Research and Development Unit of the college. The major challenge during the second year has been to drive forward on the broad front of equal opportunities (acknowledging the commonalities which exist between the policy areas) whilst continuing to address the specific issues and concerns of the distinct client groups the policies serve. A larger equal opportunities team has been formed with a coordinator and seven colleagues constituting a resource of 2.6 full-time equivalent staff members. On the advice of the team an Equal Opportunities Advisory Committee has been formed as part of the Academic Board substructure.

Much has been achieved, but much still needs to be done. For example, some colleagues continue to be uncertain about working with disabled people. Certain administrative procedures can still appear inflexible. Methods of academic assessment need review to ensure they do not penalize the disabled person. However, the committed and professional approach adopted at the college does mean that these challenges will be addressed.

The next stage of development is likely to see this initiative 'embedded' into the college following its developmental phase. Improved programmes of staff development and patterns of student support will need to be developed. New sources of financial and other support will need to be sought and here the emerging Training Enterprise Councils may prove significant as they act to respond to identified needs in their areas.

CONCLUSION

Both humanistic and economic reasons can be offered for seeking to realize the potential of disabled people through mainstream educational opportunities. The model of policy and practice developed at the Suffolk College represents one approach designed to achieve this.

REFERENCES

Funnell, P. and Johnston, B.(1989): An action approach for accessing disabled students to the Suffolk College. REPLAN Eastern Angles, 8th September.

Jolliffe, S., Impey, R. and Johnston, B.(1988): Policy for the Provision of Mainstream Opportunities for Disabled People. Suffolk College, Ipswich.

National Advisory Body 'Action for Access'(1988): Widening Opportunities in Higher Education. National Advisory Body for Public Sector Higher Education.

The Warnock Report (1978): Special Educational Needs. Her Majesty's Stationery Office, London.

Peter Funnell is currently Head of the Research and Development Unit, Suffolk College, Ipswich. Previously Senior Lecturer in Social Policy and Organizational Theory he has also been a researcher and operational manager in local government, and a service planner in the National Health Service. He is a member of the Executive Committee of the Standing Conference for Educational Development (SCED) and a member of the Council for the Centre for the Advancement of Interprofessional Education (CAIPE). He is joint contributing and series editor for the book series: 'New Directions in Vocational Education', Kogan Page 1990.

Address for correspondence: **Peter Funnell,**
Suffolk College, Rope Walk,
Ipswich, Suffolk IP4 1LT, UK

48. Should the principles of self-management be taught as standard curricula for developmentally delayed children?

Dr. Lutfi Elkhatib, Yarmouk University, Jordan.

Abstract: Mentally retarded children have a need very early in life to be guided towards short-term goals of self control in many areas of daily living. People have the power to control their own actions, but remain essentially ignorant of how to control their act. There is an emerging scientific technology for teaching and learning the skills of self-control, such as: self-observation; self-determined reinforcement; self-reinforcement; self-determined contingencies; self-instruction; self-punishment; self-recording. Programming for self-management requires a shift in the control of behaviour from an external agent to the person him/herself. To date there are few self-control procedures reported in the Arabic journals. Self-management programmes have several advantages for mentally retarded children, such as allowing them to become more fully integrated into the community, govern their own behaviour, learn the skills of daily living, and allow more time for the teacher to attend to other matters. Finally, this paper reports several elements which should be considered when we develop a self-control programme.

INTRODUCTION

The ultimate goal of any behavioural change programme should have at its core the basis of self-control techniques. In this paper I shall try to define and explore areas of self-management; with whom it has or has not been used; and indeed if the residential facilities and community at large are ready for a change in focus for the impaired persons now under the control of others. Controlling one's own choices, decisions and setting of goals is extremely important for all persons interested in living as independent and productive adults.

Children have a need very early in life to be guided towards small or short-term goals of self-control in many areas of daily living: toileting, vocal and later verbal control, eating, emotional outlets and free time or play activities. The controls are provided principally by others in the beginning, but the transfer to more self-directed behaviour comes quickly for the non-impaired youngster. With children who are impaired in cognitive or communicative areas of development, the control agents of their behavioural programmes may not be transferred to self-control techniques as soon as with non-impaired children. Often the control agents are never dropped or transferred, leaving the person in a constant state of dependence on others for choice-making, behavioural goal setting and implementation of their own programmes. As independent adults we have the freedom to instigate a programme for self-management on ourselves to lose weight, increase work output, decrease alcohol consumption or any other variety of things that effect our quality of living. We make the choices, we use the programme on ourselves as long as we see fit, we reward ourselves for efforts put in or for progress gained, and we drop the programme if it isn't working out the way we thought it would. With children and adults who are forced to live their lives in situations where choice-making is not allowed,as is the case in many institutional settings, self-management programmes are seemingly non-existent. It is difficult to tell if the professionals and others who provide services for the impaired populations either do not believe institutional persons to be capable of self-control, or think that the independence it might offer individuals trained in self-management techniques would interfere with established methods of control (i.e. control by others).

Albert Bandura has a statement about the circular effect of behaviour and behaviour management:

> Through their conduct people play an active role in producing the reinforcement contingencies that impinge upon them. Thus, behaviour partly creates the environment, and the environment influences the behaviour in reciprocal fashion. A distinguishing feature of man is that he is capable of creating self-regulative influences. By functioning as an agent as well as an object of influence, man has some power of self-direction. (Bandura, from Thoresen and Mahoney, 1974).

Developing self-directive skills and the quest for self-mastery are human characteristics that need to be fostered. People have the power to control their own actions, but remain essentially ignorant of how to control their act (Thoresen and Mahoney, 1974 pp.vii-viii). Exerting will-power or using positive thinking are not enough. There is an emerging scientific technology for teaching and learning the skills of self-control; let us look at some of them.

SELF-MANAGEMENT TECHNIQUES

There are many components to a self-management programme.

Self-observation, behaviourally, involves individuals monitoring their own behaviour and subsequently recording that behaviour. It is an initial and very important step in self-control training. Self-recording and self-evaluation are both self-observational procedures.

The mere act of observing oneself may influence the observed behaviour. The recording of one's behaviour appears to be an active intervention in its own right under conditions in which persons are motivated to change. The process seems to sensitize children to the frequency of their behaviour and its controlling variables. However, to be an effective self-change strategy, self-observation must usually be accompanied by other self-control procedures, such as self-reinforcement.

Self-determined reinforcement has to do with the person's own choice of what to reinforce themselves with, which would promote use of the target behaviour through direct involvement with the consequence. This would include self-selection of free-time activities.

Self-reinforcement reduces dependence on others; after starting programmes with some degree of external reinforcement, there is a gradual transfer to self-control. Children can be promoted from externally-administered to self-administered rewards.

Self-determined contingencies have been shown to be not only preferred by children in self-control studies, but also showed students consistently progressing more rapidly in the self-determined condition. The response-facilitation effect of being able to choose one's own contingencies has received additional support from other studies. (Brigham and Bushell, 1973; Brigham and Stoerzinger, 1976). Response maintenance, or the duration of behaviour over time, is greatly enhanced through an individual developing his own contingencies. (Wehman, 1975).

Self-instruction is another important method for developing self-control. In self-instructional training, individuals are taught to make suggestions to themselves to guide their own behaviour in a manner similar to being guided by another individual. Self-instruction can include modelling, problem solving, rehearsal and self-monitoring. The basic premise of a self-instructional programme is to understand what the goal is, accept it and set up the learning process. (Morse, 1979).

Self-punishment is a covert or internal form of self-control if it is used by internally scolding or chastising oneself. Overtly, it can be in the form of a **self-imposed response-cost** procedure, involving fining oneself from a set number of tokens available daily. Not allowing oneself to partake of a reinforcer such as watching television or drinking a milk shake are other forms of self-punishment.

Self-recording can include self-graphing of progress from one's behavioural sheets or charts. A graphic picture may provide more clear-cut feedback than other self-monitoring techniques, increasing the chances of a person becoming aware of his behaviour and the consequences of that behaviour.

Combinations of some of the above techniques can provide the basis for strong self-management programmes. Along with self-observation, a combination of environmental planning and behavioural programming seems promising as a long-term solution to self-control (Thoresen and Mahoney, 1974, p.134). But have these techniques been used to help the developmentally disabled?

WHY USE SELF-MANAGEMENT PROGRAMMES TO TEACH INDEPENDENCE TO THE MENTALLY HANDICAPPED?

Self-control is a process through which a person becomes the principal agent for regulating his/her own behaviour. In the field of education, behaviour modification research and training materials have involved almost exclusively techniques in which an external change agent is the locus of control. The agent assumes responsibility for determining target behaviours, environmental structure, and delivery of consequences. Programming for self-management or self-control requires a shift in the control of behaviour from an external agent to that person. However, the use of self-control strategies to modify, maintain, and generalize changes in the behaviour of handicapped children is relatively unexplored. To date there are few reported investigations of the use with handicapped children of cue regulation as a self-control procedure.

The long range goal of education should be self-management. In educational settings self-management procedures are preferred over teacher-imposed systems whenever the effectiveness of self-management can be clearly demonstrated. Children who are taught self-management procedures in the classroom allow more time for the teacher to be attending to other matters. Similarly, when self-management programmes are introduced into vocational settings, the first and most obvious advantage is the saving on staff time at the workshops:

> There is a critical need for the development of self-management skills for the mentally retarded if they are to be successfully absorbed into the community for education, semi-independent living facilities and workshops. The movement towards deinstitutionalization will be facilitated if self-regulation is a viable alternative to the more common externally controlled living patterns. (Wehman, 1975).

It will be the acquisition of behavioural self-control patterns that will promote an approach to a normalized lifestyle for the mentally handicapped and allow them to become more fully integrated into the community. The prospect of self-control skills with the mentally retarded is most attractive because it allows for the normalization process to occur. Development of self-control behaviours is highly congruent with the developmental-growth model which states that mentally handicapped persons can and must continue to grow. By helping the person develop self-management skills we are expanding the potential of the individual and removing the artificial ceiling which is frequently placed on the progress of many retarded persons (Wehman, 1975, p.28). Pioneer efforts in self-management strategies are showing promise for a new area of therapy. The emerging approaches have a lot to offer educators who are dedicated to developing ways of helping people assume more responsibility for their own lives. Self-management offers people an opportunity to govern their own behaviour and to learn general problem-solving strategies that can be applied to future problems. Children can learn to keep track of their own accomplishments, manage self-rewards and arrange personal prompts to promote self-selected behaviour objectives. Self-control competence may constitute a giant step towards normalization and integration of exceptional children (Kurtz and Neisworth, 1976).

CONCLUSION

Nineteen years ago one of the major conclusions of the 1970 White House Conference on Children was about the strong need for curricula to teach self-control. It found that we as educators need to teach ways of helping children to deal with feelings and emotions, cope with pressure and frustrations through the principles of self-control. They found these things to be almost totally lacking. But to me these ideas are at the core of human survival. Our society is complex, and education and behavioural management techniques do not adequately prepare our children to learn self-control. The more self-control a person has, the better that person's life can become. There is great dignity in having control over one's own life, one's choices and direction. Inner strength is increased in each person that learns successfully to use self-management techniques. Children who are exposed to a programme designed to teach them about their feelings, their choices in behavioural matters and the consequences of those choices are beginning to be seen in some schools. One model programme that I have seen used and have helped develop for the past seven years is assisting 3-7 year old handicapped and non-handicapped children learn about self-management procedures. The programme is called **Starstuff - The Twinkling Star Programme** and to date has not been marketed publicly. There are many different aspects to development of a primary programme of this sort, with the following important elements as necessary ingredients:

1. it should be available to all children;
2. it should begin as early as possible in the child`s development;
3. it should focus on the concept of health rather than illness or pathology;
4. it should be educationally focused;
5. it should emphasize normal adult-peer-self interactions;
6. it should be functional to the teacher;
7. it should be intrinsically pleasant and satisfying to the children;
8. it should be inexpensive enough to be applied on a mass basis;
9. it should increase or strengthen skills for coping effectively with stresses of living.

(Fagen and Long, 1979)

There must be other programmes in development that include some or all of the above elements besides **Starstuff**. It should be the responsibility of every teacher, administrator and concerned parent to seek out and even help develop additional programmes such as these to be used in conjunction with the otherwise standard curricula already taught to our children. I believe it to be the hope of the future for individual students as well as our society as a whole.

REFERENCES

Bandura, A.(1974): from a foreword in Thoresen and Mahoney (1974) - see below.

Brigham, T.A. and Bushell, D.(1973): Notes on autonomous environments: effects of student-selected and teacher-selected rewards on academic performance. Educational Technology, 13, pp.19-22.

Brigham, T.A. and Stoerzinger, A.(1976): An experimental analysis of children's preference for self-selected rewards. Behavioural Analysis in Education: Self-Control and Reading. Kendall-Hunt, Dubuque, Iowa.

Fagen, S.A. and Long, N.J.(1979): A psychoeducational curriculum approach to teaching self-control. Journal of Behavior Disorders, 4, 2, pp.68-82.

Kurtz, P.D. and Neisworth, J.T.(1976): Self-control possibilities for the exceptional child. Exceptional Children, 16, 3, pp.212-217.

Morse, W.C.(1979): Self-control: the Fagen-Long curriculum. Behavior Disorders, 4, 2, pp.83-91.

Thoresen, C.E. and Mahoney, M.J.(1974): Behavioral Self-Control. Holt, Rinehart and Winston, San Francisco.

Wehman, P.(1975): Behavioural self-control with the mentally retarded. Journal of Applied Rehabilitation Counseling, 6, pp.27-34.

White House Conference on Children (1971): Confronting myths of education - Report of Forum 8. U.S.Government Printing Office, Washington, D.C. Pp.121-142.

Dr. Lutfi Elkhatib is Assistant Professor in the Department of Education at Yarmouk University, Irbid, Jordan.

Address for correspondence is as above.

49. Realizing human potential through staff development in an educational context

Dave Muller

Abstract: This paper will explore the following arguments: that too much emphasis has been placed upon organizations rather than individuals in facilitating staff development and training; that in facilitating human potential it is necessary to have a model of how people behave; that there would now appear to be considerable evidence which suggests that the adult learner in particular is a purposeful autonomous individual who therefore should be treated as such in facilitating staff development and training; and finally, that staff development and training activities which result from the individual having negotiated his or her own performance indicators are more successful and lead to greater job satisfaction whilst maximizing human potential.

CONTEXT

It is self-evident that large organizations rely heavily upon the creative talents of their work force. In terms of becoming an effective organization, the wealth of ability which individuals have, needs realizing and steering towards the corporate purpose of the institution. In almost any organization, especially those of an educational nature, the bulk of fixed costs are in salaries of employees and consequently they are the most valuable and, of course, the most expensive component of the organization. There is considerable responsibility placed upon senior managers to facilitate individuals maximizing their potential for the benefit of the institution.

In an educational context realizing the potential of teachers, administrators and others enables this group to help develop other individuals in expressing their talents in a wide variety of environments.

Recently, there has been a strong move in education emphasizing the right of managers to manage. The importance of curriculum-related staff development and the need to ensure that employees are able to function within an institutional framework, can be perceived as a lessening of employees' participation. The importance of ensuring that teaching and administrative staff are fully equipped to meet the needs of learners is not questioned. However, the means by which this can be achieved is open both to theoretical and empirical debate. This paper will explore the argument that too much emphasis has been placed upon organizational considerations and not enough on the role that individuals can play in facilitating their own staff development and training.

MODELS OF PEOPLE

If it is agreed that the most valuable resource any employer has is a human one, it becomes necessary to develop sophisticated models of what people are like. The question of 'what makes people tick' has been the driving force behind the scientific, technological and humanistic endeavours of academics during the centuries. At the turn of this century it was a field of enquiry dominated by philosophy but during the last generation it has become a specialist area of study for many psychologists. Chapman and Jones (1980) convened a conference of leading psychologists in the United Kingdom inviting them to present their view of what people were like. Nearly 20 different perspectives on the nature of human behaviour were offered, each with its own theoretical and empirical base. It is not unlikely if such an event were convened today that an even greater number of perspectives would be offered. What is important is to recognize that, in applying behavioural or organizational techniques to harness a work force, the nature of what people are like is fundamental in the design of the implementation strategies. Hence, for example, if it is believed that people are only motivated by extrinsic financial rewards any strategy of staff development or training must be linked entirely to reinforcement of this kind. If, on the other hand, the view is held that people are motivated entirely by internal factors there is a need to present a different mode of staff development and training.

Few, if any, organizations have faced this issue front on. Education has been influenced more by external financial and political factors than by any view of what it is that motivates teachers and senior administrative staff to offer their skills to future generations of the work force. It is not a simple question of whether or not there is one correct view of what people are like, but the need to recognize that if one has no view at all it is difficult to influence the behaviour of the work force, and staff development and training is intended to do just this (Muller 1988).

Jahoda (1980) pushes the argument concerning the nature of people one stage further. She argues that it is more fruitful in the long run to recognize the possibility of a variety of models. She writes:

> Rubbing shoulders with other models and being confronted with what they can and cannot achieve, serves as an invaluable reminder that there are no final answers... (p.286)

What we observe and how we behave is inevitably linked to our own explicit model of what people are like but through any action such as staff training, this behaviour can change.

What is important to grasp is that the effectiveness of realizing human potential in an educational context can only be considered in the light of how individuals themselves change. It is critical to have a view of what people are like, and how the organizational climate affects individuals, in order to implement staff development and training in the first place. Yet, the aim of this intervention is to change both the organizational climate and, more significantly, the roles individuals play within it.

This does imply that the responsibility for effecting change must be invested in the individual in order for it to work and be seen to have value. The realization of human potential is the actualization of individual performance and cannot in an educational setting be driven entirely by external factors. The power of education is the ability to offer new knowledge, skills and attitudes to those engaged in it. For those of us charged with this enormous responsibility there has to be a recognition of the ownership placed by professionals on their own personal development.

DEVELOPING EFFICACY

Whilst recognizing the possibility of experimenting with different models of people, many of us would agree that our aim is to produce effective educators. There is evidence to suggest (Bandura 1989) that those individuals who perceive themselves to be effective achieve more. This belief, referred to by Bandura as 'self-efficacy', recognizes that those individuals able to take on responsibility for their own actions are potentially more effective educators. The end product of any process of staff development and training should be the development of purposeful individuals who value and believe in the contribution they can make in terms of the educational process. Such individuals are characterized by the way in which they have negotiated their own learning situations and selected appropriate knowledge, skills or attitudes which they believe make them more effective. This ownership of effectiveness through self-belief is a powerful means of realizing human potential.

Although it may be desirable to recognize that there are different ways of viewing people it is important to hold in mind the end product of any staff development or training. It is the end product that to some extent determines the ways in which people can be viewed. If it is recognized that in realizing human potential there is a need to develop self-autonomous individuals, the strategies of intervention need to facilitate purposeful, directed behaviour. This places more emphasis on models of people which internalize control rather than attribute it to external factors. The traditional behaviourist model which focuses on environmental factors in controlling behaviour may be more suited towards clinical intervention than to actualizing the potential of educationalists. We want educationalists who are rational, critical problem-solving individuals able to convey the spirit of enquiry to the students. It is recognized that the more mature adult learner is him or herself more likely to be autonomous and goal seeking (Gibbs, 1988). George Kelly developed a model of the person which emphasizes the role individuals take in creating and representing their environment (Fransella, 1980). This approach stresses the need to work within frameworks which maximize the potential of individuals to construct and to take responsibility for their own learning.

EVALUATING INTERVENTION

Is there any evidence that developing self-efficacy in individuals develops their potential? Bandura (1989) suggests that there is and reviews a number of empirical studies conducted by himself and colleagues demonstrating this. There is also evidence emerging from research in the field of occupational psychology that helping individuals develop themselves is of benefit in an industrial context. Spector (1988) found that those individuals who believe that the outcomes of the work environment are influenced by their own actions, experience greater job satisfaction. Similarly, Lane and Herriot (1990) have shown that the self-ratings of unit managers in a large leisure organization predicted subsequent performance and over a longer term led to enhanced motivation. It was suggested by Lane and Herriot that the self-ratings represented judgments of self-efficacy which in themselves improved motivation. From a macro-political perspective the emergent entrepreneurial culture emphasizes the role individuals can play in maximizing their own potential. Although speculative, it is not unreasonable to link this with the development of self-efficacy and the need to realize human potential by investing heavily in supporting entrepreneurial behaviour which places emphasis on the individual rather than the organization.

In summary, it has been argued that the value of individuals in realizing their own potential has been underplayed and that educational institutions are moving to a managerial-led model without sufficient reflection of the consequences. The views we have of people determine ways in which we implement staff development and training and these in turn are shaped by the end product we have in mind. It has also been argued that educationalists and those working in an educational environment need to develop self-efficacy and to take responsibility for their actions to become effective. It has been shown that in an industrial context this approach enhances motivation and increases productivity. There is a need to redress the balance between the requirements of institutions and the ways in which individuals function within them, in recognizing that the former can only be achieved by maximizing the potential of the latter. This should not be a surprising statement for those of us engaged in education.

REFERENCES

Bandura, A.(1989): Perceived self-efficacy in the exercise of personal agency. The Psychologist, Oct., pp.411-424.

Chapman, A.J. and Jones, D.M.(1980): Models of Man. British Psychological Society, Leicester.

Fransella, F.(1980): Man-as-Scientist. In Chapman, A.J. and Jones, D.M., Models of Man. British Psychological Society, Leicester.

Gibbs, G.(1988): Learning by Doing. Further Education Unit, London.

Jahoda, M.(1980): One model of man or many? In Chapman, A.J. and Jones, D.M., Models of Man. British Psychological Society, Leicester.

Lane, J. and Herriot, P.(1990): Self-ratings, supervisor ratings, positions and performance. British Journal of Occupational Psychology, 63, 1, pp.77-88.

Muller, D.J.(1988): Staff development: whose responsibility? Programmed Learning and Educational Technology, 25, 2, pp.101-106.

Spector, P.E.(1988): Development of the work locus of control scale. British Journal of Occupational Psychology, 61, 4, pp.335-340.

Dave Muller is Vice Principal at the Suffolk College of Higher and Further Education, with responsibility for staffing and course development. He was previously Dean of the Faculty of Science at Lancashire Polytechnic. He has published a number of papers and several books applying psychology to a wide range of topics including education, medicine and nursing. More recently he has been exploring the links between the development of policy statements, their implementation and the role of individuals in this process.

Address for correspondence: **Prof.D.Muller**
Suffolk College, Rope Walk,
Ipswich, Suffolk IP4 1LT, UK

50. Sociometric analysis applying fuzzy theory

Kazuko Nishimura and Hajime Yamashita Waseda University, Japan

Abstract: It is really more practical to represent human relations as a fuzzy graph rather than in a clear form such as a hard cluster. From the data obtained by simple questionnaires, we can measure e.g. the degree of friendship among members of a group, and can then construct the fuzzy graph for that group.
In this paper, the author proposes a method which allows members of a group to be classified by using fuzzy clustering and fuzzy ordering. The effectiveness of this analysis is illustrated by means of a case study.

INTRODUCTION

This paper presents a method, known as fuzzy theory, which can be used to analyse the human relationships and interactions within a group, and thus can find application on those occasions when the most appropriate groups need to be formed. It could be used in all spheres, but we have applied the method as an example to a kindergarten classroom and, through the application of fuzzy clustering and ordering, show the effect of this method in managing the classroom for educational purposes.

CASE STUDY

A practical analysis of the girls in a kindergarten was done as a case study. The following questionnaire (Table 1) was applied verbally in the classroom:

---

1. Select four friends with whom you would like to dance.
2. Select four friends with whom you would like to have lunch.
3. Select four friends with whom you would like to play during the lunch break.
4. Select four friends with whom you would like to go walking.

Table 1: Verbal questionnaire given to the class.

These were analysed , and we obtained the approximate graph F* given in Figure 1, and the partition tree which is illustrated as Figure 2. (The analytical method is given at the end of this paper). With these graphs, we constructed the sociogram S shown as Figure 3, where ⊙, □ etc., signify the clustered students, and △ signifies the isolated child.

The following reasons are proposed for the relationships between the children that this analysis shows:

6 , 8 : these live in the same neighbourhood and commute to the kindergarten by the same subway.
11 , 14 : their elder sisters are in the same class at the same school.
1 , 19 and 2 , 14 : their mothers are good friends.
4 : she is always too interested in everyone around her so her

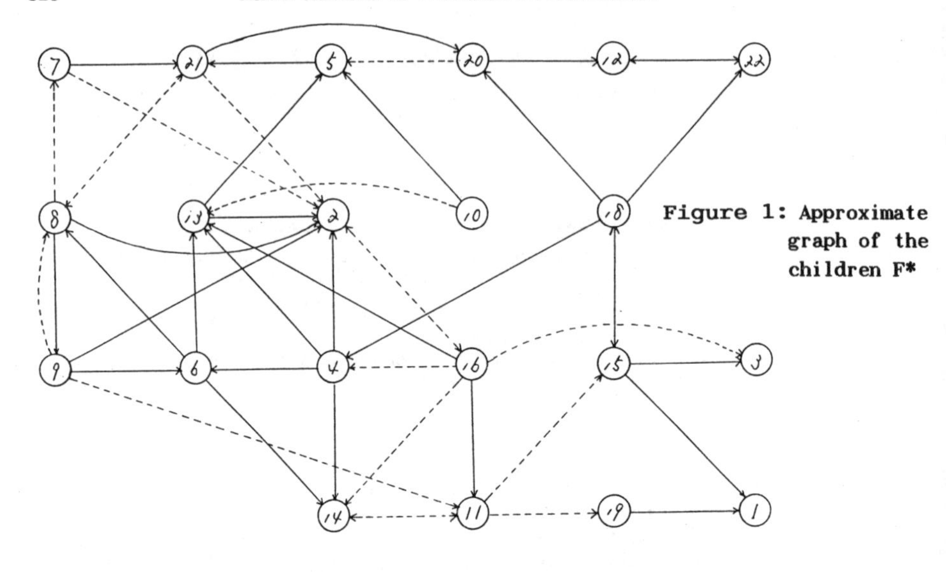

Figure 1: Approximate graph of the children F*

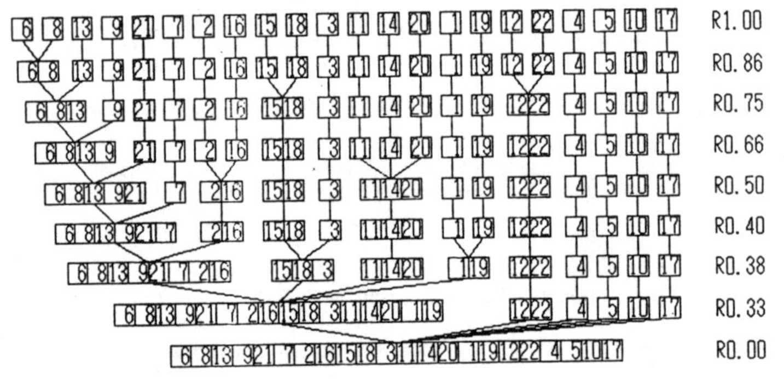

Figure 2: Partition tree of the children T.

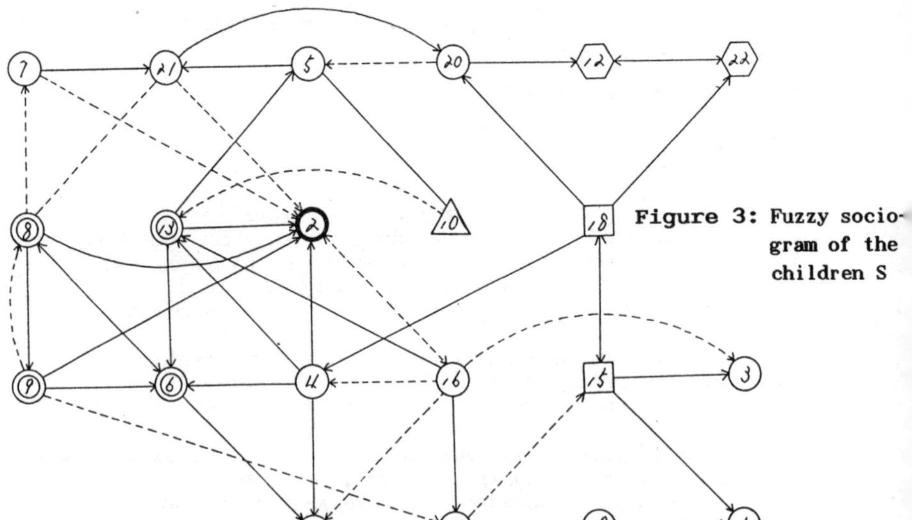

Figure 3: Fuzzy sociogram of the children S

classmates feel annoyed with her.

13 : she is a small and lovely girl, so all her classmates like her.

2 : she is always doing something different from her classmates. For instance, she plays alone in the classroom while others are dancing on the playground, in the process attracting their attention. We are unsure whether this is deliberate or not.

1 : she doesn't talk much and doesn't try to play actively with her classmates.

5 , 10 : they don't take any notice of their classmates and they do what they want to do.

Using this sociogram, it is possible to:

* confirm and update observations previously made by the class teacher;
* reveal aspects of the relationships in the class that the teacher had not noticed. For example, the relations between 18 and 15 and between 12 and 22 were not known to the teacher before our experiment.

Based on the information thus made available, the teacher could ensure that groups formed are the most appropriate, aiding the educational management of the classroom.

ANALYSIS METHOD

Suppose the questionnaire is concerned with activities and each question asks you to select some friends with whom you would like to do an activity.

If we execute n questions in a questionnaire $\{Q_k; 1 \leqslant k \leqslant n\}$ to select p friends in a classroom with m students $\{S_i; 1 \leqslant i \leqslant m\}$, then we have a response matrix

$$A=(A_{ij}), \quad 0 \leqslant a_{ij} \leqslant n \qquad (1.1)$$

where a_{ij} is the frequency with which the student S_i selects the student S_j.

Let $$f_{ij}=a_{ij}/n,$$

we could consider f_{ij} as the degree of the fuzziness with which the student i prefers the student j. Thence, we have a fuzzy graph

$$F=(f_{ij}), \quad 0 \leqslant f_{ij} \leqslant 1 \qquad (1.2)$$

Hence, the student S_i increasingly prefers student S_j as f_{ij} increases from 0 to 1.

According to the approximate algorithm, we could obtain the simplified graph F*; if a fuzzy graph is F in Figure 4A, the approximate graph F* is in Figure 4B, which shows the crisp relation and the fuzzy relation from one member to the other.

Next, if we let $2/g_{ij} = 1/f_{ij} + 1/f_{ji}$

we could consider g_{ij} as the degree of fuzziness of the extent of the preferences that students S_i and S_j have for each other. Thence, we have a fuzzy graph

$$G = (g_{ij}), \quad 0 \leqslant g_{ij} \leqslant 1 \qquad (1.3)$$

Here, g_{ij} varies from 0 to 1 as the students vary from being unfriendly to very friendly towards each other.

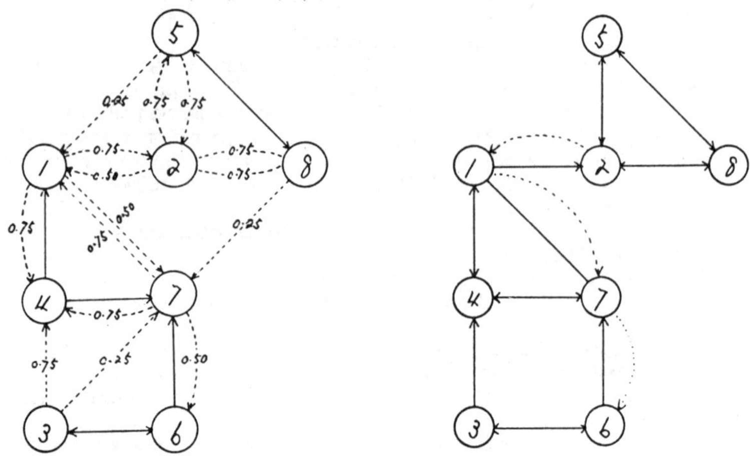

Figure 4A: Fuzzy connective graph F. **Figure 4B:** Approximate graph F*

The transitive closure $\hat{G}$ of G satisfies the symmetry, the reflexivity and the transitivity. Thus, the relation R given by $\hat{G}$ is a fuzzy equivalence relation.

If we define the t-cut matrix G^t of $\hat{G}$:

$$G^t = (g_{ij}), \quad g_{ij} = 1 \ (g_{ij} \geqslant t), \quad g_{ij} = 0 \ (g_{ij} \leqslant t) \qquad (1.4)$$

then the relation R^t given by G^t is a fuzzy equivalence relation.

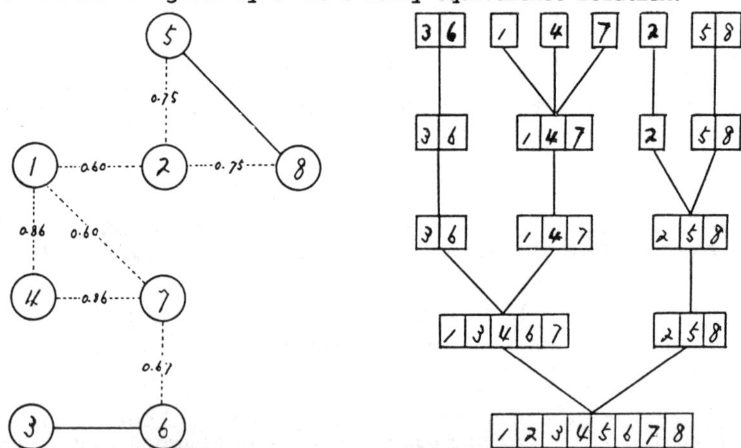

Figure 4c: Fuzzy familiarity graph G **Figure 4d:** Partition tree T

The quotient set S/R^t is composed of the cluster whose friendly degree is equal to or more than t. By changing the level t we have the partition tree T which presents the clustering and the branching structures, respectively, among the members.

For example, from the fuzzy graph F in Figure 4a, we have the fuzzy graph G which is in Figure 4c and the partition tree which is in Figure 4d. We can then connect and observe the linking structure of the sociogram S in Figure 4e, where the symbols ○, □, △ imply the members round the same cluster.

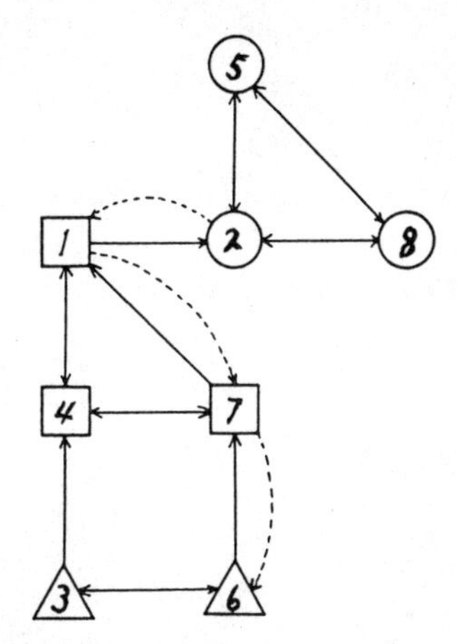

Figure 4e: Fuzzy sociogram S

ACKNOWLEDGEMENTS

The authors are grateful to Prof. H. Sunouch, Mr. Yasuo Katsumata and Mr. E. Tuda of Waseda University, and to Prof. L. Zadeh of the University of California for this research.

BIBLIOGRAPHY

Nishida, T. and Takeda, E.(1978): Fuzzy Sets and its Application. Morikita Shuppan (in Japanese).

Sunouchi, H., Yamashita, H., et al.(1987): Crisp relation and fuzzy relation of a fuzzy graph. Proceedings of NAFIPS Congress, IV, FR-b.

Tuda, E., Katsumata, Y. and Yamashita, H.(1988): Fuzzy clustering and ordering. Proceedings of-the International Conference on Fuzzy System Application, pp.173-174.

Yamashita, H.(1988): Fuzzy clustering and ordering in instructional analysis. Proceedings of the NAFIPS Congress, VII, pp.291-295.

Yamashita, H.(1989): Approximate algorithm of a fuzzy graph and its application. Proceedings of the IFSA Congress, III, pp.492-495.

Yamashita, H. and Morioka, M.(1987): On the global structure of fuzzy graph. In Bezdek, J.(ed): Analysis of Fuzzy Information. I, pp. 167-176. CRC Press.

Addresses for correspondence: **Kazuko Nishimura,**
Kawamura Gakuen University, 22-3, 2-Chome,
Mejiro, Toshima-Ku, Tokyo 171, Japan